A BOOK OF MORMON TREASURY

GOSPEL INSIGHTS FROM GENERAL AUTHORITIES AND RELIGIOUS EDUCATORS

RELIGIOUS STUDIES CENTER
BRIGHAM YOUNG UNIVERSITY

DESERET
BOOK

SALT LAKE CITY, UTAH

Visit us at deseretbook.com

Library of Congress Cataloging-in-Publication Data

A Book of Mormon treasury : Gospel insights from general authorities and religious educators.

p. cm.

Includes bibliographical references and index.

ISBN 1-59038-099-1 (alk. paper)

1. Book of Mormon—Criticism, interpretation, etc. 2. Church of Jesus Christ of Latter-day Saints—Doctrines. 3. Christian life—Mormon authors. I. Brigham Young University. Religious Studies Center. II. Title.

BX8627.B655 2003
289.3'22—dc22 2003014806

Printed in the United States of America 70582-7101
Phoenix Color Corporation, Hagerstown, MD

10 9 8 7 6 5 4 3 2 1

Contents

CONTENTS

PREFACE

In 1975 Jeffrey R. Holland, then dean of Religious Education at Brigham Young University, established the Religious Studies Center. The center (RSC) was given a charge to (1) promote and aid in the coordination of religious studies throughout the university and the Church, (2) promote the study and understanding of other cultures and religions within and beyond the Judeo-Christian traditions, and (3) promote sound scholarship that will enhance the understanding of the scriptures and history of The Church of Jesus Christ of Latter-day Saints.

In an effort to fulfill this last purpose in particular, the Religious Studies Center and Religious Education at BYU have sponsored annual symposia and conferences on the scriptures and history of the Restoration. From these symposia, outstanding papers and presentations have been published in books produced by the RSC. For over thirty years the annual Sidney B. Sperry Symposium on the Scriptures has been held at BYU. Named in honor of the former BYU dean of Religious Education and eminent gospel scholar, the Sperry Symposium has been a blessing to many members of the Church in their quest for greater understanding of the restored gospel of Jesus Christ. Each year the RSC publishes selected papers from the Sperry Symposium in a book. Five of those symposia and subsequent books were devoted exclusively to the Book of Mormon.

In addition, the RSC sponsored an annual Book of Mormon

symposium for nearly a decade. Nine volumes were published containing well over a hundred articles from some of the Church's most respected gospel scholars and religious educators. Additional publications on the Book of Mormon, not associated with these annual symposia, have also been published by the RSC during the last quarter of a century.

Unfortunately, many of those outstanding and important publications are no longer in print. The purpose of this volume is to bring together some of the most insightful articles on the Book of Mormon into a single volume. It is hoped that the articles contained herein will be a blessing to every faithful and serious student of the Book of Mormon, increasing knowledge, strengthening testimony, and motivating to greater personal righteousness. Other similar volumes of compiled classic articles dealing with each of the standard works of the Church are forthcoming.

At many of the symposia there were general authority keynote speakers. We have included six of those addresses as the first chapters of this volume. The rest of the book is organized, more or less, in the order of the books in the Book of Mormon—giving "coverage" of the books and the main doctrines contained therein. It is impossible to include in a single volume, or in many volumes for that matter, all of the doctrines, insights, and applications that are to be gained from a study of the Book of Mormon. What we have included, however, will hopefully provide many "gold nuggets" as the reader seeks to "mine" the hidden treasures contained in the "keystone of our religion." It is our hope that these classic articles will enrich the reader's love for and understanding of the Book of Mormon. The more we study the Book of Mormon, the more we will come to know that it is deeper and broader than all of us.

Religious Studies Center
Brigham Young University
Provo, Utah

1

The Book of Mormon: A Great Answer to "The Great Question"

Elder Neal A. Maxwell

The Book of Mormon provides resounding and great answers to what Amulek designated as "the great question"—namely, is there really a redeeming Christ? (Alma 34:5–6). The Book of Mormon with clarity and with evidence says, "Yes! Yes! Yes!" Moreover, in its recurring theme, the book even declares that "all things which have been given of God from the beginning of the world, unto man, are the typifying of [Christ]" (2 Nephi 11:4). How striking its answers are, considering all that God might have chosen to tell us! He, before whom all things—past, present, and future—are continually (see D&C 130:7), has chosen to tell us about the "gospel" (3 Nephi 27:13–14, 21; D&C 33:12; D&C 39:6; 76:40–41)—the transcending "good news," the resplendent answers to "the great question."

Astoundingly, too, God, who has created "worlds without number" (Moses 1:33, 37–38; see Isaiah 45:18), has chosen to reassure us on this tiny "speck of sand" that he "doeth not anything save it be for the benefit of [this] world; for he loveth [this] world" (2 Nephi 26:24); and "for behold, this is my work and my glory—to bring to pass the immortality and eternal life of man" (Moses 1:39).

It should not surprise us that this glorious gospel message is more

---

Elder Neal A. Maxwell is a member of the Quorum of the Twelve Apostles.

perfect than any of its messengers, save Jesus only. Nor should it surprise us that the gospel message is more comprehensive than the comprehension of any of its bearers or hearers, save Jesus only.

Apparently translated by Joseph Smith at an average rate of eight or more of its printed pages a day, the Book of Mormon's full significance could not have been immediately and fully savored by the Prophet Joseph. Given this average, according to Professor Jack Welch, only one and a half days, for instance, would have been spent translating all of the first five chapters of Mosiah, a remarkable sermon about which books will be written.

Coming forth as the Book of Mormon did in Bible Belt and revival conditions early in this dispensation, we of the Church have been slow to appreciate its special relevance to the erosive conditions in our time, the latter part of this dispensation. Questioning and doubting has grown rapidly on the part of some scholars and even some clerics about the historicity of Jesus. Such, however, was not the America of 1830. Demographically speaking, therefore, the majority of the "ministry" of the Book of Mormon is occurring in a time of deep uncertainty and unrest concerning "the great question"—the very question which the Book of Mormon was created to answer!

Another strong impression is how the Book of Mormon foretells the latter-day emergence of "other books" of scripture (1 Nephi 13:39), of which it is one, "proving to the world that the holy scriptures are true, and that God does inspire men and call them to his holy work in this age and generation, as well as in generations of old" (D&C 20:11).

With regard to omissions from the precious Holy Bible, in just one chapter of 1 Nephi, chapter 13, four phrases appear: *taken away,* four times; *taken out,* once; *kept back,* twice; and *taken away out of,* once. Eight indications of omissions because of transmission deficiencies appear in one chapter! Moreover, as Nephi indicated, it was the "precious things" which had been lost. You will recall that Joseph Smith's translation of Luke 11:52 shows Jesus criticizing those, then, who had "taken away the key of knowledge, the fulness of the scriptures" (Joseph Smith Translation, Luke 11:52).

While we do not know precisely what was "kept back" or "taken away" (see 1 Nephi 13:40), logically there would be a heavy representation of such plain and precious truths in the Restoration. Therefore, the "other books" provide precisely that which God is most anxious to have "had again" among the children of men, so that we might know the truth of things, in Jacob's felicitous phrase, of "things as they really are" (Jacob 4:13).

The convergence of these "other books" of scripture with the precious Bible is part of the rhythm of the Restoration. The rhythm would have been impossible except for devoted and heroic individuals, including the Jewish prophets and the Jewish people of antiquity who, in the words of the Book of Mormon, had "travails," "labors," and "pains" to preserve the Bible for us. Lamentably, as foreseen, for that contribution the Jews have been unthanked, as a people, and instead have been "cursed," "hated," and made "game" of (see 2 Nephi 29:4–5; 3 Nephi 29:4, 8). A much later expression of the rhythm of the Restoration is symbolically reflected, too, in the graves of some Church members of the 1830s buried in Ohio and Indiana. Recently discovered, there is a trail of testifying tombstones which display, in stone, replicas of both the Bible *and* the Book of Mormon. These members felt doubly blessed and wanted the world to know it.

The existing scriptures advise of more than twenty other books to come forth[1] (see 1 Nephi 19:10–16). One day, in fact, "all things shall be revealed unto the children of men which ever have been . . . and which ever will be" (2 Nephi 27:11). Hence, the ninth article of faith is such an impressive statement! My personal opinion, however, is that we will not get additional scriptures until we learn to appreciate fully those we already have.

The "other books," particularly the Book of Mormon, fulfill—if constitutional lawyers will forgive me—Nephi's "establishment clause": "These last records . . . shall *establish* the truth of the first, which are of the twelve apostles of the Lamb" (1 Nephi 13:40). What the latter-day seer, Joseph Smith, brought forth will actually aid some people in accepting God's word which had already gone forth, namely the Bible (see 2 Nephi 3:11), by convincing them "that the records of the prophets and of the twelve apostles of the Lamb are true" (1 Nephi 13:39). There is high drama ahead!

Meanwhile, even as the criticism of the Book of Mormon continues to intensify, the book continues to testify and to diversify its displays of interior consistency, conceptual richness, and its connections with antiquity.

The plentitude of the Restoration followed as foreseen by Amos: "a famine in the land, not a famine of bread, nor a thirst for water, but of hearing the words of the Lord" (Amos 8:11). The end of that famine was marked by the coming of the Book of Mormon and the "other books."

Such books have been and are the Lord's means of preserving the spiritual memory of centuries past. Without moral memory, spiritual tragedy soon follows: "Now . . . there were many of the rising generation that . . . did not believe what had been said concerning the resurrection of the dead, neither did they believe concerning the coming of Christ" (Mosiah 26:1–2).

And on another occasion: "And at the time that Mosiah discovered them . . . they had brought no records with them; and they denied the being of their Creator" (Omni 1:17).

Belief in Deity and the Resurrection are usually the first to go. Ironically, though we gratefully accept the Bible as the word of God, the very process of its emergence has, alas, caused an unnecessary slackening of the Christian faith on the part of some. Because available Bible sources are not original but represent dated derivations and translations, "other books" of scripture, which have come to us directly from ancient records and modern revelations, are even more prized.

Paul, for instance, wrote his first epistle to the Corinthians about A.D. 56. We do not, of course, have that original parchment. Instead, the earliest document involving the first epistle to the Corinthians was discovered in the 1930s and is dated to about A.D. 200. By comparison, King Benjamin's sermon was given in about 124 B.C. by a prophet. In the late fourth century A.D. it was selected by another prophet—Mormon—to be a part of the Book of Mormon. Benjamin's sermon was translated into English in A.D. 1829 by Joseph Smith, another prophet. There was, therefore, an unbroken chain of a prophet-originator, a prophet-editor, and a prophet-translator collaborating in a remarkable process.

Even so, some discount the Book of Mormon because they cannot see the plates from which it was translated. Furthermore, they say that we do not know enough about the process of translation. But Moroni's promise to serious readers, to be discussed shortly, involves reading and praying over the book's substance, not over the process of its production. We are "looking beyond the mark" (Jacob 4:14), therefore, when, figuratively speaking, we are more interested in the physical dimensions of the cross than what was achieved thereon by Jesus. Or, when we neglect Alma's words on faith because we are too fascinated by the light-shielding hat reportedly used by Joseph Smith during some of the translating of the Book of Mormon.[2]

Most of all, I have been especially struck in rereading and pondering the Book of Mormon with how, for the serious reader, it provides a very, very significant response to what might be called modern man's architectonic needs—that is, our deep needs to discern some design, purpose, pattern, or plan regarding human existence.

No less than fifteen times, the Book of Mormon uses the word *plan* in connection with the plan of salvation or its components. The very use of the word *plan* is itself striking. In bringing back this particular "plain and precious" truth—namely, God not only lives but does have a plan for mankind—the Book of Mormon is unusually relevant for our age and time. Phrases about God's planning from the "foundation of the world" appear not at all in the Old Testament but ten times in the New Testament and three times as often in the other books.[3] *Foundation,* of course, thus denotes a creation overseen by a loving and planning God.

The Book of Mormon lays further and heavy emphasis on how the gospel, in fact, has been with mankind from Adam on down. Only six pages into the book, we read of the testifying words of all the prophets "since the world began" (1 Nephi 3:20); five pages later, a recitation notes the words of the "holy prophets, from the beginning" (1 Nephi 5:13). This one verse represents many: "For behold, did not Moses prophesy unto them concerning the coming of the Messiah, and that God should redeem his people? Yea, and even all the prophets who have prophesied ever since the world began—have they not spoken more or less concerning these things?" (Mosiah 13:33; see also 2 Nephi 25:19).

It seems probable that there will be some additional discoveries of ancient records pertaining to the Old and New Testaments, further shrinking the time between the origination of those scriptures and the earliest available documentation. However, this *shrinking* will not automatically lead to an *enlarging* of the faith—at least of some. Future discoveries of ancient documents that may "throw greater views upon [His] gospel" (D&C 10:45) may also focus on portions of Jesus' gospel which existed *before* Jesus' mortal ministry. Unfortunately, a few may unjustifiably use such discoveries to diminish the divinity of the Redeemer, inferring that Jesus is therefore not the originator, as previously thought. However, the restored gospel, including the Book of Mormon, gives us such a clear reading of the spiritual history of mankind, showing God's "tender mercies" (see 1 Nephi 1:20; Ether 6:12) from Adam on down. There is thus no need for us to be anxious about finding a reliable portion of Christ's gospel before Christ's mortal ministry. The gospel was preached and known from the beginning (see Moses 5:58–59).

The detailed, interior correlation of the Book of Mormon—indeed of all true scripture—is marvelous to behold. Centuries before Christ's birth, King Benjamin prophesied: "And he shall be called Jesus Christ, the Son of God, the Father of heaven and earth, the Creator of all things from the beginning" (Mosiah 3:8).

The resurrected Jesus introduced Himself to the Nephites with strikingly similar words centuries later: "Behold, I am Jesus Christ the Son of God. I created the heavens and the earth, and all things that in them are. I was with the Father from the beginning" (3 Nephi 9:15).

But back to God's enfolding plan: Alma, after a discussion of the Fall, declared it was "expedient that man should know concerning the things whereof [God] had appointed unto them; therefore [God] sent angels to converse with them . . . and [make] known unto them the plan of redemption, which had been prepared from the foundation of the world" (Alma 12:28–30). This is the very process which was followed, of course, in North America in the first half of the nineteenth century through angelic visitations to Joseph Smith.

At the center of this architectonic responsiveness, with its related dispensational emphasis, is the Book of Mormon's steady, Christian core. Jacob wrote, "We knew of Christ . . . many hundred years before his coming; . . . also all the holy prophets which were before us. Behold, they believed in Christ and worshipped the Father in his name, . . . [keeping] the law of Moses, it pointing our souls to him" (Jacob 4:4–5). Jacob was emphatic: "None of the prophets have written . . . save they have spoken concerning this Christ" (Jacob 7:11).

God witnesses to us in so many ways: "Yea, and all things denote there is a God; yea, even the earth, and all things that are upon the face of it, yea, and its motion, yea, and also all the planets which move in their regular form do witness that there is a Supreme Creator" (Alma 30:44; see also Moses 6:63).

A believing British scientist has observed that our planet is especially situated: "Just a bit nearer to the sun, and Planet Earth's seas would soon be boiling; just a little farther out, and the whole world would become a frozen wilderness." This scientist noted: "If our orbit happened to be the wrong shape, . . . then we should alternately freeze like Mars and fry like Venus once a year. Fortunately for us, our planet's orbit is very nearly a circle."[4]

"The 21 percent of oxygen is another critical figure. Animals would have difficulty breathing if the oxygen content fell very far below that value. But an oxygen level much higher than this would also be disastrous, since the extra oxygen would act as a fire-raising material. Forests and grasslands would flare up every time lightning struck during a dry spell, and life on earth would become extremely hazardous."[5]

When, therefore, we know the affirmative answers to "the great question," we can, in Amulek's phrase, "live in thanksgiving daily" (Alma 34:38) with gratitude for the many special conditions which make daily life on this earth possible.

God's encompassing purposes are set forth to the very end of the

Book of Mormon. Moroni urged a precise method of study and verification which, if followed, will show among other things how merciful the Lord has been unto mankind "from the creation of Adam" (Moroni 10:3). Foretelling can be convincing too, along with remembering, in showing the sweep of God's love. "Telling them of things which must shortly come, that they might know and remember at the time of their coming that they had been made known unto them beforehand, to the intent that they might believe" (Helaman 16:5; see also Mormon 8:34–35).

Every age needs this architectonic message, but none more desperately than our age, which is preoccupied with skepticism and hedonism: "For how knoweth a man the master whom he has not served, and who is a stranger unto him, and is far from the thoughts and intents of his heart?" (Mosiah 5:13).

If, however, one gets too caught up in the warfare in the Book of Mormon, or if he is too preoccupied with the process of the book's emergence, such transcendent truths as the foregoing can easily be overlooked.

Even the title page[6] declares, among other things, that the Book of Mormon was to advise posterity "what great things the Lord hath done for their fathers." The very lack of such a spiritual memory once led to a decline of ancient Israel: "There arose another generation after them, which knew not the Lord, nor yet the works which he had done for Israel" (Judges 2:10).

Why was it so difficult for a whole people—or for Laman and Lemuel—to maintain faith? Because they were uninformed and unbelieving as to "the dealings of that God who had created them" (1 Nephi 2:12; 2 Nephi 1:10). Many efforts were made: "I, Nephi, did teach my brethren these things; . . . I did read many things to them, which were engraven upon the plates of brass, that they might know concerning the doings of the Lord in other lands, among people of old" (1 Nephi 19:22).

The prophetic emphasis on the Book of Mormon, therefore, is so pertinent!

Even the criticisms of the book will end up having their usefulness in God's further plans. Granted, the great answers in the book will not now be accepted by disbelievers. Such people would not believe the Lord's words—whether coming through Paul or Joseph Smith—even if they had an original Pauline parchment or direct access to the gold plates. The Lord once comforted Joseph Smith by saying such individuals "will not believe my words . . . if [shown] all these things" (D&C 5:7).

Thus, some decry the Book of Mormon. However, for those who have ears to hear, it represents an informing but haunting "cry from the dust" (2 Nephi 3:20). It is the voice of a fallen people sent to lift us. Described as a "whisper out of the dust" (2 Nephi 26:16) from "those who have slumbered" (2 Nephi 27:9), this sound from the dust is the choral cry of many anguished voices with but a single, simple message. Their spiritual struggles span a few centuries but concern the message of the ages—the gospel of Jesus Christ! The peoples of the Book of Mormon were not on the center stage of secular history. Instead, theirs was a comparatively little theater. Yet it featured history's largest message.

Not pleasing to those who crave other kinds of history, the Book of Mormon is pleasing to those who genuinely seek answers to "the great question" (Alma 34:5). Contrary to the sad conclusion now reached by many, the Book of Mormon declares to us again and again that the universe is not comprised of what has been called "godless geometric space."[7]

Granted, too, usually the "learned shall not read [these things], for they have rejected them" (2 Nephi 27:20). This is not solely a reference to Professor Anthon, since the plural pronoun *they* is used. The reference suggests a mind-set of most of the learned of the world, who, by and large, do not take the Book of Mormon seriously. Even when they read it, they do not *really* read it, except with a mind-set which excludes miracles, including the miracle of the book's coming forth by the "gift and power of God." Their flawed approach diverts them from scrutinizing the substance. Sometimes, as has been said, certain mortals are so afraid of being "taken in," they cannot be "taken out" of their mind-sets.[8]

How dependent mankind is, therefore, upon emancipating revelation: "Behold, great and marvelous are the works of the Lord. How unsearchable are the depths of the mysteries of him; and it is impossible that man should find out all his ways. And no man knoweth of his ways save it be revealed unto him; wherefore, brethren, despise not the revelations of God" (Jacob 4:8).

Now to Moroni's promise, which is a promise that rests on a premise, a promise with several parts. The reader is (1) to read and ponder, (2) while remembering God's mercies to mankind from Adam until now, and (3) to pray in the name of Christ and ask God with real intent if the book is true, (4) while having faith in Christ, then (5) God will manifest the truth of the book. The reverse approach, scanning while doubting, is the flip side of Moroni's methodology and produces flippant conclusions. Moroni's process of verification is surely not followed by many readers or reviewers of this book. This leads to misapprehension—like mistakenly labeling rumor with her thousand tongues as the gift of tongues!

Therefore, we should not be deluded into thinking that these "other books" will be welcomed, especially by those whose sense of sufficiency is expressed thus: "There cannot be any more" such books and "we need no more" such books (2 Nephi 29:3, 6).

Another strong impression from my rereading is how the Book of Mormon peoples, though Christians, were tied, until Jesus came, much more strictly to the preexilic law of Moses than we in the Church have fully appreciated. "And, notwithstanding we believe in Christ, we keep the law of Moses, and look forward with steadfastness unto Christ, until the law shall be fulfilled" (2 Nephi 25:24).

People back then were thus to "look forward unto the Messiah, and believe in him to come as though he already was" (Jarom 1:11). Moses indeed prophesied of the Messiah, but not all of his words are in the treasured Old Testament. Recall the walk of the resurrected Jesus with two disciples on the road to Emmaus? Their walk probably covered about twelve kilometers and provided ample time for Jesus' recitation of not merely three or four, but many prophecies by Moses and others concerning Christ's mortal ministry (Luke 24:27).

Scriptures attesting to Jesus' divinity are vital in any age. Otherwise, as the Book of Mormon prophesies, He will be considered a mere man (Mosiah 3:9) or a person of "naught" (1 Nephi 19:9). Over the decades, what has been called the "dilution of Christianity from within"[9] has resulted in a number of theologians not only diminishing their regard for Christ but likewise regarding the Resurrection as merely "a symbolic expression for the renewal of life for the disciple."[10] Once again we see the supernal importance of the "other books" of scripture: they reinforce the reality of the Resurrection, especially the Book of Mormon's additional gospel with its report of the visitation of and instruction by the resurrected Jesus. The resurrection of many others occurred and, by Jesus' pointed instruction, was made record of (see 3 Nephi 23:6–13).

Thus the Book of Mormon resoundingly, richly, and grandly answers the "great question." Granted, in our day, the post-Christian era, many who are preoccupied are not even asking that great question anymore, regarding Christianity "not as untrue or even as unthinkable, but simply irrelevant,"[11] just like some in Benjamin and Mosiah's times (see Mosiah 28:1–2; Omni 1:17).

If the answer to the "great question" were "no," there would quickly come a wrenching surge of what Professor Hugh Nibley has called the "terrible questions."

Even the historical, political, and geographical setting of the emergence of the Book of Mormon was special. President Brigham Young boldly declared: "Could that book have been brought forth and published to the world under any other government but the Government of the United States? No. [God] has governed and controlled the settling of this continent. He led our fathers from Europe to this land . . . and inspired the guaranteed freedom in our Government, though that guarantee is too often disregarded."[12]

In the midst of this continually unfolding drama, a few members of the Church, alas, desert the cause; they are like one who abandons an oasis to search for water in the desert. Some of these few will doubtless become critics, and they will be welcomed into the "great and spacious building." Henceforth, however, so far as their theological accommodations are concerned, they are in a spacious but third-rate hotel. All dressed up, as the Book of Mormon says, "exceedingly fine" (1 Nephi 8:27), they have no place to go except—one day, hopefully, home.

The great answers to the "great question" repeatedly focus us, therefore, on the reality of the "great and last sacrifice." "This is the whole meaning of the law, every whit pointing to that great and last sacrifice; and that great and last sacrifice will be the Son of God, yea, infinite and eternal" (Alma 34:14). These great answers reaffirm that mortal melancholy need not be, however frequently and poignantly expressed.

Furthermore, what we receive in the Book of Mormon is not a mere assemblage of aphorisms, nor is it merely a few individuals offering their philosophical opinions. Instead, we receive the cumulative witness of prophetic individuals, especially those who were eyewitnesses of Jesus, including Lehi, Nephi, Jacob, Alma, the brother of Jared, Mormon, and Moroni. The biblical account of the five hundred brothers and sisters witnessing the resurrected Jesus (1 Corinthians 15:6) is joined by the witnessing throng of twenty-five hundred in the land of Bountiful (3 Nephi 17:25). All of these are thus added to the burgeoning cloud of witnesses about whom the Apostle Paul wrote (Hebrews 12:1).

The Book of Mormon might have been another kind of book, of course. It could have been chiefly concerned with the ebb and flow of governmental history; that is, "Princes come and princes go, an hour of pomp, an hour of show." Such would not have offset, however, the many despairing books and the literature of lamentation so much of which we have already, each reminiscent in one way or another of the hopelessness of these lines from Shelley:

> *. . . Two vast and trunkless legs of stone*
> *Stand in the desert. Near them, on the sand,*
> *Half sunk, a shattered visage lies, . . .*
> *And on the pedestal, these words appear:*
> *"My name is Ozymandias, king of kings:*
> *Look on my works, ye Mighty, and despair!"*

Nothing beside remains. Round the decay
Of that colossal wreck, boundless and bare
The lone and level sands stretch far away.[13]

Because the editing of the Book of Mormon, with its gospel of hope, occurred under divine direction, it has a focus which is essentially spiritual. Yet some still criticize the Book of Mormon for not being what it was never intended to be, as if one could justifiably criticize the phone directory for lack of a plot!

Some verses in the Book of Mormon are of tremendous salvational significance, others less so. The book of Ether has a verse about lineage history: "And Jared had four sons" (and names them) (Ether 6:14). However, Ether also contains another verse of tremendous salvational significance:

"And if men come unto me I will show unto them their weakness. I give unto men weakness that they may be humble; and my grace is sufficient for all men that humble themselves before me; for if they humble themselves before me, and have faith in me, then will I make weak things become strong unto them" (Ether 12:27).

We read of a battle "when . . . they slept upon their swords . . . were drunken with anger, even as a man who is drunken with wine. . . . And when the night came there were thirty and two of the people of Shiz, and twenty and seven of the people of Coriantumr" (Ether 15:20–26). Such, however, is of a much lower spiritual significance for the development of our discipleship than are these next lines. In all of scripture, these constitute the most complete delineation of Jesus' requirement that we become as little children (see Matthew 18:3): ". . . and becometh as a child, submissive, meek, humble, patient, full of love, willing to submit to all things which the Lord seeth fit to inflict upon him, even as a child doth submit to his father" (Mosiah 3:19).

One reason to "search the scriptures" is to discover these sudden luxuriant meadows of meaning, these green pastures to nourish us in our individual times of need. The Book of Mormon surely has its share and more of these. Immediately after words about economic conditions in the now vanished city of Helam, we encounter an enduring and bracing truth: "Nevertheless the Lord seeth fit to chasten his people; yea, he trieth their patience and their faith" (Mosiah 23:20–21; see also D&C 98:12; Abraham 3:25).

Similarly, the Book of Mormon provides us with insights we may not yet be ready to manage fully. Astonishingly, Alma includes our pains, sicknesses, and infirmities, along with our sins, as being among that which Jesus would also "take upon him" (Alma 7:11–12). It was part of the perfecting of Christ's mercy by His experiencing "according to the flesh." Nephi in exclaiming "O how great the plan of our God" (2 Nephi 9:13) also declared how Jesus would suffer "the pains of all . . . men, women, and children, who belong to the family of Adam" (2 Nephi 9:21). The soul trembles at those implications. One comes away weeping from such verses, deepened in his adoration of our Redeemer.

Given such richness, it is unsurprising that the prophets urge us to read the Book of Mormon. In closing his writings to those who do not respect (1) the words of the Jews (the Bible), (2) his words (as found in the Book of Mormon), and (3) also the words from Jesus (from the future New Testament), Nephi said simply, "I bid you an everlasting farewell" (2 Nephi 33:14).

Mormon is equally emphatic regarding this interactiveness between the Bible and the Book of Mormon (see Mormon 7:8–9). The interactiveness and cross-supportiveness of holy scripture was attested to by Jesus: "For had ye believed Moses, ye would have believed me: for he wrote of me. But if ye believe not his writings, how shall ye believe my words?" (John 5:46–47).

Meanwhile, from those who say, "We have enough, from them shall be taken away even that which they have" (2 Nephi 28:30). Obviously, this refers not to the physical loss of the Bible, which may still be on the bookshelf or may be used as a bookend, but to a sad loss of conviction concerning it on the part of some.

When we "search the scriptures," the luminosity of various verses in the various books is focused, laserlike. This illumination arcs and then converges, even though we are dealing with different authors, people, places, and times: "Wherefore, I speak the same words unto one nation like unto another. And when the two nations shall run together the testimony of the two nations shall run together also" (2 Nephi 29:8).

Believing, however, is not a matter of accessing antiquity with all its evidence, though we welcome such evidence. Nor is it dependent upon accumulating welcomed historical evidence either. Rather, it is a matter of believing in Jesus' words. Real faith, like real humility, is developed "because of the word"—and not because of surrounding circumstances (Alma 32:13–14)!

How fitting it is that it should be so! The test is focused on the message, not on the messengers; on principles, not on process; on doctrines, not on plot. The emphasis is on belief, per se, "because of the word." As Jesus told Thomas on the Eastern Hemisphere, "Blessed are they that have not seen, and yet have believed" (John 20:29). He proclaimed to the Nephites: "More blessed are they who shall believe in your words because that ye shall testify that ye have seen me" (3 Nephi 12:2).

True faith therefore, is brought about by overwhelming and intimidating divine intervention. The Lord, the Book of Mormon tells us, is a shepherd with a mild and pleasant voice (see Helaman 5:30–31; 3 Nephi 11:3)—not a shouting and scolding sheepherder. Others may, if they choose, demand a "voiceprint" of the "voice of the Lord," but even if so supplied, they would not like His doctrines anyway (see John 6:66). The things of the Spirit are to be "sought by faith"; and they are not to be seen through slit-eyed skepticism.

Without real faith, individuals sooner or later find one thing or another to stumble over (Romans 9:32). After all, it is a very difficult thing to show the proud things which they "never had supposed," especially things they do not really want to know. When Jesus was speaking about Himself as the bread of life, a powerful doctrine laden with life-changing implications, there was murmuring. Jesus asked them, "Doth this offend you?" (John 6:61). "Blessed is he, whosoever shall not be offended in me" (Luke 7:23).

As if all this were not enough, the splendid Book of Mormon

advises that a third scriptural witness is yet to come from the lost tribes (see 2 Nephi 29:12–14). Its coming is likely to be even more dramatic than the coming forth of the second testament. Those who doubt or disdain the second testament of Christ will not accept the third either. But believers will then possess a triumphant triad of truth (see 2 Nephi 29:12–13). Were it not for the Book of Mormon, we would not even know about the third set of records!

We do not know when and how this will occur, but we are safe in assuming that the third book will have the same fundamental focus as the Book of Mormon: "that . . . their seed [too] . . . may be brought to a knowledge of me, their Redeemer" (3 Nephi 16:4). If there is a title page in that third set of sacred records, it is not likely to differ in purpose from the title page in the Book of Mormon, except for its focus on still other peoples who likewise received a personal visit from the resurrected Jesus (see 3 Nephi 15:20–24; 16:1–4).

Thus in the dispensation of the fulness of times there is not only a "welding together" (D&C 128:18) of the keys of all the dispensations but there will also be a "welding together" of all the sacred books of scripture given by the Lord over the sweep of human history. Then, as prophesied, "my word also shall be gathered in one" (2 Nephi 29:14). Then there will be one fold, one shepherd, and one stunning scriptural witness for the Christ!

Given all the foregoing, it is touching that a jailed Joseph Smith, during his last mortal night, 26 June 1844, bore "a powerful testimony to the guards of the divine authenticity of the Book of Mormon, the restoration of the Gospel, the administration of angels"[14] (see Alma 12:28–30). The guards apparently did not hearken then any more than most of the world hearkens now. Heeded or unheeded, however, the Book of Mormon has a further rendezvous to keep: "Wherefore, these things shall go from generation to generation as long as the earth shall stand; and they shall go according to the will and pleasure of God; and the nations who shall possess them shall be judged of them according to the words which are written" (2 Nephi 25:22).

For my part, I am glad the book will be with us "as long as the earth shall stand." I need and want additional time. For me, towers, courtyards, and wings await inspection. My tour of it has never been completed. Some rooms I have yet to enter, and there are more flaming fireplaces waiting to warm me. Even the rooms I have glimpsed contain further furnishings and rich detail yet to be savored. There are panels inlaid with incredible insights and design and decor dating from Eden. There are also sumptuous banquet tables painstakingly prepared by predecessors which await all of us. Yet, we as Church members sometimes behave like hurried tourists, scarcely venturing beyond the entry hall to the mansion.

May we come to feel as a whole people beckoned beyond the entry hall. May we go inside far enough to hear clearly the whispered truths from those who have "slumbered," which whisperings will awaken in us individually the life of discipleship as never before.

NOTES

1. Wars of the Lord, Jasher, more from Samuel, the Acts of Solomon, the book of Nathan, Shemaiah, Ahijah, Iddo, Jehu, the Sayings of the Seers, at least two epistles of Paul, books of Enoch, Ezias, Adam's Book of Remembrance, and Gad the Seer. Thus we are dealing with over twenty missing books. We also have certain prophecies from Jacob, or Israel, and extensive prophecies by Joseph in Egypt, only a portion of which we have (see 2 Nephi 3:1–25; 4:1–3; Joseph Smith Translation, Genesis 50:24–37; Alma 46:24–26).

2. Furthermore, too few people are inclined to follow the counsel of Moroni regarding the book's substance: "Condemn me not because of mine imperfection, neither my father, because of his imperfection, neither them who have written before him; but rather give thanks unto God that he hath made manifest unto you our imperfections, that ye may learn to be more wise than we have been" (Mormon 9:31).

3. Twenty-two times in the Book of Mormon, ten times in the Doctrine and Covenants, and three times in the Pearl of Great Price.

4. Alan Hayward, *God Is* (Nashville: Thomas Nelson, 1980), 62–63.

5. Hayward, *God Is,* 68.

6. Joseph Smith, *Teachings of the Prophet Joseph Smith,* comp. Joseph Fielding Smith (Salt Lake City: Deseret Book, 1976), 7.

7. Michael Harrington, *The Politics at God's Funeral: The Spiritual Crisis of Western Civilization* (New York: Holt, Rinehart, and Winston, 1983), 114.

8. C. S. Lewis, *The Last Battle* (New York: Collier, 1970), 148.

9. Harrington, *Politics,* 153.

10. Harrington, *Politics,* 164.

11. Penelope Fitzgerald, *The Knox Brothers* (New York: Coward, McCann & Geoghegen, 1977), 106–7.

12. Brigham Young, in *Journal of Discourses* (London: Latter-day Saints' Book Depot, 1854–86), 8:67.

13. Percy Bysshe Shelley, "Ozymandias," *Norton Anthology of English Literature* (New York: W. W. Norton & Company, 1986), 2:691.

14. Smith, *Teachings,* 383.

2

Jesus the Christ—Our Master and More

Elder Russell M. Nelson

My lifelong interest in the human heart took an unexpected turn in April 1984, when I was called to leave the operating room of the hospital and enter the upper room of the temple. There I became an ordained Apostle of the Lord Jesus Christ. I did not seek such a call but have humbly tried to be worthy of that trust and privilege of being His representative, now hoping to mend hearts spiritually as I previously did surgically.

So I come to you as one who has been called, sustained, and ordained—one of the twelve special witnesses of our Lord and Master. In speaking with you, I sense our mutual desire and sacred responsibility to follow this vital theme from the Book of Mormon: "We talk of Christ, we rejoice in Christ, we preach of Christ, [and] we prophesy of Christ" (2 Nephi 25:26). We honor Him as the most important individual ever to live on planet Earth. He is Jesus the Christ—our Master and more. He has numerous names, titles, and responsibilities, all of eternal significance.[1] The Topical Guide has eighteen pages (240–58) under the heading "Jesus Christ," filled with references listed under fifty-seven subheadings. In the space allotted we could not fully consider or comprehend all of these important facets of His life. But I

Elder Russell M. Nelson is a member of the Quorum of the Twelve Apostles.

would like to review, even briefly, ten of those mighty responsibilities of Jesus the Christ. I will not number these responsibilities—not wanting to imply any order of priority—because all that He accomplished was equally supernal in scope.

CREATOR

Under the direction of the Father, Jesus bore the responsibility of CREATOR. His title was *the Word*—spelled with a capital *W.* In the Greek language of the New Testament, that Word was *Logos,* or "divine Expression." It was another name for the Master. That terminology may seem strange, but it is so reasonable. We use words to convey our expression to others. So Jesus was the "Word" or "Expression" of His Father to the world.

The Gospel of John begins with this important proclamation:

"In the beginning was the Word, and the Word was with God, and the Word was God.

"The same was in the beginning with God.

"All things were made by him; and without him was not any thing made that was made" (John 1:1–3; see also D&C 93:21).

The book of Helaman records similar testimony, declaring that "Jesus Christ [is] . . . the Creator of all things from the beginning" (Helaman 14:12). Another clarifying quotation came from "the Lord God [who] said unto Moses: For mine own purpose have I made these things. . . .

"And by the word of my power, have I created them, which is mine Only Begotten Son, who is full of grace and truth.

"And worlds without number have I created; and I also created them for mine own purpose; and by the Son I created them, which is mine Only Begotten" (Moses 1:31–33).

In modern revelation, Jesus' responsibility as Creator of many worlds is again affirmed:

"Therefore, in the beginning the Word was, for he was the Word, even the messenger of salvation—

"The light and the Redeemer of the world; the Spirit of truth, who came into the world, because the world was made by him, and in him was the life of men and the light of men.

"The worlds were made by him; men were made by him; all things were made by him, and through him" (D&C 93:8–10; see also 1 Corinthians 8:6; Hebrews 1:2; 2 Nephi 9:5; 3 Nephi 9:15; D&C 76:23–24; 88:42–48; 101:32–34).

This hallowed Creator provided that each of us may have a physical body, unique, yet in many respects comparable to every other human body. Just as a well-educated musician can recognize the composer of a symphony by its style and structure, so a well-educated surgeon can recognize the Creator of human beings by the similarity of style and structure of our anatomy. Individual variations notwithstanding, this similarity provides additional evidence and deep spiritual confirmation of our divine creation by our same Creator. It enhances the understanding of our relationship to Him:

"The Gods went down to organize man in their own image, in the image of the Gods to form they him, male and female to form they them.

"And the Gods said: We will bless them" (Abraham 4:27–28).

Indeed, they have blessed each of us. Our bodies can repair and defend themselves. They regenerate new cells to replace old ones. Our bodies carry seeds that allow reproduction of our own kind with our individual characteristics. Little wonder our Creator is also known as the Great Physician (see Matthew 9:12)—able to heal the sick (see 3 Nephi 9:13; D&C 35:9; 42:48–51), restore sight to the blind (see John 9:1–11), unstop the ears of the deaf (see Isaiah 35:5; 3 Nephi 26:15), and raise the dead (see Matthew 9:23–26; John 11:5–45). And in these latter days, He has revealed a code of health known as the Word of Wisdom that has blessed the lives of all who have obeyed those teachings in faith. So we honor Jesus as our Creator, divinely directed by His Father.

JEHOVAH

Jesus was JEHOVAH. This sacred title is recorded only four times in the King James Version of the Holy Bible (see Exodus 6:3; Psalms

83:18; Isaiah 12:2; 26:4). The use of this holy name is also confirmed in modern scripture (see Moroni 10:34; D&C 109:68; 110:3; 128:9). *Jehovah* is derived from the Hebrew word *Hayah,* which means "to be" or "to exist." A form of the word *Hayah* in the Hebrew text of the Old Testament was translated into English as "I Am" (Exodus 3:14).

Remarkably, "I Am" was used by Jehovah as a name for Himself (see D&C 29:1; 38:1; 39:1). Listen to this intriguing dialogue from the Old Testament. Moses had just received a divine appointment that he did not seek—a commission to lead the children of Israel out of bondage. The scene takes place atop Mount Sinai:

"Moses said unto God, Who am I, that I should go unto Pharaoh, and that I should bring forth the children of Israel out of Egypt?" (No doubt Moses felt inadequate for his calling, even as you and I may when given a challenging assignment.)

"And Moses said [again] unto God, Behold, when I come unto the children of Israel, and shall say unto them, The God of your fathers hath sent me unto you; and they shall say to me, What is his name? what shall I say unto them?

"And God said unto Moses, I Am that I Am: and he said, Thus shalt thou say unto the children of Israel, I Am hath sent me unto you.

"And God said moreover unto Moses, Thus shalt thou say unto the children of Israel, The Lord God of your fathers, the God of Abraham, the God of Isaac, and the God of Jacob, hath sent me unto you: this is my name for ever" (Exodus 3:11, 13–15).

Jehovah had thus revealed to Moses this very name that He had meekly and modestly chosen for His own premortal identification—"I Am."

Later in His mortal ministry, Jesus occasionally repeated this name. Do you remember His terse response to tormenting questioners? Note the double meaning in His reply to Caiaphas, the chief high priest:

"The high priest asked him, . . . Art thou the Christ, the Son of the Blessed?

"And Jesus said, I am" (Mark 14:61–62).

He was declaring both His lineage and His name. Another instance occurred when Jesus was taunted about His acquaintanceship with Abraham:

"Then said the Jews unto him, . . . hast thou seen Abraham?

"Jesus said unto them, Verily, verily, I say unto you, Before Abraham was, I am" (John 8:57–58).

Jehovah—the great I Am and God of the Old Testament—clearly identified Himself when the resurrected Jesus personally appeared in His glory to the Prophet Joseph Smith and Oliver Cowdery in the Kirtland Temple on 3 April 1836. I quote from their written testimony:

"We saw the Lord standing upon the breastwork of the pulpit, before us; and under his feet was a paved work of pure gold, in color like amber.

"His eyes were as a flame of fire; the hair of his head was white like the pure snow; his countenance shone above the brightness of the sun; and his voice was as the sound of the rushing of great waters, even the *voice of Jehovah,* saying:

"I am the first and the last; I am he who liveth, I am he who was slain" (D&C 110:2–4; emphasis added; see also D&C 76:23).

Jesus fulfilled His responsibility as Jehovah, "the Great I Am," with eternal consequence.

ADVOCATE WITH THE FATHER

Jesus is our ADVOCATE WITH THE FATHER (see 1 John 2:1; D&C 29:5; 32:3; 45:3; 110:4). The word *advocate* comes from Latin roots meaning a "voice for," or "one who pleads for another." Other related terms are used in scripture, such as *intercessor* or *mediator* (see 1 Timothy 2:5; 2 Nephi 2:28; D&C 76:69). From the Book of Mormon we learn that this responsibility was foreseen before His birth: "[Jesus] shall make intercession for all the children of men; and they that believe in him shall be saved" (2 Nephi 2:9).

This mission was clearly evident in the compassionate intercessory prayer of Jesus. Picture Him in your mind, kneeling in fervent supplication. Listen to the beautiful language of His prayer and sense His feeling for His weighty responsibility as Mediator:

"I have manifested thy name unto the men which thou gavest me out of the world: thine they were, and thou gavest them me; and they have kept thy word.

"Now they have known that all things whatsoever thou hast given me are of thee.

"For I have given unto them the words which thou gavest me; and they have received them, and have known surely that I came out from thee, and they have believed that thou didst send me.

"I pray for them" (John 17:6–9).

He is also known as the Mediator of the new testament or covenant (see Hebrews 9:15; 12:24). Comprehending Him as our Advocate, Intercessor, and Mediator with the Father gives us assurance of His unequalled understanding, justice, and mercy (see Alma 7:12).

IMMANUEL

Jesus was foreordained to be the Promised Immanuel. Remember Isaiah's remarkable prophecy: "The Lord himself shall give you a sign; Behold, a virgin shall conceive, and bear a son, and shall call his name Immanuel" (Isaiah 7:14). Fulfillment of that prophecy was not just unlikely—it was humanly impossible. Incredible! Everyone knew that a virgin could not bear a child. And then for that child to be given such a pretentious name was doubly daring. The Hebrew name Isaiah announced—*Immanuel*—literally means "With us is God"! (see Isaiah 7:14, footnote *e*). That holy name was subsequently given to Jesus in the New Testament, the Book of Mormon, and the Doctrine and Covenants (see Matthew 1:23; 2 Nephi 17:14; D&C 128:22). *Immanuel* could be such only at the will of His Father.

SON OF GOD

Jesus alone bore His responsibility as the SON OF GOD—the Only Begotten Son of the Father (see John 1:14, 18; 3:16). Jesus was literally "the Son of the Highest" (Luke 1:32, 35). In more than a dozen verses of scripture, the solemn word of God, the Father bears testimony that Jesus was truly His Beloved Son. That solemn testimony was often coupled with God's pleading for mankind to hear and obey the voice of His revered Son (see Matthew 3:17; 17:5; Mark 1:11; 9:7; Luke

3:22; 9:35; 2 Peter 1:17; 2 Nephi 31:11; 3 Nephi 11:7; 21:20; D&C 93:15; Moses 4:2; JS–H 1:17). Through the condescension of God, that most unlikely prophecy of Isaiah had become reality.

The unique parentage of Jesus was also announced to Nephi, who was thus instructed by an angel: "Behold, the virgin whom thou seest is the mother of the Son of God, after the manner of the flesh. . . . Behold the Lamb of God, yea, even the Son of the Eternal Father!" (1 Nephi 11:18, 21).

From His mother, Jesus inherited His potential for mortality and death (see Genesis 3:15; Mark 6:3). From His Heavenly Father, Jesus inherited His potential for immortality and eternal life. Prior to His crucifixion, He spoke these words of clarification:

"I lay down my life, that I might take it again.

"No man taketh it from me, but I lay it down of myself. I have power to lay it down, and I have power to take it again. This . . . have I received of my Father" (John 10:17–18).

Though separate from His Heavenly Father in both body and spirit, Jesus is one with His Father in power and purpose. Their ultimate objective is "to bring to pass the immortality and eternal life of man" (Moses 1:39).

Some of you may wonder why the Son is occasionally referred to as "the Father." The designation used for any man can vary. Every man here is a son but may also be called "father," "brother," "uncle," or "grandfather," depending on conversational circumstance. So we must not allow ourselves to become confused regarding divine identity, purpose, or doctrine. Because Jesus was our Creator, He is known in scripture as "the Father of all things" (Mosiah 7:27; see also 15:3; 16:15; Helaman 14:12; Ether 3:14). But please remember, as the First Presidency taught, "Jesus Christ is not the Father of the spirits who have taken or yet shall take bodies upon this earth, for He is one of them. He is The Son, as they are sons or daughters of Elohim."[2]

We comprehend that distinction well when we pray to our Heavenly Father in the name of His Son, Jesus Christ, through the power of the Holy Ghost. And as we do so regularly, we honor our heavenly and earthly parentage, just as Jesus honored His, as the Son of God.

ANOINTED ONE

"God anointed Jesus of Nazareth with the Holy Ghost and with power" (Acts 10:38). So Jesus was the ANOINTED ONE. Because of this fact, He was accorded two specific titles. One was the *Messiah,* which in Hebrew means "the anointed." The other was the *Christ,* which comes from the Greek word that also means "the anointed." Thus, "Jesus is spoken of as the Christ and the Messiah, which means he is the one anointed of the Father to be his personal representative in all things pertaining to the salvation of mankind" (Bible Dictionary, "Anointed One," 609). Scriptures declare that *Christ* is the only name under heaven whereby salvation comes (see 2 Nephi 25:20). So you may add either of these titles to signify your adoration for Jesus—as "the Christ," or as "the Messiah"—anointed by God for that supernal responsibility.

SAVIOR AND REDEEMER

Jesus was born to be the SAVIOR and REDEEMER of all mankind (see Isaiah 49:26; 1 Nephi 10:5). He was the Lamb of God (see 1 Nephi 10:10), who offered Himself without spot or blemish (see 1 Peter 1:19) as a sacrifice for the sins of the world (see John 1:29). Later, as the resurrected Lord, He related that sacred responsibility to the meaning of the *gospel,* which He described in one powerful passage: "Behold I have given unto you my gospel, and this is the gospel which I have given unto you—that I came into the world to do the will of my Father, because my Father sent me. And my Father sent me that I might be lifted up upon the cross" (3 Nephi 27:13–14).

Thus, Jesus personally defined *gospel.* This term comes from the Old English *godspell,* which literally means "good news." The LDS Bible Dictionary notes the following: "The good news is that Jesus Christ has made a perfect atonement for mankind that will redeem all mankind from the grave and reward each individual according to his/her works. This atonement was begun by his appointment in the premortal world but was worked out by Jesus during his mortal sojourn" (Bible Dictionary, "Gospels," 682).

Jesus' atonement had been foretold long before He was born in Bethlehem. Prophets had prophesied His advent for many generations. For example, let us sample the record of Helaman, which was written some thirty years before the Savior's birth: "Remember that there is no other way nor means whereby man can be saved, only through the atoning blood of Jesus Christ, who shall come; yea, remember that he cometh to redeem the world" (Helaman 5:9). His atonement blesses each of us in a very personal way. Listen carefully to this explanation from Jesus:

"For behold, I, God, have suffered these things for all, that they might not suffer if they would repent;

"But if they would not repent they must suffer even as I;

"Which suffering caused myself, even God, the greatest of all, to tremble because of pain, and to bleed at every pore, and to suffer both body and spirit—and would that I might not drink the bitter cup, and shrink—

"Nevertheless, glory be to the Father, and I partook and finished my preparations unto the children of men" (D&C 19:16–19).

Jesus fulfilled His glorious promise made in pre-earthly councils by atoning for the Fall of Adam and Eve unconditionally, and for our own sins upon the condition of our repentance. His responsibility as Savior and Redeemer was indelibly intertwined with His responsibility as Creator. To shed additional insight on this relationship, I would like to share a remarkable quotation that I found in a rare book in London one day while searching through the library of the British Museum. It was published as a twentieth-century English translation of an ancient Egyptian text. It was written by Timothy, Archbishop of Alexandria, who died in A.D. 385. This record refers to the creation of Adam. The premortal Jesus is speaking of His Father:

"He . . . made Adam according to Our image and likeness, and He left him lying for forty days and forty nights without putting breath into him. And He heaved sighs over him daily, saying, 'If I put breath into this [man], he must suffer many pains.' And I said unto My Father,

"'Put breath into him; I will be an advocate for him.' And My Father said unto Me, 'If I put breath into him, My beloved Son, Thou wilt be obliged to go down into the world, and to suffer many pains for him before Thou shalt have redeemed him, and made him to come back to his primal state.' And I said unto My Father, 'Put breath into him; I will be his advocate, and I will go down into the world, and will fulfil Thy command.'"[3]

Jesus' responsibility as Advocate, Savior, and Redeemer was foredetermined in premortal realms and fulfilled by His atonement (see Job 19:25–26; Matthew 1:21). Your responsibility is to remember, to repent, and to be righteous.

JUDGE

Closely allied to the Lord's status as Savior and Redeemer is His responsibility as JUDGE. Jesus revealed this interrelationship after He had declared His definition of *gospel* that we just cited: "As I have been lifted up [upon the cross] by men even so should men be lifted up by the Father, to stand before me, to be judged of their works, whether they be good or whether they be evil—therefore, according to the power of the Father I will draw all men unto me, that they may be judged according to their works" (3 Nephi 27:14–15).

The Book of Mormon sheds further light on how that judgment will occur. So does the temple endowment. When we approach that threshold of the eternal court of justice, we know who will personally preside: "The keeper of the gate is the Holy One of Israel; and he employeth no servant there; and there is none other way save it be by the gate; for he cannot be deceived, for the Lord God is his name. And whoso knocketh, to him will he open" (2 Nephi 9:41–42).

Scriptures indicate that the Lord will receive apostolic assistance when exercising judgment upon the house of Israel (see 1 Nephi 12:9; D&C 29:12). Your personal encounter at judgment will be aided by your own "bright recollection" (Alma 11:43) and "perfect remembrance"

(Alma 5:18) of your deeds, as well as by the desires of your heart (see D&C 137:9).

EXEMPLAR

Another responsibility of the Lord is that of Exemplar. To people of the Holy Land, He said, "I have given you an example, that ye should do as I have done to you" (John 13:15; see also 14:6; 1 Peter 2:21). To people of ancient America, He again emphasized His mission as Exemplar: "I am the light; I have set an example for you" (3 Nephi 18:16, see also 27:27; 2 Nephi 31:9, 16). In His Sermon on the Mount, Jesus challenged His followers with this admonition: "Be ye therefore perfect, even as your Father which is in heaven is perfect" (Matthew 5:48).

Sinless and flawless as Jesus was in mortality, we should remember that He viewed His own state of physical perfection as being yet in the future (see Luke 13:32). Even He had to endure to the end. Can you and I be expected to do any less?

When the crucified and resurrected Lord appeared to the people in ancient America, He again stressed the importance of His example. But now He included Himself as a perfected personage: "I would that ye should be perfect even as I, or your Father who is in heaven is perfect" (3 Nephi 12:48).

Are you vexed by your own imperfections? For example, have you ever locked your keys inside the car? Or to accomplish a task, have you ever moved from one room to another only to find you had forgotten what you wanted to do? (Incidentally, troubles of that nature don't disappear as you grow older.) Meanwhile, please do not be discouraged by the Lord's expression of hope for your perfection. You should have faith to know that He would not require development beyond your capacity. Of course you should strive to correct habits or thoughts which are improper. Conquering of weakness brings great joy. You can attain a certain degree of perfection in some things in this life. And you can become perfect in keeping various commandments. But the Lord was not necessarily asking for your errorless and perfect behavior in all things. He was pleading for more than that. His hopes are for your full potential to be realized—to become as He is! That includes the perfection of your physical body, when it will be changed to an immortal state that cannot deteriorate or die.

So while you earnestly strive for continuing improvement in your life here, remember your resurrection, exaltation, and perfection await you in the life to come. That precious promise of perfection could not have been possible without the Lord's Atonement and His example.

MILLENNIAL MESSIAH

I have chosen to speak last of the Lord's ultimate responsibility, which lies yet in the future. That will be His masterful status as the Millennial Messiah. When that day comes, the physical face of the earth will have been changed: "Every valley shall be exalted, and every mountain and hill shall be made low: and the crooked shall be made straight, and the rough places plain" (Isaiah 40:4). Then Jesus will return to the earth. His second coming will be no secret. It will be broadly known: "The glory of the LORD shall be revealed, and all flesh shall see it together" (Isaiah 40:5).

Then, "the government shall be upon his shoulder: and his name shall be called Wonderful, Counsellor, The mighty God, The everlasting Father, The Prince of Peace" (Isaiah 9:6). He will govern from two world capitals—one in old Jerusalem (see Zechariah 14:4–7; D&C 45:48–66; 133:19–21) and the other in the New Jerusalem, "built upon the American continent" (Articles of Faith 1:10; see also Ether 13:3–10; D&C 84:2–4). From these centers He will direct the affairs of His Church and kingdom. Then He "shall reign for ever and ever" (Revelation 11:15; see also Exodus 15:18; Psalm 146:10; Mosiah 3:5; D&C 76:108).

In that day He will bear new titles and be surrounded by special Saints. He will be known as "Lord of lords, and King of kings: and they that [will be] with him [will be those who] are called, and chosen, and faithful" to their trust here in mortality (Revelation 17:14; see also 19:16).

He is Jesus the Christ—our Master and more. We have discussed but ten of His many responsibilities: Creator, Jehovah, Advocate with the Father, Immanuel, Son of God, Anointed One, Savior and Redeemer, Judge, Exemplar, and Millennial Messiah.

As His disciples, you and I bear mighty responsibilities too. Wherever I walk, it is my divine calling and sacred privilege to bear fervent testimony of Jesus the Christ. He lives! I love Him. Eagerly I follow Him, and willingly I offer my life in His service. As His special witness, I solemnly teach of Him. I testify of Him. It is my hope and blessing that you will bear your responsibility to know the Lord, love Him, follow Him, serve Him, teach and testify of Him, as I do.

NOTES

1. See Daniel H. Ludlow, "Jesus Christ Is Basis of LDS Beliefs," *Church News,* 29 March 1980, 9–10, 13.

2. James R. Clark, comp. *Messages of the First Presidency of The Church of Jesus Christ of Latter-day Saints* (Salt Lake City: Bookcraft, 1965–75), 5:34.

3. Timothy, Archbishop of Alexandria, "Discourse on Abbatôn," in *Coptic Martyrdoms etc. in the Dialect of Upper Egypt,* ed. and trans. E. A. Wallis Budge (New York: AMS, 1977), brackets appear in printed text; see also Moses 3:7; 6:8–9, 22, 29.

3

Agency and Freedom

Elder Dallin H. Oaks

Second Nephi, the focus of this symposium, provides some of our most important doctrinal insights on the significance of agency in the gospel plan. I have therefore chosen to speak about agency and freedom.

The scriptural terms are *agency* and *free.* When we refer to agency, we sometimes combine the two words and say *free agency.* But we sometimes use this term to refer to *freedom* as well as *agency.* And the scriptural term *free* sometimes means *agency* and sometimes means *freedom.*

In view of this confusion, I need to define the terms I will use. When I say *agency,* I refer to an exercise of the will, the power to choose. When I say *freedom,* I mean the power and privilege to carry out our choices. This includes everything from thoughts, such as hate, to actions, such as running.

In the first part of this message I will discuss the doctrine of the Church. In the second part I will describe some applications of that doctrine.

I. DOCTRINE

Sister Oaks is my best critic. She tells me that when I speak about doctrine my talks are pretty dry, probably more understandable to read

---

Elder Dallin H. Oaks is a member of the Quorum of the Twelve Apostles.

than to hear. Perhaps it would help if I began with an outline of the nine points I will make from the scriptures.

1. Before the world was created, we existed in the presence of God.

2. Agency is a gift of God.

3. We had agency in the premortal existence.

4. There Satan presented a plan that would have taken away our agency.

5. When God rejected Satan's plan, Satan and those who followed him rebelled and were cast out of heaven.

6. Pursuant to God's plan, Adam and Eve made the choice that caused the Fall, making mankind subject to mortality and sin in the world.

7. We are here to be tested, and this cannot occur without opposition in all things.

8. To provide that opposition, Satan is permitted to try to persuade us to use our agency to choose evil.

9. If we choose evil and do not repent, we can ultimately become captives of Satan.

To appreciate the significance of the added gospel knowledge restored in this dispensation, notice how many of these essential gospel truths are revealed or clarified in the Book of Mormon, especially 2 Nephi, and in the Doctrine and Covenants and the Pearl of Great Price.

1. *Before the world was created, we existed in the presence of God* (see D&C 93:29). Abraham saw that God stood in the midst of these spirits and chose some of them to make His rulers (see Abraham 3:23). We do not know much about the premortal existence. The scriptures sometimes refer to preexistent "intelligences" and sometimes to preexistent "spirits" (see Moses 6:36; Abraham 3:18–23; 5:7; D&C 93:29–33). For present purposes it is unnecessary to distinguish between the two. The important thing is that in the premortal existence we had individual identity and we dwelt in the presence of God.

2. *Agency, the power to choose, is a gift of God.* As we read in 2 Nephi 2:16: "Wherefore, the Lord God gave unto man that he should act for himself." Further, "Therefore, cheer up your hearts, and remember that

ye are free to act for yourselves—to choose the way of everlasting death or the way of eternal life" (2 Nephi 10:23). And in modern revelation the Lord said, "Behold, I gave unto him that he should be an agent unto himself" (D&C 29:35).

The Prophet Joseph Smith described agency as "that free independence of mind which heaven has so graciously bestowed upon the human family as one of its choicest gifts."[1] The word *free* is also used to describe agency in this hymn Latter-day Saints have been singing since our first hymnbook was printed in 1835:

Know this, that ev'ry soul is free
To choose his life and what he'll be;
For this eternal truth is giv'n
That God will force no man to heav'n.

He'll call, persuade, direct aright,
And bless with wisdom, love, and light,
In nameless ways be good and kind,
But never force the human mind.[2]

3. *We had agency in the premortal existence.* This is evident from the fact that more than one plan was put forward in the Council in Heaven and that a third of the hosts of heaven could choose to follow Satan and rebel against the Father.[3]

4. *Satan's plan, presented in the premortal existence, would have taken away our agency.* During what we call the Council in Heaven, the Father explained the conditions of the next step in the progression of His spirit children. They needed to receive a mortal body, and it was necessary for God to "prove them herewith, to see if they will do all things whatsoever the Lord their God shall command them" (Abraham 3:25).

Satan came before God with this proposal: "Behold, here am I, send me, I will be thy son, and I will redeem all mankind, that one soul shall not be lost, and surely I will do it; wherefore give me thine honor" (Moses 4:1). But the Beloved Son, our Savior, who was "chosen from the beginning" (Moses 4:2), said to the Father, "Here am I, send me"

(Abraham 3:27) and "Father, thy will be done, and the glory be thine forever" (Moses 4:2).

In the book of Moses, God describes Satan's effort:

"Wherefore, because that Satan rebelled against me, and sought to destroy the agency of man, which I, the Lord God, had given him, and also, that I should give unto him mine own power; by the power of mine Only Begotten, I caused that he should be cast down;

"And he became Satan, yea, even the devil, the father of all lies, to deceive and to blind men, and to lead them captive at his will, even as many as would not hearken unto my voice" (Moses 4:3–4).

Satan's method of assuring "that one soul shall not be lost" (Moses 4:1) would be to "destroy the agency of man" (Moses 4:3). Under his plan, Satan would have been our master, and he would have led us "captive at his will" (Moses 4:4). Without the power of choice, we would have been mere robots or puppets in his hands.

5. *When God rejected Satan's plan, Satan and those who followed him rebelled and were cast out of heaven.* The contest the scriptures call the "war in heaven" (Revelation 12:7) concerned Satan's attempts to usurp the power of God and to destroy the agency of God's children. One-third of the hosts of heaven exercised their agency to follow Satan. The Bible describes this in veiled references to Lucifer's attempt to exalt himself and to a war in which the dragon and his agents were cast out of heaven (see Isaiah 14:12–15; Revelation 12:7–9; Abraham 3:28). The event is described more clearly in modern revelation:

"For [the devil] rebelled against me, saying, Give me thine honor, which is my power; and also a third part of the hosts of heaven turned he away from me because of their agency;

"And they were thrust down, and thus came the devil and his angels" (D&C 29:36–37; see also D&C 76:25–26).

In his great poem "Immanuel—A Christmas Idyll," Elder Orson F. Whitney describes this event in the council of Gods when "The destiny of worlds unborn / Hung trembling in the scale." One arose:

A stature mingling strength and grace,
Of meek though Godlike mien,

The lustre of whose countenance
Outshone the noon-day sheen.
The hair was white as purest foam,
Or frost of Alpine hill.
He spake—attention grew more grave—
The stillness e'en more still.
"Father!"—the voice like music fell,
Clear as the murmuring flow
Or mountain streamlet, trickling down
From heights of virgin snow—
"Father!" it said, "since One must die
Thy children to redeem,
Whilst Earth—as yet unformed and void—
With pulsing life shall teem;
"And thou, great Michael, foremost fall,
That mortal man may be,
And chosen Savior yet must send,
Lo, here am I, send me!
I ask—I seek no recompense,
Save that which then were mine;
Mine be the willing sacrifice,
The endless glory—Thine!"
He ceased and sat; when sudden rose
Aloft a towering Form,
Proudly erect, as lowering peak
That looms above the storm.
A presence bright and beautiful,
With eye of lashing fire,
A lip whose haughty curl bespoke
A Sense of inward ire.
"Give me to go," he boldly cried,
With scarce concealed disdain,
"And none shall hence, from heaven to earth,
That shall not rise again.
My saving plan exception scorns—

Man's agency unknown.
As recompense, I claim the right
To sit on yonder Throne!"
Ceased Lucifer. The breathless hush
Resumed and denser grew.
All eyes were turned; the general gaze
One common magnet drew.
A moment there was solemn pause—
Then, like the thunder-burst,
Rolled forth from lips Omnipotent,
The words: "I'LL SEND THE FIRST!"
'Twas done. From congregation vast,
Tumultuous murmurs rose;
Waves of conflicting sound, as when
Two meeting seas oppose.
'Twas finished—but the heavens wept—
And still their annals tell
How God's elect was chosen Christ,
O'er One who fighting fell.[4]

6. *Pursuant to God's plan, Adam and Eve made the choice that caused the Fall, making mankind subject to mortality and sin in the world.* "But of the tree of the knowledge of good and evil, thou shalt not eat of it [the Lord told Adam and Eve], nevertheless, thou mayest choose for thyself, for it is given unto thee; but, remember that I forbid it, for in the day thou eatest thereof thou shalt surely die" (Moses 3:17). Adam and Eve were able to bring about the Fall by choice because they had alternatives and they had agency, whose essence is described in these words: "Thou mayest choose for thyself, for it is given unto thee."

Thus we see that what we call "the Fall" and "the transgression of Adam" was a necessary step that resulted from our first parents' exercise of their gift of agency. In 2 Nephi, Lehi explained, "But behold, all things have been done in the wisdom of him who knoweth all things. Adam fell that men might be; and men are, that they might have joy" (2 Nephi 2:24–25).

With the Fall came mortality and an opportunity to be tested. The Lord proclaimed that Adam's children were given "to know good from evil; wherefore they are agents unto themselves" (Moses 6:56). Alma taught that with the Fall men became "as Gods, knowing good from evil, placing themselves in a state to act, or being placed in a state to act according to their wills and pleasures, whether to do evil or to do good" (Alma 12:31; see also 42:7).

Similarly, the prophet Samuel taught: "For behold, ye are free; ye are permitted to act for yourselves; for behold, God hath given unto you a knowledge and he hath made you free" (Helaman 14:30). Note that in this teaching the word *free* refers to agency.

7. *We are here to be tested, and this cannot occur without opposition in all things.* On this subject, 2 Nephi enlarges our understanding. Father Lehi taught his son Jacob, "It must needs be, that there is an opposition in all things. If not so, my first-born in the wilderness, righteousness could not be brought to pass, neither wickedness, neither holiness nor misery, neither good nor bad. Wherefore, all things must needs be a compound in one" (2 Nephi 2:11).

In other words, if we did not have opposition, we could not exercise our agency by making choices. "Wherefore," Father Lehi explained, "the Lord God gave unto man that he should act for himself. Wherefore, man could not act for himself save it should be that he was enticed by the one or the other" (2 Nephi 2:16).

Without opposition in all things, we could not achieve righteousness. All things would be a "compound in one," a mixture—no distinction between wickedness and holiness. In that state of innocence, God's children would be "having no joy, for they knew no misery; doing no good, for they knew no sin" (2 Nephi 2:23). As we read in modern revelation, "And it must needs be that the devil should tempt the children of men, or they could not be agents unto themselves; for if they never should have bitter they could not know the sweet" (D&C 29:39).

8. *To provide the needed opposition, Satan is permitted to try to persuade us to use our agency to choose evil.* In 2 Nephi 2:26, Lehi declares that the Messiah will come "in the fulness of time, that he may redeem

the children of men from the fall." Then he gives us this important explanation:

"And because that they are redeemed from the fall they have become free forever, knowing good from evil; to act for themselves and not to be acted upon, save it be by the punishment of the law at the great and last day, according to the commandments which God hath given.

"Wherefore, men are free according to the flesh; and all things are given them which are expedient unto man. And they are free to choose liberty and eternal life, through the great Mediator of all men, or to choose captivity and death, according to the captivity and power of the devil; for he seeketh that all men might be miserable like unto himself" (2 Nephi 2:26–27).

"Free . . . to act for themselves" and "free to choose" refer to agency. "Free according to the flesh" refers to freedom, as I will illustrate later.

9. *If we choose evil and do not repent, we can ultimately become captives of Satan.* Lehi's assurance that we are free "to act for [ourselves] and not to be acted upon" has this exception: "save it be by the punishment of the law at the great and last day" if we have chosen "captivity and death, according to the captivity and power of the devil" (2 Nephi 2:26–27). He then pleads with his sons not to "choose eternal death, according to the will of the flesh and the evil which is therein, which giveth the spirit of the devil power to captivate, to bring you down to hell, that he may reign over you in his own kingdom" (2 Nephi 2:29).

Similarly, Amulek taught, "For behold, if ye have procrastinated the day of your repentance even until death, behold, ye have become subjected to the spirit of the devil, and he doth seal you his; therefore, the Spirit of the Lord hath withdrawn from you, and hath no place in you, and the devil hath all power over you; and this is the final state of the wicked" (Alma 34:35).

In summary, agency, the power to choose, is a gift of God, conferred on His children and exercised by them in the premortal life. It is an essential precondition of the further progression we seek in mortality. But agency cannot be exercised unless there is opposition in all things. That opposition is provided by Satan, who once sought to destroy our agency. His effort continues. He tries to persuade us to do evil and to make those choices that will finally give him the mastery he was denied in the preexistence—to have all power over us, to lead us captive at his will.

II. APPLICATION

Now I will discuss some applications of these scriptural principles.

First, because *agency* is a God-given precondition to the purpose of mortal life, no person or organization can take away our agency in mortality.

Second, what can be taken away or reduced by the conditions of mortality is our *freedom,* the power to act upon our choices. Agency is absolute, but in the circumstances of mortality freedom is always qualified.

Freedom may be qualified or taken away (1) by physical laws, including the physical limitations with which we are born, (2) by our own actions, and (3) by the actions of others, including governments.

Lehi taught his son Jacob that "men are free [have freedom] according to the flesh" (2 Nephi 2:27). For example, in the flesh we are subject to the physical law of gravity. If I should hang from the catwalk in the Marriott Center at Brigham Young University and release my grip, I would not be free to will myself into a soft landing. And I cannot choose to run through a brick wall.

A loss of freedom reduces the extent to which we can act upon our choices, but it does not deprive us of our God-given agency. A woman who has spent much of her life confined to a wheelchair expressed that thought in verse. Annie Johnson Flint writes:

I cannot walk, but I can fly;
No roof can house me from the stars.
No dwelling pen me in its bounds,
Nor keep me fast with locks and bars.
No narrow room my thoughts can cage,
No fetters hold my roving mind;
From these four walls that shut me in,

My soaring soul a way can find. . . .
And when the long, long day is done,
I clasp the dearest book of all,
And through the dim, sweet silences,
I hear my Father's accents fall.
Then, though in chains, yet I am free;
Beyond the pressure of my care,
Above earth's night, my spirit mounts
On eagle wings of Faith and Prayer.[5]

Other limitations on freedom are self-imposed, such as the immobility we seek when we buckle our seat belt or the commitment we make when we sign a contract. In these examples we limit one freedom in order to achieve a larger and more important one.

Many losses of freedom are imposed upon us by others. The science of government is a consideration of the procedures and extent to which the official representatives of one group of citizens can impose restrictions on the freedom of another group. Decisions on the extent to which government power should restrict the freedom of individuals are among the most difficult ones we face in an organized society. How much should zoning laws restrict a person's right to use his own property? How many taxes should we extract, and what compulsory functions should government perform with them? How much harm can society allow a person to do to himself, such as by self-mutilation or drug abuse? These are all questions of freedom.

We have to accept some government limitations on freedom if we who live in communities are to have life, liberty, and the pursuit of happiness. A condition of uninhibited individual freedom would allow the strong to oppress the weak. It would allow the eccentric desires of one person to restrict the freedom of many.

Interferences with our freedom do not deprive us of our agency. When Pharaoh put Joseph in prison, he restricted Joseph's freedom, but he did not take away his agency. When Jesus drove the money changers out of the temple, He interfered with their freedom to engage in a particular activity at a particular time in a particular place, but He did not take away their agency.

The Lord has told us in modern revelation that He established the Constitution of the United States to assure "that every man may act . . . according to the moral agency which I have given unto him" (D&C 101:78). In other words, God established our Constitution to give us the vital political freedom necessary for us to act upon our personal choices in civil government. This revelation shows the distinction between *agency* (the power of choice), which is God-given, and *freedom,* the right to act upon our choices, which is protected by the Constitution and laws of the land.

Freedom is obviously of great importance, but as these examples illustrate, freedom is always qualified in mortality. Consequently, when we oppose a loss of freedom, it would be better if we did not conduct our debate in terms of a loss of our agency, which is impossible under our doctrine. We ought to focus on the legality or wisdom of the proposed restriction of our freedom.

Third, we receive assurance from our doctrine that Satan, who sought to take away our agency in the preexistence, is not permitted to take it from us in this life. The Prophet Joseph Smith taught that the devil cannot compel men to do evil; he has "power over us only as we permit him."[6] Elder James E. Faust elaborated on this when he said, "Certainly he can tempt and he can deceive, but he has no authority over us which we do not give him."[7]

Fourth, as suggested by these teachings, Satan is still trying to take away our agency by persuading us to voluntarily surrender our will to his.

This subject has a morbid fascination for mankind. The long-lived German legend of Faust concerns a man who sold his soul to the devil in exchange for knowledge and power. This is also the theme of Stephen Vincent Benet's "The Devil and Daniel Webster." A variety of modern practices tend toward this surrender, and they carry eternal dangers. As Elder Faust warned us, "The mischief of devil worship, sorcery, casting spells, witchcraft, voodooism, black magic, and all other forms of demonism should be avoided like the plague."[8]

Fifth, we should also avoid any practices in which one person attempts to surrender even part of his will to another person or another person attempts to take it. Whether the means are chemical, behavioral, electronic, or others not yet dreamed of, such attempts run counter to the heavenly plan and further the adversary's. Agency, the power to choose and direct our thoughts and our actions, is a gift of God, and we should resist any means that would compromise it.

Sixth, we should avoid any behavior that is addictive. Whatever is addictive compromises our will. Subjecting our will to the overbearing impulses imposed by any form of addiction serves Satan's purposes and subverts our Heavenly Father's. This applies to addictions to drugs (such as narcotics, alcohol, nicotine, or caffeine), addiction to practices such as gambling, and any other addictive behavior. We can avoid addictions by keeping the commandments of God.

Seventh, we should be aware that some people are more susceptible to some addictions than others are. Perhaps such susceptibility is inborn, like the unnamed ailment the Apostle Paul called "a thorn in the flesh, the messenger of Satan to buffet me, lest I should be exalted above measure" (2 Corinthians 12:7). One person has a taste for nicotine and is easily addicted to smoking. Another person cannot take an occasional drink without being propelled into alcoholism. Another person samples gambling and soon becomes a compulsive gambler.

Perhaps these persons, as the saying goes, were "born that way." But what does that mean? Does it mean that persons with susceptibilities or strong tendencies have no choice, no agency in these matters? Our doctrine teaches us otherwise. Regardless of a person's susceptibility or tendency, his will is unfettered. His agency is unqualified. It is his freedom that is impaired. Other persons are more free, because when they unwisely sample the temptations, they seem immune to the addiction. But regardless of the extent of our freedom, we are all responsible for the exercise of our agency.

As Lehi taught, in mortality we are only free "according to the flesh" (2 Nephi 2:27). Most of us are born with thorns in the flesh, some more visible, some more serious than others. We all seem to have susceptibilities to one disorder or another, but whatever our susceptibilities, we have the will and the power to control our thoughts and our actions. This must be so. God has said that He holds us accountable for what we do and what we think, so our thoughts and actions must be controllable by our agency. Once we have reached the age or condition of accountability, the claim "I was born that way" does not excuse actions or thoughts that fail to conform to the commandments of God. We need to learn how to live so that a weakness that is mortal will not prevent us from achieving the goal that is eternal.

God has promised that He will consecrate our afflictions for our gain (see 2 Nephi 2:2). The efforts we expend in overcoming any inherited weakness build a spiritual strength that will serve us throughout eternity. Thus, when Paul prayed thrice that his "thorn in the flesh" would depart from him, the Lord replied, "My grace is sufficient for thee: for my strength is made perfect in weakness." Obedient, Paul concluded: "Most gladly therefore will I rather glory in my infirmities, that the power of Christ may rest upon me. Therefore I take pleasure in infirmities, in reproaches, in necessities, in persecutions, in distresses for Christ's sake: for when I am weak, then am I strong" (2 Corinthians 12:9–10).

Whatever our susceptibilities or tendencies, they cannot subject us to eternal consequences unless we exercise our agency to do or think the things forbidden by the commandments of God. For example, a susceptibility to alcoholism impairs its victim's freedom to partake without addiction, but his agency allows him to abstain and thus escape the physical debilitation of alcohol and the spiritual deterioration of addiction.

Eighth, beware the argument that because a person has strong drives toward a particular act, he has no power of choice and therefore no responsibility for his actions. This contention runs counter to the most fundamental premises of the gospel of Jesus Christ.

Satan would like us to believe that we are not responsible in this life. That is the result he tried to achieve by his contest in the premortal life. A person who insists that he is not responsible for the exercise of his agency because he was "born that way" is trying to ignore the outcome of the War in Heaven. We *are* responsible, and if we argue otherwise, our efforts become part of the propaganda effort of the adversary.

Individual responsibility is a law of life. It applies in the law of man and the law of God. Society holds people responsible to control their impulses so we can live in a civilized society. God holds His children responsible to control their impulses in order that they can keep His commandments and realize their eternal destiny. The law does not excuse the short-tempered man who surrenders to his impulse to pull a trigger on his tormentor, or the greedy man who surrenders to his impulse to steal, or the pedophile who surrenders to his impulse to satisfy his sexual urges with children.

I suppose it is inevitable that those who have surrendered to impulse would try to use the defense of "irresistible impulse." But in the courts on high, this defense will be transparent to the Great Judge, who sees our actions and "knows all the thoughts and intents of the heart" (Alma 18:32).

There is much we do not know about the extent of freedom we have in view of the various thorns in the flesh that afflict us in mortality. But this much we do know: we *all* have our agency and God holds us accountable for the way we use it in thought and deed. That is fundamental.

God has commanded us in modern revelation not to become entangled in sin (see D&C 88:86). He has said: "Go ye out from among the wicked. Save yourselves. Be ye clean that bear the vessels of the Lord" (D&C 38:42). This principle of individual responsibility and these commands to go out from among the wicked and to be clean apply to a multitude of circumstances. In terms of agency and freedom, I urge you to apply these commands in this way: If you have a weakness or a susceptibility to some particular transgression, especially one that can be addictive, use your agency and your freedom to steer a course far from the circumstances of that particular transgression.

May God bless us to live our lives so as to avoid entangling ourselves in sin and compromising our precious and unique gift of agency. May we accept responsibility for our thoughts and our actions. May we use our agency to make righteous choices and to act upon them as we have the freedom to do so.

For my conclusion I come back to the words of Nephi in 2 Nephi 33, the concluding chapter:

"I, Nephi, have written what I have written, and I esteem it as of great worth, and especially unto my people. . . .

"And it speaketh harshly against sin, according to the plainness of the truth. . . .

"And if ye shall believe in Christ ye will believe in these words, for they are the words of Christ, and he hath given them unto me; and they teach all men that they should do good. . . .

"And I pray the Father in the name of Christ that many of us, if not all, may be saved in his kingdom at that great and last day" (2 Nephi 33:3, 5, 10, 12).

NOTES

1. Joseph Smith, *Teachings of the Prophet Joseph Smith,* comp. Joseph Fielding Smith (Salt Lake City: Deseret Book, 1976), 49.

2. "Know This, That Every Soul Is Free," *Hymns* (Salt Lake City: The Church of Jesus Christ of Latter-day Saints, 1985), no. 240.

3. See Joseph Fielding Smith, *Doctrines of Salvation* (Salt Lake City: Bookcraft, 1954), 1:64–65, 70.

4. Orson F. Whitney, "Immanuel—A Christmas Idyll," in *The Poetical Writings of Orson F. Whitney* (Salt Lake City: Juvenile Instructor Office, 1889), 136–39.

5. Annie Johnson Flint, "My Wants," unpublished copy in author's possession.

6. Smith, *Teachings,* 181; see also 187, 189.

7. James E. Faust, "'The Great Imitator,'" *Ensign,* November 1987, 35.

8. Faust, "'Great Imitator,'" 33.

4

Rending the Veil of Unbelief

Elder Jeffrey R. Holland

If one were to ask a casual reader of the Book of Mormon to name the principal character in that book, the responses would undoubtedly vary. For one thing, any record covering more than a thousand years of history—with all the persons such a history would include—is unlikely to have any single, central figure emerge over such an extended period as the principal character. Nonetheless, after acknowledging that limitation, perhaps some might list any one of several favorite, or at least memorable, persons. Such names as Mormon, the abridger for whom the book is named; or Nephi, the book's early and very recognizable young prophet; or Alma, to whom so many pages are devoted; or Moroni, the fearless captain who flew the title of liberty; or his namesake, who concluded the book and delivered it some fourteen hundred years later to the young Joseph Smith—these would undoubtedly be among some of those figures mentioned.

All of these responses would be provocative, but they would also be decidedly incorrect. The principal and commanding figure in the Book of Mormon, from first chapter to last, is the Lord Jesus Christ, of whom the book is truly "another testament." From the first page—indeed, from the book's title page—to the last declaration in the text,

---

Elder Jeffrey R. Holland is a member of the Quorum of the Twelve Apostles.

this testament reveals, demonstrates, examines, and underscores the divine mission of Jesus Christ as recorded in the sacred accounts of two New World dispensations, accounts written for the benefit of a third dispensation, the last and greatest of all dispensations, the dispensation of the fulness of times. This sacred record, written by prophets and preserved by angels, was written for one crucial, fundamental, eternally essential reason: "to the convincing of the Jew and Gentile that Jesus is the Christ, the Eternal God, manifesting himself unto all nations" (Book of Mormon, title page).

In a remarkable vision recorded early in the Book of Mormon, the young prophet Nephi sees the eventual preparation and circulation of the Holy Bible, "a record of the Jews, which contains the covenants of the Lord, which he hath made unto the house of Israel" (1 Nephi 13:23). But, alarmingly, he also sees the abuse and doctrinal decimation of that book as it moves down through the ages and passes through many hands.

It was foretold in this vision that the Bible record would be clear and untarnished in the meridian of time, that in its beginning "it contained the fulness of the gospel of the Lord," with both Old and New Testaments going "from the Jews in purity unto the Gentiles" (1 Nephi 13:24–25). But over time, through both innocent error and malicious design, many doctrines and principles, especially those emphasizing covenantal elements of "the gospel of the Lamb," were lost—and sometimes were simply willfully expunged—from "the book of the Lamb of God" (1 Nephi 13:26, 28). Unfortunately, these missing elements were both "plain and precious" (1 Nephi 13:28)—plain, we presume, in their clarity and power and ability to be understood; precious surely in their profound worth, gospel significance, and eternal importance. Whatever the reason for or source of the loss of these truths from the biblical record, that loss has resulted in "pervert[ing] the right ways of the Lord, . . . blind[ing] the eyes and harden[ing] the hearts of the children of men" (1 Nephi 13:27). In painful understatement, "an exceedingly great many do stumble" (1 Nephi 13:29). Honest women and men are less informed of gospel truths and less secure in the salvation of

Christ than they deserve to be because of the loss of vital truths from the biblical canon as we have it in modernity (see 1 Nephi 13:21–29).

But in His love and foreknowledge, the great Jehovah, the premortal Christ, promised Nephi, and all who have received Nephi's record, that "after the Gentiles do stumble exceedingly, because of the most plain and precious parts of the gospel of the Lamb which have been kept back . . . I will be merciful unto the Gentiles in that day, insomuch that I will bring forth unto them, in mine own power, much of my gospel, which shall be plain and precious, saith the Lamb.

"For, behold, saith the Lamb: I will manifest myself unto thy seed, that they shall write many things which I shall minister unto them, which shall be plain and precious. . . .

"And in them shall be written my gospel, saith the Lamb, and my rock and my salvation" (1 Nephi 13:34, 36).

This promised record, now known to the world as the Book of Mormon, along with "other books" that have now come forth by the revelatory power of the Lamb, "shall make known the plain and precious things which have been taken away from [the Bible]; and shall make known to all kindreds, tongues, and people, *that the Lamb of God is the Son of the Eternal Father, and the Savior of the world; and that all men must come unto him, or they cannot be saved.*

"And they must come according to the words which shall be established by the mouth of the Lamb; and the words of the Lamb shall be made known in the records of thy seed, as well as in [the Bible]; wherefore they both shall be established in one; for there is one God and one Shepherd over all the earth" (1 Nephi 13:39–41; emphasis added).

Surely the most plain and precious of all truths lost from the Bible, particularly the Old Testament, are the clear, unequivocal, and extensive declarations regarding the coming of Christ and the eternal, essential covenantal elements of His gospel that have been taught beginning with Adam and continuing in each dispensation of time. Thus, the highest and most revered purpose of the Book of Mormon is to restore to Abraham's seed that crucial message declaring Christ's divinity, convincing all who read its pages "with a sincere heart, with real intent" that Jesus is the Christ (Moroni 10:4).

The fact that four-fifths of this record comes out of a period *before* Christ's birth, the fact that it is a record of an otherwise unknown people, the fact that inspiring insights and deep doctrines regarding Jesus are revealed here and found nowhere else in the biblical canon—or all of Christendom, for that matter—and the fact that the Book of Mormon reaffirms the truthfulness and divinity of that Bible insofar as the latter has been translated correctly are just a few of the reasons that the book should rightly be considered the most remarkable and important religious text produced since the New Testament gospels were compiled nearly two millennia ago. Indeed, in light of the plain and precious portions that have been lost from the New Testament as well as the Old Testament, it could be said that in restoring ancient biblical truths and adding scores of new ones about the Only Begotten Son of the Living God of us all, the Book of Mormon links with the Holy Bible to form the most remarkable and important religious text ever given to the world in any age of time.

The Book of Mormon has many purposes, and it contains many true and stimulating principles, but one purpose transcends all others in both kind and degree. That purpose is "the convincing of the Jew and Gentile that Jesus is the Christ" (Book of Mormon, title page).

A very special contribution the Book of Mormon makes in this matter is to our knowledge of the *premortal* Christ. Christ as Jehovah, Christ as the God of Lehi and Nephi and the brother of Jared before His birth as well as the Redeemer of Mormon and Moroni after it, is one of the prominent messages of this record.

In modern times many students of religion have great difficulty in linking Old Testament theology and divinity with that which is presented in the New Testament. The Book of Mormon does so very much to bridge that gap, not only in terms of actual history, beginning six hundred years before Christ and ending four hundred years afterward, but also in the continuity of doctrine and consistent image of divinity that is taught through that period. We talk about the two sticks of Judah and Joseph coming together, as prophesied by Ezekiel, as one of the great latter-day contributions of the Book of Mormon (see Ezekiel 37:15–28); however, I think it is nearly as important to note, in bringing "sticks" together, what the Book of Mormon does to unite the Old Testament with the New Testament in a way that is not recognized or sometimes even seen as a possibility in other religious traditions.

EARLY WITNESSES OF CHRIST

Nephi, Jacob, and Isaiah—all living and prophesying before Christ—are positioned where they are at the beginning of the book to serve as the three ancient witnesses of the Book of Mormon or, more specifically, three special Book of Mormon witnesses of Christ, which surely they are. But that role of witness is shared by many, many others in the Book of Mormon, most of them prior to Christ's birth and ministry in mortality.

Amulek says to his fellow citizens of Ammonihah (about 74 B.C.), "My brethren, I think that it is impossible that ye should be ignorant of the things which have been spoken concerning the coming of Christ, who is taught by us to be the Son of God; yea, *I know that these things were taught unto you bountifully* before your dissension from among us" (Alma 34:2; emphasis added).

The coming of Christ and the particulars of His mission and message were taught bountifully throughout the entire course of the Book of Mormon. It should not be surprising that the book as we now have it begins with a vision of "One descending out of the midst of heaven, and [Lehi] beheld that his luster was above that of the sun at noon-day" (1 Nephi 1:9). This vision of the premortal Christ, accompanied in spirit by "twelve others," brought forth a book in which Lehi was bidden to read. The book spoke of "many great and marvelous things," including the plain declaration "of the coming of a Messiah, and also the redemption of the world" (1 Nephi 1:14, 19).

From these opening passages onward, the Book of Mormon speaks continually of Christ before His mortal birth, during His sojourn among both the Jews and the Nephites, and in His postmortal rule and reign in the eternities that follow. Even though His contemporaries in Jerusalem rejected that message given by Lehi, that great prophet nevertheless continued his prophecies of "a Messiah, or, in other words, a

Savior of the world" (1 Nephi 10:4). Included in Lehi's very specific knowledge of the coming of Christ to mortality were such revelatory details as a vision that the Messiah would be slain and "should rise from the dead, and should make himself manifest, by the Holy Ghost, unto the Gentiles" (1 Nephi 10:11).

Whether it was this kind of revelation or something even more definitive (a personal appearance of Christ?) we do not know, but Lehi obviously had some very special manifestations regarding the Son of God. Shortly before his death, he testified to his sons, "Behold, the Lord hath redeemed my soul from hell; *I have beheld his glory,* and I am encircled about eternally in the arms of his love" (2 Nephi 1:15; emphasis added).

As early as Nephi's writings we learn the name which the Messiah shall carry, but that same Nephi is quick to acknowledge that other ancient prophets knew the name as well. "For according to the words of the prophets," he writes, "the Messiah cometh in six hundred years from the time that my father left Jerusalem; and according to the words of the prophets, and also the word of the angel of God, his name shall be Jesus Christ, the Son of God" (2 Nephi 25:19).

Nephi's brother Jacob follows that acknowledgment with a powerful testimony of the breadth of revelation and widespread knowledge of Christ that had been given to those ancient prophets. He writes:

"For this intent have we written these things, that they may know that we knew of Christ, and we had a hope of his glory many hundred years before his coming; and not only we ourselves had a hope of his glory, but also all the holy prophets which were before us.

"Behold, they believed in Christ and worshiped the Father in his name, and also we worship the Father in his name. And for this intent we keep the law of Moses, it pointing our souls to him. . . .

"Wherefore, we search the prophets, and we have many revelations and the spirit of prophecy; and having all these witnesses we obtain a hope, and our faith becometh unshaken, insomuch that we truly can command in the name of Jesus and the very trees obey us, or the mountains, or the waves of the sea" (Jacob 4:4–6).

In that bold and persuasive spirit he pleads with his brethren:

"Behold, will ye reject these words? Will ye reject the words of the prophets; and will ye reject all the words which have been spoken concerning Christ, after so many have spoken concerning him; and deny the good word of Christ, and the power of God, and the gift of the Holy Ghost, and quench the Holy Spirit, and make a mock of the great plan of redemption, which hath been laid for you?" (Jacob 6:8).

But soon enough one came doing exactly those things: Sherem, the first of the anti-Christs in the Book of Mormon. Sherem came declaring "that there should be no Christ" and in every way attempted to "overthrow the doctrine of Christ" (Jacob 7:2). Knowing that Jacob "had faith in Christ who should come," Sherem sardonically made particular effort to confront and challenge him on the practice of what Sherem called "preaching that which ye call the gospel, or the doctrine of Christ" (Jacob 7:3, 6). His argument was based on the feeble and tediously predictable reasoning of all anti-Christs—that "no man knoweth of such things; for he cannot tell of things to come" (Jacob 7:7).

Of Sherem, Jacob asks: "Believest thou the scriptures? And he said, Yea.

"And I said unto him: Then ye do not understand them; for they truly testify of Christ. Behold, I say unto you that none of the prophets have written, nor prophesied, save they have spoken concerning this Christ" (Jacob 7:10–11).

THE BROTHER OF JARED

One of the greatest of those prophets in the Book of Mormon—indeed, a very strong case could be made for calling him *the* greatest of the prophets in the Book of Mormon—goes unnamed in the record that documents Christ's remarkable life. That prophet is identified to the modern reader only as "the brother of Jared." Yet even in such near anonymity, the revelation that unfolded before this man's eyes was so extraordinary that his life and legacy to us have become synonymous with bold, consummate, perfect faith.

In the dispersion required of them at the time of the Tower of Babel, the people of Jared arrived at "the great sea which divideth the lands" (Ether 2:13), where they pitched their tents, awaiting further revelation regarding the crossing of a mighty ocean. For four years they awaited divine direction, but apparently they waited too casually—without supplication and exertion. Then this rather remarkable moment presented itself:

"And it came to pass at the end of four years that the Lord came again unto the brother of Jared, and stood in a cloud and talked with him. And for the space of three hours did the Lord talk with the brother of Jared, and chastened him because he remembered not to call upon the name of the Lord" (Ether 2:14).

It is difficult to imagine what a three-hour rebuke from the Lord might be like, but the brother of Jared endured it. With immediate repentance and immediate prayer, this prophet once again sought guidance for the journey they had been assigned and for those who were to pursue it. God accepted his repentance and lovingly gave further direction for this crucial mission.

For such an oceanic crossing, these families and their flocks needed seaworthy crafts similar to the barges they had constructed for earlier water travel—small, light, dish-shaped vessels identical in design above and beneath so that they were capable of staying afloat even when facing overwhelming waves or, worse yet, when they might be overturned by them. These "exceedingly tight" crafts (Ether 2:17) were obviously boats of unprecedented design and undiminished capability, made under the direction of Him who ruled the seas and the winds that rend them, to the end that the vessels might travel with the "lightness of a fowl upon the water" (Ether 2:16).

These were miraculously designed and meticulously constructed ships. But they had one major, seemingly insoluble limitation. In such a tight, seaworthy design, there was no means of allowing light for the seafarers who would travel in them. The brother of Jared "cried again unto the Lord saying: O Lord, behold I have done even as thou hast commanded me; and I have prepared the vessels for my people, and behold there is no light in them. Behold, O Lord, wilt thou suffer that we shall cross this great water in darkness?" (Ether 2:22).

Then comes an extraordinary and unexpected response from the

Creator of heaven and earth and all things that in them are, He who boldly declared to Abraham, "Is anything too hard for the Lord?" (Genesis 18:14): "And the Lord said unto the brother of Jared: *What will ye that I should do* that ye may have light in your vessels?" (Ether 2:23; emphasis added).

Then, as if such a disarming inquiry from omnipotent deity is not enough, the Lord proceeds to verbalize the very problems that the brother of Jared already knows only too well.

"For behold, ye cannot have windows, for they will be dashed in pieces; neither shall ye take fire with you, for ye shall not go by the light of fire.

"For behold, ye shall be as a whale in the midst of the sea; for the mountain waves shall dash upon you. . . . *Therefore what will ye that I should prepare for you* that ye may have light when ye are swallowed up in the depths of the sea?" (Ether 2:23–25; emphasis added).

Clearly the brother of Jared was being tested. The Lord had done His part—miraculously, profoundly, ingeniously. Unique, resolutely seaworthy ships for crossing the ocean had been provided. The brilliant engineering had been done. The hard part of this construction project was over. Now He wanted to know what the brother of Jared would do about incidentals.

After what has undoubtedly been a great deal of soul-searching and head-scratching, the brother of Jared comes before the Lord—perhaps red-faced but not empty-handed. In a clearly apologetic tone, he says:

"Now behold, O Lord, and do not be angry with thy servant because of his weakness before thee; for we know that thou art holy and dwellest in the heavens, and that we are unworthy before thee; because of the fall our natures have become evil continually; nevertheless, O Lord, thou hast given us a commandment that we must call upon thee, that from thee we may receive according to our desires.

"Behold, O Lord, thou hast smitten us because of our iniquity, and hast driven us forth, and for these many years we have been in the wilderness; nevertheless, thou hast been merciful unto us. O Lord, look upon me in pity, and turn away thine anger from this thy people, and suffer not that they shall go forth across this raging deep in darkness;

but behold these things which I have molten out of the rock" (Ether 3:2–3).

Things—the brother of Jared hardly knows what to call them. *Rocks* probably doesn't sound any more inspiring. Here, standing next to the Lord's magnificent handiwork, these *ne plus ultra,* impeccably designed, and marvelously unique seagoing barges, the brother of Jared offers for his contribution: *rocks.* As he eyes the sleek ships the Lord has provided, it is a moment of genuine humility.

He hurries on: "And I know, O Lord, that thou hast all power, and can do whatsoever thou wilt for the benefit of man; therefore touch these stones, O Lord, with thy finger, and prepare them that they may shine forth in darkness; and they shall shine forth unto us in the vessels which we have prepared, that we may have light while we shall cross the sea.

"Behold, O Lord, thou canst do this. We know that thou art able to show forth great power, which looks small unto the understanding of men" (Ether 3:4–5).

For all of his self-abasement, the faith of the brother of Jared is apparent. In fact, we might better say *transparent* in light of the purpose for which these stones will be used. Surely God, as well as the reader, feels something very striking in the childlike innocence and fervor of this man's faith. *"Behold, O Lord, thou canst do this."* Perhaps there is no more powerful single line of faith spoken by man in scripture. It is almost as if he is encouraging God, emboldening Him, reassuring Him. Not "Behold, O Lord, I am sure that thou canst do this." Not "Behold, O Lord, thou hast done many greater things than this." However uncertain the prophet is about his own ability, he has *no* uncertainty about God's power. There is nothing here but a single, clear, bold, and assertive declaration with no hint or element of vacillation. It is encouragement to Him who needs no encouragement but who surely must have been touched by it. "Behold, O Lord, thou canst do this."

THE RENDING OF THE VEIL

What happened next ranks among the greatest moments in recorded history, surely among the greatest moments in recorded faith.

It forever established the brother of Jared among the greatest of God's prophets. As the Lord reaches forth to touch the stones one by one with His finger—a response, it would seem, coming in undeniable response to the commanding faith of the brother of Jared—"the veil was taken from off the eyes of the brother of Jared, and he saw the finger of the Lord; and it was as the finger of a man, like unto flesh and blood; and the brother of Jared fell down before the Lord, for he was struck with fear" (Ether 3:6).

The Lord, seeing the brother of Jared fall to the earth, commands him to rise and asks, "Why hast thou fallen?" (Ether 3:7).

The reply: "I saw the finger of the Lord, and I feared lest he should smite me; for I knew not that the Lord had flesh and blood" (Ether 3:8).

Then this marvelous declaration from the Lord: "Because of thy faith thou hast seen that I shall take upon me flesh and blood; and never has man come before me with such exceeding faith as thou hast; for were it not so ye could not have seen my finger. Sawest thou more than this?" (Ether 3:9).

The brother of Jared answers, "Nay; Lord, show thyself unto me" (Ether 3:10). The Lord removed the veil completely from the eyes of the brother of Jared and came into full view of this resolutely faithful man.

Then this most remarkable revelation of the premortal Jehovah: "Behold, I am he who was prepared from the foundation of the world to redeem my people," He said. "Behold, I am Jesus Christ. I am the Father and the Son. In me shall all mankind have life, and that eternally, even they who shall believe on my name; and they shall become my sons and my daughters.

"And never have I showed myself unto man whom I have created, for never has man believed in me as thou hast. Seest thou that ye are created after mine own image? Yea, even all men were created in the beginning after my own image.

"Behold, this body, which ye now behold, is the body of my spirit; and man have I created after the body of my spirit; and even as I appear unto thee to be in the spirit will I appear unto my people in the flesh" (Ether 3:14–16).

Before examining the doctrinal truths taught in this divine encounter, it will be useful to note two seemingly problematic issues here, issues that would seem to have reasonable and acceptable resolutions.

The first issue is suggested in two questions the Lord asks the brother of Jared during the vision as it unfolds: "Why hast thou fallen?" and "Sawest thou more than this?" It is a basic premise of Latter-day Saint theology that God "knoweth all things, and there is not anything save he knows it" (2 Nephi 9:20). The scriptures, both ancient and modern, are replete with this assertion of omniscience. Nevertheless, God has frequently asked questions of men, usually as a way to test their faith, measure their honesty, or allow their knowledge greater development. For example, he called unto Adam in the Garden of Eden, "Where art thou?" and later asked Eve, "What is this that thou hast done?" (Genesis 3:9, 13), yet an omniscient parent clearly knew the answer to both questions, for He could see where Adam was and He had watched what Eve had done. It is obvious that the questions are for the children's sake, giving Adam and Eve the responsibility of replying honestly. Later, in trying Abraham's faith, God repeatedly called out regarding Abraham's whereabouts, to which the faithful patriarch would answer: "Here am I" (Genesis 22:11). The purpose in this scriptural moment was not to provide God with information He already knew but to reaffirm Abraham's fixed faith and unwavering position in the most difficult of all parental tests. These kinds of rhetorical questions are frequently used by God, particularly in assessing faith, honesty, and the full measure of agency, allowing the "students" the freedom and opportunity to express themselves as revealingly as they wish, even though God knows the answer to His own and all other questions.

The second issue that requires preliminary comment stems from the Lord's exclamation, "Never has man come before me with such exceeding faith as thou hast; for were it not so ye could not have seen my finger" (Ether 3:9). And later, "Never have I showed myself unto man whom I have created, for never has man believed in me as thou hast" (Ether 3:15). The potential for confusion here comes with the realization that many—indeed, we would assume all—of the major prophets living prior to the brother of Jared had seen God. How then does one account for the Lord's declaration? Adam's face-to-face conversations with God in the Garden of Eden can be exempted because of the paradisiacal, prefallen state of that setting and relationship. Furthermore, other prophets' visions of God, such as those of Moses and Isaiah in the Bible, or Nephi and Jacob in the Book of Mormon, came after this "never before" experience of the brother of Jared. But before the era of the Tower of Babel, the Lord did appear unto Adam and "the residue of his posterity who were righteous" in the valley of Adam-ondi-Ahman three years before Adam's death (see D&C 107:53–55). And we are left with Enoch, who said very explicitly, "I saw the Lord; and he stood before my face, and he talked with me, even as a man talketh one with another, face to face" (Moses 7:4). We assume there would have been other prophets living in the period between Adam's leaving the Garden of Eden and the building of the Tower of Babel who also saw God in a similar manner, including Noah, who "found grace in the eyes of the Lord" and "walked with God" (Genesis 6:8–9), the same scriptural phrase used to describe Enoch's relationship with the Lord (see Genesis 5:24).

This issue has been much discussed by Latter-day Saint writers, and there are several possible explanations, any one—or all—of which may cast some light upon the larger truth of this passage. Nevertheless, without additional scriptural revelation or commentary on the matter, any conjecture is only that—conjecture—and as such is inadequate and incomplete.

One possibility is that this is simply a comment made in the context of one dispensation and as such applies only to the Jaredites and Jaredite prophets—that Jehovah has never before revealed Himself to one of their seers and revelators. Obviously this theory has severe limitations when measured against such phrases as "never before" and "never has man" and combined with the realization that Jared and his brother are the fathers of this dispensation, the first to whom God could have revealed Himself in their era.

Another suggestion is that the lowercase reference to "man" is the key to this passage, suggesting that the Lord has never revealed Himself to the unsanctified, to the nonbeliever, to temporal, earthy, natural man. The implication here is that only those who have put off the natural man, only those who are untainted by the world—in short, the sanctified (such as Adam, Enoch, and now the brother of Jared)—are entitled to this privilege.

Some have believed that the Lord here means He has never before revealed Himself to this degree or to this extent. This theory would suggest that divine appearances to earlier prophets had not been with this same "fulness," that never before had the veil been lifted to give such a complete revelation of Christ's nature and being.

A further possibility is that this is the first time Jehovah has appeared and identified Himself as Jesus Christ, the Son of God, thus the interpretation of the passage being "never have I showed myself [as Jesus Christ] unto man whom I have created" (Ether 3:15). This possibility is reinforced by one way of reading Moroni's later editorial comment: "Having this perfect knowledge of God, he could not be kept from within the veil; therefore he saw *Jesus*" (Ether 3:20; emphasis added).

Yet another interpretation of this passage is that the faith of the brother of Jared was so great he saw not only the *spirit* finger and body of the premortal Jesus (which presumably many other prophets had also seen) but also had some distinctly more revealing aspect of Christ's body of flesh, blood, and bone. Exactly what insight into the flesh-and-blood nature of Christ's future body the brother of Jared might have had is not clear, but Jehovah does say to him, "Because of thy faith thou hast seen that I shall take upon me flesh and blood" (Ether 3:9), and Moroni does say that Christ revealed Himself in this instance "in the likeness of the same body even as he showed himself unto the Nephites" (Ether 3:17). Some have taken that to mean literally "the same body" the Nephites would see—a body of flesh and blood. A safer position would be that it was at least the exact spiritual likeness of that future body. Jehovah says, "Behold, this body, which ye now behold, is the body of my spirit . . .

and even as I appear unto thee to be in the spirit will I appear unto my people in the flesh" (Ether 3:16), and Moroni says, "Jesus showed himself unto this man in the spirit" (Ether 3:17).

A final—and in terms of the faith of the brother of Jared (which is the issue at hand) surely the most persuasive—explanation for me is that Christ is saying to the brother of Jared, "Never have I showed myself unto man *in this manner, without my volition, driven solely by the faith of the beholder.*" As a rule, prophets are invited into the presence of the Lord, are bidden to enter His presence by Him and only with His sanction. The brother of Jared, on the other hand, stands alone then (and we assume now) in having thrust himself through the veil, not as an unwelcome guest but perhaps technically an uninvited one. Says Jehovah, *"Never has man come before me with such exceeding faith as thou hast; for were it not so ye could not have seen my finger. . . . Never has man believed in me as thou hast"* (Ether 3:9, 15; emphasis added). Obviously the Lord Himself is linking unprecedented faith with this unprecedented vision. If the vision is not unique, then it has to be the faith—and how the vision is obtained—that is so remarkable. The only way this faith could be so remarkable would be in its ability to take this prophet, uninvited, where others had only been able to go by invitation.

Indeed it would appear that this is Moroni's own understanding of the circumstance, for he later writes, "Because of the knowledge [which has come as a result of faith] of this man *he could not be kept from beholding within the veil. . . .*

"Wherefore, having this perfect knowledge of God, *he could not be kept from within the veil;* therefore he saw Jesus" (Ether 3:19–20; emphasis added).

This may be one of those very provocative examples (except that it is real life and not hypothetical) about God's power. Schoolboy philosophers sometimes ask, "Can God make a rock so heavy that He cannot lift it?" or "Can God hide an item so skillfully that He cannot find it?" Far more movingly and importantly we may ask here, "Could God have stopped the brother of Jared from seeing through the veil?" At first blush one is inclined to say, "Surely God could block such an experience if He wished to." But think again. Or, more precisely, read again.

"This man . . . *could not be kept from beholding within the veil; . . . he could not be kept from within the veil*" (Ether 3:19–20; emphasis added).

No, this may be an absolutely unprecedented case of a prophet's will and faith and purity so closely approaching that of heaven's that the man moves from understanding God to being actually like Him, with His same thrust of will and faith, at least in this one instance. What a remarkable doctrinal statement about the power of a mortal man's faith! And not an ethereal, unreachable, select category of a man, either. This is one who once forgot to call upon the Lord, one whose best ideas focused on rocks, and one who doesn't even have a traditional name in the book that has immortalized his remarkable feat of faith. Given such a man with such faith, it should not be surprising that the Lord would show this prophet much, show him visions that would be relevant to the mission of all the Book of Mormon prophets and to the events of the latter-day dispensation in which the book would be received.

After the prophet stepped through the veil to behold the Savior of the world, he was not limited in seeing the rest of what the eternal world revealed. Indeed, the Lord showed him "all the inhabitants of the earth which had been, and also all that would be; and he withheld them not from his sight, even unto the ends of the earth" (Ether 3:25). The staying power for such an experience was once again the faith of the brother of Jared, for "the Lord could not withhold anything from him, for he knew that the Lord could show him all things" (Ether 3:26).

A REMARKABLE VISION

This vision of "all the inhabitants of the earth which had been, and also all that would be, . . . even unto the ends of the earth" (Ether 3:25) was similar to that given to Moses and others of the prophets (see Moses 1:27–29). In this case, however, it was written down in great detail and then sealed up. Moroni, who had access to this recorded vision, wrote on his plates "the very things which the brother of Jared saw" (Ether 4:4). Then he, too, sealed them up and hid them again in the earth before his death and the final destruction of the Nephite civilization. Of this vision given to the brother of Jared, Moroni wrote,

"There never were greater things made manifest than those which were made manifest unto the brother of Jared" (Ether 4:4).

Those sealed plates constitute the sealed portion of the Book of Mormon which Joseph Smith did not translate. Furthermore, they will remain sealed, literally as well as figuratively, until "they shall exercise faith in me, saith the Lord, even as the brother of Jared did, that they may become sanctified in me, then will I manifest unto them the things which the brother of Jared saw, even to the unfolding unto them all my revelations, saith Jesus Christ, the Son of God, the Father of the heavens and of the earth, and all things that in them are" (Ether 4:7).

The full measure of this unprecedented and unexcelled vision—"there never were greater things made manifest"—is yet to be made known to the children of men. But consider what was made known in one man's experience in receiving it, consider that the time was approximately two thousand years before Christ's birth, and consider what is *not* presently contained in the Old Testament canon of that period regarding Jehovah and His true characteristics. These twenty-five items are all drawn from Ether 3 and 4:

1. Jehovah, the God of the pre-Christian era, was the premortal Jesus Christ, identified here by that name (see Ether 3:14).

2. Christ is both a Father and a Son in His divine relationship with the children of men (see Ether 3:14).

3. Christ was "prepared from the foundation of the world to redeem [his] people" (Ether 3:14), knowledge which had been shared before with Enoch and later would be shared with John the Revelator (see Moses 7:47; Revelation 13:8).

4. Christ had a spirit body, which looked like and was in the premortal form of His physical body, "like unto flesh and blood," including fingers, voice, face, and all other physical features (Ether 3:6).

5. Christ assisted in the creation of man, fashioning the human family "after the body of my spirit" (Ether 3:16).

6. With a spirit body and the divinity of His calling, the premortal Christ spoke audibly, in words and language understood by mortals (see Ether 3:16).

7. Christ is a God, acting for and with His Father, who is also a God (see Ether 3:14; 4:7).

8. Christ reveals some truths to some that are to be kept from others until an appointed time—His "own due time" (Ether 3:24).

9. Christ uses a variety of tools and techniques in revelation, including the interpreting power of "two stones": the Urim and Thummim (see Ether 3:23–24; D&C 17:1).

10. Christ's later atoning, redeeming role is clearly stated even before it has been realized in His mortal life. Furthermore, in a most blessed way for the brother of Jared, it is immediately efficacious. "I am he who was prepared from the foundation of the world to redeem my people," Christ says. "In me shall all mankind have life, and that eternally, even they who shall believe on my name; and they shall become my sons and my daughters" (Ether 3:14).

Then the brother of Jared has his redemption pronounced, as though the Atonement had already been carried out. "Because thou knowest these things ye are redeemed from the fall," Christ promises him, "therefore ye are brought back into my presence; therefore I show myself unto you" (Ether 3:13).

This statement underscores the eternal nature of the Atonement, its effects reaching out to all those who lived before the Savior's birth as well as all those living after it. All who in Old Testament times were baptized in Christ's name had the same claim upon eternal life that the brother of Jared had, even though Christ had not yet even been born. In matters of the Atonement, as in all other eternal promises, "time only is measured unto men" (Alma 40:8).

11. Christ had past knowledge of "all the inhabitants of the earth which had been" and foreknowledge of "all that would be," showing all of these to the brother of Jared (Ether 3:25).

Moroni, in recording the experience of the brother of Jared, adds these insights and revelations which come from the same encounter:

12. Future Saints will need to be sanctified in Christ to receive all of His revelations (see Ether 4:6).

13. Those who reject the vision of the brother of Jared will be shown "no greater things" by Christ (Ether 4:8).

14. At Christ's command "the heavens are opened and are shut," "the earth shall shake," and "the inhabitants thereof shall pass away, even so as by fire" (Ether 4:9).

15. Believers in the vision of the brother of Jared will be given manifestations of Christ's spirit. Because of such spiritual experience, belief shall turn to knowledge and they "shall know that these things are true" (Ether 4:11).

16. "Whatsoever thing persuadeth men to do good" is of Christ. Good comes of none except Christ (Ether 4:12).

17. Those who do not believe Christ's words would not believe Him personally (see Ether 4:12).

18. Those who do not believe Christ would not believe God the Father, who sent Him (see Ether 4:12).

19. Christ is the light and the life and the truth of the world (see Ether 4:12).

20. Christ will reveal "greater things" (Ether 4:13), "great and marvelous things" (Ether 4:15), and knowledge hidden "from the foundation of the world" (Ether 4:14) to those who rend the veil of unbelief and come unto Him.

21. Believers are to call upon the Father in the name of Christ "with a broken heart and a contrite spirit" if they are to "know that the Father hath remembered the covenant which he made" unto the house of Israel (Ether 4:15).

22. Christ's revelations to John the Revelator will be "unfolded in the eyes of all the people" in the last days, even as they are about to be fulfilled (Ether 4:16).

23. Christ commands all the ends of the earth to come unto Him, believe in His gospel, and be baptized in His name (see Ether 4:18).

24. Signs shall follow those who believe in Christ's name (see Ether 4:18).

25. Those faithful to Christ's name at the last day shall be "lifted up to dwell in the kingdom prepared for [them] from the foundation of the world" (Ether 4:19).

Indeed, an appeal like that of the brother of Jared is given by the

Father to both Gentile and Israelite, to whom this record is sent. Asking the latter-day reader to pierce the limits of shallow faith, Christ cries:

"Come unto me, O ye Gentiles, and I will show unto you the greater things, the knowledge which is hid up because of unbelief.

"Come unto me, O ye house of Israel, and it shall be made manifest unto you how great things the Father hath laid up for you, from the foundation of the world; and it hath not come unto you, because of unbelief.

"Behold, *when ye shall rend that veil of unbelief* which doth cause you to remain in your awful state of wickedness, and hardness of heart, and blindness of mind, then shall the great and marvelous things which have been hid up from the foundation of the world from you—yea, when ye shall call upon the Father in my name, with a broken heart and a contrite spirit, then shall ye know that the Father hath remembered the covenant which he made unto your fathers, O house of Israel" (Ether 4:13–15; emphasis added).

The Book of Mormon is predicated on the willingness of men and women to "rend that veil of unbelief" in order to behold the revelations—and the Revelation—of God (Ether 4:15). It would seem that the humbling experience of the brother of Jared in his failure to pray and his consternation over the sixteen stones were included in this account to show just how mortal and just how normal he was—so very much like the men and women we know and at least in some ways so much like ourselves. His belief in himself and his view of himself may have been limited—much like our view of ourselves. But his belief in God was unprecedented. It was without doubt or limit: "I know, O Lord, that thou hast all power, and can do whatsoever thou wilt for the benefit of man; therefore touch these stones, O Lord, with thy finger" (Ether 3:4).

And from that command given to the Lord, for it does seem to be something of a command, the brother of Jared and the reader of the Book of Mormon would never be the same again. Ordinary individuals with ordinary challenges could rend the veil of unbelief and enter the realms of eternity. And Christ, who was prepared from the foundation of the world to redeem His people, would be standing at the edge of that veil to usher the believer through.

5

LIKENING THE SCRIPTURES UNTO US

Elder Dean L. Larsen

As I have studied the Book of Mormon, I have become convinced that, in addition to its being another powerful witness for Jesus Christ and His gospel plan, it has unusual value for us by virtue of what we can learn from the experiences of the people whose record it is. In some respects, our review of the historical events in the book permits us to see a reflection of ourselves. As we compare circumstances and conditions in our own time with those we see in relevant segments of the Book of Mormon history, we may be able to predict with some degree of accuracy the consequences of human behavior in our day. We can also gain vital insight into how we may continue to merit the Lord's blessings and thus avoid the calamities that so often befell these ancient people.

The book of Alma is as useful in this kind of review as any of the scriptures we possess. In this paper, I am going to look beyond the significant doctrinal teachings that make Alma such a rich treasury and invite you to look with me at the lives of the people from this part of the record and compare them with conditions and events in our present day. In doing so, I intend to draw upon other relevant sources, some from the Book of Mormon, and some from other documents that may

Elder Dean L. Larsen is an emeritus member of the First Quorum of the Seventy.

help us to see ourselves in the continuing historic panorama of God's dealings with His earthly children.

"AND THUS THEY DID DWINDLE IN UNBELIEF"

As the book of Mosiah concludes, the people of Nephi have been established under a government of elected judges. Alma, the son of Alma, has been named as the "first chief judge" (Mosiah 29:42). He is also the presiding officer of the Church.

It is a good time. The great love felt by the people for King Mosiah has laid a strong foundation for the new government. The Church is well established, and the people rejoice because of the liberty which has been granted unto them (see Mosiah 29:39).

Challenges soon confront the leaders in this new system. Alma is faced with a seditious movement against the government as well as against the Church. Gideon, one of the most loved and respected of the senior citizens, is murdered. Nehor, who has instigated the insurrection, and who is personally guilty of Gideon's murder, is summarily tried and executed for his crime. But his apostate influence has taken root among the people, for, as the record says, "there were many who loved the vain things of the world," and "the hearts of many were hardened" (Alma 1:16, 24).

By the time five years have passed, the Nephite nation is torn by civil war, and there are many defections from the Church. In the midst of these difficulties, the Nephites are invaded by Lamanite armies. In the ensuing battles, so many Nephites are slain that they are "not numbered, because of the greatness of their number" (Alma 3:1). It is a time of great remorse among the Nephites.

"And so great were their afflictions that every soul had cause to mourn; and they believed that it was the judgments of God sent upon them because of their wickedness and their abominations; therefore they were awakened to a remembrance of their duty.

"And they began to establish the church more fully; yea, and many were baptized in the waters of Sidon and were joined to the church of God" (Alma 4:3–4).

In this resurgence of faith the Nephites prosper again. Peace returns. Remarkably, it does not last for long. Within a period of three years, defection and apostasy begin to manifest themselves within the Church.

"And it came to pass in the eighth year of the reign of the judges, that the people of the church began to wax proud, because of their exceeding riches, and their fine silks, and their fine-twined linen, and because of their many flocks and herds, and their gold and their silver, and all manner of precious things, which they had obtained by their industry; and in all these things were they lifted up in the pride of their eyes" (Alma 4:6).

The dissension spreads rapidly. Alma, perplexed by the drift of his people toward another tragedy, resigns from his position as chief judge and turns his full energy and attention to the collapsing Church.

"And this he did that he himself might go forth among his people, or among the people of Nephi, that he might preach the word of God unto them, to stir them up in remembrance of their duty, and that he might pull down, by the word of God, all the pride and craftiness and all the contentions which were among his people, seeing no way that he might reclaim them save it were in bearing down in pure testimony against them" (Alma 4:19).

Alma then goes to the major cities of the land to accomplish his purpose—Zarahemla, Gideon, Melek, Ammonihah, Sidom, among the Zoramites, and eventually Jershon. Much of Alma's record is composed of the great doctrinal discourses preached by Alma and his companions in their efforts to reclaim this people. It is a labor of many years and demands the utmost of Alma's faith and perseverance.

In the course of these events, we can observe the manner in which the Lord tests and tries His people. We note, as well, the afflictions that He permits them to bring upon themselves in order to humble them and keep them from falling completely away from the course He has marked out for them. The warfare and suffering described in the latter chapters of Alma are grim reminders of the tragedies that people can bring upon themselves when they drift away from the Lord's standard.

In each dispensation of the gospel prior to the one in which we live, there has come a time when the people of God have succumbed to the worldly influences that have encompassed them. Periods of spiritual darkness have followed as the earth's inhabitants have turned themselves away from God and have suffered the consequences of their folly. The saddest recorded accounts in the scriptural and historical records are those of once-favored people who drift into apostasy.

Following the Savior's visit to the Nephites and Lamanites here in the Americas, the people who responded to His ministry enjoyed a period of unprecedented prosperity and happiness. In 4 Nephi we find this description of them:

"And the Lord did prosper them exceedingly in the land; yea, insomuch that they did build cities again where there had been cities burned. . . .

"And . . . the people of Nephi did wax strong, and did multiply exceedingly fast, and became an exceedingly fair and delightsome people. . . .

"And it came to pass that there was no contention among all the people, in all the land; . . .

"And there were no envyings, nor strifes, nor tumults, nor whoredoms, nor lyings, nor murders, nor any manner of lasciviousness; and surely there could not be a happier people among all the people who had been created by the hand of God" (4 Nephi 1:7, 10, 13, 16).

For almost two hundred years the people lived in these favored circumstances. Then, almost inconceivably, they left the pattern of life that had brought them such great blessings.

Mormon's commentary on the spiritual decline of this people merits careful, thoughtful review:

"And now I, Mormon, would that ye should know that the people had multiplied, insomuch that they were spread upon all the face of the land, and that they had become exceedingly rich, because of their prosperity in Christ.

"And now, . . . there began to be among them those who were lifted up in pride. . . .

"And from that time forth they did have their goods and their substance no more common among them.

"And they began to be divided into classes. . . .

"And . . . there were many . . . which professed to know the Christ, and yet they did deny the more parts of his gospel. . . .

" . . . The people did harden their hearts, for they were led . . . to do all manner of iniquity. . . . And thus they did dwindle in unbelief and wickedness, from year to year" (4 Nephi 1:23–27, 34).

"But wickedness did prevail upon the face of the whole land, insomuch that the Lord did take away his beloved disciples, and the work of miracles and of healing did cease because of the iniquity of the people.

"And there were no gifts from the Lord, and the Holy Ghost did not come upon any, because of their wickedness and unbelief. . . .

"For behold they had wilfully rebelled against their God" (Mormon 1:13–14, 16).

SIMILAR CHALLENGES IN OUR TIME

We have been assured that in this last dispensation of the fulness of times, there will be no universal apostasy. When the Lord appears again in His glory, He will find a people who will have remained faithful and who will be ready to receive Him and join with Him in the completion of His work.

But the fact that there will not be a complete apostasy in this last dispensation does not mean all who have received the gospel and become members of the Church will remain faithful. Prophetic references to our own day, in fact, seem to indicate that there will be many who have known the truth and have tasted of the Lord's goodness that will then allow themselves to be tempted away from the course the Lord has marked out for them.

In the 1965 October general conference, Elder Harold B. Lee spoke of the test that would come, and in his remarks he cited the words of President Heber C. Kimball, who said:

"We think we are secure here in the chambers of the everlasting hills, . . . but I want to say to you, . . . the time is coming when we will be mixed up in these now peaceful valleys to that extent that it will be difficult to tell the face of a Saint from the face of an enemy to the people of God. Then, brethren, look out for the great sieve, for there will be a great sifting time, and many will fall; for I say unto you there is a test, a TEST, a TEST coming, and who will be able to stand?"[1]

In Lehi's vision of the tree of life, he describes those who would be tempted away from the path of eternal happiness, even after they have followed the rod of iron to the tree and tasted of its fruit. This is Lehi's description of what he saw:

"And it came to pass that there arose a mist of darkness; yea, even an exceedingly great mist of darkness, insomuch that they who had commenced in the path did lose their way, that they wandered off and were lost.

"And it came to pass that I beheld others pressing forward, and they came forth and caught hold of the end of the rod of iron; and they did press forward through the mist of darkness, clinging to the rod of iron, even until they did come forth and partake of the fruit of the tree.

"And after they had partaken of the fruit of the tree they did cast their eyes about as if they were ashamed.

"And I also cast my eyes round about, and beheld, on the other side of the river of water, a great and spacious building; and it stood as it were in the air, high above the earth.

"And it was filled with people, both old and young, both male and female; and their manner of dress was exceedingly fine; and they were in the attitude of mocking and pointing their fingers towards those who had come at and were partaking of the fruit.

"And after they had tasted of the fruit they were ashamed, because of those that were scoffing at them; and they fell away into forbidden paths and were lost" (1 Nephi 8:23–28).

Nephi later declared, "And it came to pass that I saw and bear record, that the great and spacious building was the pride of the world" (1 Nephi 11:36).

In reference to the calamities that will come upon the disobedient in the last days, the Lord revealed to Joseph Smith:

"Nevertheless, Zion shall escape if she observe to do all things whatsoever I have commanded her.

"But if she observe not to do whatsoever I have commanded her, I will visit her according to all her works, with sore affliction, with pestilence, with plague, with sword, with vengeance, with devouring fire" (D&C 97:25–26).

"Behold, vengeance cometh speedily upon the inhabitants of the earth, a day of wrath, a day of burning, a day of desolation, of weeping, of mourning, and of lamentation; and as a whirlwind it shall come upon all the face of the earth, saith the Lord.

"And upon my house shall it begin, and from my house shall it go forth, saith the Lord;

"First among those among you, saith the Lord, who have professed to know my name and have not known me, and have blasphemed against me in the midst of my house, saith the Lord" (D&C 112:24–26).

"Behold, I tell you these things, even as I also told the people of the destruction of Jerusalem; and my word shall be verified at this time as it hath hitherto been verified" (D&C 5:20).

With these direful warnings and predictions the Lord combines remarkable promises to those who will remain faithful and who will not yield to the temptations the world offers. But these are conditional promises. The Lord will not be mocked in these last days by those who make covenants of obedience and then violate them with a sense of impunity or with the deceitful intent of one day repenting and coming back into line after purposeful excursions into forbidden paths.

Nephi was allowed to see our time in vision, and he knew of the efforts the adversary would make to delude and confuse the members of the Church as well as others of God's children. Nephi said:

"For behold, at that day shall he rage in the hearts of the children of men, and stir them up to anger against that which is good.

"And others will he pacify, and lull them away into carnal security, that they will say: All is well in Zion; yea, Zion prospereth, all is well—and thus the devil cheateth their souls, and leadeth them away carefully down to hell" (2 Nephi 28:20–21).

We live in a time of rapid Church growth. Large numbers are being baptized throughout the world. Many countries that have not been accessible to the missionary effort are now opening their doors. In many respects Zion is prospering, and things seem to be going well.

In the midst of this apparent general prosperity of the Church, it is well for us to look carefully and honestly into our own lives to see if some of the evidences of spiritual infirmity are beginning to reappear, particularly in light of the warnings the Lord has given to us.

MAINTAINING CENTERS OF SPIRITUAL STRENGTH

Historically, the drifting away from the course of life marked out by the Lord has occurred as individuals begin to make compromises with the Lord's standard. This is particularly true when the transgression is willful and no repentance occurs. Remember Mormon's description of those who turned away from the true path in his day. They did not sin in ignorance. They willfully rebelled against God. It did not occur as a universal movement. It began as individual members of the Church knowingly began to make compromises with the Lord's standard. They sought justification for their diversions in the knowledge that others were compromising as well. Those who willfully sin soon seek to establish a standard of their own with which they can feel more comfortable and which justifies their misconduct. They also seek the association of those who are willing to drift with them along this path of self-delusion.

As the number of drifting individuals increases, their influence becomes more powerful. It might be described as the "great and spacious building syndrome." The drifting is the more dangerous when its adherents continue to overtly identify with and participate with the group that conforms to the Lord's way. Values and standards that were once clear become clouded and uncertain. The norm of behavior begins to reflect this beclouding of true principles. Conduct that would once have caused revulsion and alarm now becomes somewhat commonplace.

Alma was faced with this challenge as he began his efforts to reestablish the order of the Church among his people. To them he said:

"All you that are desirous to follow the voice of the good shepherd, come ye out from the wicked, and be ye separate, and touch not their unclean things; and behold, their names shall be blotted out, that the names of the wicked shall not be numbered among the names of the righteous. . . .

"For what shepherd is there among you having many sheep doth not watch over them, that the wolves enter not and devour his flock? And behold, if a wolf enter his flock doth he not drive him out? Yea, and at the last, if he can, he will destroy him.

"And now I say unto you that the good shepherd doth call after you; . . . and he commandeth you that ye suffer no ravenous wolf to enter among you, that ye may not be destroyed" (Alma 5:57, 59–60).

Alma's father, you will recall, had been faced with this problem in the days of King Mosiah. He consulted with the king, and it was determined that the matter should be dealt with within the Church. Alma, therefore, went to the Lord to learn what should be done. The Lord's response is of great significance.

"Therefore I say unto you, Go; and whosoever transgresseth against me, him shall ye judge according to the sins which he has committed; and if he confess his sins before thee and me, and repenteth in the sincerity of his heart, him shall ye forgive, and I will forgive him also.

"Now I say unto you, Go; and whosoever will not repent of his sins the same shall not be numbered among my people; and this shall be observed from this time forward" (Mosiah 26:29, 32).

Zeezrom's story in the book of Alma is an excellent example of the effectiveness of repentance. Zeezrom, who once taunted and defied Alma, made a dramatic change in his life and became one of the stalwarts in the effort to strengthen the Church and reconvert his people. He was one of the few who became companions with Alma in his missionary labors, obviously deserving of the complete trust and confidence of his priesthood leader.

The safe course to follow is to adhere strictly to the standards set by the Lord, without compromise. Those who do so give support to one another in righteousness and faith. They have compassion for the sinner, but an intolerance for sin. They deal with the unrepentant sinner in such a way that that person cannot persist in working any evil, insidious influence among them.

Such was the case with the people of Enoch. Time will not permit a review of the circumstances in Enoch's day, but a careful study of that episode may give some insight into the manner in which the Lord will preserve a righteous people in our time in a world that is ripening in iniquity as it was before the flood.

Within the framework of the gospel of Jesus Christ, the Savior has provided a refuge from the evils of the world. Wherever a congregation or community of Saints is found, there should be the sustaining influence of the gospel and the assurance that those who identify themselves as Saints are applying themselves to gospel principles.

As in the days of Enoch, the Lord makes promises to the faithful of this dispensation who will maintain such centers of spiritual strength.

"And the glory of the Lord shall be there, and the terror of the Lord also shall be there, insomuch that the wicked will not come unto it, and it shall be called Zion. And it shall come to pass among the wicked, that every man that will not take his sword against his neighbor must needs flee unto Zion for safety. And there shall be gathered unto it out of every nation under heaven" (D&C 45:67–69).

"And the nations of the earth shall honor her, and shall say: Surely Zion . . . cannot fall, neither be moved out of her place, for God is there, and the hand of the Lord is there;

"And he hath sworn by the power of his might to be her salvation and her high tower.

" Therefore, verily, thus saith the Lord, let Zion rejoice, for this is Zion—the pure in heart" (D&C 97:19–21).

In conforming to the instruction given by the Lord to Alma, leaders have an obligation to exercise the judicial processes essential to preserving a refining gospel environment, free from the corrupting influences that otherwise intrude within the group and threaten its spiritual base.

In establishing the honor code at Brigham Young University, Church leaders have attempted to foster an institution of higher learning that can offer those who come here as faculty or students the assurance of a place where academic studies can be pursued in a gospel environment uncontaminated by the influences that are destructive to faith and spiritual well-being.

All who enroll at Brigham Young University make a pledge to which they affix their signatures as an affidavit that they will abide by the honor code or be subject to dismissal.

You will know, individually, whether you have integrity to that pledge. I think you will have some sense, collectively, as to whether this code of honor is being upheld by the student body of BYU. May I give it as my strong personal conviction that to the degree you, individually, violate this code, you invite into this campus community a spirit of dissent that will inevitably have its effect upon you as well as upon this institution.

May I express profound admiration and gratitude to those of you who retain your commitment to this honor code as well as to the principles of the gospel of Jesus Christ. Your integrity will not go unnoticed by a just and loving Father in Heaven. You represent a moral strength that is greatly needed today. You continue to contribute to the perpetuation of a condition here on this campus that will bless many lives.

It should not surprise us, in light of the counsel we have been given, that we occasionally observe some of the things Alma saw among the members of the Church for whom he had concern and to whom he made this appeal:

"Behold, I say unto you, that the good shepherd doth call you; yea, and in his own name he doth call you, which is the name of Christ; and if ye will not hearken unto the voice of the good shepherd, to the name by which ye are called, behold, ye are not the sheep of the good shepherd.

"And now if ye are not the sheep of the good shepherd, of what fold are ye? . . .

"For I say unto you that whatsoever is good cometh from God, and whatsoever is evil cometh from the devil.

"And now, my brethren, I would that ye should hear me, for I speak in the energy of my soul; for behold, I have spoken unto you plainly that ye cannot err" (Alma 5:38–40, 43).

At the conclusion of his record in the Book of Mormon, Enos

speaks of the struggle that was necessary to keep the people of his day from falling into disobedience and despair. He says:

"And there was nothing save it was exceeding harshness, preaching and prophesying of wars, and contentions, and destructions, and continually reminding them of death, and the duration of eternity, and the judgments and the power of God, and all these things—stirring them up continually to keep them in the fear of the Lord. I say there was nothing short of these things, and exceedingly great plainness of speech, would keep them from going down speedily to destruction" (Enos 1:23).

I do not believe conditions among the members of the Church today are as severe as they were in Enos's time. However, I believe it is a time for great plainness in speech. Against the backdrop of conditions in Alma's day and the prophecies the Lord has given pertaining to our own time, I have tried to speak to you in plainness and forthrightness about the conditions in which we live and the reasons for feeling some concern about whether we are fully qualifying for the blessings the Lord has promised. I have hoped to confirm two things with you that the Lord has made clear in His revelations. One is that while the Lord has made it clear that He will not permit apostate influences to engulf His Church in this dispensation, He may, from time to time, require a purging of those who fail to withstand the tests, in a manner that He has described in unmistakable terms. Such purging, if it is required in our day, will be as painful and devastating as any experienced by God's children at any time on the earth. The suffering of the disobedient in the time of Alma gives us some idea today of the terrible circumstances that a wayward people can bring upon themselves.

The second thing I wish to confirm with you is that if we will be faithful to the gospel plan of life, if we will keep the commandments of God without compromise, without attempting to willfully, purposefully cheat against that which we know to be right and pure and good, we will have the preserving, protecting power of the Lord to be with us, regardless of the course the world may take and its inevitable consequences.

We have a solemn obligation to the Lord, to ourselves, to our posterity, and to the many good people in the world who are looking for the right way, to preserve a community of Saints whom the Lord can bless and who can serve as a beacon and a sanctuary to all who love the Lord and seek to do His will. May we be wise enough and honest enough with ourselves to learn from the scriptural examples preserved for us and avoid the tempting of the adversary, who desires to cheat our souls and lead us carefully down to his depths of despair and misery. May we be fervent enough in our faith and love of the Lord and His work that we will be more than passive camp followers in our Church membership. May we be assertive and aggressive in standing for all that is right and pure and good.

NOTE

1. Harold B. Lee, "Watch! Be Ye Therefore Ready," *Improvement Era,* December 1965, 68:1152–54; see also Conference Report, October 1965, 127.

6

The Liahona Triad

Elder Robert E. Wells

Some time ago I had a dream on a spiritual subject. It was an allegory centered on the Book of Mormon. I have never referred to it before, but when I was invited to write about some facet of the Book of Mormon, my thoughts turned to that most unusual dream, and I felt that it might have been given to me for this purpose.

In the dream I saw multitudes milling around aimlessly. A few people were being propelled toward a beautiful goal in the distance. The force moving them was both constant and invisible, but only a few moved directly and quickly toward the goal. Most wavered, slowed down, wandered around, or became totally disoriented, and although the force that was there to propel them was steady and constant, most people were not able to take advantage of it. I asked, "Why don't they all use the force the same way? What is happening? What does this all mean?" The answer came from a personage whose presence I sensed but did not see. He said, "The ability to take advantage of the power attracting people to Jesus Christ, the desirable goal, depends entirely upon each person's faith, diligence, and heed."

I awoke suddenly, knowing exactly where that phrase came from—

Elder Robert E. Wells is an emeritus member of the First Quorum of the Seventy.

the Liahona story. I have not recounted the details of the dream, only the overall impression, because the experience was quite long.

Since the allegorical dream occurred, I have stayed alert for additional information about the tradition of the Liahona. I will call my remarks "The Liahona Triad." A triad is a group of three closely associated items or concepts. Musicians know that the word *triad* can also mean a chord of three tones: a root tone played with its third tone and fifth tone, constituting the harmonic basis of tonal music. I believe that there is a kind of celestial music that comes from the Book of Mormon and from the three closely associated qualities of *faith, diligence,* and *heed*—a celestial music that lifts the soul. I quote from Nephi, recounting the appearance of the strange instrument:

"And it came to pass that as my father arose in the morning, and went forth to the tent door, to his great astonishment he beheld upon the ground a round ball of curious workmanship; and it was of fine brass. And within the ball were two spindles; and the one pointed the way whither we should go into the wilderness. . . .

"And it came to pass that I, Nephi, beheld the pointers which were in the ball, that they did work according to the *faith and diligence and heed* which we did give unto them.

"And there was also written upon them a new writing, which was plain to be read, which did give us understanding concerning the ways of the Lord; and it was written and changed from time to time" (1 Nephi 16:10, 28–29; emphasis added).

The application of the symbolism of the Liahona to our personal lives was recorded about five hundred years later. The chapter heading of Alma 37 reads, "As the Liahona guided the Nephites, so the word of Christ leads men to eternal life."

Alma explains: "My son, . . . for as our fathers were slothful to give heed to this compass . . . they did not prosper; even so it is with things which are spiritual.

"For behold, it is as easy to give heed to the word of Christ, which will point to you a straight course to eternal bliss, as it was for our fathers to give heed to this compass, which would point unto them a straight course to the promised land" (Alma 37:43–44).

President Spencer W. Kimball used the symbolism of the Liahona in a fascinating illustration about fifteen years ago while talking to the young men of the Church:

"Wouldn't you like to have that kind of a ball—each one of you—so that whenever you were in error it would point the right way and write messages to you, . . . so that you would always know when you were in error or in the wrong way?

"That, my young brethren, you all have. The Lord gave to every boy, every man, every person, a conscience which tells him everytime he starts to go on the wrong path. . . .

"You must realize that you have something like the compass, like the Liahona, in your own system."[1]

President Monson also used the illustration of the Liahona in a general conference talk. He said: "The same Lord who provided a Liahona for Lehi provides for you and for me today a rare and valuable gift to give direction to our lives, to mark the hazards to our safety, and to chart the way, even safe passage—not to a promised land, but to our heavenly home. The gift to which I refer is known as your *patriarchal blessing.*"[2]

So this unusual instrument has fascinated the prophets and been used in their sermons for centuries, by both Book of Mormon and modern prophets.

But is there any independent evidence that such an instrument might actually have existed twenty-six hundred years ago? Some may be familiar with an article in the February 1961 *Improvement Era* by Hugh Nibley entitled "The Liahona's Cousins." In that article, Dr. Nibley traced "belomancy" in ancient times, especially in the Near East. "Belomancy is the practice of divination [fortune-telling] by shooting, tossing, shaking, or otherwise manipulating rods, darts, pointers, or other sticks, all originally derived from arrows."[3]

The Liahona, as we know, had moving spindles or pointers.

Brother Nibley continued: "Whenever divination arrows are described, they are invariably found to have writing on them, like the Zuni 'word-painted arrows of destiny.' . . .

" . . . And what person after considering the divination arrows, portable or enshrined, of other travelers in the desert will deny that in the Liahona we have an implement which, far from being the invention of a brain-sick imagination, was not without its ancient counterparts?"[4]

If Lehi brought the Liahona to the Americas, can we find any trace of such an instrument in the legends of the Lamanites before Columbus? Well, almost. Last year, while living in Mexico City, I went to the famous Museum of Anthropology in Chapultepec Park. There on display was the famous tapestry of Jucutacato, about six feet by eight feet. It has thirty-six frames, like a comic strip, and obviously depicts the migration of a people. In eleven of the first twelve frames, a peculiar round object with a bird, or dove, above it appears in front of the leader. The object seems to be suspended by three strings or chains, but it also has a base to stand on.

In the book *In Search of Cumorah,* we read: "The concept of a sacred ball was not unique to the Tarascan Indians. The Guatemalan Quiche and Cakchiquel histories mention a sacred ball or rock in connection with their legends of migration across the sea."[5]

"The Totonicapan version tells of four great leaders bringing their people from the other side of the sea. . . . Before leaving [the main leader] was given a present by the god Nacxit. It was called the Giron Gagal [meaning *sacred bundle*]. Taking it with him, by miraculous means Balam Quitze [the leader] was able to lead his people across the sea."[6]

In my years in South America, I heard of other similar legends. So perhaps there are signs remaining of an ancient spiritual compass. And, although these concepts regarding the Liahona may be interesting, I find of much greater importance the contents of the Book of Mormon and the power and magnetic attraction of the triad of *faith, diligence,* and *heed* as a formula designed to lead or pull us toward Christ. Faith in Christ, diligence in seeking and following Christ, and heed in obeying Christ are an intrinsic part of all the pages of the Book of Mormon.

I would like to share with you some of my favorite illustrations of each principle of the triad.

FAITH

The Book of Mormon was written by holy prophets for the purpose of building the faith of the reader—faith in Heavenly Father and Jesus Christ and faith in The Church of Jesus Christ of Latter-day Saints as the Lord's kingdom once again established on earth.

Nephi. In the opening pages of the epic saga, young Nephi was quickly identified as a person of singular faith. "Blessed art thou, Nephi, because of thy faith, for thou has sought me diligently" (1 Nephi 2:19). Nephi's faith was directly related to the quality of his seeking and searching for the Lord. Then in 1 Nephi 3, we find an inspired insight into the ways of the Lord that will bless our lives if we have the kind of faith that Nephi had. This oft-quoted passage illustrates the practical and universal faith that made young Nephi so outstanding: "I will go and do the things which the Lord hath commanded, for I know that the Lord giveth no commandments unto the children of men, save he shall prepare a way for them that they may accomplish the thing which he commandeth them" (1 Nephi 3:7).

Nephi's faith that the Lord would open the way has encouraged and inspired countless prophets, leaders, missionaries, and members. Every reader of the Book of Mormon remembers it. It is one of those jewels of truth that jump out at one from the Book of Mormon.

The first story in the Book of Mormon demonstrating Nephi's indomitable faith took place when the four brothers were given the commandment to return to Jerusalem to obtain the genealogy of their forefathers that was engraved on brass plates. Twice they failed dismally. But on the third attempt at this seemingly impossible mission, Nephi (with total faith in the Lord) sneaked into the city alone, not knowing beforehand the things which he should do. Nephi's unwavering faith that the Lord would prepare the way allowed the Lord to bless him with success, overcoming all obstacles (see 1 Nephi 3–4). The Book of Mormon records many other examples of this kind of faith.

I also love the ship story. The Lord commanded Nephi to build a ship that would hold together during an ocean voyage of more than ten thousand miles and for about one year's time—without putting into port for supplies or repairs. That is some boat! This was a family of desert people who knew about camels and tents and dry sand but little or nothing about ships, water, nautical engineering, and ship construction techniques.

The brothers called Nephi a fool for thinking he could build a ship (see 1 Nephi 17:17). But Nephi's faith told him that God would prepare the way. He reminded the family that the Lord had led Israel out of Egyptian slavery, had divided the waters of the Red Sea for Moses, and had made Israel mighty to drive the wicked out of the promised land. After reviewing these faith-promoting experiences, Nephi said to his brothers, "[God] ruleth high in the heavens," and "God had commanded me that I should build a ship. . . . If God had commanded me to do all things I could do them" (1 Nephi 17:39, 49, 50). The clincher is in verse 51: "If the Lord has such great power, and has wrought so many miracles among the children of men, how is it that he cannot instruct me [a man of the desert], that I should build a ship?"

And Nephi did build a ship—a seaworthy ship—and it did take them across half the circumference of the globe, bringing them safely to the New World, their promised land.

Alma. There is in Alma 32 perhaps the finest doctrinal explanation of faith in any of the scriptures. "*Faith* is not to have a perfect knowledge of things; therefore if ye have *faith* ye hope for things which are not seen, which are true" (Alma 32:21; emphasis added).

Remember, the main test of this life on earth is to see if we, not remembering the premortal existence with Heavenly Father and not being able to prove His existence by material evidence, will still have faith in Him, trust Him, and obey His commandments, no matter the hazard or sacrifice that may be required of us.

Listen to Alma's persuasive words about experimenting with faith and about faith as a seed requiring care and nourishment: "If ye will awake and arouse your faculties, even to an *experiment* upon my words, and exercise a particle of *faith,* yea, even if ye can no more than desire to believe, let this desire work in you, even until ye believe. . . .

"Now, we will compare the word [faith] unto a seed. Now, if ye give place, that a seed may be planted in your heart, . . . behold, it will begin to swell within your breasts; and when you feel these swelling motions, ye will begin to say within yourselves—It must needs be that this is a good seed, or that the word is good, for it beginneth to enlarge my soul; yea, it beginneth to enlighten my understanding. . . .

". . . As the tree beginneth to grow, ye will say: Let us nourish it with great care, that it may get root, that it may grow up, and bring forth fruit unto us. . . .

"But if ye neglect the tree [faith], and take no thought for its nourishment, behold it will not get any root; . . . it withers away. . . .

"Now, this is not because the seed was not good, . . . but it is because your ground is barren, and ye will not nourish the tree" (Alma 32:27–28, 37–39; emphasis added).

There is no more clear, more powerful, more faith-developing explanation of this vital process in all the world's books than is found here in Alma's masterful discourse.

A question frequently thought of but seldom asked is: "Just how much faith do I need for the atonement of Christ to work for me?" In other words, how much faith do I need to receive salvation? In the book of Alma, and nowhere else, we find the answer. The prophet Amulek taught this simple but grand principle: "The Son of God . . . bringeth about means unto men that they may have faith *unto repentance*" (Alma 34:14–15; emphasis added).

Please note those three words: "faith unto repentance." That is the clue. Four times in three verses Amulek uses that expression (see Alma 34:15–17). May I quote the part that is the strongest:

"Thus mercy can satisfy the demands of justice, and encircles them in the arms of safety, while he that exercises no *faith unto repentance* is exposed to the whole law of the demands of justice; therefore only unto him that has *faith unto repentance* is brought about the great and eternal plan of redemption" (Alma 34:16; emphasis added).

So the combination of faith in Christ plus faith unto repentance is vitally important. That concept is one of the greatest insights we have into the importance of simple, clear faith—faith sufficient to repent. Apparently faith great enough to move mountains is not required; faith enough to speak in tongues or to heal the sick is not needed; all that we need is enough faith to recognize that we have sinned and need to repent of our sins, to feel remorse for them, and to desire to sin no more but to please Christ the Lord. Then the greatest miracle of all, the Atonement, whereby Christ rescues us from our deserved punishment, is in effect in our behalf.

The Book of Mormon has three outstanding stories illustrating this dual principle of salvation through faith in Christ plus faith enough to repent. They are the stories of Enos, King Benjamin, and Alma.

Enos. Enos said: "My soul hungered [part of repentance and change of attitude]; and I kneeled down before my Maker, and I cried unto him in mighty prayer and supplication . . . [This is repentance and faith] all the day long . . . and when the night came I did still raise my voice high that it reached the heavens.

"And there came a voice unto me, saying: Enos, thy sins are forgiven thee. . . .

"And I said: Lord, how is it done?

"And he said unto me: Because of thy faith in Christ, whom thou hast never before heard nor seen" (Enos 1:4–5, 7–8).

Note that both faith to repent and faith in Christ are present.

King Benjamin. King Benjamin had just finished delivering a great sermon that an angel had given to him to preach to the people. When he finished, he noticed that the people had all fallen to the earth, for the fear of the Lord had come upon them. The record says:

"They all cried aloud with one voice, saying: O have mercy [they are repenting], and apply the atoning blood of Christ that we may receive forgiveness of our sins, . . . for we believe in Jesus Christ, the Son of God."

Note both principles—faith in Christ and faith enough to repent.

"After they had spoken these words the Spirit of the Lord came upon them, and they were filled with joy, having received a remission of their sins, and having peace of conscience, because of the exceeding *faith* which they had in Jesus Christ who should come" (Mosiah 4:2–3; emphasis added).

Alma. Alma said to his son Helaman: "I was racked with eternal torment. . . .

"Yea, I did remember all my sins and iniquities. . . . [He is repenting.]

"... While I was harrowed up by the memory of my many sins, behold, I remembered also to have heard my father prophesy unto the people concerning the coming of one Jesus Christ, a Son of God, to atone for the sins of the world.

"Now, as my mind caught hold upon this thought, I cried within my heart: O Jesus, thou Son of God, have mercy on me, who am in the gall of bitterness. ... [He is very repentant.]

"... When I thought this, I could remember my pains no more. ...

"And oh, what joy, and what marvelous light I did behold. ...

"... There can be nothing so exquisite and sweet as was my joy" (Alma 36:12–13, 17–21).

Thus, one of the major teachings about faith that I find in the Book of Mormon is the dual concept that the Atonement of Christ works because of the combination of simple faith in Christ and faith enough to repent.

Moroni. At the end of the Jaredite history, Moroni, the historian, interjected a short sermon on faith. It is a jewel in itself, worthy of being on everyone's list of favorite scriptures on faith:

"And now, I, Moroni, would speak somewhat concerning these things; I would show unto the world that *faith* is things which are hoped for and not seen; wherefore, dispute not because ye see not, for ye receive no witness until after the trial of your *faith*. ...

"For the brother of Jared said unto the mountain Zerin, Remove—and it was removed. And if he had not had *faith* it would not have moved; wherefore thou workest after men have *faith*" (Ether 12:6, 30; emphasis added).

Thus, the Book of Mormon is a great source for learning about and increasing our faith in Christ. It pulls us—like the invisible magnetic power in my dream—towards Christ.

DILIGENCE

Faith in combination with diligence (the second part of the Liahona triad) creates an unbeatable combination to produce success in any venture. The Book of Mormon is replete with both. If we would be drawn to Christ, we need to understand *diligence.* As it is used in the Book of Mormon, *diligence* is synonymous with such terms as *perseverance, persistence, dedication, determination, steadiness, dependability*—so much needed and so much sought after in our uncertain world.

One of my favorite heroes of the Book of Mormon is the principal compiler himself, General Mormon, who exemplifies diligence. His tragic end does not do justice to his long life of diligently serving his people in spite of their sins and unworthiness. Here is a great man who literally and figuratively gave his life for his nation and his people.

Mormon was large enough of stature and sober enough of mind that by age sixteen he was chosen by the people to be the leader of their armies. He served as their general for forty-five years. Other great generals of history—Washington, Napoleon, and Wellington—served for much shorter periods. Mormon was dedicated, courageous, persistent, and endured to the bitter end of the final nine years of the Nephite nation. This was after a thirteen-year interruption to his military service because the Lord commanded him to step down, perhaps partly so Mormon could get the sacred records ready to turn over to his son Moroni and partly to try to get the Nephites to listen to his warnings. Unfortunately, the Nephite nation did not listen to General Mormon, nor repent, so he finally, and diligently, returned to lead his people in their tragic final years.

General Mormon wrote an affectionate letter to his son Moroni that is recorded in Moroni 9: "And now, my beloved son, notwithstanding their hardness, let us labor *diligently;* for if we should cease to labor, we should be brought under condemnation; for we have a labor to perform whilst in this tabernacle of clay, that we may conquer the enemy of all righteousness, and rest our souls in the kingdom of God" (Moroni 9:6; emphasis added).

The sons of Mosiah. Alma and the sons of Mosiah became very dedicated missionaries. The sons of Mosiah were grandsons of King Benjamin and were princes of the kingdom; one of them could have become the king when their father died. Instead, they all turned to the ministry of Christ. One most distinguishing feature of these great missionaries was their steadfast *diligence* in carrying out their duties and responsibilities. In Alma 17 we find several of their most outstanding attributes listed. The word *diligent* is not used often, but it obviously applies all the way through. Listen to the kind of men they had become:

"They had waxed strong in the knowledge of the truth; for they were men of a sound understanding and they had searched the scriptures *diligently,* that they might know the word of God.

"But this is not all [they were diligent in other things, too]; they had given themselves to much prayer, and fasting; therefore they had the spirit of prophecy, and the spirit of revelation, and when they taught, they taught with power and authority of God" (Alma 17:2–3; emphasis added).

They served longer than missionaries do today. Verse 4 says that they had been on their mission for fourteen years (now that is true diligence) and had much success among the Lamanites, bringing many to the knowledge of the truth.

Furthermore, they were diligent in spite of difficult circumstances. They did not have it easy at all: "Now these are the circumstances which attended them in their journeyings, for they had many afflictions; they did suffer much, both in body and in mind, such as hunger, thirst and fatigue, and also much labor in the spirit" (Alma 17:5).

These great missionaries were heroic examples of diligence, persistence, and long-suffering in preaching the word of the Lord.

Jacob. Jacob, the son of Lehi, was a powerful teacher. As a boy, he saw the Savior. For some time he was the custodian of the small plates, having received them from his brother Nephi. Nephi had ordained him to continue as a consecrated priest and teacher of the people. Jacob accounted for his heavy stewardship with these beautiful words that serve as an example to all today who hold the priesthood: "We did magnify our office unto the Lord, taking upon us the responsibility, answering the sins of the people upon our own heads if we did not teach them the word of God with all *diligence;* wherefore, by laboring with our might [this is diligence again] their blood might not come upon our garments" (Jacob 1:19; emphasis added).

In chapter 5 of his record, Jacob quoted Zenos's allegory relative to the tame and wild olive trees that had to be nourished, pruned, digged about, dunged, rooted up and replanted, pruned again, grafted, burned, and so forth. Then he stated, "How blessed are they who have labored *diligently* in his vineyard; and how cursed are they who shall be cast out into their own place!" (Jacob 6:3; emphasis added).

In addition, we can understand the powerful spirit of Jacob better as we meditate upon the hard work of engraving the plates for the benefit of future generations. He said, "We labor *diligently* to engraven these words upon plates, hoping that our beloved brethren and our children will receive them with thankful hearts" (Jacob 4:3; emphasis added).

And then he bore this wonderful testimony:

"For, for this intent have we written these things, that they may know that we knew of Christ, and we had a hope of his glory many hundred years before his coming; and not only we ourselves had a hope of his glory, but also all the holy prophets which were before us.

"Behold, they believed in Christ and worshiped the Father in his name, and also we worship the Father in his name" (Jacob 4:4–5).

The Book of Mormon has many examples from which we can learn to be more diligent in our service to Christ—truly, diligence is an attribute which will draw us unto Christ, as I saw in my dream.

HEED

The word *heed* is not in common usage today, but in the days of the Book of Mormon it was a strong and frequently used synonym for "hear," "hearken," "listen to," "pay attention to," or "keep." Today we would probably use "obey" or "be obedient to." If we would be drawn to Christ, we need to understand *heed* as used in the Book of Mormon. Here are a few brief examples:

1. "I, Nephi, did exhort them to give *heed* unto the word of the Lord" (1 Nephi 15:25; emphasis added).

2. "Take *heed* that ye do not transgress" (Mosiah 5:11; emphasis added).

3. "It is . . . easy to give *heed* to the word of Christ" (Alma 37:44; emphasis added).

An often-repeated message of the Book of Mormon—right from

its first pages—is closely related to the injunction to obey or "heed the commandments." Remember the promise of the Lord to Nephi: "Inasmuch as thy seed shall *keep my commandments,* they shall prosper in the land of promise" (1 Nephi 4:14; emphasis added). We can safely substitute the word *heed* for *keep* or *obey,* and then one of the significant promises of the entire Book of Mormon comes into focus. Just as the Book of Mormon is truly written to help the reader increase in faith, it also leads to an increase in "heeding" or "obeying" the Lord—which will lead to prosperity in this land of promise.

The opposite of "heed" is, as Alma said, to be "slothful to give heed":

"For as our fathers were slothful to give *heed* to this compass . . . they did not prosper; even so it is with things which are spiritual.

"For behold, it is as easy to give *heed* to the word of Christ, which will point to you a straight course to eternal bliss, as it was for our fathers to give *heed* to this compass" (Alma 37:43–44; emphasis added).

To heed is to remain righteous. "Heed," as it is used in the Book of Mormon, has a certain permanency about it that is opposite to temporary obedience or alternating "on again, off again" obedience. It is understood that as you continue to heed the Lord, you will not waver, vacillate, or complain, but rather you will weather the storm and persevere no matter what you may be called upon to endure:

"And now my brethren, if ye were righteous and were willing to *hearken* to the truth, and give *heed* unto it, that ye might walk uprightly before God, then ye would not murmur because of the truth" (1 Nephi 16:3; emphasis added).

To heed is to be careful. Sometimes *heed* can mean to be careful. In King Benjamin's great sermon at the temple, he tells us that we must take upon ourselves the name of Christ and then be careful to avoid transgression: "Therefore, *take heed* [be careful] that ye do not transgress, that the name be not blotted out of your hearts" (Mosiah 5:11; emphasis added).

And another illustration, this one from Mormon:

"Wherefore, take heed, my beloved brethren, that ye do not judge that which is evil to be of God, or that which is good and of God to be of the devil" (Moroni 7:14).

Pride is an obstacle to heeding. Pride frequently causes people to choose not to listen or pay attention to prophets and leaders. That occurred from time to time in the Book of Mormon:

"After Helaman and his brethren had appointed priests and teachers over the churches . . . there arose a dissension among them, and they would not give *heed* to the words of Helaman and his brethren;

"But they grew proud, being lifted up in their hearts, because of their exceedingly great riches; therefore they grew rich in their own eyes, and would not give *heed* to their words, to walk uprightly before God" (Alma 45:23–24).

To heed is to pay attention. The Prophet Joseph used the word *heed* in telling the brethren that their mind, or intellect, could learn more than they thought. Contrary to the "Fixed I.Q. Theory," he taught, "God has created man with a mind capable of instruction, and a faculty which may be enlarged in proportion to the heed and diligence given to the light communicated from heaven to the intellect."[7] Could not this same principle apply to the spirit?

Giving heed, or obedience, to the commandments, ordinances, and prophets, will draw you powerfully and invisibly to Christ, just as I saw in my dream.

"NEW WRITING" ON THE LIAHONA

One fascinating peculiarity of the Liahona was that not only did its pointers guide Lehi's family in the wilderness but "a new writing, which was plain to be read" appeared on the pointers to give them "understanding concerning the ways of the Lord; and it was written and changed from time to time, according to [their] faith and diligence" and heed (1 Nephi 16:29). Very little is said about this phenomenon. In fact, I can find no further reference to this changeable writing. As I read the Book of Mormon, however, something strange seems to happen to me. Passages of scriptures that I have read many times in one light seem to change—and suddenly there is a new meaning to that old and familiar scripture. I like to think that the Book of

Mormon is truly like the Liahona of old. Not only does it point us in the way of the Lord and to the Lord according to the faith, diligence, and heed we give it, but if we are interested enough to read it again and again, from cover to cover, there are times when a "new writing"—plain to be read—seems to appear. I would like to share two personal examples of such an experience:

As you are undoubtedly aware, the leaders of the Church are prone to choose a passage of scripture and use it as a kind of theme. For a few years, we have had the principal subject of "Come unto Christ," a phrase that is often repeated in the Book of Mormon. Before that, the theme was the threefold mission of the Church:

1. Proclaim the gospel.
2. Perfect the Saints.
3. Redeem the dead.

I had read chapter 10 of Moroni many times because it is the closing chapter of the great Book of Mormon, it is Moroni's farewell to the Lamanites, and it has the wonderful promise to readers of the Book of Mormon that if they will read, ponder, and ask of God with a sincere heart and faith in Christ, they will receive an answer to their prayer and know by the power of the Holy Ghost that the book is true.

I happened to be reading Moroni 10 again when verse 31 seemed to jump out in a different way. I don't know if a general conference speaker pointed it out or if I heard it used by some other person—but there it was: the theme of proclaim, perfect, and redeem was in verse 31—only in reverse! Let me show you this "new writing," hidden there all of the time. Verse 31 says: "Awake, and arise from the dust, O Jerusalem; yea, and put on thy *beautiful garments.*" Then, *"strengthen thy stakes"* follows, and, lastly, "*enlarge thy borders forever*" (emphasis added). I could clearly see that "enlarge thy borders" meant to enlarge the Church through missionary work and to *proclaim* the gospel to all the world. It seemed that I could also see clearly that "strengthen thy stakes" meant to *perfect* the Saints through the priesthood organizations and the auxiliaries. And it seemed to me that "put on thy beautiful garments" referred to the temple robes and going to the temples of the Lord to *redeem* our beloved ancestors. To me, it was enlightening—it was a new writing, a new emphasis on an old and familiar verse of the scriptures which I already loved but which now had a new thought that made it even more important to me.

I love to talk to missionaries and train them in proselyting techniques that produce greater than ordinary success. One hot afternoon in the tropics, I stood before a zone conference of missionaries. I was telling them that missionaries should so conduct themselves and be so spiritually prepared in their way of teaching and be such perfect gentlemen and ladies that the investigators and members would actually see them as "angels." I usually tell some stories about people who have seen the missionaries as angel messengers. In fact, *angel* means "messenger" in Hebrew *(malak).* I quoted from Moroni 7:29: "Have miracles ceased? Behold I say unto you, Nay; neither have angels ceased to minister unto the children of men." And right there—on my feet, in front of the missionaries—a strange thing happened. My eyes darted across the column to verse 31 and it glowed—it jumped out at me. So I read it as well, and while I was reading it out loud to the missionaries I saw it as a new writing with a new meaning. Let me quote it to you, and then I will interpret it to you as I did to the missionaries that day. It says, "The office of their ministry [the ministry of angels] is to call men unto repentance, and to fulfil and to do the work of the covenants of the Father, . . . to prepare the way among the children of men, by declaring the word of Christ unto the chosen vessels of the Lord."

It was made clear to me at that moment that angels and missionaries do the very same work—the very same things. They (both missionaries and angels) call people to repentance, and they fulfill and do the work of the covenants of the Father (both missionaries and unseen angels work to get people to be baptized, to receive the gift of the Holy Ghost, etc.). They also prepare the children of men by declaring the word of Christ unto them (both missionaries and unseen angels). In other words, no wonder some special, elect people are so in tune with the Spirit that they see the missionaries as angels. They see only the missionaries, but they feel angels present, so they believe the missionaries to be angels too.

The Liahona triad of faith, diligence, and heed pulling us to

Christ—with each point illustrated throughout the Book of Mormon—plus the concept of a "new writing" every time I reread the Book of Mormon has been of immeasurable help to me in my life. I leave you my witness that the gospel is true. Any person who reads, ponders, and prays with *faith, diligence,* and *heed* about the Book of Mormon will come to know that Jesus Christ is the Savior of the world, that Joseph Smith was His revelator and prophet in these last days, and that The Church of Jesus Christ of Latter-day Saints is the Lord's kingdom once again established on the earth, preparatory to the Second Coming of the Messiah.

NOTES

For additional reading about the Liahona, see Robert F. Smith, "Lodestone and the Liahona," in *Reexploring the Book of Mormon,* ed. John W. Welch (Salt Lake City and Provo, Utah: Deseret Book and FARMS, 1992), 44–46; Robert L. Bunker, "The Design of the Liahona and the Purpose of the Second Spindle," *Journal of Book of Mormon Studies* 3, no. 2 (fall 1994): 1–11; Hugh W. Nibley, "The Liahona and Murmurings in the Wilderness," in *Teachings of the Book of Mormon, Semester One* (Provo, Utah: FARMS, 1993), 464–66.

1. Spencer W. Kimball, "Our Own Liahona," *Ensign,* November 1976, 79.
2. Thomas S. Monson, "Your Patriarchal Blessing: A Liahona of Light," *Ensign,* November 1986, 65; emphasis added.
3. Hugh W. Nibley, "The Liahona's Cousins," *Improvement Era,* February 1961, 104.
4. Nibley, "Liahona's Cousins," 106, 110.
5. David A. Palmer, *In Search of Cumorah: New Evidences for the Book of Mormon from Ancient Mexico* (Bountiful, Utah: Horizon, 1981), 157.
6. Adrian Recinos, ed., *Título de los Señores de Totonicapan, Anales de los Cakchiqueles, Memorial de Solola* (Mexico, D.F.: Fondo de Cultura Económica, 1950), as cited in Palmer, *In Search of Cumorah,* 157.
7. Joseph Smith, *Teachings of the Prophet Joseph Smith,* comp. Joseph Fielding Smith (Salt Lake City: Deseret Book, 1976), 51.

7

THE TITLE PAGE

Daniel H. Ludlow

I am grateful to have been asked to discuss the title page of the Book of Mormon.[1] I was both surprised and dismayed when I reviewed my book *A Companion to Your Study of the Book of Mormon*—in which I consider each book in the Book of Mormon, chapter by chapter and verse by verse—to find that I did not discuss there or even mention the title page. As I reviewed other commentaries on the Book of Mormon, I found that, almost without exception, they begin with the first verse of the first chapter of 1 Nephi and end with the last verse of the tenth chapter of Moroni. I soon became convinced that the title page of the Book of Mormon is one of the least studied and least understood parts of this holy scripture. Articles and comments on the title page are indeed few and far between.

Perhaps more disturbing, some of us may have been applying a misleading personal interpretation to the origin and the meaning of some of the statements in the title page because of the lack of thoughtful consideration we have given to these statements. For example, one statement in the title page is quoted very frequently (and I believe correctly) as referring to the entire Book of Mormon: "Which is to show

---

Daniel H. Ludlow is an emeritus professor of ancient scripture and former dean of Religious Education at Brigham Young University.

unto the remnant of the House of Israel what great things the Lord hath done for their fathers; and that they may know the covenants of the Lord, that they are not cast off forever—And also to the convincing of the Jew and Gentile that Jesus is the Christ, the Eternal God, manifesting himself unto all nations." Yet many people would say that in the present paragraphing of the title page that passage should refer only to Moroni's abridgment of the book of Ether.

Now let me share with you the steps I followed in my study of the title page. First, I read and reread the following statement by Joseph Smith about the title page, which appears in the standard histories of the Church:

"I wish to mention here that the title-page of the Book of Mormon is a literal translation, taken from the very last leaf, on the left hand side of the collection or book of plates, which contained the record which has been translated, the language of the whole running the same as all Hebrew writing in general; and that said title page is not by any means a modern composition, either of mine or of any other man who has lived or does live in this generation."[2]

Next, I obtained copies of the title pages from all major editions of the Book of Mormon—1830, 1837, 1840, 1852, 1879, 1920, and 1981. I noted that in the 1981 edition the text of the title page is divided into twelve major statements. I then compared the wording, spelling, capitalization, and punctuation of each of the twelve statements in all of the major editions. Later in this essay, I will share with you the results of these comparisons.

I also studied the earliest sources of the title page text. The earliest available source is the "printer's manuscript," which is largely in the handwriting of Oliver Cowdery. It is now in the possession of the Community of Christ in Independence, Missouri. With assistance from the staff of the Church Historical Library in Salt Lake City, I obtained a copy of the title page from that manuscript. I have prepared a typewritten copy of that manuscript page, listing its text word-for-word and letter-by-letter. I will include that copy at a later point.

Furthermore, I obtained copies of the two other early documents which contain the title page. The first is a handwritten copy on the copyright application form of 11 June 1829, and the second is a printed copy from the 26 June 1829 *Wayne Sentinel.*

With all these copies gathered, let us now examine some of the items I have noted in analyzing the text of the Book of Mormon title page.

But first, let me propose an experiment. Below is a typewritten copy of the title page of the Book of Mormon as it appears in the printer's manuscript. The spelling, capitalization, and punctuation are as shown.

Assume that (1) you are a typesetter working in a publishing house in 1830, and (2) you have the assignment to set this material in type after correcting obvious errors. Now go ahead, edit the material, and punctuate it into sentences and paragraphs.

"The Book of Mormon An account written by the hand of Mormon upon plates taken from the plates of Nephi Wherefore it is an abridgment of the record of the People of Nephi & also of the Lamanites written to the Lamanites which are a remnant of the house of Israel & also to Jew & Gentile written by way of commandment & also by the spirit of Prophesy & of revelation written & sealed up & hid up unto the Lord that they might not be destroid to come forth by the gift & power of God unto the interpretation thereof sealed by the hand of Moroni & hid up unto the Lord to come forth in due time by the way of Gentile the enterpretation thereof by the gift of God an abridgment taken from the Book of Ether also which is a record of the People of Jared which were scattered at the time the Lord confounded the language of the People when they were building a tower to get to heaven which is to shew unto the remnant of the house of Israel how great things the Lord hath done for their fathers & that they may know the covenants of the Lord that they are not cast off forever & also to the convincing of the Jew & Gentile that Jesus is the Christ the Eternal God manifesting himself unto all Nations & now if there be fault it be the mistake of men wherefore condemn not the things of God that ye may be found spotless at the judgment seat of Christ—By Joseph Smith Juniour, Author & proprietor"

How did you do? Did you edit it in the same way it was edited for the 1830 edition? The possibility that you did it differently is quite high. You saw that the copy of the title page in the printer's manuscript contains virtually no punctuation marks, but you also saw that it is capitalized quite carefully. The experiment you just completed is what the typesetter for E. B. Grandin had to do. According to the following statement by B. H. Roberts in *A Comprehensive History of the Church,* the foreman in the Grandin printing establishment, John H. Gilbert, claimed that he was largely responsible for the punctuation and capitalization (possibly not all) of the first edition, which would include determining the sentences and the paragraphs: "It is said by Mr. Gilbert, Grandin's foreman printer and chief compositor on the *Book of Mormon,* that the manuscript as sent to him was neither capitalized nor punctuated, and that the capitalization and punctuation in the first edition was done by him."[3]

Previously I mentioned two early documents of the title page text. The earliest of these two versions is the copy of the copyright application of 11 June 1829 (see figure 1). You will note that in the space on the application form for the title of the book, the Prophet Joseph Smith included all of the text of what we now call the title page. You will note also that the text is written with some capitalization and a considerable degree of punctuation but is not divided into paragraphs.

The later of these two documents is the 26 June 1829 *Wayne Sentinel* (see figure 2). You will note that the text is separated into the following clauses, sentences, and paragraphs:

1. An introduction: "The Book of Mormon, an account, written by the hand of Mormon upon plates, taken from the plates of Nephi."

2. A first paragraph beginning, "Wherefore it is an abridgment of the record of the people of Nephi," and ending, "an abridgment taken from the book of Ether."

3. A second paragraph beginning, "Also, which is a record of the people of Jared," and ending, "that ye may be found spotless at the judgment seat of Christ."

The *Wayne Sentinel* was published by the E. B. Grandin publishing concern. Undoubtedly this 26 June 1829 version reflects the punctuation and paragraphing that had already been determined for the first printing of the Book of Mormon.

You will notice (see figure 3) in the reproduction of the title page in

Nathern District of New York } To wit:

Be it remembered, That on the Eleventh day of June in the fifty third year of the Independence of the United States of America, A. D. 1829 Joseph Smith Junior of the said District, hath deposited in this Office the title of a Book the right whereof he claims as author in the words following, to wit: The Book of Mormon; an account written by the hand of Mormon upon plates taken from the plates of Nephi. Wherefore it is an abridgment of the record of the people of Nephi and also of the Lamanites, written to the Lamanites which are a remnant of the House of Israel; and also to Jew & Gentile, written by way of commandment; and also by the spirit of prophecy & of revelation. Written & sealed & hid up unto the Lord that they might not be destroyed to come forth by the gift & power of God unto the interpretation thereof, sealed up by the hand of Moroni & hid up unto the Lord, to come forth in due time by the way of Gentile, the interpretation thereof by the gift of God; an abridgment taken from the book of Ether, also, which is a record of the people of Jared, which were scattered at the time the Lord confounded the language of the people when they were building a tower to get to Heaven; which is to shew unto the remnant of the House of Israel how great things the Lord hath done for their fathers; & that they may know the covenants of the Lord that they are not cast off forever; and also to the convincing of the Jew & Gentile that Jesus is the Christ the Eternal God, manifesting himself unto all nations. And now if there be a fault it be the mistake of men; wherefore condemn not the things of God, that ye may be found spotless at the judgment seat of Christ. By Joseph Smith Junior, author & Proprietor.

In conformity to the act of the Congress of the United States, entitled "An act for the encouragement of learning, by securing the copies of Maps, Charts, and Books, to the authors and proprietors of such copies, during the times therein mentioned;" and also, to the act entitled "An act supplementary to an act entitled 'An act for the encouragement of learning, by securing the copies of Maps, Charts, and Books, to the authors and proprietors of such copies during the times therein mentioned,' and extending the benefits thereof to the arts of Designing, Engraving and Etching historical and other prints."

R. R. Lansing Clerk of the United States Dist. Court for the Nathern Dist. of New York.

Figure 1. Copyright application form for the Book of Mormon, 11 June 1829
Courtesy Archives, The Church of Jesus Christ of Latter-day Saints

It is pretended that it will be published as soon as the translation is completed. Meanwhile we have been furnished with the following, which is represented to us as intended for the title page of the work—we give it as a curiosity:—

"The *Book of Mormon*, an account, written by the hand of Mormon upon plates, taken from the plates of Nephi:—

"Wherefore it is an abridgment of the record of the people of Nephi, and also of the Lamanites, written to the Lamanites, which are a remnant of the house of Israel; and also to Jew and Gentile; written by way of commandment, and also by the spirit of prophecy, and of revelation; written and sealed and hid up unto the Lord, that they might not be destroyed,—to come forth by the gift and power of God unto the interpretation thereof—sealed up by the hand of Moroni, and hid up unto the Lord, to come forth in due time by the way of Gentile—the interpretation thereof by the gift of God: an abridgment taken from the book of Ether.

"Also, which is a record of the people of Jared, which were scattered at the time the Lord confounded the language of the people, when they were building a tower to get to Heaven; which is to shew unto the remnant of the house of Israel how great things the Lord hath done for their fathers: and that they may know the covenants of the Lord, that they are not cast off forever: and also to the convincing of the Jew and Gentile that Jesus is the Christ, the Eternal God, manifesting himself unto all nations. And now, if there be fault, it be the mistake of men: wherefore condemn not the things of God, that ye may be found spotless at the judgment seat of Christ.—By Joseph Smith, Junior, Author and Proprietor"

Figure 2. Text of the title page as printed in the *Wayne Sentinel,* 26 June 1829

the first edition (1830) that the wording, the essential punctuation, and the paragraphing are identical to that in the article already published in the *Wayne Sentinel.* These two versions established the pattern of publishing the title page in three sections: a brief introduction and two paragraphs. This same format has been used in all subsequent editions published in English.

One change was made in the title page in the second edition (1837). The clause "An abridgment taken from the book of Ether" was moved from the last part of the first paragraph to the beginning of the second paragraph, bringing the two elements about the book of Ether together. This clause has remained in this position in all subsequent editions in English, including both those of The Church of Jesus Christ of Latter-day Saints and those of the Community of Christ.

The 1840 edition of the title page is virtually identical to the 1837 edition, except that the word *Moroni* appears after the second paragraph. The name *Moroni* also is printed in the same place both in the LDS edition of 1852 and in the RLDS editions of 1874 and 1908.

The only changes between the 1830 and the 1981 editions in the language or spelling are shown in the following list:

1830 Edition	*1981 Edition*
which [are a remnant]	who [are a remnant]
[spirit of] prophesy	[spirit of] prophecy
by the way of Gentile	by way of the Gentile
which [were scattered]	who [were scattered]
[Which is to] shew	[Which is to] show
how [great things the Lord hath done]	what [great things the Lord hath done]
if there be fault, it be	if there are faults they are
the mistake of men	the mistakes of men
judgment seat	judgment-seat
By Joseph Smith, Junior, Author and Proprietor	Translated by Joseph Smith Jun.

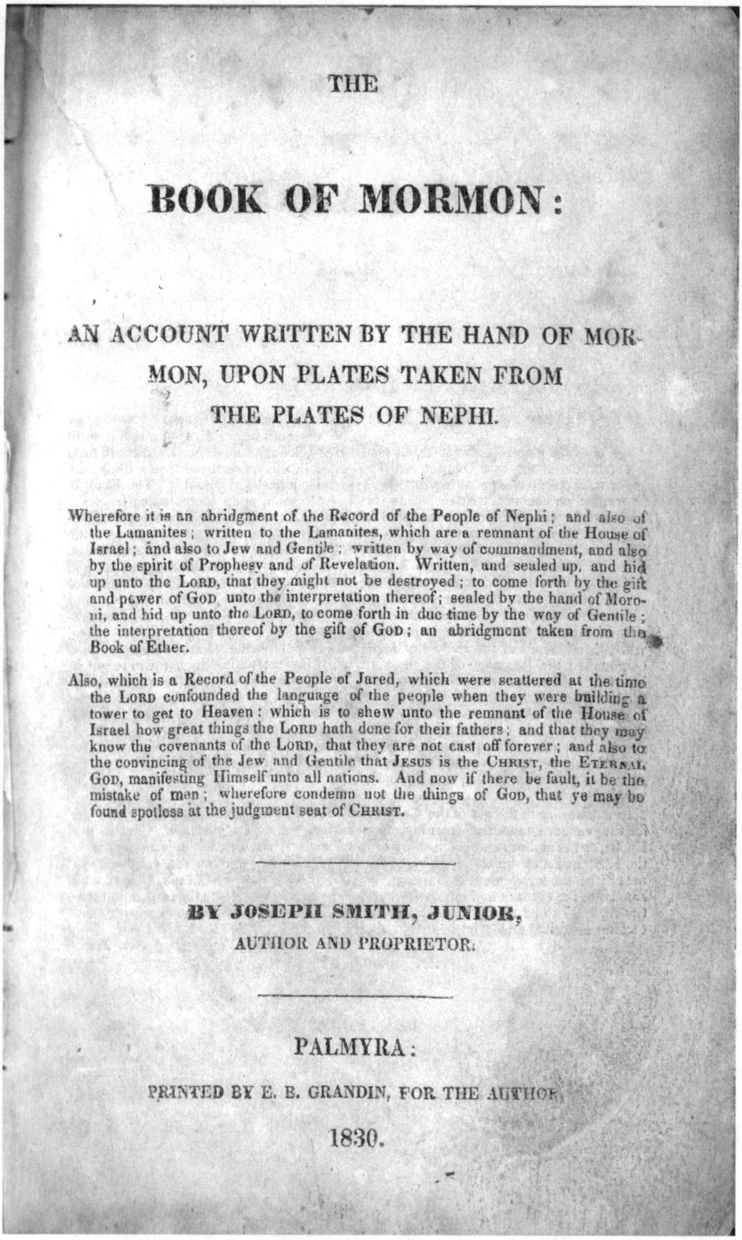

THE

BOOK OF MORMON:

AN ACCOUNT WRITTEN BY THE HAND OF MORMON, UPON PLATES TAKEN FROM THE PLATES OF NEPHI.

Wherefore it is an abridgment of the Record of the People of Nephi; and also of the Lamanites; written to the Lamanites, which are a remnant of the House of Israel; and also to Jew and Gentile; written by way of commandment, and also by the spirit of Prophesy and of Revelation. Written, and sealed up, and hid up unto the LORD, that they might not be destroyed; to come forth by the gift and power of GOD unto the interpretation thereof; sealed by the hand of Moroni, and hid up unto the LORD, to come forth in due time by the way of Gentile; the interpretation thereof by the gift of GOD; an abridgment taken from the Book of Ether.

Also, which is a Record of the People of Jared, which were scattered at the time the LORD confounded the language of the people when they were building a tower to get to Heaven: which is to shew unto the remnant of the House of Israel how great things the LORD hath done for their fathers; and that they may know the covenants of the LORD, that they are not cast off forever; and also to the convincing of the Jew and Gentile that JESUS is the CHRIST, the ETERNAL GOD, manifesting Himself unto all nations. And now if there be fault, it be the mistake of men; wherefore condemn not the things of GOD, that ye may be found spotless at the judgment seat of CHRIST.

BY JOSEPH SMITH, JUNIOR,

AUTHOR AND PROPRIETOR.

PALMYRA:

PRINTED BY E. B. GRANDIN, FOR THE AUTHOR.

1830.

Figure 3. Title page of the 1830 edition of the Book of Mormon
Courtesy L. Tom Perry Special Collections,
Harold B. Lee Library, Brigham Young University

Some of the non-English editions of the title page have paragraphing different from that of the English editions. The 1980 edition in Fijian has four paragraphs, and the Rarotongan edition has three paragraphs.

Interestingly, changing the number of paragraphs might lead to additional insights as we ask such questions as: (1) *who* the author is (or who the authors are) of the various statements of the title page, and (2) *when* the various statements were written. For example, publishing the title page in two paragraphs and adding the word *Moroni* in some editions undoubtedly influenced virtually all early students of the Book of Mormon to conclude that Moroni was the only author of the title page. According to this reasoning, one would conclude that the title page must have been written after about A.D. 385 when Moroni received the plates from his father, Mormon. This view has been expressed by different scholars, including Dr. Sidney B. Sperry, who concluded that Moroni wrote the entire title page at two distinctively different times in his life:

"In the opinion of the writer this statement [Mormon 8:12–13] was Moroni's original farewell. A careful study of what precedes and what follows these words must lead one to realize the possibility of this being so. Verse 13 is a logical point for a chapter division.

"It is quite likely that at this point Moroni wrote the first paragraph (as we now have it) of the title page of the Book of Mormon.

"'Wherefore, it is an abridgment of the record of the people of Nephi, and also of the Lamanites—Written to the Lamanites, who are a remnant of the house of Israel; and also to Jew and Gentile—Written by way of commandment, and also by the spirit of prophecy and of revelation—Written and sealed up, and hid up unto the Lord, that they might not be destroyed—To come forth by the gift and power of God unto the interpretation thereof—Sealed by the hand of Moroni, and hid up unto the Lord, to come forth in due time by way of the Gentile—The interpretation thereof by the gift of God.'

"He did not write the second paragraph of the title page at this time for the very good and sufficient reason that he had not yet abridged the Book of Ether which is mentioned therein."[4]

Dr. Sperry then reviewed the contents of Mormon 8:14–9:37 and added:

"There may be those who will prefer to believe that this is the point at which Moroni wrote the first paragraph of the title page rather than at Mormon 8:13, as I have advocated. But no matter—Moroni finds that he still has space left on the plates upon which he may write something of value. He ponders the matter and finally decides on making an abridgment of the Book of Ether for the benefit of future generations. . . .

"Having finished his task of abridgment, Moroni then proceeded to add another paragraph to his title page. This was a logical necessity. Thus we read:

"'An abridgment taken from the Book of Ether also, which is a record of the people of Jared, who were scattered at the time the Lord confounded the language of the people, when they were building a tower to get to heaven—Which is to show unto the remnant of the House of Israel what great things the Lord hath done for their fathers; and that they may know the covenants of the Lord, that they are not cast off forever—And also, to the convincing of the Jew and Gentile that Jesus is the Christ, the Eternal God, manifesting himself unto all nations—And now, if there are faults they are the mistakes of men; wherefore, condemn not the things of God, that ye may be found spotless at the judgment-seat of Christ.'"[5]

According to Dr. Sperry, Moroni then proceeded to give us the text now found in Moroni chapters 1 through 10.

Virtually all other scholars and students of the Book of Mormon who have written commentary about the title page have reached exactly the same two conclusions: (1) the title page was written entirely by Moroni, and (2) he wrote it at two different times in his life.

Just as a matter of interest, however, let us change the paragraphing of the title page into a brief title (The Book of Mormon) and six paragraphs that we will number 1 through 6 for ease of reference in this discussion. The title page then would appear as follows:

THE BOOK OF MORMON

1. "An account written by the hand of Mormon upon plates taken from the plates of Nephi. Wherefore, it is an abridgment of the record of the people of Nephi, and also of the Lamanites. Written to the

Lamanites, who are a remnant of the house of Israel; and also to Jew and Gentile. Written by way of commandment, and also by the spirit of prophecy and of revelation. Written and sealed up, and hid up unto the Lord, that they might not be destroyed, to come forth by the gift and power of God unto the interpretation thereof.

2. "Sealed by the hand of Moroni, and hid up unto the Lord, to come forth in due time by way of the Gentile, the interpretation thereof by the gift of God.

3. "An abridgment taken from the Book of Ether also, which is a record of the people of Jared, who were scattered at the time the Lord confounded the language of the people, when they were building a tower to get to heaven.

4. "Which is to show unto the remnant of the House of Israel what great things the Lord hath done for their fathers, and that they may know the covenants of the Lord that they are not cast off forever.

5. "And also to the convincing of the Jew and Gentile that Jesus is the Christ, the Eternal God, manifesting himself unto all nations.

6. "And now, if there are faults they are the mistakes of men; wherefore, condemn not the things of God, that ye may be found spotless at the judgment-seat of Christ."

Let us now reread the entire title page word-for-word but with this new paragraphing and consider additional possibilities as to the *person* who might have written certain paragraphs and as to the *time* when those paragraphs might have been written.

The brief four-word title (The Book of Mormon) has appeared on the title page of all editions.

In reading the first paragraph, let us change our mind-set and assume that Mormon wrote it rather than Moroni. After all, Mormon was the major abridger or compiler of the writings we have in our present Book of Mormon. Surely, he would have been justified in writing a preface of some type for his work.

"An account, written by the hand of Mormon upon plates, taken from the plates of Nephi. Wherefore, it is an abridgment of the record of the people of Nephi, and also of the Lamanites.

"Written to the Lamanites, who are a remnant of the house of Israel, and also to Jew and Gentile. Written by way of commandment, and also by the spirit of prophecy and of revelation. Written and sealed up, and hid up unto the Lord, that they might not be destroyed, to come forth by the gift and power of God unto the interpretation thereof."

Everything in that paragraph could reasonably and logically have been written by Mormon. Some might say that Mormon would have been too modest to include his own name. But at the time he would have written this paragraph, he was the *only* writer who had written on the plates that he refers to throughout the record as the "plates of Mormon." Also, the word *Mormon* appears only twice on the entire title page: once in the four-word title, and once in the first paragraph of ninety-eight words. In Mosiah 18:30, however, Mormon used the word *Mormon* six times in the first forty-two words of the verse!

Let us now read the next paragraph, assuming as we do so that Moroni is its author. He has received the plates from his father and has engraved on the plates the text of Mormon chapters 8 and 9. Then he adds these words to the title page that his father had written:

"Sealed by the hand of Moroni, and hid up unto the Lord, to come forth in due time by way of the Gentile, the interpretation thereof by the gift of God."

These words obviously were written by Moroni. Therefore, the remainder of the title page also must have been written by Moroni, because he was the only one to engrave on the plates after his father, Mormon.

The assumption that Mormon wrote the first paragraph and Moroni wrote the second paragraph helps explain other difficulties that scholars have pointed out. Note, for example, the close parallels in wording and thought patterns between the last sentence of the first paragraph and the sentence now comprising the second paragraph of our illustration:

"Written and sealed up, and hid up unto the Lord, that they might not be destroyed, to come forth by the gift and power of God unto the interpretation thereof.

"Sealed by the hand of Moroni, and hid up unto the Lord, to come forth in due time by way of the Gentile, the interpretation thereof by the gift of God."

If Moroni had written both of these sentences, why would he have repeated himself so closely? But if Mormon wrote the first of these sentences and intended it to be the final sentence of his title page, could not Moroni logically have used almost the same wording in writing his sentence, which at that time he intended to be the final sentence of the title page?

As indicated earlier, Moroni definitely wrote the remainder of the title page *after* he had completed his abridgment of the plates of Ether. Notice the wording of the next sentence, which in our example forms one paragraph:

"An abridgment taken from the Book of Ether also, which is a record of the people of Jared, who were scattered at the time the Lord confounded the language of the people, when they were building a tower to get to heaven."

Now let us read the final three paragraphs, assuming that Moroni wrote them at the very end of his writing and assuming that they pertain to the entire record on the plates of Mormon, both to the writings of Mormon and to the writings of Moroni:

"Which is to show unto the remnant of the House of Israel what great things the Lord hath done for their fathers, and that they may know the covenants of the Lord that they are not cast off forever.

"And also to the convincing of the Jew and Gentile that Jesus is the Christ, the Eternal God, manifesting himself unto all nations.

"And now, if there are faults they are the mistakes of men; wherefore, condemn not the things of God, that ye may be found spotless at the judgment-seat of Christ."

In the traditional printings, these paragraphs appear to pertain *only* to the "abridgment taken from the Book of Ether," although most of us have quoted them as though they pertain to the entire Book of Mormon. The paragraphing suggested here would indicate that they do indeed pertain to the entire book, which is the most logical interpretation.

Let me emphasize that I am not suggesting that the present paragraphing of the title page is necessarily wrong. However, the decision to publish the title page text in two paragraphs was not determined by the Prophet Joseph Smith but by John H. Gilbert, the typesetter at E. B. Grandin's publishing house, *before* he had the opportunity to read and study the entire Book of Mormon. Thus he would not have understood the separate and different contributions of Mormon and Moroni in the Book of Mormon: Mormon's contribution to "the record of the people of Nephi" and Moroni's contribution to the "abridgment taken from the Book of Ether." Mr. Gilbert's lack of understanding is evident in his decision to divide the introductory statement pertaining to the book of Ether in the title page into two sentences in two different paragraphs. Thus in the first edition of the Book of Mormon the wording "an abridgment taken from the Book of Ether" appears as the last part of paragraph 1, whereas the wording, "also, which is a record of the people of Jared," appears as the first part of paragraph 2. As noted earlier, these two elements were combined in the 1837 edition to comprise the beginning of paragraph 2, where they have remained ever since.

Concerning the setting of the type for the title page, Mr. Gilbert has written: "In the forepart of June 1829, Mr. E. B. Grandin, the printer of the 'Wayne Sentinel,' came to me and said he wanted I should assist him in . . . printing 5000 copies of a book. . . . Hyrum Smith brought the first installment of manuscript, of 24 pages, closely written on common foolscap paper. . . . The title page was first set up, and after proof was read and corrected, several copies were printed."[6]

That first setting of the type for the title page text into two paragraphs by Mr. Gilbert in "the forepart of June 1829" obviously established the two-paragraph pattern followed (1) in the 26 June 1829 article in the *Wayne Sentinel,* (2) in the first edition of the Book of Mormon, and (3) in all subsequent editions of the Book of Mormon in English.

Thus, I believe we may at least consider dividing the text of the title page into more than two paragraphs, knowing that the Book of Mormon is true and that the paragraphing of the title page in no way detracts from its divine nature. I give my testimony that I know the

Book of Mormon is the true word of God, revealed to and written by earlier prophets and translated by the Prophet Joseph Smith through the gift and power of God.

NOTES

1. The author gave two separate presentations on this subject at the Second Annual Book of Mormon Symposium (1986). This written account contains material from both presentations.

2. Joseph Smith Jr., *History of The Church of Jesus Christ of Latter-day Saints,* ed. B. H. Roberts (Salt Lake City: Deseret News, 1932–51), 1:71.

3. B. H. Roberts, *A Comprehensive History of The Church of Jesus Christ of Latter-day Saints* (Salt Lake City: The Church of Jesus Christ of Latter-day Saints, 1930), 1:159.

4. Sidney B. Sperry, "The Story of the Writing of the Title Page to the Book of Mormon," in *A Book of Mormon Treasury* (Salt Lake City: Bookcraft, 1959), 123–24.

5. Sperry, "Title Page," 123–24.

6. Wilford C. Wood, *Joseph Smith Begins His Work* (Salt Lake City: Wilford C. Wood, 1958), introductory section.

8

Early Christianity and 1 Nephi 13–14

Stephen E. Robinson

In chapters 13 and 14 of 1 Nephi, the prophet Nephi describes the vision in which he saw the future of the world and its kingdoms as it related to his posterity. Nephi's vision is the type of revelation known in biblical literature as apocalyptic, and it is represented in the New Testament most fully by the Revelation of John. The revelations of Nephi and John have more in common, however, than merely the apocalyptic form, for Nephi's vision (see 1 Nephi 14:19–28) anticipates that of John. The two are complementary, centering in part on the same characters and themes: the Lamb and His Church, the Apostasy, the great and abominable church of the devil, and the Restoration of the gospel in the latter days. The purpose of this inquiry is to see whether the descriptions given by Nephi, specifically those of the Apostasy and of the great and abominable church, when added to the information of John and other pertinent scriptures, help us draw some historical conclusions about the nature of the Apostasy and the identity of the great and abominable church.

Before proceeding, however, we must define our terms. The Greek word *apostasia* (apostasy) means "rebellion" or "revolution." It conveys

---

Stephen E. Robinson is a professor of ancient scripture at Brigham Young University.

the sense of an internal takeover within an organization or institution by factions hostile to the intentions of its previous leaders. I personally prefer the translation "mutiny" for *apostasia,* as it calls up the image of a ship being commandeered by those who are not authorized to do so and being taken in a direction the ship was not intended to go. Since early Christians often thought of the Church as a ship, I think "mutiny" conveys exactly the right sense of what Paul and others meant by the term *apostasy.*

We must also analyze and define the component parts of the phrase *great and abominable church.* The word *great* in this context is an adjective of size rather than of quality and (like the Hebrew *gadol* or the Greek *megas*) informs us of the great size of the abominable entity. Secondary meanings might refer to great wealth or power.[1] The term *abominable* is used in the Old Testament to describe that which God hates, which cannot fail to arouse His wrath. In the book of Daniel the abomination of desolation is that thing which is so hateful to God that its presence in the temple causes the divine presence to depart, leaving the sanctuary desolate (see Daniel 11:31; 12:11; Matthew 24:15; Joseph Smith—Matthew 1:12–20). In the Old Testament the terms translated into English as abominable or abomination (Hebrew roots *shiqqutz, ta'ab, piggul;* Greek Septuagint and New Testament *bdelugma*) are usually associated with one of two practices—idolatrous worship or gross sexual immorality.[2]

The term *church* (Hebrew *qahal* or *edah;* Greek *ekklesia*) had a slightly broader meaning anciently than it does now and referred to an assembly, congregation, or association of people that bonded them together and commanded their loyalties. Thus, the term was not necessarily restricted to religious associations and in fact was used at Athens to denote the legislative assembly of government.[3] When we put all this together, it appears that the phrase *great and abominable church* means an immense assembly or association of people bound together by their loyalty to that which God hates. Most likely this will be a religious association involved specifically in sexual immorality or idolatry (that is, false worship—abandoning the God of Israel and worshiping anything else).

While the revelation of John does not use the exact term *great and abominable church,* the entity so described by Nephi is clearly the harlot described by John in Revelation 17–18, since the identical terms *mother of abominations, mother of harlots,* and *the whore who sitteth upon many waters* are used by both prophets (see 1 Nephi 14:10–12, 16; Revelation 17:1, 5).

Major characteristics of the great and abominable church in 1 Nephi may be listed as follows:

1. It persecutes, tortures, and slays the Saints of God (see 1 Nephi 13:5).

2. It seeks wealth and luxury (see 1 Nephi 13:7).

3. It is characterized by sexual immorality (see 1 Nephi 13:7).

4. It has excised plain and precious things from the scriptures (see 1 Nephi 13:26–29).

5. It has dominion over all the earth, among all nations, kindreds, tongues, and people (see 1 Nephi 14:11).

6. Its fate is to be consumed by a world war, in which the nations it incited against the Saints turn to war among themselves until they destroy the great and abominable church itself (see 1 Nephi 22:13–14).

These same characteristics are also attributed to the whore (Babylon) in the Revelation of John:

1. She is drunk with the blood of the Saints and with the blood of the martyrs of Jesus and of the prophets (see Revelation 17:6; 18:24).

2. She is characterized by the enjoyment of great wealth and luxury (see Revelation 17:4; 18:3, 11–16).

3. She (naturally) is characterized by sexual immorality (see Revelation 17:1–2, 5).

4. She has dominion over all nations (see Revelation 17:15, 18; 18:3, 23–24).

5. Her fate is to be consumed by the very kings who have made war on the Lamb under the influence of her deceptions (see Revelation 17:14–16; 18:23).

It should be noted that one characteristic not common to both prophetic descriptions is Nephi's statement that the great and abominable church has held back important parts of the canon of scripture.

But because John's record is one of the very scriptures Nephi refers to (see 1 Nephi 14:20–23), this omission in John's account is not surprising.

It must also be noted that in John's revelation the whore cannot be equated with the two beasts; they do not represent the same things. The whore and the beasts are motivated by the same evil genius, Satan. The one beast supports the whore (see Revelation 17:3), but the beast and the whore are separate entities with separate functions in the evil empire. The whore of Revelation 17–18 is specifically the satanic counterpart of the woman in chapter 12, who symbolizes the Church of Jesus Christ that was forced into the wilderness (that is, it became inaccessible to human beings). Symbolizing the great and abominable church (the counterfeit) as a whore underscores the nature of her evil—she is physically and spiritually unfaithful; that is, she represents both sexual immorality and idolatry, the twin abominations of the Old Testament. Thus, she is the "mother of abominations." It seems that in John's revelation the symbol of the whore is used narrowly to represent false religion, while the beasts, the image of the beast, and the horns of the beast serve to represent other aspects of the kingdom of the devil. Moreover, if the symbol of the virtuous woman of Revelation 12 is intended to represent specifically the true Church of Jesus Christ (as the crown of twelve apostles and her being driven into the wilderness so indicate),[4] it follows that the whore, her counterpart, represents specifically false and counterfeit religion. Satan has more than one institution at his disposal, but the whore is false religion. The whore cannot represent kingdoms or governments—the beast and its horns do (see Revelation 17:12).[5] But she can represent the false beliefs and ideologies that often capture or motivate governments. The whore provides the theory; government provides the muscle. When the false religion represented by the whore is joined to the civil governments (the kings of the earth) represented by the horns of the beast with whom she fornicates, then the wine of their fornication (the results of the union of church and state, or of ideology and police power) plunders the resources of the earth and makes all the world drunk. That is, the power of the state church, or of the church state, seeks to dominate the economy of nations and destroys the spiritual equilibrium and discernment of human beings (see Revelation 17:2; 18:3).

Moreover, because the great and abominable church from 1 Nephi is identified in every aspect with the whore, while the beast is never even mentioned in Nephi's vision, it follows that when we discuss *the* great and abominable church, we must not confuse the whore which Nephi saw and described with the beast which he did not. There are no references to the beasts of Revelation in Nephi's vision of the great and abominable church. As both John and Nephi make clear, the nations outlast the whore and eventually destroy her. Both beast and whore are component parts of the kingdom of the devil, but they are *separate* parts even though they sometimes work together.

Perhaps the greatest difficulty in Nephi's description of the great and abominable church is an apparent contradiction between chapters 13 and 14. In 1 Nephi 13 the great and abominable church is one specific church among many. Indeed, Nephi's description of it as "most abominable above all other churches" (1 Nephi 13:5, 26) is nonsense otherwise. Moreover, it has a specific historical description: it is formed among the Gentiles *after* the Bible has been transmitted in its purity to the Gentiles by the Jews (see 1 Nephi 13:26), and it is the specific historical agent responsible for excising plain and precious truths from the scriptural record. It would appear that in chapter 13 Nephi is describing a specific historical institution as the great and abominable church. To this we must add the information given in Doctrine and Covenants 86:1–4, which states that the great and abominable church did its work after the apostles had fallen asleep; that is, around the end of the first century A.D. Similarly, in the revelation of John the role of the whore has a historical frame. She comes into the picture after the beasts, upon which she rides and which give her support, and she is eliminated from the picture while they yet continue. Again, the great and abominable church (Babylon) is not a term identical with "the kingdom of the devil," for the whore is only one of the component parts of a larger empire, together with the beasts, the image, the horns, and the false prophet—and also with other false churches. This last idea is clearly brought out in 1 Nephi 22:22–23:

"But it is *the kingdom of the devil,* which shall be built up among the children of men, which kingdom is established among them which are in the flesh—

"For the time speedily shall come that *all churches* which are built up to get gain, and all those who are built up to get power over the flesh, and those who are built up to become popular in the eyes of the world, and those who seek the lusts of the flesh and the things of the world, and to do all manner of iniquity; yea, in fine, *all those who belong to the kingdom of the devil* are they who need fear, and tremble" (emphasis added).

Indisputably, the full kingdom of the devil is made up of many churches (or denominations) and will be until the end of the world. Taking 1 Nephi 13 and 22 as our starting points, we might be justified in asking just which of all those false denominations is the *actual* great and abominable church of the devil. The apparent contradiction comes in 1 Nephi 14:10, where we are told that there are only *two* churches: "And he said unto me: Behold there are save two churches only; the one is the church of the Lamb of God, and the other is the church of the devil."

How can this be? How can the devil's church or churches be one and many at the same time? The apparent contradiction actually gives us the solution to the larger puzzle and ultimately our identification of the great and abominable church.

The answer is that the term is used in two different ways in these two chapters. In chapter 13 it is used historically, and in chapter 14 it is used typologically, or apocalyptically. In apocalyptic literature (remember that both Revelation and 1 Nephi 13–14 are apocalyptic in nature) the seer is caught up in vision and sees things from God's perspective. Time ceases to be an important element. This is why the chronology of John's revelation at times seems to be scrambled—with God there is no time. Apocalyptic visions are highly symbolic, usually requiring an angelic interpreter for the seer to understand what he sees. But the symbols are inclusive; that is, they stand for archetypical categories into which all specific instances of something can be placed. This is why the whore can be called Nineveh (some of John's language comes from Nahum's description of Nineveh in Nahum 3), or Babylon, Sodom,

Egypt, Jerusalem, or Rome. It doesn't matter; the names change, but the character—"that great city"—remains the same in every dispensation. To illustrate, let us take the name of the whore, or great and abominable church, *Babylon.* A literal reading would lead us to believe that some particular city is being described, and we would want to know which city it was. But if we read carefully, we see that Babylon in John's revelation is not one city but many cities, all of which fall into the larger category of "that great city" which is the antithesis of the city of God, the heavenly Jerusalem, or Zion. Just as Zion is wherever the pure in heart dwell (see Doctrine and Covenants 97:21), so Babylon is where the whore lives. Since Latter-day Saints understand that Zion is a spiritual category, which may in different contexts mean Salt Lake City, Far West, Jerusalem, or the city of Enoch, why do we have such a hard time understanding Zion's opposite, Babylon, in the same way? It is precisely this variable identity that Jacob teaches to us when he says: "Wherefore, he that fighteth against Zion, both Jew and Gentile, both bond and free, both male and female, shall perish; *for they are they who are the whore of all the earth; for they who are not for me are against me, saith our God*" (2 Nephi 10:16; emphasis added).

In other words Babylon, "the whore of all the earth," is in this context anyone who fights against Zion. In apocalyptic literature the cast of characters is constant in every dispensation; they are these same archetypical categories into which all things can be placed. From the apocalyptic point of view there is only one script, one plot, from the foundation of the world until its end. The characters in the play and the lines they deliver are always the same from dispensation to dispensation, although the individual actors who play the roles and speak the lines may change with time. Therefore, there is always the role of "that great city," though the part might be played at different times in history by Sodom, Egypt, Nineveh, Babylon, Rome, Berlin, Moscow, or Washington, D.C. The important thing is to know what the archetypical patterns are and their identifying characteristics. Then we can orient ourselves in any time or place and know who functions *now* in the role of Babylon and where Zion is located.

Once we understand that the term *great and abominable church* has two extensions, the one open, inclusive, and archetypical, and the other limited and historical, the rest is easy. In chapter 14, Nephi describes the archetypical roles themselves: "There are save two churches only" (that is, Zion and Babylon). But in chapter 13 he is referring to the specific institution (the actor, if you will) who played the role of Babylon in the Roman Empire in the second century A.D. Nevertheless, it won't do us much good in the twentieth century to know who played Babylon in the second. We need to recognize Babylon now, in our time, although the actors have been changed.

Apocalyptic literature is also dualistic. Since it deals with archetypes, it boils everything down to opposing principles: love and hate, good and evil, light and dark. There are no gray areas in apocalyptic scripture. At the very least, everything can be reduced to the opposing categories of A and not-A ("They who are not for me are against me, saith our God" [2 Nephi 10:16]). In the realm of religion there are only two categories: religion that will save and religion that will not. The former is the church of the Lamb, and the latter—no matter how well intentioned—is a counterfeit. Thus, even a "good" church must still be part of the devil's kingdom in the sense used in 1 Nephi 14 ("there are save two churches only"), for it cannot do what it pretends to do. Nevertheless, such a church cannot be called the great and abominable church in the sense used in 1 Nephi 13, for its intentions are good and honorable, and quite often such churches teach people enough truth that they can then recognize the true church when they meet it. These churches do not slay the Saints of God, they do not seek to control civil governments, nor do they pursue wealth, luxury, and sexual immorality. Such churches may belong to the kingdom of the devil in the apocalyptic sense, where there are only two categories, A and not-A, but they cannot be called the great and abominable church in the historical sense—the description is just not accurate. Furthermore, individual orientation to the Church of the Lamb or to the great and abominable church is not only by membership but by loyalty. Just as there are those on the records of The Church of Jesus Christ of Latter-day Saints who belong to the great and abominable church by virtue of their loyalty to Satan and his lifestyle (see 2 Nephi 10:16), so there are members of other churches who will eventually belong to the Lamb by virtue of their loyalty to Him and to His lifestyle, which will lead to their accepting the saving ordinances. The distinction is based on who has your heart, not on who has your records.

It seems to me that many Latter-day Saints have made one of two errors in trying to identify the great and abominable church. The first is to believe that some specific denomination or other, to the exclusion of all others, has been the great and abominable church since the beginning of time. This is dangerous, for if we understand the great and abominable church to be one specific church, some will want to know which one it is, and an antagonistic relationship with that church or denomination will inevitably follow. It might, for example, be argued that Judaism was the great and abominable church. After all, the Jewish religious establishment of that day would seem to qualify on several points. They persecuted the Church and spilled the blood of the Saints. They crucified the Messiah, the Savior of the world. They joined religion together with civil government and used the police power to enforce their religious views. Both Pharisees and Sadducees were reproved by Jesus for their pursuit of wealth at the expense of justice. Jesus told the Pharisees that Satan was their father, and John referred to certain Jewish meetinghouses in Asia as "synagogues of Satan" (Revelation 2:9; 3:9). It was precisely this kind of religious argument—that the Jews were the infidels, the beast, the anti-Christ—that contributed to the Holocaust and that still fans the moral insanity of neo-Nazi religious groups. Has Satan's hand ever been more clearly discernible in any human undertaking? Latter-day Saints do not want to indulge in witch hunting.

But while Jerusalem in A.D. 30 might have been one manifestation of Babylon (see Revelation 11:8), Judaism cannot be the great and abominable church described by Nephi and John. First, the Jews did not and clearly will not enjoy dominion over all the nations of the earth. Second, Nephi says that the scriptures were complete when they came forth from the mouth of a Jew but were excised by the great and abominable church, which had its formation among the Gentiles. And finally, according to the scriptures, it does not seem to be the fate of the

Jews to be utterly consumed by the nations of the earth; it appears quite the opposite.

More often it has been suggested that the Roman Catholic Church might be the great and abominable church of 1 Nephi 13, but this is also untenable, primarily because Roman Catholicism as we know it did not yet exist when the crimes described by Nephi were being committed. In fact, the term *Roman Catholic* makes sense only after A.D. 1054, when it began to be used to distinguish the Western, Latin-speaking Orthodox church, which followed the bishop of Rome, from the Eastern, Greek-speaking Orthodox church, which followed the bishop of Constantinople (in association with others). Indeed, in the period between Peter and Constantine, there were other Christian churches besides the orthodox: Ebionites, Syrian and Egyptian Christians, Donatists, Gnostics, Marcionites, and so on. We don't know very much about how they were related to each other.

Even if we were to use the term "Roman" Catholic for the church which Constantine began making his state religion in A.D. 313 (and the other orthodox churches would object to this), still the New Testament as we know it (that is, without the excised plain and precious parts) had already been widely circulated by then. In other words, the work of the great and abominable church in slaying the apostles and excising the scriptures had already been done. By the time Constantine joined church and state together in the fourth century, the apostles had been dead for centuries, and the true church and its keys had already been lost. The commonly held notion of shifty-eyed medieval monks rewriting the scriptures as they copied is bigoted and unfair. In fact, we owe those monks a debt of gratitude that anything was saved at all. Besides, in comparison to some of the other Christian groups around, the orthodox Christians had quite a high standard of morality. By this time they had gone to the extremes of asceticism and can hardly be accused (in this period, anyway) of having many harlots and practicing gross immorality. In fact, in some areas of the ancient world, orthodoxy replaced an earlier more corrupt form of Christianity. Finally, during most of the period before 313, the orthodox were hardly in a position to persecute the Saints, as the orthodox were being thrown to the lions themselves.

The Catholic (that is, "universal") Church of the fourth century was the result of the Apostasy, its end product—not its cause. To find the real culprits in the case of the excised texts, we need to look at a much earlier period in Christian church history. None of the Presidents of The Church of Jesus Christ of Latter-day Saints has ever identified Roman Catholicism as the great and abominable church. And, in speaking of Catholic and Protestant faiths, the Prophet Joseph Smith said:

"The old Catholic church traditions are worth more than all you have said. Here is a principle of logic that most men have no more sense than to adopt. I will illustrate it by an old apple tree. Here jumps off a branch and says, I am the true tree, and you are corrupt. If the whole tree is corrupt, are not its branches corrupt? If the Catholic religion is a false religion, how can any true religion come out of it? If the Catholic church is bad, how can any good thing come out of it? The character of the old churches have always been slandered by all apostates since the world began."[6]

It was Martin Luther, not Joseph Smith, who identified the Roman Catholic Church as Babylon and the pope as the anti-Christ.[7] Besides, are we really to believe that Satan had no ministers in the world before there were Roman Catholics? Was there no Babylon to oppose Zion in the days of Cain, Nimrod, Pharaoh, or Herod?

Finally, I would like to submit that no single historical church or denomination known to us can be *the* great and abominable church in an exclusive sense. No single organization meets all the requirements:

1. It must have been formed among the Gentiles and must have controlled the distribution of the New Testament scriptures, which it edited and from which it deleted plain and precious things.

2. It must have slain the Saints of God and killed the apostles and prophets.

3. It must be in league with civil governments and use their police power to enforce its religious views.

4. It must have dominion over all the earth.

5. It must pursue wealth, luxury, and sexual immorality and must last until essentially the end of the world.

No one denomination fits the entire description. Neither does world Communism in our own day. The conclusion is inescapable—no *single* entity can be *the* great and abominable church from the beginning of the world to the end. Rather, the role has been played by many different actors in many different times, and the great and abominable church that Nephi described in 1 Nephi 13 is not the same one that crucified Christ or that martyred Joseph and Hyrum.

So the one error, as I see it, is to try to blame some modern denomination for the activities of an ancient great and abominable church described by both Nephi and John. The other error is to go too far the other way and remove the great and abominable church from history altogether. This latter approach does not acknowledge that there ever was or ever will be a historical manifestation of the great and abominable church. It allegorizes the term completely, so that it becomes merely a vague symbol for all the disassociated evil in the world. We cannot accept this in the face of clear and explicit scripture to the contrary, for if we do, we shall not be able to recognize the historical manifestations of the great and abominable church in our own time or in the times to come. On the one hand, we must avoid the temptation to identify the role of the great and abominable church so completely with one particular denomination that we do not recognize the part when it is played by some other organization, but on the other hand we must remember that the role *will* be played by *some* agency. Will we be able to recognize it?

To return to our original topic, can we identify the historical agency that acted as the great and abominable church in earliest Christianity and which Nephi and others describe? I would like to argue that the great and abominable church Nephi describes in chapter 13 had its origins in the second half of the first century and had essentially done its work by the middle of the second century. This period might be called the blind spot of ecclesiastical history, for it is here that the fewest primary historical sources have been preserved. Essentially, what happened is that we have good sources for New Testament

Christianity (the New Testament documents themselves); then the lights go out (that is, we have very few historical sources), and in the dark we hear the muffled sounds of a great struggle. When the lights come on again a hundred years or so later, we find that someone has rearranged all the furniture and that Christianity is something very different from what it was in the beginning. That different entity can be accurately described by the term *hellenized Christianity.* The hellenization of Christianity is a phenomenon which has long been recognized by scholars of Christian history, but it is one which Latter-day Saints know better as the Great Apostasy. Hellenization means imposing Greek culture on the native cultures of the East. The result was a synthesis of East and West, with elements of the Greek West predominating, a melting-pot of popular culture that was virtually worldwide.

But in the realm of religion, synthesis means compromise, and when we speak in terms of the gospel, compromise with the popular culture of the world means apostasy from the truth. When Jewish Christianity and Greek culture met head-on in the Gentile mission field in the middle of the first century, the Greeks eventually won, and Jewish Christianity was ultimately "revised" to make it more attractive and appealing to a Greek audience. Primary prejudices of the Hellenistic world were the "absolute" nature of God (that is, he cannot be bound or limited by anything) and the impossibility of anything material or physical being eternal. In order to accommodate these ideas and thus appeal to a broader Gentile audience, Christianity had to discard the doctrines of an anthropomorphic God and the resurrection of the dead or else "reinterpret" them in a manner that had the same effect.[8] This is precisely what some Greek Christians at Corinth had already done and against which Paul responds with such force in 1 Corinthians 15:12: "Now if Christ be preached that he rose from the dead, how say some among you that there is no resurrection of the dead?"

One assumption necessary to my line of reasoning is that the earliest apostates from the true primitive Church constituted the great and abominable church among the Gentiles. Therefore we need something to link the Apostasy with the great and abominable church, and I think we have such a link in many places, but two will suffice to make my point here. In 2 Thessalonians 2:3, Paul says, "That day shall not come, except there come a falling away [literally, an apostasy] first, and that man of sin be revealed, the son of perdition." This man of sin will sit in the temple of God showing himself that he is God (see 2 Thessalonians 2:4). The "mystery of iniquity" (2 Thessalonians 2:7) was already under way as Paul wrote, and you will recall that one of the names of Babylon is "mystery" (Revelation 17:5). Paul mentions that this son of perdition, or man of sin, is the counterfeit for the Man of Holiness—he is Satan.[9] And the temple in which he sits is the church now desolated of the divine presence by the abomination of apostasy and become the church of the devil.[10] The church of the devil is any church that teaches the philosophies of men mingled with scripture, which dethrones God in the church and replaces him with man (2 Thessalonians 2:4) by denying the principle of revelation and turning instead to human intellect. It is for this reason that creeds which are the product of human intellect are an *abomination* to the Lord (see JS–H 1:19), for they are idolatry—men worshiping the creations not of their own hands but of their own minds and knowing all along it is a creation of their intellect that is being worshiped.

Perhaps my point could be made more quickly by citing Doctrine and Covenants 86:3, where the Lord explicitly identifies the whore, Babylon, as the apostate church: "And after they have fallen asleep the great persecutor of the church, the apostate, the whore, even Babylon, that maketh all nations to drink of her cup, in whose hearts the enemy, even Satan, sitteth to reign—behold he soweth the tares; wherefore, the tares choke the wheat and drive the church into the wilderness."

Clearly, whatever denominational name we choose to give it, the great and abominable church described by Nephi and John and the earliest apostate church are identical. The fact is that we do not really know what name to give it. I have proposed hellenized Christianity, but that is a description rather than a name. Babylon in the first and second centuries may even have been a collection of different movements. The Jewish Christians could not let go of the law of Moses and so eventually gave up Christ instead. The "orthodox" adopted Greek philosophy. The

Gnostics wallowed in the mysteries and in unspeakable practices on the one hand or in mysteries and a neurotic asceticism on the other. Tatian and Marcion rewrote the scriptures, the latter boldly chopping out anything he did not like, and all of them together forced the virtuous woman, the true Church of Jesus Christ, into the wilderness.

NOTES

1. See, for example, *gadol* and its cognates in W. L. Holladay, *A Concise Hebrew and Aramaic Lexicon of the Old Testament* (Leiden: E. J. Brill, 1971), 55.

2. Where the context is given, a large majority of occurrences of *abomination* and its forms refer to immorality or idolatry. Compare Robert Young, *Analytical Concordance to the Bible* (Grand Rapids, Mich.: Eerdmans, 1978), 6.

3. Originally, the term *ekklesia,* from two Greek words meaning "call" and "out," referred to those citizens who were called out or summoned to their public meetings by the heralds. Thus, it was an ideal word to represent the body of individuals "called" by God "out" of the world through the Holy Ghost—the Church. The civil dimension of the word can be seen in Acts 19:32, where "assembly" in the Greek text is *ekklesia,* elsewhere translated as "church." However, we must remember that we don't know the original word behind "church" on the plates, but whatever it was, Joseph Smith chose to render it *church* and not *assembly* or something else.

4. This was also the view of the Prophet Joseph Smith. The Joseph Smith Translation of Revelation 12:7 reads: "nor the woman which was the church of God, who had been delivered of her pains, and brought forth the kingdom of our God and his Christ."

5. Compare also the Joseph Smith Translation of Revelation 13:1: "And I saw another sign, in the likeness of the kingdoms of the earth; a beast rise up out of the sea."

6. Joseph Smith, *History of the Church of Jesus Christ of Latter-day Saints,* ed. B. H. Roberts, 2d ed., rev. (Salt Lake City: Deseret Book, 1957), 6:478.

7. One of the many instances which might be cited is found in *Table Talk,* no. 4487 (11 April 1539): "I believe the pope is the masked and incarnate devil because he is the Antichrist. As Christ is God incarnate, so the Antichrist is the devil incarnate." See also Helmut T. Lehman and Jaroslav Jan Pelikan, eds, *Luther's Works* (Philadelphia: Concordia Fortress Press, 1955–76), 54:346.

8. An example might be cited in Acts 17:32–33 where the mere mention to the Greeks of the physical resurrection breaks up Paul's meeting with the Areopagus council.

9. The Joseph Smith Translation makes this identification even more apparent: "for there shall come a falling away first, and that man of sin be revealed, the son of perdition. . . . For the mystery of iniquity doth already work, and he it is who now worketh, and Christ suffereth him to work, until the time is fulfilled that he shall be taken out of the way" (2 Thessalonions 2:3, 7).

10. For Lucifer as the man of sin, see Bruce R. McConkie, *Doctrinal New Testament Commentary* (Salt Lake City: Bookcraft, 1973), 3:62–64.

9

Nephi's Message to the "Gentiles"

S. Michael Wilcox

And also to the convincing of the Jew and Gentile that Jesus is the Christ, the Eternal God, manifesting himself unto all nations. (Book of Mormon, title page)

Chapters 25 through 33 of 2 Nephi contain Nephi's final messages. They had a profound influence on later Book of Mormon prophets and have great relevancy today. Nephi addresses his comments to three main groups of people: the Jews, the descendants of Lehi, and the Gentiles. His commentary can be read as a unified discourse that serves as his final testimony; much of it contains an explanation of the Isaiah chapters he has just quoted. There is a logic and organization that flows from chapter to chapter. In this paper I will not attempt to deal with the entire message in detail but will isolate Nephi's teachings to and about the Gentiles in the overall context of the broader discourse. I will focus primarily on chapters 26 and 27. In order to do this I will first give a brief chapter-by-chapter summary of Nephi's major points.

S. Michael Wilcox is an instructor at the Salt Lake University Institute of Religion.

NEPHI'S ORGANIZATION

Chapter 25. Nephi speaks primarily of the Jews who will eventually reject the gospel and the Savior and will slip into the darkness of apostasy. Verses 23 through 30 contain a message to Nephi's own seed relative to their acceptance of the Savior.

Chapter 26:1–22. Nephi speaks of Lehi's descendants and the Gentiles. They too will eventually reject the gospel and the Savior and will go into apostasy.

Chapter 26:23–33. Nephi describes the loving nature of Christ and notes the Savior's invitation to all the world to partake of His goodness. In essence he asks, "How can you reject a God who is so full of mercy and goodness and turn His gospel into darkness?"

Chapter 27. Nephi teaches that because the Jews, the Gentiles, and Lehi's descendants are all in a state of apostasy, and because of the loving nature of Christ, another opportunity will be given to them to learn of the Savior and the saving principles of His gospel through a restoration. The key to that restoration will be the Book of Mormon. It will testify of the truths lost in the apostasy and provide a firm witness of Jesus Christ. The majority of this chapter comes from Isaiah 29.

Chapter 28. Nephi declares that Satan will not be idle. He will use any weapons at his disposal to negate the Restoration and keep the world in the darkness of apostasy. These weapons will come primarily from the philosophies, pride, learning, and lifestyles of mankind.

Chapter 29. Satan will make a specific attack on the Book of Mormon in an attempt to get people to reject it as well as the gospel of Christ and the Restoration. That attack is best stated by the phrase, "A Bible! A Bible! We have got a Bible, and there cannot be any more Bible" (2 Nephi 29:3).

Chapter 30. In spite of all opposition, the light of the Restoration will spread. The coming of the Jews, the Lamanites, and the Gentiles to the light of the gospel will cause a great "division" between the righteous and the wicked. In the end Christ will be victorious, and Satan will have power over men "no more, for a long time" (2 Nephi 30:18). Again, Isaiah is heavily quoted.

Chapters 31–32. Nephi teaches in simple terms what each individual must do to be part of the final victory of Christ. Each person must accept the Savior, repent, be baptized, receive the Holy Ghost, and then endure to the end by following the example of Christ, specifically His example of obedience to the Father.

Chapter 33. Nephi expresses his love for all three groups of people and pleads with them to believe in Christ. If they have faith in Christ, they will rejoice in Nephi's words and in the Book of Mormon.

With this overall perspective we can now examine the specifics of Nephi's message to the Gentiles.

JESUS IS THE CHRIST

Nephi begins his message to the Gentiles by stating:

"It must needs be that the Gentiles be *convinced* also that Jesus is the Christ, the Eternal God;

"And that he manifesteth himself unto all those who believe in him, by the power of the Holy Ghost; yea, unto every nation, kindred, tongue, and people, working mighty miracles, signs, and wonders, among the children of men according to their faith" (2 Nephi 26:12–13; emphasis added).

This is the central message of the sermon. It is also the major purpose of the Book of Mormon. Moroni's statement of intent given in the title page proclaims that the Book of Mormon is written to convince "the Jew and Gentile that Jesus is the Christ, the Eternal God, manifesting himself unto all nations." This so closely parallels Nephi's words that it cannot be coincidental. Nephi shows in chapter 27 that God will use the Book of Mormon in the latter days to bear witness of Christ's divinity to all nations, particularly the Gentile nations.

To be "convinced" that Jesus is the Christ indicates faith in Him, which is the first principle of the gospel. Nephi stated that Christ manifested Himself to "every nation" in various ways "according to their faith" (2 Nephi 26:13). What kind of faith is convincing faith, and how does it apply to the Gentiles?

In the *Lectures on Faith,* the Prophet Joseph Smith explains "that three things are necessary in order that any rational and intelligent being may exercise faith in God unto life and salvation. First, the idea that he [God] actually exists. Secondly, a *correct* idea of his character, perfections, and attributes. Thirdly, an actual knowledge that the course of life which [one] is pursuing is according to his [God's] will."[1] Convincing faith would, by definition, lead one to life and salvation.

THE ETERNAL GOD

For the Gentiles to have convincing faith in Christ, they need to establish and maintain the above three principles clearly in their minds. Nephi, however, is not at all convinced that they have sufficient faith in Christ to lead them to salvation. This is ironic in light of the fact that the Gentile nations most frequently alluded to in the writings of Nephi are the Christian nations of Europe and the United States. In most places throughout Nephi's writings the terms *Gentile nations* and *Christian nations* are interchangeable (see 1 Nephi 13; 14; 22; see also 2 Nephi 30–33).

What then do the Christian or Gentile nations lack, since most of them already accept Christ in their own way? Nephi's own words supply the beginnings of an answer. They must be convinced not only of Christ's messiahship, but that He is (1) the Eternal God, (2) that He manifests Himself to all (every nation, kindred, tongue, and people) who believe in Him by the power of the Holy Ghost, and (3) that He manifests Himself by mighty miracles, signs, and wonders. We are left to ask if the Gentile Christians accept these basic truths about Christ.

What does Nephi mean by calling Christ the "Eternal God"? The Book of Mormon witnesses several profound and basic truths about Christ which have been largely lost by the Christian world. It teaches that Christ is the Jehovah of the Old Testament; the God of Abraham, Isaac, and Jacob; the Creator of the world. The brother of Jared saw and understood the divinity and premortal nature of Jesus Christ. For bearing testimony of Christ as God, Abinadi was burned at the stake. King Noah told him, "Thou art worthy of death. For thou hast said that God himself should come down among the children of men" (Mosiah 17:7–8). Abinadi taught the true doctrine of the Savior to the wicked priests, explaining why Christ was called both the Father and the Son:

"And because he dwelleth in flesh he shall be called the Son of God, and having subjected the flesh to the will of the Father, being the Father and the Son—

"The Father, because he was conceived by the power of God; and the Son, because of the flesh; thus becoming the Father and Son" (Mosiah 15:2–3).

Amulek taught the truth concerning Christ when challenged by the lawyer Zeezrom, who had tried to trick him through the doctrine of the Godhead:

"Now Zeezrom saith again unto him: Is the Son of God the very Eternal Father?

"And Amulek said unto him: Yea, he is the very Eternal Father of heaven and of earth, and all things which in them are; he is the beginning and the end, the first and the last" (Alma 11:38–39).

These pronouncements should not be confusing to those who have a correct understanding of the Godhead. It was not confusing to Amulek in spite of Zeezrom's attempt at confusing him. Amulek later speaks of the judgment, when men shall "be arraigned before the bar of Christ the Son, and God the Father, and the Holy Spirit, which is one Eternal God" (Alma 11:44). The Book of Mormon does not teach that Christ and God the Father are the same being, as the creeds of Christendom do. This is plainly seen by the Savior's own teachings in 3 Nephi, which stress the importance of Christ as a God in much the same way that John the Beloved does in John 1. This emphasis on the eternal nature of Christ's divinity was plainly stated by Nephi, who testified: "For if there be no Christ there be no God; and if there be no God we are not, for there could have been no creation. But there is a God, and he is Christ, and he cometh in the fulness of his own time" (2 Nephi 11:7).

Elder Bruce R. McConkie pointedly and plainly testified of Christ. In his testimony we find a full meaning to Book of Mormon truths as they relate to Christian creeds and Nephi's statement that the Gentiles must needs be convinced "that Jesus is the Christ, the Eternal God."

"Christ-Messiah is God!

"Such is the plain and pure pronouncement of all the prophets of all the ages. In our desire to avoid the false and absurd conclusions contained in the creeds of Christendom, we are wont to shy away from this pure and unadorned verity; we go to great lengths to use language that shows there is both a Father and a Son, that they are separate Persons and are not somehow mystically intertwined as an essence of spirit that is everywhere present. Such an approach is perhaps essential in reasoning with the Gentiles of sectarianism; it helps to overthrow the fallacies formulated in their creeds.

"But having so done, if we are to envision our Lord's true status and glory, we must come back to the pronouncement of pronouncements, the doctrine of doctrines, the message of messages, which is that Christ is God. And if it were not so, he could not save us."[2]

We need to see Christ in his transfigured glory as the Eternal God, much as Peter, James, and John did on the Mount of Transfiguration. The timeliness and importance of the Book of Mormon in a world that more and more humanizes the Savior becomes blatantly apparent.

TO ALL MEN THROUGH THE HOLY GHOST

Nephi also knew that the Gentiles needed to be convinced that Christ "manifesteth himself unto all those who believe in him, by the power of the Holy Ghost; yea, unto every nation, kindred, tongue, and people" (2 Nephi 26:13). It is not difficult to understand Nephi's concern in light of the Christian creeds. The Christian world largely rejects the Book of Mormon because it claims to be another witness for Christ. "A Bible! A Bible!" the world cries, "We have got a Bible, and there cannot be any more Bible" (2 Nephi 29:3). The Gentiles have no true doctrinal explanation for the vast majority of God's children throughout the world who have not heard the message of salvation through the atonement of Christ. At best the Christian churches consign them to a purgatorial state; at worst, to hell.

Nephi spoke of "the Holy Ghost." The Christian world today denies the gifts of the Spirit and the revelatory power of the Holy

Ghost. Moroni spoke of this denial after receiving the plates from his father:

"And again I speak unto you who deny the revelations of God, and say that they are done away, that there are no revelations, nor prophecies, nor gifts, nor healing, nor speaking with tongues, and the interpretation of tongues;

"Behold I say unto you, he that denieth these things knoweth not the *gospel of Christ;* yea, he has not read the scriptures; if so, he does not understand them" (Mormon 9:7–8; emphasis added).

When asked by President Martin Van Buren "wherein we differed in our religion from the other religions of the day[,] Brother Joseph said we differed in mode of baptism, and the gift of the Holy Ghost by the laying on of hands. We considered that all other considerations were contained in the gift of the Holy Ghost."[3]

With the loss of the priesthood through the Christian apostasy, the gift of the Holy Ghost was also lost. Hence the Gentiles need to be convinced that Christ manifests Himself by the testifying power of the Holy Ghost and the confirming power of the gifts of the Spirit.

MIGHTY MIRACLES, SIGNS, AND WONDERS

This leads to the third teaching to the Gentiles. They need to be convinced that Christ, the Eternal God, works "mighty miracles, signs, and wonders, among the children of men according to their faith" (2 Nephi 26:13). Christ-centered faith is the key to these miracles and wonders. For the most part the Christian world denies miracles, signs, and wonders, claiming they were done away after the first century A.D. Nephi saw this future denial and wrote, "And they deny the power of God, the Holy One of Israel; and they say unto the people: Hearken unto us, and hear ye our precept; for behold there is no God today, for the Lord and the Redeemer hath done his work, and he hath given his power unto men" (2 Nephi 28:5).

Moroni taught that the disappearance of "signs" indicates a loss of faith:

"And if there were miracles wrought then, why has God ceased to be a God of miracles and yet be an unchangeable Being? And behold, I say unto you he changeth not; if so he would cease to be God; and he ceaseth not to be God, and is a God of miracles.

"And the reason why he ceaseth to do miracles among the children of men is because that *they dwindle in unbelief,* and depart from the right way, *and know not the God in whom they should trust"* (Mormon 9:19–20; emphasis added).

Signs, wonders, and miracles will accompany faith, hence Nephi's concern that the Gentiles be "convinced" that Jesus is the Christ and that He works "mighty miracles." The Lord's own words proclaim Him to be a God of miracles: "I will show unto the world that I am the same yesterday, today, and forever; and I work not among the children of men save it be according to their faith" (2 Nephi 27:23).

THE GENTILE STUMBLING BLOCK

After Nephi details the Gentile overthrow of "the seed of my brethren," he states that the Gentiles have "stumbled, because of the greatness of their stumbling block" (2 Nephi 26:15, 20). An explanation of the Gentile stumbling block is given by the angel who instructs Nephi while he views the dream of his father. The angel says, "Because of these things [plain and precious truths] which are taken away out of the gospel of the Lamb, an exceedingly great many do stumble, yea, insomuch that Satan hath great power over them" (1 Nephi 13:29). Some of those losses include an understanding of the Godhead, baptism, the Resurrection of Christ, revelation, the gift of the Holy Ghost, the sacrament, the priesthood, the Fall, and many other essential truths pertaining to the salvation of mankind. The angel also instructs Nephi that the "plain and precious parts of the gospel of the Lamb . . . have been kept back by that abominable church" (1 Nephi 13:34). The Christian apostasy destroyed faith in Christ to the extent that the Gentiles need to be reconvinced of His divinity and gospel. Their stumbling block is the direct result of the Apostasy. Even though they are "Christian" nations, in Nephi's mind they do not have convincing faith in Christ. As Christ Himself stated to Joseph Smith, "They teach for doctrines the commandments of men, having a form of godliness, but they deny the power thereof" (JS–H 1:19). This idea was spoken to Isaiah centuries before (see Isaiah 29:13) and recorded by Nephi in 2 Nephi 27:25. Both Isaiah and Nephi clearly understood the Gentile stumbling block.

The plain and precious truths removed by the Christian or Gentile apostasy dealt in part with Joseph Smith's three pillars of faith: the idea that God exists, a correct understanding of His attributes, and a knowledge of the course necessary to pursue in order to please Him. These truths were in large measure lost with the formation of the great and abominable church. Apostasy always strikes at the foundations of faith, seeking to replace revelation and testimony with emotional zeal, intellectual bargaining, and state religion. A brief summary of conditions in the Christian nations and churches of today will suffice to prove our point.

Nephi prophesied of the conditions the Gentile apostasy would bring. "They have built up many churches"; they are "lifted up in the pride of their eyes"; "they put down the power and miracles of God"; they seek "gain and grind upon the face of the poor" (2 Nephi 26:20). They "cause envyings, and strifes, and malice" (2 Nephi 26:21). "There are also secret combinations . . . and works of darkness" (2 Nephi 26:22). It is not difficult to verify Nephi's words in modern society. All these things are the results of apostasy and the loss of convincing faith. Speaking of the conditions that existed among the Christian, Gentile nations during World War I, Joseph F. Smith said, "Would it be possible, could it be possible, for this condition to exist if the people of the world possessed *really the true knowledge of the gospel of Jesus Christ?*"[4]

THE PRECEPTS AND LEARNING OF MEN

Nephi gives a clear and repeated testimony as to the primary cause of human, particularly Gentile, apostasy. They "preach up unto themselves *their own wisdom* and *their own learning*" (2 Nephi 26:20; emphasis added). They are full of priestcrafts that stand in opposition to and replace the priesthood of God. Nephi defines them as follows: "Priestcrafts are that men preach and *set themselves up for a light* unto the world, that they may get gain and praise" (2 Nephi 26:29; emphasis added). Nephi then teaches that the apostate Christians of the Gentile world proclaim that God "hath given *his power unto men;* . . . [therefore] hearken ye unto *my precept*" (2 Nephi 28:5; emphasis added). He warns that even the "humble followers of Christ . . . err because they are taught by the *precepts of men*" (2 Nephi 28:14; emphasis added). The words of the Savior to Joseph Smith in the Sacred Grove concerning the teachings of the various Christian churches echo these ideas (see JS–H 1:19). The doctrines of men do not have the "power" to build convincing faith; therefore, they cannot bring salvation.

The learning, pride, and precepts of men standing in opposition to the revelations of God cause apostasy. There is an immense difference between inquiring after religion with "all the powers of both reason and sophistry" (JS–H 1:9) and humbly calling upon our Father in Heaven for light and truth as did Joseph. Men in a state of apostasy set *themselves* up for a light unto the world instead of holding up the Savior's light. "Behold I am the light which ye shall hold up," Christ taught the Nephites (3 Nephi 18:24).

The Book of Mormon bears multiple witnesses that this aspect of Gentile society is the principle cause of apostasy. In the allegory of the olive tree, Zenos explains apostasy with the following words:

"Who is it that has corrupted my vineyard?

"And it came to pass that the servant said unto his master: Is it not the *loftiness* of thy vineyard—have not *the branches* thereof *overcome the roots* which are good? And because the branches have overcome the roots thereof, behold they grew faster than the strength of the roots, *taking strength unto themselves.* Behold, I say, is not this the cause that the trees of thy vineyard have become corrupted?" (Jacob 5:47–48; emphasis added).

Ironically, the *stumbling block* of the Gentiles is their own learning. This learning replaces the plain and precious truths, causing them to stumble.

THE ATTRIBUTES OF CHRIST

To offset the "doctrine of Christ" taught by the precepts of men, Nephi gives a beautiful description of the Savior. A correct understanding of His "perfections" will do much to "convince" the Gentiles that Jesus is the Christ and that they must build a saving faith. Christ describes the Gentiles in the following words: "The Gentiles . . . shall be lifted up in the pride of their hearts above all nations, and above all the people of the whole earth" (3 Nephi 16:10). In opposition to the pride of the Gentile world, Nephi, echoing the words of Isaiah, describes the humble invitation of Christ.

"He doeth not anything save it be for the benefit of the world; for he loveth the world, even that he layeth down his own life that he may draw all men unto him. Wherefore, he commandeth none that they shall not partake of his salvation.

"Behold, doth he cry unto any, saying: Depart from me? Behold, I say unto you, Nay; but he saith: Come unto me all ye ends of the earth, buy milk and honey, without money and without price.

"Behold, hath he commanded any that they should depart out of the synagogues, or out of the houses of worship? Behold, I say unto you, Nay.

"Hath he commanded any that they should not partake of his salvation? Behold I say unto you, Nay; but he hath given it free for all men; and he hath commanded his people that they should persuade all men to repentance.

"Behold, hath the Lord commanded any that they should not partake of his goodness? Behold I say unto you, Nay; but all men are privileged the one like unto the other, and none are forbidden" (2 Nephi 26:24–28).

With this true picture of Christ, convincing faith can be renewed. It is also Nephi's invitation to the Gentiles to return to the simple purity of Christ's doctrines and love. An attitude of condemnation, exclusion, superiority, or exploitation is antithetical to the true Christian spirit. The Christian Gentile world has largely forgotten Christ's teaching, "By this shall all men know that ye are my disciples, if ye have love one to another" (John 13:35).

DRUNKEN IN INIQUITY

Nephi begins chapter 27 with a general statement of the iniquity that will exist "in the last days, or in the days of the Gentiles, . . . all the lands of the earth . . . will be drunken with iniquity and all manner of abominations" (2 Nephi 27:1). According to the Revelation of John, "The inhabitants of the earth have been made drunk with the wine of her [the great and abominable church's] fornication" (Revelation 17:2). It is apparent that this iniquity results in large measure from the Apostasy. This is plainly taught to Nephi during his vision as recorded in 1 Nephi 14 and by the Prophet Joseph Smith, who records that "grief, sorrow, and care . . . [brought on by] murder, tyranny, and oppression [are] supported and urged on and upheld by the influence of that spirit which hath so strongly riveted the creeds of the fathers, who have inherited lies, upon the hearts of the children, and filled the world with confusion." The Prophet also warns that the confusion and oppression of apostasy are "growing stronger" and are "the very mainspring of all corruption, and the whole earth groans under the weight of its iniquity" (D&C 123:7). Then, in language reminiscent of the angel's words in 1 Nephi 13:5, describing "the formation of a [great] church" of apostasy, Joseph Smith concludes, "It is an iron yoke, it is a strong band; they are the very handcuffs, and chains, and shackles, and fetters of hell" (D&C 123:8).

"THE FULNESS OF THE EVERLASTING GOSPEL"

Nephi sees, however, that in spite of a world drunken in iniquity, the love of God will be manifested. The Gentiles and all the world will be given the knowledge necessary to have convincing faith in Christ. In essence the world is given another opportunity to accept the gospel in its fulness. A restoration is promised. That restoration hinges on a book that contains "the fulness of the everlasting Gospel" (JS–H 1:34). Its pages restore the true knowledge of God—His attributes, characteristics, perfections—and teach men the course they must walk in order to know their lives are in accordance with His will. True convincing and saving faith in Christ is the book's purpose and its central theme. For this purpose the Book of Mormon will always be the main pillar upon which the Latter-day Saints build their testimonies of Christ.

In chapter 27, Nephi describes the Book of Mormon in detail:

"The Lord God shall bring forth unto you the words of a book, and they shall be the words of them which have slumbered" (2 Nephi 27:6). He explains in words of plainness the coming forth of the Book of Mormon. He mentions the "three witnesses" and "a few" others (2 Nephi 27:12–13), which we identify as the eight witnesses. He gives special instructions to the Prophet Joseph Smith regarding the final sealing up of the book again that the Lord "may preserve [its] words" (2 Nephi 27:22).

THE LEARNED AND THE UNLEARNED

By far the major thrust of chapter 27 deals with the conflict between the "learned" and the "unlearned," between the blind and those who see. This is a continuation of the same theme described by Nephi in chapter 26. Nephi records that the book is "sealed." There are several interpretations that can be gleaned from this word. Certainly in a historical or literal context, the plates were sealed and Joseph Smith, Martin Harris, and Professor Charles Anthon fulfilled the prophetic dialogue between the learned and the unlearned. Parts of the Book of Mormon plates were also literally sealed and translation was not given.

Taken in a larger symbolic context, the learned represent the "world and the wisdom thereof" (1 Nephi 11:35). To the learned, proud, worldly-wise Gentile society, the depth, spirit, truth, and edifying power of the Book of Mormon are "sealed." The book will always be sealed to the proud. "I cannot read it," the learned declare (2 Nephi 27:18). Those words have been proven true by generations of critics who claim to see the gnat-like flaws in the Book of Mormon and cannot see the camel-like truths when they are written "as plain as word can be" (2 Nephi 32:7). The Book of Mormon remains "sealed" to the stiffnecked, "for they will not search knowledge, nor understand great knowledge, when it is given unto them in plainness" (2 Nephi 32:7). Nephi testifies that these learned people "cast many things away which are written and esteem them as things of naught" (2 Nephi 33:2). "Behold, ye have closed your eyes," he warns (2 Nephi 27:5). Because of this self-inflicted blindness, many of the Gentiles continue to "stumble," rejecting the Book of Mormon and thus failing to see the truths necessary to obtain "convincing" faith in Christ unto salvation.

Nephi speaks of the overt opposition that the learned will mount against the Book of Mormon and warns that "all that watch for iniquity are cut off; and they that *make a man an offender for a word,* and lay a snare for him . . . and *turn aside the just for a thing of naught"* (2 Nephi 27:31–32; emphasis added). The Book of Mormon and Joseph Smith have suffered this type of attack since 1830. How many critics have tried to "disprove" the Book of Mormon because of a single word or phrase? How many have searched it meticulously for flaws and contradictions? How many have rejected its goodness, judging it to be worth nothing?

In spite of the attacks, however, the Book of Mormon and Joseph Smith will continue to be accepted by the meek and unlearned. Humble searchers for truth will learn greater truths than the worldly wise. They will "read a sealed book."

A great restoration of truth accompanies the Book of Mormon, even "a marvelous work and a wonder" (2 Nephi 27:26). Nephi teaches that the truths which proceed from the unlearned will cause "the wisdom of their wise and learned [to] perish" (2 Nephi 27:26). Those who "fight against Zion and . . . distress her" are compared to "a hungry man which dreameth, and behold he eateth but he awaketh and his soul is empty" (2 Nephi 27:3). As Elder McConkie so graphically stated, "What does it matter if a few barking dogs snap at the heels of the weary travelers? Or that predators claim those few who fall by the way? The caravan moves on."[5]

To the unlearned and humble who are maimed (made spiritually "deaf" and "blind") by the apostasy, Nephi gives a message of hope: "In that day shall the deaf hear the words of the book, and the eyes of the blind shall see out of obscurity and out of darkness. . . . They also that erred in spirit shall come to understanding, and they that murmured shall learn doctrine" (2 Nephi 27:29, 35). The stumbling block of apostasy is removed for the Gentiles who are given eyes to see and ears to hear by the Book of Mormon. It restores true sight, and with that vision, convincing faith in Christ is once again on the earth and men are prepared for salvation.

THE FINAL VICTORY

Nephi presents a more detailed picture of Satan's opposition in 2 Nephi 28 and 29. Chapter 29, especially, speaks of a direct attack against the Book of Mormon as a second witness of Christ. The "learned" Gentiles say to God, "Enough! We have your words and will not accept any more" (see 2 Nephi 29:3).

So that all men will know the final outcome of the conflict between Satan and Christ, between the learned and the unlearned, between apostasy and restoration, Nephi wrote chapter 30. In it he announces that members of the Jews, the Lamanites, and the Gentiles (the three major groups spoken of throughout his farewell), will accept the Book of Mormon, come to Christ, lose their "scales of darkness," and be convinced (2 Nephi 30:6). Nephi clearly states that the Book of Mormon will be the key to this conversion: "And now, I would prophesy somewhat more concerning the Jews and the Gentiles. For after the book of which I have spoken shall come forth, and be written unto the Gentiles, and sealed up again unto the Lord, there shall be many which shall believe the words which are written" (2 Nephi 30:3). The success of the restoration begins with the Gentiles, who carry the Book of Mormon to Lehi's descendants and the Jews, that they might "be restored unto . . . the knowledge of Jesus Christ" (2 Nephi 30:5). The last are first and the first last.

The Restoration results in "a great division" (2 Nephi 30:10), and leads to a final separation at the Millennium when the wicked are destroyed, and, as Nephi teaches, "Satan shall have power over the hearts of the children of men no more, for a long time" (2 Nephi 30:18).

Although chapters 31 through 33 are discussed in other papers, it is good to mention one thing about the last three chapters in the context of the message to the Gentiles. Those chapters contain "the doctrine of Christ" (2 Nephi 31:21). As if to validate his own words and restore a plain and precious truth, Nephi gives a pure and simple explanation of the truths of the plan of salvation and the atonement of Christ. He shows his Gentile readers "the way" to be "saved in the kingdom of God" (2 Nephi 31:21). Since Christ is "the way," it is not surprising to find Nephi exhorting all mankind to "endure to the end, in following the example of the Son of the living God" (2 Nephi 31:16). Only in this way can the Gentiles be "convinced" that Jesus is the Christ and find salvation through His name.

THE FINAL TESTIMONY

The Book of Mormon must always be at the center of our attempt to convince the Gentiles, Lamanites, or Jews of the divinity of Jesus Christ and the truths of His gospel. To try any other way is bound to end in frustration. Nephi concludes his words with a very powerful testimony of the Book of Mormon and Christ. That testimony links them together with an inseparable unity. "And now, my beloved brethren, and also Jew, and all ye ends of the earth, hearken unto these words and believe in Christ; and if ye believe not in these words believe in Christ. And if ye shall believe in Christ ye will believe in these words, for they are the words of Christ, and he hath given them unto me; and they teach all men that they should do good" (2 Nephi 33:10).

NOTES

1. Joseph Smith, *Lectures on Faith* (Salt Lake City: Deseret Book, 1985), 38.

2. Bruce R. McConkie, *The Promised Messiah: The First Coming of Christ* (Salt Lake City: Deseret Book, 1978), 98.

3. Joseph Smith, *The History of the Church of Jesus Christ of Latter-day Saints,* ed. B. H. Roberts, 2d ed., rev. (Salt Lake City: Deseret Book, 1976), 4:42.

4. Joseph F. Smith, *Gospel Doctrine* (Salt Lake City: Deseret Book, 1949), 416; emphasis added.

5. Bruce R. McConkie, "The Caravan Moves On," *Ensign,* November 1984, 85; emphasis added.

10

Recovering the Missing Record of Lehi

S. Kent Brown

The Book of Mormon teems with references to works known by its compilers and authors but not included in its final collection of texts. Documents comprising the plates of brass, for instance, are mentioned merely in passing.[1] Further, Mormon alludes to a substantial collection from which he distilled the nearly thousand-year history of his people.[2] These countless unnamed texts, moreover, do not include the so-called "sealed plates," which formed part of what was entrusted to Joseph Smith but remained untranslated.[3] Among these accounts, the record of Lehi is singled out by name. It constituted, I propose, both a major source behind and an important influence on the writings of Lehi's two literary sons, Nephi and Jacob.[4] In fact, a hint exists that Lehi's record-keeping served as a model for scribes in later centuries.[5] Furthermore, a surprising amount of information exists that allows us to determine substantially the content and compass of Lehi's record.[6]

As he opens his own story, Nephi announces that he is writing "a record of my proceedings in my days" (1 Nephi 1:1). But a few lines later, after reporting the divine calling of his father to be a prophet (see 1 Nephi 1:5–15), he adds this important notation: "I, Nephi, do not

---

S. Kent Brown is a professor of ancient scripture and director of ancient studies at Brigham Young University.

make a full account of the things which my father hath written, for he hath written many things which he saw in visions and in dreams; and . . . many things which he prophesied and spake unto his children. . . . But I shall make an account of my proceedings in my days. Behold, I make an abridgment of the record of my father . . . ; wherefore, after I have abridged the record of my father then will I make an account of mine own life" (1 Nephi 1:16–17). Thus, even though he intended to "make a record of [his] proceedings," Nephi introduces his own account with the news of his father's calling (see 1 Nephi 1:5–15), adding a note that he is abridging his father's record. According to verse 16—and this sets our agenda—this record includes (a) the notice of Lehi's prophetic call, (b) "things which he saw in visions and in dreams," and (c) "things which he prophesied and spake unto his children."[7]

LEHI'S RECORD IN THE LARGE AND SMALL PLATES

It is important to notice that Nephi inscribed two records on metal plates: the first on the large plates of Nephi[8] and the second on his small plates,[9] each making use of his father's journal.[10] Concerning the large plates, Nephi recounts: "And upon the plates . . . I did engraven the record of my father, and also our journeyings in the wilderness, and the prophecies of my father" (1 Nephi 19:1). Notably, this verse outlines the material found in 1 Nephi and in the first three chapters of 2 Nephi. To illustrate, (a) "the record of my father" corresponds roughly to 1 Nephi 1–10; (b) the "journeyings in the wilderness" appear in 1 Nephi 16–18, beginning with the discovery of the Liahona compass; and (c) the "prophecies of my father" would include 2 Nephi 1–3 and, possibly, 1 Nephi 10. This overall scheme is interrupted only by Nephi's dream (see 1 Nephi 11–15) and his discourse to the extended family (see 1 Nephi 19–22), both of which digress from the main story that focuses primarily on Lehi.

It was evidently after Lehi's death that Nephi began his second account—the small plates—which came to include the first six records of the Book of Mormon.[11] Nephi himself states: "I, Nephi, had kept the records upon my [large] plates . . . thus far.

"And it came to pass that the Lord God said unto me: Make other plates; and thou shalt engraven many things upon them which are good in my sight, for the profit of thy people.

"Wherefore, I, Nephi . . . went and made these [small] plates upon which I have engraven these things.

"And I engraved that which is pleasing unto God. . . .

"And if my people desire to know . . . the history of my people they must search mine other [large] plates" (2 Nephi 5:29–33).

According to this view, the books of 1 and 2 Nephi comprise Nephi's second record. In the case of this narrative, too, Nephi acknowledges that his father's work underlays its foundation; for only "after I have abridged the record of my father," Nephi affirms, "will I make an account of mine own life" (1 Nephi 1:17). Plainly it was Nephi's avowed purpose to incorporate parts of his father's work into this second composition.[12]

The structure of the early verses of 1 Nephi 1 shows Nephi's dependence on his father's account, preserving the opening of Lehi's record itself. As a matter of custom, ancient prophets introduced an account of their divine callings near the beginning of their records, coupling it with a colophon about the year of the reign of the local king[13]—precisely what we find in 1 Nephi 1:4–15. Directly after Nephi's opening remark about himself (see 1 Nephi 1:1–3) there is a notation that the story began during the first year of King Zedekiah's reign (see 1 Nephi 1:4). Next, as expected, we read of God commissioning the prophet (see 1 Nephi 1:5–15). But it is not the call of Nephi; it is Lehi's call.[14] In this light, I believe that Nephi inserted the opening of his father's book into 1 Nephi 1:4–15.[15]

WHEN AND ON WHAT DID LEHI WRITE?

Lehi must have completed much of his record by the time Nephi began to write his first narrative: "Upon the [large] plates which I made I did engraven the record of my father" (1 Nephi 19:1). If so, when and how did Lehi's book come into existence? Clearly Lehi's account was already extant when Nephi inscribed it on the large plates. Further, someone apparently kept a journal, possibly on perishable material, during the years that Lehi's family lived in the desert (see 1 Nephi 17:4). We turn now to evidence for these observations.

The report of the voyage of Lehi's family to the promised land appears in 1 Nephi 18, followed by Nephi's comment that he then manufactured plates for writing by smelting ore (see 1 Nephi 19:1–2).[16] By Nephi's account, he already possessed (a) the record of Lehi, (b) the genealogy of Lehi's fathers, and (c) an itinerary of the family's travels in the desert. Nephi, of course, could have obtained the genealogy from the brass plates (see 1 Nephi 5:16). But Lehi's narrative, including the desert wanderings, must have come from another source. It seems, then, that Lehi's account, basically complete when Nephi began his first record, served as one of Nephi's sources. Thus Lehi evidently was already composing his narrative while traveling in the desert and crossing the sea.

Another indicator of a running log of the family's travel experiences is that after relating Lehi's discovery of the compass in 1 Nephi 16:10, Nephi begins to narrate the family's trek by a series of "we" passages (see 1 Nephi 16:11–19, 33; 17:1–6).[17] These passages, narrated in first person plural, bear the marks of a summary of a diary-like record. That Nephi was evidently summarizing such an account appears in 1 Nephi 17:4 where, after mentioning the physical well-being that the family enjoyed in the desert (see 1 Nephi 17:2–3), he compresses his long story into a few words, "We did sojourn for the space of many years, yea, even eight years in the wilderness."[18]

We have no way of knowing what material Lehi originally used for record keeping. However, Lehi's fifth son, Jacob, makes an incidental remark that may shed light on this question as well as on the reason the Lord commanded Nephi to keep records on metal plates. After acknowledging the difficulty of inscribing on metal, Jacob says: "We know that the things which we write upon plates must remain; But whatsoever things we write upon anything save it be upon plates must perish and vanish away" (Jacob 4:1–2).

In this connection, it is worth noting that Nephi had obtained the brass plates before Jacob was born.[19] And Jacob must have noticed their durability since he could read and teach from them after he had become a grown man. Consequently, his remark that writing "remains" when engraved on metal tablets no doubt derived from his own experience, as did his assertion that other types of material for writing "must perish and vanish away." How had Jacob observed this? The most natural answer is that someone in his father's family had written on nonmetallic substances. Compared to the durability of the brass plates, these materials had evidently proven unsatisfactory for permanent records.[20]

Other hints, or the lack of them, suggest that Lehi initially kept his record neither on metallic plates nor on empty leaves (if any) of the brass plates. First, no reason appears for Lehi to carry engraving tools into the desert. It was only after he had left Jerusalem, in fact, that the Lord instructed him to seek custody of the brass plates (see 1 Nephi 3:2–4). Furthermore, the only item that Nephi seems to have brought later to his father from Jerusalem, along with the brass plates, was the sword of Laban (see 2 Nephi 5:14; Jacob 1:10). No tools are mentioned.[21] Finally, no account even hints that anyone in Lehi's family smelted ore either for plates or for tools while living in the desert. On the contrary, they avoided kindling fires even for cooking (see 1 Nephi 17:2, 12). To be sure, Nephi possessed the skill to refine ore for metal plates, since after crossing the desert he crafted metal tools for constructing his ship (see 1 Nephi 17:16).[22] These observations, then, when coupled with Jacob's note about nonmetallic writing substances, lead one to postulate that records kept in the desert were written on something other than metal, although we cannot be certain of the material.[23]

What can we distill from our discussion thus far? In the first place, Lehi's record both served as a source for Nephi's two accounts, those on the large and small plates, and specifically underlies most of the opening of 1 Nephi, a text from the small plates. Second, Lehi's record was essentially complete by the time he and his family reached the land of promise, since Nephi employed it as a source for his annals on the large plates soon after arriving. Third, we surmise that Lehi initially wrote his narrative on a substance less durable than metal, and that it was Nephi who first inscribed it on metallic leaves when he recopied it onto his large plates.

THE SCOPE OF LEHI'S BOOK ON THE SMALL PLATES

Our next task is to determine how extensively Lehi's account underlies 1 and 2 Nephi as well as Jacob's book. We shall first explore direct quotations and afterwards, passages that Jacob and Nephi appear to paraphrase from the account of their father. In this connection, two of the most important and lengthy quotations from Lehi are his portrayal of the vision of the tree of life (see 1 Nephi 8:2–28) and the report of his last instructions and blessings to his family (see 2 Nephi 1:4–3:25; 4:3–7, 9, 11).

The quotations. The vision of the tree certainly comes from Lehi's own record. The piece in 1 Nephi 8:2–28 stands in the first person singular, an important criterion. By the way Nephi introduces the story, he is obviously quoting from his father: "He [Lehi] spake unto us, saying: Behold, I have dreamed a dream" (1 Nephi 8:2). Additionally, Nephi leaves no doubt as to when he ceases quoting Lehi and begins to paraphrase: "And now I, Nephi, do not speak all the words of my father. But, to be short in writing, behold, he saw other multitudes pressing forward; and they came and caught hold of the end of the rod of iron" (1 Nephi 8:29–30).

Concerning Lehi's last blessings and instructions to his family, there is some question whether they formed part of his record.[24] We cannot be entirely certain, chiefly because the scenes occurred close to Lehi's death. Of course, it is probable that not many years had passed between Lehi's arrival in the promised land (see 1 Nephi 18:23) and his death (see 2 Nephi 4:12).[25] During this period, Nephi had been keeping a record of his people on the large plates "thus far" (2 Nephi 5:29). Had Lehi also continued to write? If he had, we would expect him to include his last blessings and instructions; for, as Nephi tells us, "[Lehi] also hath written many things which he prophesied and spake unto his children" (1 Nephi 1:16), observations which fit Lehi's last blessings. Perhaps most significantly, the section of 2 Nephi comprising Lehi's last instructions exhibits the expected first person singular narrative. This characteristic, especially in such a long section, impels us toward the view that Lehi himself was responsible for the report. Of course, someone may have written Lehi's words as he spoke and, afterwards, Nephi inserted them into the large plates.[26] Whichever the case, we should view Lehi's last words to his family as a continuation of what he had written simply because they match, according to Nephi's description, what Lehi had already recorded.

One other long quotation, preserved by Jacob, also came from Lehi's record. It lies in Jacob 2:23–33, a discussion of fidelity in marriage. After chastising his people for their pride (see Jacob 2:12–22) and then for their "grosser crimes," Jacob declares, "For behold, thus saith the Lord: This people begin to wax in iniquity; . . . for they seek to excuse themselves in committing whoredoms, because of the things which were written concerning David, and Solomon his son" (Jacob 2:23). A quotation from the Lord begins in this verse and runs through verse 33. But who received these instructions? At first glance it appears that Jacob was repeating what he himself had received, since a few lines earlier he had written, "As I inquired of the Lord, thus came the word unto me, saying: Jacob, get thou up into the temple on the morrow, and declare the word which I shall give thee unto this people" (Jacob 2:11). Was Jacob carrying out the Lord's instructions by retelling what he had been told? Not really.[27] A more careful look at chapter 2 reveals that the counsel concerning one wife indeed came from the Lord but that Jacob was not the first to receive it. In fact, the recipient of these directions was Lehi. After the long quotation from the Lord (see Jacob 2:23–33), including Jacob's short commentary (see Jacob 2:27), we find this statement: "And now behold, my brethren, ye know that these commandments [concerning fidelity to one's wife] were given to our father, Lehi; wherefore, ye have known them before" (Jacob 2:34). Therefore, as Jacob insists, it was Lehi who previously received "these commandments."

An equally compelling passage occurs a few lines later in which Jacob accusingly announces: "Behold, the Lamanites your brethren . . . are more righteous than you; for they have not forgotten the commandments of the Lord, which was given unto our father—that they should have save it were one wife, and concubines they should have none, and there should not be whoredoms committed among them" (Jacob 3:5). Except for punctuation, this verse stood thus in the printer's manuscript.[28] Every printed edition of the Book of Mormon has changed the word *commandments* in this passage to the singular, and, except in the 1981 edition, the word *father* has appeared as plural. Significantly, the printer's manuscript demonstrates unequivocally that these "commandments" were delivered to Jacob's father, Lehi. Consequently, we conclude that in Jacob 2:23–33 we find instructions that the Lord entrusted to Lehi. Jacob, in his sermon, quotes them to his hearers from Lehi's record, which "ye have known" (Jacob 2:34).

Other quotations likely from Lehi's record are shorter, and all occur in 1 Nephi.[29] We must use caution, however, in attributing these extractions to Lehi's record, since, because of their brevity, they may be based on the memory of one or another family member.

The paraphrases. As one might expect, the paraphrases from Lehi outnumber the quotations. With two exceptions (see 2 Nephi 1:1–3; Jacob 3:5), all of the restatements which may go back to Lehi's record turn up in 1 Nephi. The two visions associated with Lehi's call must of course be included since Nephi has apparently recast the account from first person to third person (see 1 Nephi 1:4–12, 13–14, 15). This report, as already noted, is sprinkled with direct quotations, presumably from Lehi's original narration (see 1 Nephi 1:13–14). Then follows Nephi's summary, which indicates that he is restating his father's chronicle: "And now I, Nephi, do not make a full account of the things which my father hath written, for he hath written many things which he saw in visions and in dreams" (1 Nephi 1:16).

Much of chapter 2 may also depend on Lehi's narrative.[30] Mixed with these lines are Lehi's own words[31] as well as Nephi's observations both about his brothers' attitudes at having to leave Jerusalem (see 1 Nephi 2:11–13) and about a revelation that he himself received (see 1 Nephi 2:16–24). At the end of the summary from Lehi, Nephi concludes by saying, "And my father dwelt in a tent" (1 Nephi 2:15).

A third important paraphrase occurs in chapter 8, summarizing the remainder of Lehi's dream and his consequent exhortation to Laman and Lemuel (see 1 Nephi 8:30–33; 8:35–9:1). Nephi introduces this restatement by conceding that he cannot repeat "all the words of [his] father" (1 Nephi 8:29) and closes it thus: "And all these things did my father see, and hear, and speak, as he dwelt in a tent, . . . and also a great many more things, which cannot be written upon these [small] plates" (1 Nephi 9:1). Nothing in this verse states specifically that Lehi had written down what Nephi had just recapitulated. But Lehi's dream and the accompanying exhortations to his family fit so well with Nephi's description of his father's written work (see 1 Nephi 1:16) that I feel confident that all of chapter 8, except Nephi's inserted remarks, goes back to Lehi's record.

Another very important summary from Lehi's record stands in 1 Nephi 10:1–16, which Nephi prefaces in an unusual way: "And now I, Nephi, proceed to give an account . . . of my proceedings, and my reign and ministry; wherefore, to proceed with mine account, *I must speak somewhat of the things of my father*" (1 Nephi 10:1; emphasis added). After a synopsis of Lehi's prophecies to his sons about the coming Messiah and the scattering and gathering of the Nephites and Lamanites, Nephi concludes: "And after this manner of language did my father prophesy and speak unto my brethren, and also many more things which I do not write in this book; for I have written as many of them as were expedient for me in mine other book.

"And all these things . . . were done as my father dwelt in a tent" (1 Nephi 10:15–16).[32] Although Nephi does not claim here that he is paraphrasing Lehi's prophetic words from a written source, he does acknowledge that he already included them in his "other book" (i.e., the large plates), from which he likely took the material for 1 Nephi 10:1–16. Remembering that his father's record contained "many things which he prophesied and spake unto his children" (1 Nephi 1:16), it would be surprising indeed if Nephi were not ultimately dependent in this instance upon Lehi's own written account.

In his original record, this segment (1 Nephi 10:1–16), which sets out Lehi's teachings on the coming Messiah and the scattering and gathering of Israel, may well have continued the earlier account of his vision and exhortation to his sons (see 1 Nephi 8:2–9:1). Two observations are relevant. First, just a few lines separate these two longer sections (see 1 Nephi 9:2–6). Apparently Nephi's attention to "these [small] plates" in 1 Nephi 9:1 presented an opportunity to discuss them briefly in verses 2 through 6 before resuming his father's account in chapter 10. Second, when we compare the content of these two units with the content of Nephi's own analogous dream of the tree of life (see 1 Nephi 11–14), it seems obvious that the two pieces belong together. Although it is not apparent from the narrative of Lehi's dream of the tree that the prophecies regarding Israel's destiny and the Messiah (see 1 Nephi 10:1–16) are parts of a whole, their connection becomes clear from Nephi's parallel dream. Hence we conclude that the discussion in 1 Nephi 9:2–6 stands between two sections which likely formed a unit in Lehi's narrative.

The last paraphrase requiring review is the desert itinerary (see 1 Nephi 16:11–17, 33; 17:1–6). To be sure, Nephi himself could have kept the log in the desert. One observation, however, inclines toward the view that the itinerary was Lehi's. Nephi mentions the desert journal twice in 1 Nephi 19:1–2. In verse 1, when itemizing sources for the large plates, Nephi lists "the record of my father, and also [the record of] our journeyings in the wilderness, and the prophecies of my father." It is worth noting that Nephi mentions the desert journal *between* items from Lehi. Only after naming the sources from his father does Nephi say, "And also many of mine own prophecies have I engraven upon [the large plates]" (1 Nephi 19:1). Verse 2 paints a similar picture. Here, too, Nephi itemizes the sources that he drew on when composing his record on the large plates: "the record of my father, and the genealogy of his fathers, and the more part of all our proceedings in the wilderness." Again Nephi has associated the "proceedings" of the desert period with his father's work. Consequently, the itinerary almost certainly came from Lehi's pen.

In sum, the following segments of 1 Nephi paraphrase Lehi's record: Lehi's two visions at the time of his call (see 1 Nephi 1:4–15), his departure into the desert (see 1 Nephi 2:1–10, 14–15), parts of Lehi's vision of the tree of life (see 1 Nephi 8:30–33; 8:35–9:1), his prophecies concerning Israel and the Messiah (see 1 Nephi 10:1–16), and the desert itinerary (see 1 Nephi 16:11–17, 33; 17:1–6). There are others shorter in length which almost all appear in 1 Nephi: Lehi's prophecies and subsequent rejection in Jerusalem (see 1 Nephi 1:18–20), his prophecies regarding the brass plates (see 1 Nephi 5:17–19),[33] Lehi sending for Ishmael and his family (see 1 Nephi 7:1–2), Nephi's interpretation of Lehi's words concerning Israel's destiny (see 1 Nephi 15:17–18),[34] the Lord's command to Lehi to move on and the accompanying discovery of the compass (see 1 Nephi 16:9–10),[35] and the revelation to Lehi by means of the compass (see 1 Nephi 16:25–27).[36]

CHARACTER OF THE RECORD

To portray the content of Lehi's record is a formidable task, since we possess only fragments and summarized accounts. Consequently, we run the risk of overstatement or underestimation. But we can discern a tentative outline. So far, three ingredients have appeared: prophecies, visions, and teachings.

The prophecies. Concerning prophecies, Nephi informs us that his father included many among his writings (see 1 Nephi 1:16; 19:1). Although Lehi prophesied on several occasions about his family (see 1 Nephi 7:1), a unique opportunity presented itself when he blessed and instructed them before his death, assuring them that their posterity would survive to the last days (see 2 Nephi 1:1–4:12). With an eye to the future, Lehi mentions first the promised land "which the Lord God hath covenanted with me should be a land for the inheritance of . . . my children forever" (2 Nephi 1:5). Of course, dwelling in the land is conditional upon obedience to the Lord and His principles (see 2 Nephi 1:7). Sadly, Lehi prophesies of a time when his posterity will turn their backs on "their Redeemer and their God" (2 Nephi 1:10). In that day, he foresees, the Lord "will bring other nations . . . and he will give unto them power, and he will take away from [Lehi's descendants] the lands of their possessions, and he will cause them to be scattered and smitten" (2 Nephi 1:11). Although this prospect grieves Lehi deeply, he acknowledges that the Lord's "ways are righteousness forever" (2 Nephi 1:19).

Even in the face of such gloomy prospects, Lehi beams a light on the divine pledge that the family's progeny will survive these most vexing times (see 2 Nephi 4:7, 9). He agrees with a vow made to Joseph of Egypt that God would preserve Joseph's offspring (see 2 Nephi

3:16), a promise recorded on the brass plates (see 2 Nephi 4:2). In fact, much of the prophetic radiance that Lehi draws from this Joseph promise (see 2 Nephi 3:6–21) shines on a special seer (see 2 Nephi 3:7, 11) who in the last days will carry the word of the Lord both to Joseph's seed through Lehi (see 2 Nephi 3:7) and to the house of Israel (see 2 Nephi 3:13).[37] Then Lehi prophesies to his own son Joseph that this seer will be "an instrument in the hands of God . . . and do that thing which is great in the sight of God, unto the bringing to pass much restoration unto the house of Israel, and unto the seed of thy brethren" (2 Nephi 3:24).

One aspect of Lehi's prophecies about his descendants holds out the promise that their records will come forth to the world (see 2 Nephi 29:2). A similar assurance came to Joseph of Egypt, to whom the Lord declared regarding the seer: "I will give unto him that he shall write the writing of the fruit of thy loins, unto the fruit of thy loins. . . . And it shall be as if the fruit of thy loins had cried unto them from the dust" (2 Nephi 3:18–19).

Lehi simply obtained the same divine commitment awarded to Joseph—that his posterity's writings would cry out as if "from the dust" to others of his descendants (2 Nephi 3:19).

Because he knows the destiny of his progeny, Lehi compares his family to an olive tree whose branches have been broken off (see 1 Nephi 10:12–14; 15:12–13), a comparison tied to the prophet Zenos's allegory of the olive tree, also found in the brass plates.[38] In this allegory, the house of Israel is likened to an olive tree whose branches are removed and grafted elsewhere but eventually restored to the main trunk of the tree. Such a prophetic image had a deep influence on Lehi, for Nephi relates that his father spoke "concerning the house of Israel, that they should be compared like unto an olive-tree, whose branches should be broken off and . . . scattered upon all the face of the earth.

"Wherefore, he said it must needs be that we should be led . . . into the land of promise, unto the fulfilling of the word of the Lord, that we should be scattered upon all the face of the earth" (1 Nephi 10:12–13). That these words were prophetic is evident in Nephi's summarizing remark a few lines later: "After this manner of language did my father prophesy" (1 Nephi 10:15).[39]

The coming Messiah also enlivens Lehi's prophecies. Almost predictably, in his last blessings to his family, Lehi turns to the Messiah, illuminating His mission as Redeemer from the Fall, as Guarantor of human freedom, and as Mediator of eternal life (see 2 Nephi 2:26–28). An earlier prophecy about the Messiah played a role in Lehi's preaching in Jerusalem (see 1 Nephi 1:19), the inspiration coming from his vision of a book (see 1 Nephi 1:8–14). In that vision, Lehi at first seemed not to recognize the "One descending out of the midst of heaven" whose brightness "was above that of the sun at noon-day" (1 Nephi 1:9), even though Lehi had been rather certain that he saw God "sitting upon his throne" earlier in the vision (1 Nephi 1:8). But this second figure who descended, followed by "twelve others," apparently remained unknown to Lehi until he began to read in the book brought to him: "The things which [Lehi] read in the book, manifested plainly of the coming of a Messiah" (1 Nephi 1:10, 19). At the same time, Lehi learned of the threatening destruction of Jerusalem because of the inhabitants' wickedness (see 1 Nephi 1:13).[40] This mournful outlook, along with the prediction of the Messiah's coming, formed the core of his prophesying to the people in the city (see 1 Nephi 1:19).

Lehi also accentuates the Messiah when he recounts his vision of the tree of life (see 1 Nephi 10:4–11), much of his prophecy evidently growing out of this later vision. This vision of the tree, and of the Messiah and his forerunner, appears to considerably expand Lehi's knowledge of the Messiah's ministry in Palestine. In the earlier vision (see 1 Nephi 1:8–13), Lehi had learned of His coming for "the redemption of the world" (1 Nephi 1:19). But whether this prior occasion had taught Lehi more remains uncertain since Nephi offers only a sketchy summary (see 1 Nephi 1:14, 19). In contrast, Lehi relates many more specific details about the Redeemer in the later prophecy (see 1 Nephi 10:4–11) than we find in chapter 1.

It is worth making a point here concerning Lehi's expressions for the Messiah. Whether his words are paraphrased or quoted directly, Lehi never used the Greek title *Christ* when speaking of the Messiah,[41] nor did he ever call Him *Son of God* or the like.[42] Only Lehi's sons Nephi and Jacob employed titles of this sort.[43] To be sure, Lehi would have known the designation *Son* from the works of Zenos and Zenock, whose works appeared on the brass plates.[44] But in the few quotations from these latter two prophets, whose works Alma also cited when speaking of the coming Messiah (see Alma 33:11, 13, 16), nowhere do Zenos and Zenock expand the title to *Son of God* or something related.[45]

Did Lehi know expressions such as *Son of God* and *Christ?* Concerning both the title *Christ* and the name *Jesus,* the answer is a definite no. According to 2 Nephi 10:3, an angel revealed the title *Christ* to Jacob only after Lehi's death, and Nephi makes use of this term only after narrating Jacob's experience (see 2 Nephi 11:4). In addition, Nephi writes the name *Jesus* for the first time only near the end of his second book (see 2 Nephi 26:12), and Jacob records it but once in the latter half of his work (see Jacob 4:6). Therefore, we can safely conclude that Lehi did not know these expressions. In the case of *Son of God* and related titles, we cannot be sure that Lehi did not know them, but at least he did not use them.[46]

Visions and dreams. Besides Lehi's prophecies, we know of seven of his visions and inspired dreams if we include the instructions given to him by means of the compass (see 1 Nephi 16:26–27). Nephi recounts that Lehi had included such in his record: "[Lehi] hath written many things which he saw in visions and in dreams" (1 Nephi 1:16). In this connection, Lehi himself admits that he was "a visionary man" (1 Nephi 5:4). Incidentally, Lehi saw little difference between the terms *dream* and *vision.*[47]

Lehi's earliest vision likely stood at the beginning of his own record. Nephi recounts that "as [Lehi] prayed unto the Lord, there came a pillar of fire and dwelt upon a rock before him; and he saw and heard much. And it came to pass that he returned to his own house at Jerusalem; and he cast himself upon his bed, being overcome with the Spirit and the things which he had seen" (1 Nephi 1:6–7).

That Lehi's experience constituted a vision grows out of the emphasis on what he saw. Remarkably, while Nephi repeats nothing of the vision's content, it certainly must have included Lehi's calling as a prophet. And it is reasonable that some of the content of this vision coincided with what Lehi saw immediately thereafter in the vision of the book. Nephi possibly thought that juxtaposing the two visions would indicate corresponding content.[48] We come to this view when we realize that Nephi must have abbreviated as much as possible, owing to the difficulty of inscribing on metal plates.

Nephi opens his summary of Lehi's second vision, the vision of the book, by picturing what Lehi saw when he was caught away by the Spirit: "And being thus overcome with the Spirit, he was carried away in a vision, even that he saw the heavens open, and he thought he saw God sitting upon his throne, surrounded with numberless concourses of angels" (1 Nephi 1:8).[49] Lehi then saw "One descending out of the midst of heaven" and "twelve others following him" (1 Nephi 1:9–10). Nephi continues, "The first came and stood before my father, and gave unto him a book, and bade him that he should read. . . . And he read, saying: Wo, wo, unto Jerusalem, for I have seen thine abominations! Yea, and many things did my father read concerning Jerusalem—that it should be destroyed, and the inhabitants thereof; . . . and many should be carried away captive into Babylon" (1 Nephi 1:11, 13).

This passage captures the warning of Lehi's vision: Jerusalem had become iniquitous and was to be ravaged. This warning, of course, formed the core of the messages of contemporary prophets at Jerusalem.[50] Although Nephi does not allude to it here, at some point Lehi had also learned about the approaching Redemption through the Messiah, for Nephi's tight summary of Lehi's later preaching reads: "And [Lehi] testified that the things which he saw and heard, and also the things which he read in the book, manifested plainly of the coming of a Messiah, and also the redemption of the world" (1 Nephi 1:19).

In narrating his father's third vision, Nephi includes words of divine assurance as well as forewarning: "The Lord spake unto my father, yea, even in a dream, and said unto him: Blessed art thou Lehi, because of the things which thou hast done; and because thou hast been faithful and declared unto this people the things which I commanded thee, behold, they seek to take away thy life" (1 Nephi 2:1). In this same vision the Lord also charged Lehi to leave Jerusalem, the first step in a very long journey that would take him halfway around the world: "The Lord commanded my father, even in a dream, that he should take his family and depart into the wilderness" (1 Nephi 2:2). Lehi's response to this command eventually led him and his family to a distant land of promise: the Americas.

Lehi's fourth vision directs the return of his sons to Jerusalem for the record on the plates of brass (see 1 Nephi 3:2–6). Nephi quotes the very words of Lehi: "[Lehi] spake unto me [Nephi], saying: Behold I have dreamed a dream, in the which the Lord hath commanded me that thou and thy brethren shall return to Jerusalem.

"For behold, Laban hath the record of the Jews and also a genealogy of my forefathers, and they are engraven upon plates of brass" (1 Nephi 3:2–3).

Nephi and his brothers were to go to Laban and "seek the records, and bring them down hither" (1 Nephi 3:4). Notably, Lehi received this vision only after he and his family had established a base camp near the Red Sea (see 1 Nephi 2:5–9).

The fifth vision has to do with the tree of life and the Messiah (see 1 Nephi 8:2–28). As we have seen, this section preserves a long excerpt from Lehi's record. There were elements of the vision, however, that Lehi apparently left out.[51] The most notable illuminates the time of the Messiah's coming. Oddly, neither Lehi nor Nephi relates this detail in the accounts of their visions—at least not in the small plates. It is only afterward that Nephi brings up this particular while recollecting his vision (see 1 Nephi 19:7–10). Nephi speaks thus: "And behold [the Messiah] cometh, according to the words of the angel, in six hundred years from the time my father left Jerusalem" (1 Nephi 19:8). If "the angel" in this passage (see 1 Nephi 11:14) is the same as the "man . . . dressed in a white robe" of Lehi's vision (1 Nephi 8:5)—and this seems apparent—then we can reasonably assume that Lehi had learned what Nephi learned concerning when the Messiah would come.

In my reckoning, the revelation written on the compass constitutes Lehi's sixth vision (see 1 Nephi 16:26).[52] On this occasion, Lehi had prayed to know where Nephi should go to find food. In His response, the Lord chastised Lehi and his family for complaining because of their hardships (see 1 Nephi 16:24–25). Nephi then writes that "when my father beheld the things which were written upon the ball, he did fear and tremble exceedingly, and also my brethren and the sons of Ishmael and our wives" (1 Nephi 16:27). Like the Urim and Thummim among the ancient Israelites, the compass served as an important means of revelation.[53]

The last recorded vision is noted briefly in 2 Nephi 1:4, "For, behold, said [Lehi], I have seen a vision, in which I know that Jerusalem is destroyed; and had we remained in Jerusalem we should also have perished." That Lehi was granted a vision of the destruction of Jerusalem should not surprise us. Other prophets beheld the same.[54] For example, Lehi's son Jacob recounts seeing "that those who were at Jerusalem . . . have been slain and carried away captive" (2 Nephi 6:8). And Ezekiel was transported in vision from Babylon to Jerusalem, where he witnessed the abominable practices of the priests and the consequent withdrawal of the Lord from the temple before the city fell (see Ezekiel 8:3–10:19).

The doctrines. Among the important doctrines taught by Lehi, in addition to those already noted, three stand out: fidelity in marriage, opposition in all things, and Adam's role. Concerning fidelity to one's spouse, Lehi linked this principle to the question of plurality of wives. Jacob, we recall, quotes at some length the relevant words of Lehi (see Jacob 2:23–26, 27–33). While the occasion when Lehi received this divine injunction remains unknown, according to Jacob the Lord had told Lehi that "this people[55] begin to wax in iniquity; . . . for they seek to excuse themselves in committing whoredoms" (Jacob 2:23). More to the point, people had sought "to excuse themselves" on scriptural grounds, "because of the things . . . written concerning David, and Solomon his son" (Jacob 2:23). God, through Lehi, was very emphatic that no "man among you [shall] have save it be one wife" (Jacob 2:27) unless God Himself reverses this commandment: "For if I will, saith the Lord of Hosts, raise up seed unto me, I will command my people" (Jacob 2:30). What had angered the Lord in Jacob's day was having "seen the sorrow, and heard the mourning of the daughters of my people . . . because of the wickedness and abominations of their husbands" (Jacob 2:31). In Lehi's account of it, fidelity to one's marriage partner was so crucial to his family's presence in the promised land that, if not observed, God would soundly curse "the land for their sakes" (Jacob 2:29).

A second significant teaching of Lehi elucidates the doctrine of opposition in all things. As part of his last instructions to his son Jacob (see 2 Nephi 2), Lehi testifies that God's final judgment leads either to "punishment which is affixed" or to "happiness which is affixed" (2 Nephi 2:10). He then reasons, "It must needs be, that there is an opposition in all things. If not so . . . righteousness could not be brought to pass, neither wickedness, neither holiness nor misery" (2 Nephi 2:11). Lehi further maintains that without opposition we have no power to be righteous or unrighteous. We note the dramatic result that Lehi says would ensue: "And if these things are not there is no God. And if there is no God we are not, neither the earth; for there could have been no creation" (2 Nephi 2:13). According to Lehi, then, the totality of existence would cease if opposition disappeared. He repeats this perception in different terms: "All things must needs be a compound in one; wherefore, if it should be one body it must needs remain as dead, having no life neither death, nor corruption nor incorruption, happiness nor misery, neither sense nor insensibility. Wherefore, it must needs have been created for . . . naught; wherefore there would have been no purpose in the end of its creation" (2 Nephi 2:11–12).

The stance that all existence would be utterly wasted if no antithetical relationships existed leads Lehi to say: "Wherefore, this thing [no opposition] must needs destroy the wisdom of God and his eternal purposes, and also the power, and the mercy, and the justice of God" (2 Nephi 2:12). Since Lehi has just previously been dealing with the coming Redemption through the Messiah (see 2 Nephi 2:6–10), we should probably understand this doctrine in terms of the Redeemer's work. That is, if no opposition exists, there is no reason for a Redeemer who can bring about God's mercy *and* justice.

A third element of Lehi's teaching ties into his concerns about the role of the Redeemer and about opposition in all things—the role of Adam in the drama of salvation (see 2 Nephi 2:15–27). Lehi insists that two ingredients were joined together in Adam's situation—a choice along with the freedom to make that choice: "It must needs be that there was an opposition; even the forbidden fruit in opposition to the tree of life. . . .

"Wherefore, the Lord God gave unto man that he should act for himself" (2 Nephi 2:15–16).

For Lehi, the opposition facing Adam was necessary so that the choice could be made—the forbidden fruit versus the tree of life. In fact, had Adam not been enticed to make the choice that brought both mortality and the capability of parenthood, the earth would never have been peopled, thus frustrating God's plan:

"And now, behold, if Adam had not transgressed he would not have fallen, but he would have remained in the garden of Eden. . . .

"And [Adam and Eve] would have had no children. . . .

"Adam fell that men might be" (2 Nephi 2:22–23, 25).

The whole point is that if Adam had not fallen, the human race would never have existed. But since he did fall, "the Messiah cometh . . . that he may redeem the children of men from the fall. And because that they are redeemed from the fall they have become free forever. . . .

"To choose liberty and eternal life, through the great Mediator of all men, or to choose captivity and death, according to the captivity and power of the devil" (2 Nephi 2:26–27).

The reasons for opposition, then, are (a) to perpetuate existence—and Adam's fall led to this—and (b) to bring about God's plan, which is to save us through the Messiah's redemption.[56]

CONCLUSION

In summary, a strong case exists for the argument that Lehi's written record underlay much in the writings of Nephi and Jacob. The most persistent problem, of course, is whether a particular quotation or paraphrase indeed goes back to Lehi's written source. Naturally, Nephi's brief characterizations of his father's writings (see 1 Nephi 1:16; 19:1–2) enable us to grasp important clues regarding the nature of

Lehi's work. Yet in the final analysis we can be certain about only a portion; the rest remains merely suggestive. Far from being a futile exercise, however, our review has made it abundantly clear that Lehi's writings and teachings deeply impressed his sons Nephi and Jacob, a fact which allows us to assess with increased accuracy the positive influences of Lehi, the man and the prophet.

NOTES

1. These included, for instance, the books of Moses and Jeremiah's prophecies (see 1 Nephi 5:11–14; Alma 18:36).

2. See, for example, Words of Mormon 1:3–11; Mormon 4:23; 6:6.

3. See Ether 4:1–7; 5:1; see also 2 Nephi 27:6–10.

4. In an article entitled "Nephi's Outline," *BYU Studies* 20, no. 2 (winter 1980): 131–49, Noel B. Reynolds argues that a literary framework undergirding the first book of Nephi takes the form of a chiasmatic balancing of themes throughout. While it may be possible that Nephi indeed succeeded in doing what Reynolds says he did, I believe it possible to demonstrate (a) that Nephi utilized Lehi's record as the basis for his own, and (b) that Nephi included a brief outline—a virtual "table of contents"—of his historical narrative in 1 Nephi 19:1.

5. About five hundred years after Lehi left Jerusalem, during a transfer of sacred records from King Mosiah to Alma, Mosiah charged Alma to "keep a record of the people, handing them down . . . even as they had been handed down from the time that Lehi left Jerusalem" (Mosiah 28:20), revealing a tie between the tradition of keeping records and the name of Lehi.

6. As with any study of literary sources, difficulties persist. The major problem is how to distinguish written reports from oral communications, an issue not easily solved in every instance affecting Lehi. On the one hand, we can be certain that Nephi and Jacob appealed to a written source (a) when they say they have done so and (b) when they quote their father at some length, cases which clearly point to an extant document. On the other hand, we may in fact be dealing with oral reports when a written source is neither mentioned nor apparently quoted extensively. While bearing this in mind, I shall deal with the Lehi materials as if they were largely derived from his written record unless reasons exist for understanding them otherwise.

7. As observed in 1 Nephi 1:16, Lehi's record apparently did not include

much, if anything, from Lehi's brief ministry in Jerusalem (see 1 Nephi 1:18–20). Concerning prophecies, as Nephi details them, Lehi's writings contained primarily those which were directed to his family, "his children."

8. The relationship between (a) the large plates of Nephi, (b) the book of Lehi which was translated by Joseph Smith and then lost (see the first edition of the Book of Mormon [E. B. Grandin of Palmyra, N.Y., 1830, p. 1]), and (c) the remainder of the Book of Mormon has been graphically worked out most recently by Grant R. Hardy and Robert E. Parsons, "Book of Mormon Plates and Records," in *Encyclopedia of Mormonism,* ed. Daniel H. Ludlow (New York: Macmillan, 1992), 1:195–201. The book of Lehi, translated by Joseph Smith, consisted of an abridgment by Mormon of the record begun by Lehi's son Nephi (ca. 590 B.C.) and continued by succeeding scribes virtually down to the era of King Mosiah (ca. 130 B.C.). Aside from employing his name honorifically, this work apparently was not written in any part by Lehi and thus does not come within the purview of this study.

9. See 1 Nephi 19:1–2. Discussions appear in George Reynolds and Janne M. Sjodahl, *Commentary on the Book of Mormon,* 4th ed. (Salt Lake City: Deseret News, 1962), 1:194; Sidney B. Sperry, *Book of Mormon Compendium* (Salt Lake City: Bookcraft, 1968), 16, 43, 282; and Eldin Ricks, *Book of Mormon Commentary,* 2d ed. (Salt Lake City: Deseret News, 1953), 226.

10. Others have also noticed that Nephi employed Lehi's written account when compiling his own. For instance, Sidney B. Sperry suggests that the nine opening chapters of 1 Nephi were based upon Lehi's record, Nephi's personal work beginning only with chapter 10 (*Compendium,* 94). Although the commentary compiled from the work of George Reynolds and Janne M. Sjodahl expresses a similar view regarding the early chapters of 1 Nephi, it indicates that the division between the works of Lehi and Nephi occurs at the end of chapter 8 rather than chapter 9 (*Commentary,* 1:10; it may be important to note that Reynolds and Sjodahl did not collaborate to produce this commentary). In a discussion of the early segments of the Book of Mormon, Eldin Ricks basically adopts the position of Reynolds and Sjodahl (*Commentary,* 110). A close inspection of these and later chapters, however, indicates that these suggestions must be modified considerably since (a) Nephi includes important material in his opening chapters about himself and (b) both he and Jacob quote and paraphrase their father's words in later chapters.

11. Lehi's death is recorded in 2 Nephi 4:12, just before Nephi wrote that the Lord directed him to make the second, smaller set of plates (see 2 Nephi 5:30).

12. There remains the question why the "table of contents" for the large

plates (see 1 Nephi 19:1) seems to correspond so accurately to the content of 1 Nephi and 2 Nephi 1–3, which derive from the small plates. It is clear thus far that Lehi's record underpins both works of Nephi. If only because Lehi's record is reported to underlie both accounts (see 1 Nephi 19:1; 2 Nephi 5:29–33), the "table of contents" for the large plates would, in my view, approximate the content of the small plates. Furthermore, since 1 Nephi 19:1 describes so plainly what we find in 1 Nephi and 2 Nephi 1–3, it seems thoroughly safe to maintain that the two records of Nephi roughly paralleled one another (see again 1 Nephi 1:16–17).

13. Jeremiah, for example, opens his book by mentioning the kings whose reigns his ministry spanned (see Jeremiah 1:2–3) just before the account of his call (see Jeremiah 1:4–10). Similar juxtapositions occur in Isaiah 6:1; Ezekiel 1:1; Zephaniah 1:1; and Zechariah 1:1.

14. In fact, Lehi's call consisted of two visions that came in rapid succession. In the first, he had a surprising manifestation of a pillar of fire resting on a nearby rock, accompanied by a voice (see 1 Nephi 1:6). In the second, after returning home bewildered and fatigued by his first vision, Lehi saw the divine council as well as the coming Messiah, who brought him a book containing a prophecy of Jerusalem's fate (see 1 Nephi 1:8–15).

15. In addition, Nephi probably altered the opening account of Lehi's visions from first to third person. Nephi's narrative exhibits clear evidences of summarizing his father's report in at least two passages: (a) after a direct quotation in verse 13, Nephi outlines in verses 13 and 14 what his father had seen in the second vision; (b) verse 15 also forms a summary of what Lehi said (and sang) in response to his visions.

16. It may be argued that Nephi made the plates while still traveling in the Arabian wilderness, before coming to the ocean. In my opinion, however, the phrase "and it came to pass," found at the beginning of 1 Nephi 19:1, indicates that these events followed those recounted in chapter 18, since this expression in Hebrew serves to continue the story. Had Nephi smelted and fashioned this set of plates while still in the desert, he would doubtlessly have said so.

17. Sandwiched between these "we" passages are the accounts of how Nephi was able to find food after breaking his bow (see 1 Nephi 16:20–32) and of what occurred when Nephi's father-in-law, Ishmael, died (see 1 Nephi 16:34–39), incidents constituting digressions in the travel narrative.

18. The question naturally arises as to why I view the itinerary as the work of Lehi, not of Nephi. The matter cannot be decisively settled, for it remains possible that Nephi himself was largely responsible for the chronicle of "our journeyings in the wilderness" (1 Nephi 19:1). However, a review of the possibilities suggests that

Lehi was responsible for the desert itinerary. These are the options: (a) Lehi himself wrote the whole record (in this instance, the question would be solved); (b) Lehi dictated the record to a member of his family who served as scribe (in this case as well, the record would be attributed to Lehi); (c) Lehi directed Nephi or another family member to keep a desert diary (in this event, it is most probable that the record would reflect the name of the person who commissioned the work, that is, Lehi); (d) Nephi, with permission of and input from his father, wrote the wilderness record (to my mind, there is serious question whether the account would have been attributed to Nephi even in this instance, since it was a record of the desert wanderings of the family of Lehi, he being the patriarch); and (e) Nephi kept a diary in the desert without the knowledge of Lehi (a highly dubious proposition).

19. Nephi mentions only three other brothers when Lehi moved his family into the desert (see 1 Nephi 2:5). Later, in 2 Nephi 2:1, Lehi calls Jacob his firstborn "in the wilderness," clarifying that Jacob was born after the departure from Jerusalem.

20. The use of impermanent writing materials for certain purposes seems to have continued in Nephite society, because some 450 years later King Mosiah hypothetically describes the actions of a wicked king who "*teareth up* the laws of . . . righteousness" (Mosiah 29:22; emphasis added). In addition, the observation that a name can be "blotted out" (Mosiah 5:11) may point to a use of ink, besides engraving tools for metals.

21. Whether Nephi or Lehi would have mentioned engraving tools, even if Nephi had brought them back from Jerusalem along with the brass plates, is certainly open to question. As illustration, the sword of Laban is not mentioned with the annotated list of the contents of the brass plates (see 1 Nephi 5:11–16)—even though Nephi brought it. Rather, it is noted in contexts widely removed from concerns for records and record keeping (see 2 Nephi 5:14; Jacob 1:10). It is also possible, though unlikely, that one of Lehi's family members may have acquired engraving tools along the way.

22. The problem for Nephi was not how to refine ore but where he should go to find it (see 1 Nephi 17:9–10). An intriguing though unprovable suggestion is that if Lehi's family traveled through the Aqaba region (at the northern tip of the east arm of the Red Sea), where ore has been refined for millennia, Nephi may have learned his smelting skills there. See Lynn M. and Hope Hilton, *In Search of Lehi's Trail* (Salt Lake City: Deseret Book, 1976), 107, 110.

23. Ricks (*Commentary,* 227) suggests that "Nephi copied his father's record in its entirety from manuscript or scroll form to the durability of metal sheets." But he does not adduce any evidence.

24. It would be interesting to compare Lehi's last words to his family with the multiplying testamental literature which claims to record, in rather standardized ways, the last instructions of ancient patriarchs and prophets to their children. For recent studies on Lehi's last instructions, see Monte S. Nyman and Charles D. Tate Jr., eds., *The Book of Mormon: Second Nephi, The Doctrinal Structure* (Provo, Utah: Religious Studies Center, Brigham Young University, 1989).

25. Sperry (*Compendium,* 151–52) observes that "we are told neither how old Lehi was at the time of his death nor how many years had elapsed from the time the party had left Jerusalem before he passed away. This we do know—that less than thirty years had passed away after the Nephites left Jerusalem before his death" (see 2 Nephi 5:28).

26. In 1 Nephi 2:9–10, Nephi relates that "when my father saw that the waters of the river emptied into the fountain of the Red Sea, he spake unto Laman, saying: O that thou mightest be like unto this river, continually running into the fountain of all righteousness! And he also spake unto Lemuel: O that thou mightest be like unto this valley, firm and steadfast, and immovable in keeping the commandments of the Lord!" Hugh W. Nibley, in *An Approach to the Book of Mormon,* 3d ed. (Salt Lake City: Deseret Book and FARMS, 1988), 268, maintains that "Nephi seems to have been standing by, for he takes most careful note of the circumstance. The common practice was for the inspired words of the leader to be taken down in writing immediately."

27. On this occasion, in Jacob's discussion of pride, the other major topic (see Jacob 2:13–22), it does not once appear that he quotes directly what the Lord told him the night before (see Jacob 2:11). Instead, he paraphrases the Lord's words and intermingles his own observations with them. Only in verses 23–33 does he repeat directly the Lord's words, those pertaining to having one wife.

28. See Stanley R. Larson, "A Study of Some Textual Variations in the Book of Mormon Comparing the Original and Printer's Manuscripts and the 1830, the 1837, and the 1840 Editions" (master's thesis, Brigham Young University, 1974), 95–96. The printer's manuscript of the Book of Mormon was copied by Oliver Cowdery from the one originally dictated by Joseph Smith. The copy made by Oliver Cowdery was taken to the printer, E. B. Grandin, and became the basis for the first printed edition of the Book of Mormon. The original manuscript, written at Joseph Smith's dictation, is no longer extant for the passage in question (Jacob 3:5).

29. They consist of an extract that Lehi read from the book brought to him in the second vision of his call (see 1 Nephi 1:13), his exclamation at having read

this book (see 1 Nephi 1:14), words of the Lord spoken to Lehi in a dream (see 1 Nephi 2:1), Lehi's remark to his son Laman (see 1 Nephi 2:9) and the following comment to his son Lemuel (see 1 Nephi 2:10), his instructions to Nephi to return to Jerusalem for the brass plates (see 1 Nephi 3:2–6), Sariah's complaint against Lehi (see 1 Nephi 5:2) and his conciliatory conversation with her (see 1 Nephi 5:4–5), a further extract from Lehi's vision of the tree of life (see 1 Nephi 8:34), and what the Messiah's forerunner would say about the Messiah (see 1 Nephi 10:8).

30. 1 Nephi 2:1–10, and 14–15 all speak directly of Lehi.

31. See 1 Nephi 2:1, 9, 10.

32. This is the third time Nephi mentions that his father "dwelt in a tent." The earlier occurrences are in 1 Nephi 2:15 and 9:1. One is tempted to suggest that since these three instances all mark conclusions to sections wherein Nephi has summarized Lehi's record, Nephi may be using the phrase "dwelt in a tent" as a literary device to indicate a return to the narrative about himself. In support of this observation, I note that Nephi speaks of his father's tent twice more in 1 Nephi, the second instance underscoring my point. In the first case, Nephi merely relates that he returned there after his own vision of the tree of life (see 1 Nephi 15:1). But in the second instance, Nephi's mention of the tent forms part of a clear literary transition between two segments of his narrative (see 1 Nephi 16:6). Compare Psalms 78:55, 60; also compare Mitchell Dahood, *Psalms III,* Anchor Bible 17A (Garden City, N.Y.: Doubleday, 1970), 445.

33. It may well be that the "table of contents" of the brass plates (1 Nephi 5:11–16) also derives from Lehi's work.

34. We find several references to Lehi's dream as Nephi relates how he interpreted it for his brothers (see 1 Nephi 15:12–18, 21, 23, 26–30).

35. The commands to Lehi to move his camp may have derived from the itinerary (see 1 Nephi 2:2; 16:9; 17:44; 18:5).

36. The number of allusions to what Lehi did and said are too many to list and discuss. In most, it is impossible to determine whether we are dealing with matters from Lehi's annals. Many such references doubtless came from the memories of Nephi and Jacob.

37. The prophecy of Joseph came from the brass plates (see 2 Nephi 4:2). Lehi knew of other prophecies by Joseph since he speaks of "the prophecies which he [Joseph] wrote" (2 Nephi 4:2).

38. This allegory is quoted at length in Jacob 5. For studies on this important chapter, see Stephen D. Ricks and John W. Welch, eds., *The Allegory of the Olive Tree* (Salt Lake City: Deseret Book and FARMS, 1994); Kent P. Jackson,

"Nourished by the Good Word of God," in *Studies in Scripture, Vol. 7: 1 Nephi to Alma 29,* ed. Kent P. Jackson (Salt Lake City: Deseret Book, 1987), 185–95; and L. Gary Lambert, "Allegory of Zenos," in *Encyclopedia of Mormonism,* ed. Daniel H. Ludlow (New York: Macmillan, 1992), 1:31–32.

39. A similar point is made in 1 Nephi 15:12 as Nephi attempts to explain what Lehi meant. His brothers had not understood Lehi's comparison of themselves with the olive tree (see 1 Nephi 10:12–14). So Nephi declares to them "that the house of Israel was compared unto an olive-tree, by the Spirit of the Lord which was in our father; and behold are we not broken off from the house of Israel, and are we not a branch of the house of Israel?" (1 Nephi 15:12). This is how the verse reads in the original manuscript, after adding punctuation. Beginning with the printer's manuscript and continuing through the printed editions of the Book of Mormon, an *s* had been added to the word *father.* The original manuscript clarifies that it was Lehi who was moved by the Spirit to apply the olive tree comparison to his family and posterity, and this sense is recognized in the 1981 edition of the Book of Mormon, where the singular spelling has been restored (see Larson, "Some Textual Variations," 59).

40. On the family learning of the fulfillment of this prophecy, refer to 2 Nephi 1:4 and 6:8.

41. The titles *Christ* (Greek) and *Messiah* (Hebrew) mean the same thing: "anointed." It is possible, of course, that Joseph Smith—while translating—used the title *Christ* in contexts which dealt with the word *Messiah,* but see notes 42 and 43.

42. The terms by which Lehi designates the Messiah are *Lamb of God* (1 Nephi 10:10); *Holy One of Israel* (2 Nephi 1:10; 3:2); *God* (2 Nephi 1:10, 22, 24, 26–27; 2:2–3, 10); *Lord God* (2 Nephi 1:17); *Holy Messiah* (2 Nephi 2:6, 8); *Messiah* (1 Nephi 1:19; 10:4–5, 7, 9–11, 14, 17; 2 Nephi 1:10; 2:26; 3:5); *Lord* (1 Nephi 10:8, 14; 2 Nephi 1:15, 19, 27); *prophet* (1 Nephi 10:4); *Savior* (1 Nephi 10:4); *Redeemer* (1 Nephi 10:5–6, 14; 2 Nephi 1:10; 2:3); *One* (1 Nephi 1:9); *Firstfruits* (2 Nephi 2:9); *Holy One* (2 Nephi 2:10); *Mediator* (2 Nephi 2:28).

43. Nephi and Jacob use several titles which apparently go beyond what they could have found in the brass plates, assuming the brass plates included the full Pentateuch and many of the prophets' writings (see 1 Nephi 5:11–13; 19:21–23). 1 Nephi 19:23 presents an interesting problem. In all the printed editions except the most recent, we find the reference "the book of Moses." The original manuscript has it "the books of Moses." When Oliver Cowdery copied down the manuscript for the printer, he accidentally made *books* singular. This misreading persisted until the edition of 1981 (see Larson, "Some Textual

Variations," 67–68). The following titles and names used by Nephi seem more at home in a later era such as that of the New Testament or early Christianity: *Beloved Son* (2 Nephi 31:11); *Beloved* (2 Nephi 31:15); *Son of the living God* (2 Nephi 31:16); *Son of righteousness* (2 Nephi 26:9); *Son of the most high God* (1 Nephi 11:6); *Son of God* (1 Nephi 10:17; 11:7, 24; 2 Nephi 25:16, 19); *Only Begotten of the Father* (2 Nephi 25:12); *Jesus* (2 Nephi 26:12; 31:10; 33:4, 6); *Jesus Christ* (2 Nephi 25:19–20; 30:5); *Christ* (2 Nephi 11:4, 6–7; 25:16, 23–29; 26:1, 8, 12; 28:14; 30:7; 31:2, 13, 19–21; 32:3, 6, 9; 33:7, 9–12); *true vine* (1 Nephi 15:15); *light* (1 Nephi 17:13). The following names from Jacob fit the same situation: *Only Begotten Son* (Jacob 4:11); *Christ* (2 Nephi 10:3, 7; Jacob 1:4, 6–8; 2:19; 4:4–5, 11–12; 6:8–9; 7:2–3, 6, 9, 11, 14, 17, 19); *Jesus* (Jacob 4:6).

44. In 1 Nephi 19:10–17, Nephi summarizes points from the writings of Zenock, Neum, and particularly Zenos. In verse 21 of that chapter he indicates that these teachings were on the brass plates (see also Alma 33:12).

45. It may be urged that in the Book of Mormon we have mere hints and glimpses from the writings of Zenock and Zenos and that, consequently, it is not possible to draw very firm conclusions. In my view, however, Alma brought together the passages from the writings of these two men which proved a point about the Son of God (see Alma 33:11, 13, 16). Zenos and Zenock called the Messiah *Son* whereas Alma called Him *Son of God* (see Alma 33:14, 17, 18, 22). Had Alma known of a passage in which either Zenock or Zenos mentioned the *Son of God,* he surely would have cited it to make his point to the Zoramites.

46. The first to adopt such a title was Nephi in his narration of how he had sought to receive the vision which his father had seen of both the tree of life and the Messiah. Curiously, as soon as Nephi inscribes the title *Son of God,* he adds the parenthetical explanation, "And the Son of God was the Messiah who should come" (1 Nephi 10:17). When did Nephi initially learn this title, especially since Lehi apparently did not use it? The only clear hint occurs at the beginning of his own parallel vision of the tree of life, which he begins narrating a few lines later, starting in chapter 11. On that occasion, he was told by the Spirit that after he had seen "a man descending out of heaven," he was to "bear record that it is the Son of God" (1 Nephi 11:7). In Nephi's account on the small plates, this is the first recorded notice of Nephi's having heard the title *Son of God* (he had apparently learned from the Spirit the expanded form—*Son of the Most High God*—just before this [see 1 Nephi 11:6]). It might be argued that Nephi knew such titles but had not utilized them in 1 Nephi until this point. Against this, I should point out that thus far, when speaking of the Messiah, Nephi had consistently employed the language of his father. Then in 1 Nephi 10:17, when he introduces the term

Son of God, he even adds a note of explanation. Since evidently the first person ever to mention that title to Nephi was the Spirit in the vision (see 1 Nephi 11:6–7), we are left to presume that before this experience Nephi did not know the term.

47. The term *dream* is clearly to be understood in the inspired sense. Of the seven dreams and visions of Lehi, three are called dreams (see 1 Nephi 2:1–2; 3:2; 8:2). In the final instance, Lehi himself equates dream with vision: "Behold, I have dreamed a dream; or, in other words, I have seen a vision" (1 Nephi 8:2).

48. Nephi's employment of the phrase "saw and heard" (1 Nephi 1:19) may be intended to recall what Lehi "saw and heard" in the very first vision (the phrase occurs twice in 1 Nephi 1:6). If so, it becomes very likely that Lehi had learned about the coming Messiah in this first experience. It is impossible, however, to recover exactly how much was revealed to him concerning the Messiah on this occasion, since Nephi does not elaborate.

49. This type of vision forms the standard motif of the prophet or seer being introduced into the council of the Lord. Isaiah, for example, experienced this when he received his call (see Isaiah 6:1, 8; Jeremiah 23:18, 22; Revelation 4:2–4).

50. In 1 Nephi 1:4 we read that "many prophets" had come to Jerusalem "prophesying unto the people that they must repent, or the great city Jerusalem must be destroyed." Among those prophets would have been Jeremiah, who had already been saying this for twenty-five years, and Habakkuk, who was prophesying and writing between 608 and 598 B.C. See also Zephaniah 1.

51. One item has to do with the condition of the stream of water, which Lehi had overlooked when he saw the vision. It was Nephi who, after recounting his experience with the corroborating vision, adds this curious note: "The water which my father saw was filthiness; and so much was his mind swallowed up in other things that he beheld not the filthiness of the water" (1 Nephi 15:27). When one examines Lehi's narration, what Nephi says proves true. Lehi describes the water simply as "a river of water" (1 Nephi 8:13), not indicating whether it appeared muddy or clear. In contrast, Nephi is very explicit about its appearance, calling it "the fountain of filthy water . . . and the depths thereof are the depths of hell" (1 Nephi 12:16).

52. Incidentally, Nephi explains that "from time to time" writing would appear on the compass to give directions to Lehi's family while still in the desert (1 Nephi 16:29).

53. In regard to the Urim and Thummim in Old Testament usage, see Exodus 28:30; Leviticus 8:8; Numbers 27:21; Deuteronomy 33:8; 1 Samuel 28:6;

Ezra 2:63; and Nehemiah 7:65. See also Paul Y. Hoskisson, "Urim and Thummim," in *Encyclopedia of Mormonism,* 4:1499–1500.

54. Nahum saw a similar vision of Nineveh under siege and finally falling (see Nahum 2:1–3:3, 10–15).

55. The revelation may have concerned people at Jerusalem or it may have concerned Lehi's extended family. If the latter, Benjamin's assertion that members of the traveling party "were unfaithful" (Mosiah 1:17) takes on a more focused meaning.

56. These three major elements of Lehi's instruction—fidelity to spouse, opposition as an essential ingredient of existence, and the Adam-Redeemer relationship in the plan of salvation—are supplemented by other less-emphasized themes which, when noted, exhibit a rich variety: Lehi's teachings on the tree of life (see 1 Nephi 8:2–35), the fall of Jerusalem (see 1 Nephi 1:13, 19), the coming of the Messiah (see 1 Nephi 1:19; 10:4–11; 2 Nephi 2:6–9), the scattering and gathering of Israel (see 1 Nephi 9:3; 10:3, 12–14), and the important ministry of the seer of the latter days who is to take God's message to Lehi's descendants (see 2 Nephi 3:6–21).

— 11 —

Jacob: Prophet, Theologian, Historian

Robert J. Matthews

Inasmuch as all the doctrines that have been revealed since Adam have been communicated to us through the teachings of one prophet or another, I am honored and eager to present a paper on the life of one of the greatest of these, Jacob, son of Lehi. There have been few people in history who have possessed the combination of spirituality, intellectual capacity, judgment, literary ability, parentage, faith, and seership that Jacob did. He exhibited an inherent desire for righteousness. He was a plain-spoken man but used very descriptive language. With all these natural endowments, what an opportunity and advantage it was for him to have Lehi as a father and Nephi as an older brother to get him started right.

Our sources about Jacob consist of thirty-one pages in the Book of Mormon of Jacob's own words (thirteen in 2 Nephi; eighteen in the book of Jacob), plus eleven brief references to him by Nephi, Lehi, Enos, Alma, and Mormon (see 1 Nephi 18:7; 18:19; 2 Nephi 2:1–4; 5:6; 5:26; 11:1; 11:3; 31:1; Enos 1:1–3; Words of Mormon 1:3; Alma 3:6).

There have been but few writings in the Church giving biographical

---

Robert J. Matthews, former dean of Religious Education, is an emeritus professor of ancient scripture at Brigham Young University.

references to Jacob. In 1891 Elder George Reynolds offered a brief biographical sketch in his *Dictionary of the Book of Mormon.*[1] In 1966 I included a half-page entry on Jacob and a biographical note in my *Who's Who in the Book of Mormon.*[2] In October 1976, the *Ensign* magazine carried a short but informative article by C. Terry Warner.[3] And in 1981, the index to the new edition of the Book of Mormon offered a list of twenty-six well-documented statements about Jacob. I have benefited from each of these publications and have endeavored to include all that these previous works have offered. But beyond their separate contributions, I have tried to make this paper the most complete recitation on Jacob that I could, by basing it on the text of the Book of Mormon itself, and by avoiding unreasonable speculation. I have admired Jacob for more than forty years, and that admiration has increased with this study.

OVERVIEW OF JACOB'S LIFE

Jacob is first mentioned in 1 Nephi 18:7 when Lehi's group was about to enter the ship on the Arabian coast to sail to the promised land. Nephi introduces Jacob in this manner: "And now, my father had begat two sons in the wilderness; the elder was called Jacob and the younger Joseph."

These two sons were born during the eight years Lehi's family journeyed in the wilderness (see 1 Nephi 17:4). We do not know the exact date of Jacob's birth, but we know it had to be within the first seven years of their journey in the wilderness, since Joseph was born after Jacob and was also born within the eight-year period. Since Lehi left Jerusalem in 600 B.C., Jacob had to have been born between 600 and 593 B.C.

Lehi's group spent an undetermined length of time at Bountiful while the ship was being built. This would likely take a year or two. If the ship set sail at about 590 B.C. and arrived in the promised land about 589 B.C., the boy Jacob could be not less than three nor more than ten years old at that time. There is, however, additional information that has a bearing on the date of Jacob's birth.

Nephi's record of his family's travels in the wilderness and of the rebellions of Laman, Lemuel, and Ishmael's sons while voyaging at sea tells us that his "parents being stricken in years, and having suffered much grief because of their children . . . were brought down, yea, even upon their sickbeds" (1 Nephi 18:17). Nephi said Lehi and Sariah's sorrow was so great that it almost caused their deaths, and that "Jacob and Joseph also, being young, having need of much nourishment, were grieved because of the afflictions of their mother" (1 Nephi 18:18–19).

Lehi, recalling these trying times, especially those in the wilderness, said to Joseph, "Thou wast born in the wilderness of mine afflictions; yea, in the days of my greatest sorrow did thy mother bear thee" (2 Nephi 3:1). And to Jacob he said: "Thou art my first-born in the days of my tribulation in the wilderness. And behold, in thy childhood thou hast suffered afflictions and much sorrow, because of the rudeness of thy brethren. Nevertheless, Jacob, my first-born in the wilderness, thou knowest the greatness of God; and he shall consecrate thine afflictions for thy gain" (2 Nephi 2:1–2).

The tone of these verses suggests that certainly Jacob and possibly Joseph were old enough to remember their parents' suffering, the rebellion of Laman and Lemuel, and the goodness of Nephi while they were in the wilderness. Hence, they would not have been mere infants at the time all of this was happening. Such evidence argues for Jacob's having been born during the early part of the wilderness journey and therefore being at least seven and possibly as many as ten years old when they arrived in the promised land.

Lehi no doubt named his son Jacob in memory of the patriarch Jacob, father of the twelve tribes of Israel. It may well be that Lehi and Sariah, embarking on a journey toward a new promised land and having recently obtained the plates of brass, a record of the house of Israel, were impressed to name their new son after their great ancestor. In like manner we conclude that Lehi's next son, Joseph, was named in honor of Joseph of Egypt, who was also their direct ancestor and would have been spoken of often in the plates of brass (see 2 Nephi 3:3–4, 22).

All that we know about Jacob's life we have gleaned from the writings on the small plates of Nephi—the religious record. More detailed information would probably be found on the large plates of Nephi and also in Lehi's record (see 1 Nephi 19:1–2; see also 1 Nephi 1:16–17; 6:1; 9:1–5), which Nephi says contains genealogical information "and the more part of all our proceedings in the wilderness." I thus presume that the 116 pages of lost manuscript, which were a translation of Mormon's abridgment of the "Book of Lehi" (see heading of D&C 3), would contain considerably more about the boyhood of Jacob than does our present record.

After the death of Father Lehi in the promised land, the Lord warned Nephi to separate himself from the families of his elder brothers and to take those people with him who believed in the revelations of God. Nephi speaks of this event: "Wherefore, it came to pass that I, Nephi, did take my family, and also Zoram and his family, and Sam, mine elder brother and his family, and Jacob and Joseph, my younger brethren, and also my sisters, and all those who would go with me. And all those who would go with me were those who believed in the warnings and the revelations of God" (2 Nephi 5:6).

We know from an earlier passage (see 1 Nephi 16:7) that Laman, Lemuel, Sam, Nephi, and Zoram each married daughters of Ishmael, and it is interesting that now, a decade or so later, each of them is said to have "his family," but Jacob and Joseph are referred to only in the singular with no mention of a family. We know but little about when Jacob was married, to whom, or the manner of his family. We are informed that he did indeed have a family and that he taught them many times in the "nurture and admonition of the Lord" (Enos 1:1) and often spoke to them of "eternal life, and the joy of the saints" (Enos 1:3). We also know that he had a righteous son named Enos (see Jacob 7:27; Enos 1:1–3). A posterity is also shown in the prophetic instruction to Jacob that the small plates would be handed down through his seed from generation to generation (see Jacob 1:3).

As to how old he got or when he eventually died, we do not have much detail. The only certain date we have in the mature years of Jacob's life is found in Jacob 1:1, where he indicates that fifty-five "years had passed away from the time that Lehi left Jerusalem." This would be 545 B.C. and is near the time when Jacob became the keeper of the records and the spiritual leader of his people. This seems to be very near the time of Nephi's death (see Jacob 1:9–12; 2:1). Jacob would have been at least fifty years old at the time. All the events recorded in the book of Jacob happened after that, which as we will see took a number of years. When Jacob died, he was therefore "some years" past fifty (see Jacob 7:1).

WRITING THE BOOK OF JACOB

Nephi had been both the spiritual and secular leader. But Jacob informs us that when Nephi became old he separated the responsibilities of the Church and the secular government and conferred each upon a different person. To Jacob he gave the sacred records known as the small plates. Although the report does not specifically say it, I assume that Jacob was also appointed at that time to succeed Nephi as the spiritual leader. Nephi conferred the responsibility of the civil government upon a man who became known among the people as second Nephi (see Jacob 1:1–11).

Nephi instructed Jacob that he should write upon the small plates only those things that were "most precious" such as "preaching which was sacred, or revelation which was great, or prophesying," and that he should touch but lightly on the history of the people (Jacob 1:2–4). That type of commandment required that Jacob wait for a while before writing upon the plates, since it calls for time to make comparisons and gain perspective. We can discern that Jacob waited for some length of time after he was given the records before he began writing, for in his first chapter he speaks of the "reigns of the kings" after Nephi, and also tells us that the successors to Nephi had taken the title of second, and then third Nephi and so forth (see Jacob 1:9–11; see also Jacob 3:13). He would not have been able to make such a glance into the past had he written immediately.

The book of Jacob consists of three main sections. The first is Jacob 1:1 through 3:14, which contains a lengthy sermon by Jacob against the materialistic influence of riches and pride, and words against the grosser crime of immorality. Jacob concludes this portion of the book with these words: "These plates are called the plates of Jacob, and they were made by the hand of Nephi. And I make an end of speaking these words" (Jacob 3:14).

The second section is Jacob 4–6 and includes the marvelous allegory of Zenos. This section concludes with Jacob's farewell to his people until they meet at the "pleasing bar of God" (Jacob 6:13). It seems that Jacob had intended this "farewell" to be the end of his book.

The third and final section, Jacob 7, was written "some years" (Jacob 7:1) later than the other two parts and tells of a man named Sherem, who was an anti-Christ. Apparently Jacob's encounter with Sherem was so important that he added it to his record, even though it was some years after he had thought it was finished. Jacob concludes with an observation that his writing "has been small" (Jacob 7:27), which probably means small in comparison to the longer books of 1 and 2 Nephi.

The closing words of Jacob are these:

"And it came to pass that I, Jacob, began to be old; and the record of this people being kept on the other plates of Nephi, wherefore, I conclude this record, declaring that I have written according to the best of my knowledge, by saying that the time passed away with us, and also our lives passed away like as it were unto us a dream, we being a lonesome and a solemn people, wanderers, cast out from Jerusalem, born in tribulation, in a wilderness, and hated of our brethren, which caused wars and contentions; wherefore, we did mourn out our days.

"And I, Jacob, saw that I must soon go down to my grave; wherefore, I said unto my son Enos: Take these plates. And I told him the things which my brother Nephi had commanded me, and he promised obedience unto the commands. And I make an end of my writing upon these plates, which writing has been small; and to the reader I bid farewell, hoping that many of my brethren may read my words. Brethren, adieu" (Jacob 7:26–27).

MULTIPLE WRITINGS AND COPIES

Understanding that Jacob wrote on the small plates over a period of years with great care and selection leads to another important conclusion about his writing pattern and probably that of other Nephite prophets. A casual reader may think that what was engraved on the plates was all the writing the prophets did. However, Jacob makes an observation about the difficulty of engraving on metal compared to writing on other material:

"Now behold, it came to pass that I, Jacob, having ministered much unto my people in word, (and I cannot write but a little of my words, because of the difficulty of engraving our words upon plates) and we know that the things which we write upon plates must remain;

"But whatsoever things we write upon anything save it be upon plates must perish and vanish away; but we can write a few words upon plates, which will give our children, and also our beloved brethren, a small degree of knowledge concerning us, or concerning their fathers—

"Now in this thing we do rejoice; and we labor diligently to engraven these words upon plates, hoping that our beloved brethren and our children will receive them with thankful hearts" (Jacob 4:1–3).

We see from this explanation that the Nephites did write upon other materials, probably leather or paper. I would conclude therefore that what Jacob finally engraved on metal plates would rarely, if ever, be his first draft of a document.

JACOB'S MINISTRY

When Jacob became the chief spiritual leader and prophet of the Nephites at about 545 B.C., he had already been tried, tested, and proven worthy, and for twenty to thirty years had been a vigorous preacher of righteousness under Nephi's leadership. At an early age Jacob had a vision of the Savior. In Lehi's blessing to Jacob, recorded in 2 Nephi 2, we read: "Wherefore, thy soul shall be blessed . . . and thy days shall be spent in the service of thy God. Wherefore, I know that thou art redeemed, because of the righteousness of thy Redeemer. . . . And thou hast beheld in thy youth his glory; wherefore, thou art blessed even as they unto whom he shall minister in the flesh" (2 Nephi 2:3–4).

Relatively early in his lifetime, Jacob was consecrated a priest and a teacher "over the land of my people" by his brother Nephi (2 Nephi 5:26; see also 6:2; Jacob 1:18). That he "came in at the gate" (D&C

43:7) and was properly and regularly called to the work in the established order of the kingdom of God is shown by Jacob's own statement about his call to the ministry: "I, Jacob, [have] been called of God, and ordained after the manner of his holy order, and [have] been consecrated by my brother Nephi" (2 Nephi 6:2).

THE PRIESTHOOD AND THE LAW OF MOSES

It is necessary to say something about Jacob's consecration as "a priest and teacher." The faithful Nephites from Lehi to the time of Christ were diligent in performing the requirements of the law of Moses. It is true that they also had the gospel in its fulness and the Melchizedek Priesthood, yet they understood that it was necessary to obey the ordinances of the law of Moses until that law was fulfilled (see 2 Nephi 25:24–30; Jacob 4:5; Mosiah 13:30).

As originally established in Israel under the law of Moses, the Aaronic Priesthood was a hereditary office, and the priests were selected only from the family of Aaron. The Lord designated that the lesser priesthood was to be conferred on men called from the tribe of Levi, that within the tribe the direct descendants of Aaron should be designated as the priests (the highest office within the Levitical or Aaronic Priesthood), and that the presiding priests (high priest or "bishop") should be called only from the firstborn among the descendants of Aaron (see Exodus 30:30–31; 40:15; D&C 68:16–19; 84:18; 107:13–17). The Prophet Joseph Smith had this to say about the established order: "The Levitical Priesthood is forever hereditary—fixed on the head of Aaron and his sons forever, and was in active operation down to Zacharias the father of John."[4]

There were no descendants of Levi or Aaron among the Nephites because Lehi's family was of Joseph (see 1 Nephi 6:2), rather than Levi. Therefore, the Nephites could not be regularly called to officiate in the ordinances of the law of Moses and Aaronic Priesthood. However, since the Melchizedek Priesthood encompasses all the powers and authority of the Aaronic, worthy men among the Nephites, such as Jacob and Joseph, could be consecrated as priests and teachers and could function in the ordinances of the law of Moses, as well as the gospel, by virtue of the Melchizedek Priesthood (see D&C 68:18–20). These were not the offices of priest and teacher as we know them today in the Aaronic Priesthood. It should be clear to us that the Nephites did not have an established order of priests and Levites such as that found in ancient Israel, because there were no Levites among them. Yet there is strong evidence that the Nephite leaders held the Melchizedek Priesthood since they performed the ordinances of the law of Moses, which they could not have done unless they had priesthood authority. Since they were not of the lineage to hold the Aaronic Priesthood, they must have held this Melchizedek Priesthood, which has no limitations on tribal lineage.

After the law of Moses was fulfilled by the Atonement of Jesus Christ, the stipulations pertaining to the lineage of Levi and Aaron were no longer in effect. Hence after the coming of Christ, the Nephites could ordain non-Levite men to all of the Aaronic Priesthood offices even as we do today in the Church. However, in the restoration of all things, Aaron's lineage shall yet again be given a special assignment.[5]

JACOB'S COLORFUL METHODS

We will now return to the account of Jacob's ministry. In 2 Nephi 6 through 10, Nephi included a lengthy sermon that Jacob had delivered to the people. We are not informed what the occasion was, but we can discern that it was a conference or a special gathering, because Nephi appointed Jacob to speak and requested that his topic include those parts of Isaiah we call chapters 49 through 52. Although the written account of this sermon occupies thirteen pages in 2 Nephi, it is only a portion of what Jacob said at the time. The discourse was so long that it took Jacob two days to deliver it. Nephi was so pleased with the discourse that he recorded part of it on the small plates and then commented: "And now, Jacob spake many more things to my people at that time; nevertheless only these things [2 Nephi 6–10] have I caused to be written" (2 Nephi 11:1). The words "at that time" further suggest that this was a particular occasion or conference. And there can be no missing the fact that Nephi recognized that his younger brother had a special ability to declare the word of the Lord and teach the people.

At the beginning of this sermon, Jacob says a few things that are useful to us in learning about him as a person and as a teacher. First, he states his authority as his having been "called of God, and ordained after the manner of his holy order," and "consecrated" by Nephi. He then informs his hearers that he has already spoken to them of "exceedingly many things" but wants to speak again, for he is "desirous for the welfare of" their souls and has great anxiety for his people. He has previously exhorted them with "all diligence" and taught "the words of [his] father" and has "spoken unto [them] concerning all things which are written, from the creation of the world" (2 Nephi 6:2–3). He then explains:

"And now, behold, I would speak unto you concerning things which are, and which are to come; wherefore, I will read you the words of Isaiah. And they are the words which my brother has desired that I should speak unto you. And I speak unto you for your sakes, that ye may learn and glorify the name of your God. And now, the words which I shall read are they which Isaiah spake concerning all the house of Israel; wherefore, they may be likened unto you, for ye are of the house of Israel. And there are many things which have been spoken by Isaiah which may be likened unto you, because ye are of the house of Israel" (2 Nephi 6:4–5).

It is clear that Jacob was lively and energetic in his ministry, a preacher of the gospel, a student of the holy scriptures, and an exhorter to righteousness. Nephi respected him and approved of his preaching and his doctrine. Nephi even tells us that one of the reasons he likes Jacob so much is that Jacob is a personal eyewitness of the Redeemer and therefore has something important to say. Nephi places Jacob alongside Isaiah and himself: "And now I, Nephi, write more of the words of Isaiah, for my soul delighteth in his words. For I will liken his words unto my people, and I will send them forth unto all my children, for he verily saw my Redeemer, even as I have seen him. And my brother, Jacob, also has seen him as I have seen him; wherefore, I will send their words forth unto my children to prove unto them that my words are true. Wherefore, by the words of three, God hath said, I will establish my word" (2 Nephi 11:2–3).

The records show that early in life Jacob had exhibited those traits of stability, spiritual capacity, and doctrinal clarity that make him one of the outstanding Book of Mormon prophets.

Jacob not only covered a multitude of subjects, "all things which are written, from the creation of the world" (2 Nephi 6:3), but he demonstrated his sincerity and illustrated his seriousness in a number of ways. He was descriptive in his language, using a large number of adjectives and metaphors. In addition, he was blunt and forceful in his message. He expressed great love for the people but was not of the opinion that he must always maintain a positive image or say only nice things. Without being crude, he was nevertheless devastatingly direct in reminding the people of their sins.

He must have been animated as a speaker, for on at least one occasion as he stood before the people he shook their sins from his garments. His words are so graphic that we need to read them to feel the impact: "O, my beloved brethren, remember my words. Behold, I take off my garments, and I shake them before you; I pray the God of my salvation that he view me with his all-searching eye; wherefore, ye shall know at the last day, when all men shall be judged of their works, that the God of Israel did witness that I shook your iniquities from my soul, and that I stand with brightness before him, and am rid of your blood" (2 Nephi 9:44).

There is no way Jacob could have shaken his clothing in that manner without attracting considerable attention. It is significant that he did this while he was a relatively young man serving under the leadership of Nephi. He was not the prophet at that time, but he was a prophet in the making. From the record, we learn that Jacob was taught by the Spirit and was a bold, charismatic expounder of the gospel of Jesus Christ. By reading his words, I developed a mental image of him illustrated by terms such as *stalwart, strong, courageous, compassionate, deliberate, forthright, meek, dignified, appropriate, reflective, poetic, sensitive,* and *kind.*

It is noteworthy that in the thirty-one pages of the Book of

Mormon containing firsthand material given us from Jacob's mouth and pen, he says little about himself. When he does, he usually focuses on his ministry, his call, his preaching, his visits from an angel, and so forth. His interest is in the sacred word and the doctrine. Although that leaves us without personal details, it nevertheless tells us something about him.

SUBJECT MATTER OF JACOB'S TEACHINGS

We have already mentioned that Jacob taught the words of his father and that he taught "all things . . . from the creation" (2 Nephi 6:3) from the scriptures. We have also noted that he enjoyed using the words of Isaiah. Following is a discussion about some of Jacob's prominent teachings, specifically noting what we owe to him, or learn specifically from him, in the Book of Mormon. These are doctrines that we would not have in such clarity were it not for his teachings. In making this selection, I chose topics on which I turn to Jacob for help in teaching. That is, I chose things for which Jacob is sometimes the only source, or in some instances the best source, and always a very good source.

The scattering and gathering of Israel. Although Jacob is only one of several Book of Mormon writers who discusses the scattering and gathering of Israel, he is probably the most prolific on the subject. I don't think anyone has revealed more about this subject than he has, unless possibly Nephi. Jacob informs us that he knows whereof he speaks because it was told him by an angel (see 2 Nephi 6:9, 11), or he read of it from the writings of Isaiah or Zenos, or he was taught it by the Spirit (see Jacob 4:15). He speaks in detail of the destruction of Jerusalem by the Babylonians and also of a second destruction and scattering of the Jews after the time of Christ (see 2 Nephi 6:8–15; 9:1–2; 10:1–22). His great interest in the worldwide scattering and gathering of Israel and their eventual acceptance of the Lord Jesus Christ led him to quote the lengthy allegory of Zenos found in Jacob 5. We are ever grateful to Jacob for including this marvelous excerpt from the plates of brass, which is the most comprehensive statement we have on the scattering and gathering anywhere in scripture.

What if there were no Atonement? In 2 Nephi 9 Jacob presents a most informative explanation of the Fall of Adam and the Savior's Atonement. In this chapter Jacob explains that the great Creator Himself is the Holy One of Israel, who will come and die for all mankind and provide an infinite Atonement (see 2 Nephi 9:5–7). This statement by Jacob is the first use of the phrase "infinite atonement" in the Book of Mormon. What would have been the consequences if there had been no Atonement by Jesus Christ? Do you know the answer? Jacob knew.

He declares that because of the Fall of Adam, which has passed upon all mankind, if there were not an infinite Atonement the fleshly bodies of all mankind would return to the earth never to receive a resurrection, and the spirits of mankind would all become devils, forever miserable, and forever subject to the devil. "And our spirits must have become like unto him, and we become devils, angels to a devil . . . in misery, like unto himself" (2 Nephi 9:9). This declaration about what would have been the fate of mankind, especially of man's spirit, if there were no Savior, is plainer than is found in any other passage of scripture and is one of the greatest testimonies of the benefit mankind receives from the Atonement of our Redeemer. If you want to see how little this is known and thus how important this information is, test it on your family or friends. Ask them what the condition of our spirits would be if there had been no Atonement. Few will understand this without the help of Jacob. We find ourselves turning to 2 Nephi 9:7–9 again and again in teaching the Atonement of Jesus Christ.

Jacob's vivid use of language. Jacob continues his discourse by speaking of death, hell, the grave, paradise, resurrection, judgment, spiritual death, redemption, happiness, misery, obedience, disobedience, and other topics that belong to the plan of salvation. But Jacob doesn't call it simply the plan of salvation, he labels it the "merciful plan of the great Creator" (2 Nephi 9:6), the "great plan of our God" (2 Nephi 9:13), or the "way of deliverance of our God" (2 Nephi 9:11). Likewise, the work of the devil is "that cunning plan of the evil one" (2 Nephi 9:28).

Furthermore, Jacob does not simply speak of "death," but of "the slumber of death" (Jacob 3:11), and three times he speaks of death as an "awful monster" (2 Nephi 9:10, 19, 26). If a person neglects to keep the commandments, he is not merely disobedient; he "wasteth the days of his probation, [and] awful is his state" (2 Nephi 9:27). He doesn't say that mankind is under the eye of God, but that man is under the "all-searching eye" of God (2 Nephi 9:44). In one breath Jacob speaks of "awful fear," "awful guilt," "awful misery," and "awful reality" awaiting the ungodly (2 Nephi 9:46–47).

In describing the futility of mortal man's rebellion against God, Jacob mentions "the piercing eye of Almighty God" (Jacob 2:10) and exclaims, "O that he would show you that he can pierce you, and with one glance of his eye he can smite you to the dust" (Jacob 2:15). To illustrate the scope of the Lord's knowledge, he proclaims, "How unsearchable are the depths of the mysteries of him; . . . it is impossible that man should find out all his ways" (Jacob 4:8), and "he knoweth all things, and there is not anything save he knows it" (2 Nephi 9:20). Jacob likes adjectives to accompany his nouns, so he speaks of the "great Creator" (2 Nephi 9:5), the "merciful plan" (2 Nephi 9:6), the "infinite atonement" (2 Nephi 9:7), "captive bodies" in the grave, and "captive spirits" in hell (2 Nephi 9:12). He speaks of uncleanness, nakedness, guilt, and perfect knowledge (see 2 Nephi 9:14). Jacob glories in the majesty of God, and when he speaks of Him he exults with phrases such as, "O the greatness and the justice of our God" (2 Nephi 9:17), "O the greatness of the mercy of our God" (2 Nephi 9:19), "O how great the holiness of our God" (2 Nephi 9:20). We do not have anything else equal to Jacob's preaching. The Book of Mormon mentions "the gift of preaching" (Alma 9:21), and Jacob had such a gift.

Riches, pride, and unchastity. One of Jacob's strongest discourses is centered on the curse of trusting in material riches, the problem of harboring pride, and the damning effects of immorality. His teachings on these subjects are among the best we have in the scriptures, not only for their content but also for the directness of his message and the beauty and power of his language. In speaking of these subjects, Jacob talks of "the pleasing word of God" (Jacob 2:8) and says that "the hand of providence hath smiled upon [the people] most pleasingly" so that they have become rich in material things (Jacob 2:13), but as a consequence they have also become proud. He rebukes the men who have been untrue to their marriage vows, saying they have "broken the hearts of [their] tender wives, and lost the confidence of [their] children, because of [their] bad examples before them," and therefore "many hearts died, pierced with deep wounds" (Jacob 2:35). Jacob says this situation is like "daggers placed to pierce their souls and wound their delicate minds" (Jacob 2:9).

The name "Christ." Although the Book of Mormon speaks of the Savior a great many times, beginning in the very first chapter, it does not introduce the words *Jesus* or *Christ* until seventy-eight pages into the book. For example, the book of 1 Nephi makes 150 references to the Savior, using twenty-three different names, but it never uses the name *Jesus* or *Christ.* The first use of the name *Christ* in the Book of Mormon is in 2 Nephi 10:3, in Jacob's lengthy two-day sermon. It appears, from the way Jacob says it, that this is a new term among them: "Wherefore, as I said unto you, it must needs be expedient that Christ—for in the last night the angel spake unto me that this should be his name—should come among the Jews."

It is significant that Jacob emphasized his words by declaring that an angel had given him this new name just the night before. I am not surprised that this specific information was made known through this unusual and excellent prophet Jacob. The Nephites already knew of the Atonement and they had many different names for the Savior, but Jacob seems to have given them the very word and pronunciation of the name *Christ.*

The power of faith. Jacob's entire life is a reflection of his faith in the Lord Jesus Christ. He explains that when Sherem the anti-Christ sought him out it was in the "hope to shake me from the faith," because Sherem knew that "I, Jacob, had faith in Christ who should come" (Jacob 7:3–5). However, Jacob had had "many revelations," had "truly . . . seen angels," and had "heard the voice of the Lord speaking unto [him] in very word, from time to time; wherefore [he] could not be shaken" (Jacob 7:5).

In Jacob 4:6 he relates some of the miraculous things which accompany the kind of faith that he and the other prophets possessed:

"Wherefore, we search the prophets, and we have many revelations and the spirit of prophecy; and having all these witnesses we obtain a hope, and our faith becometh unshaken, insomuch that we truly can command in the name of Jesus and the very trees obey us, or the mountains, or the waves of the sea" (Jacob 4:6).

We do not have an account of Jacob's commanding the mountains, the waves, or the trees to obey, but he seems to be familiar with such miracles. He reasons with the reader that it should not be surprising that God can give a man power to command the elements and that the elements will obey, since God created the world in the first place by the "power of his word." So why would God not be able to command the earth, "according to his will and pleasure" (Jacob 4:7–9)?

Obtaining a hope in Christ. Closely associated with having faith is what Jacob calls "obtaining a hope in Christ" (see Jacob 2:19; 4:6). All the prophets speak of "hope," but Jacob is unique in the way he uses the word. His phrase of "obtaining *a* hope" is more than just having "hope" and seems to be the assurance or testimony that one has reached a particular state or spiritual condition and a special relationship with the Lord. Here are some of Jacob's words on the subject: "Before ye seek for riches, seek ye for the kingdom of God. And after ye have obtained a hope in Christ ye shall obtain riches, if ye seek them; and ye will seek them for the intent to do good" (Jacob 2:18–19). And also, "We knew of Christ, and we had a hope of his glory many hundred years before his coming" (Jacob 4:4). And again, "We search the prophets, and we have many revelations and the spirit of prophecy; and having all these witnesses we obtain a hope, and our faith becometh unshaken" (Jacob 4:6). Jacob urges his hearers to have faith and to be reconciled to God through the Atonement of Christ, having "obtained a good hope of glory . . . before he manifesteth himself in the flesh" (Jacob 4:11).

The phrase "a hope" is used two other times in the Book of Mormon by Alma the Younger (see Alma 13:29; 25:16), but the context of each shows that it is used differently than Jacob uses it. In all, the word *hope* appears fifty times in the Book of Mormon and is used by eight different prophets. Jacob, however, is unique in using it in the sense of obtaining "a hope," which is an achievement of something beyond simply "hoping."

All the prophets knew of Christ. That all the prophets knew of and testified of the coming of Christ is a fundamental gospel concept. The Old Testament in its present condition is not at all clear on this matter, so we look to latter-day revelation for evidence. There are numerous passages in the Book of Mormon that can be used to teach this concept, but none better than two passages in the book of Jacob. When I want a scripture that is clear and to the point on this subject I cite the following from Jacob: "We knew of Christ, and we had a hope of his glory many hundred years before his coming; and not only we ourselves had a hope of his glory, but also all the holy prophets which were before us. Behold, they believed in Christ and worshiped the Father in his name, and also we worship the Father in his name" (Jacob 4:4–5). And further, "Behold, I say unto you that none of the prophets have written, nor prophesied, save they have spoken concerning this Christ" (Jacob 7:11). Language cannot be plainer than that.

A definition of truth. Formulating a definition of "truth" has taxed the mental and philosophical resources of the world's thinkers. Pilate asked Jesus, "What is truth?" (John 18:38), as if he were saying, "Who knows what truth is?" Furthermore, we ask in one of our hymns, "O Say, What Is Truth?"[6] Jacob helps to provide an answer to these queries by defining what truth is and telling how we can learn it. These are his words: "The Spirit speaketh the truth and lieth not. Wherefore, it speaketh of things as they really are, and things as they really will be" (Jacob 4:13). In other words, Jacob says that truth is reality as learned through the Spirit.

The Lord further defined truth as "knowledge of things as they are, and as they were, and as they are to come" (D&C 93:24). The hymn "Oh Say, What Is Truth?" identifies truth as "the sum of existence," and in Doctrine and Covenants 91:4 the Lord says that "the Spirit manifesteth truth." Jacob's definition is in harmony with that in the Doctrine and Covenants and in the hymn and is especially meaningful to us because it indicates that ultimate truth is known through the voice of the Spirit. As we know, some truths are available to mortals in no other way but by the ministration of the Holy Spirit.

"To be learned is good." An oft-quoted verse from the Book of Mormon, at least in a university setting, comes from Jacob as recorded in 2 Nephi 9:29. But as recorded in verse 28, Jacob had just spoken of the cunning plan of the devil to deceive mankind and to cause men to trust vainly and foolishly in their own learning and "set . . . aside" the "counsel of God," "supposing they know of themselves." Jacob does not say there is any particular blessedness in being ignorant. He knows that it is not the learning but the pride and vanity men place in their learning that is a problem, so to set the matter straight he says: "But to be learned is good if they hearken unto the counsels of God" (2 Nephi 9:29). However, we should take note from Jacob's caution that many who are learned struggle with their faith.

A perfect knowledge of Christ. We have mentioned twice that Jacob was an eyewitness of Jesus Christ and that even in his youth he had seen the Redeemer. Jacob himself tells us that he had seen angels, had received ministration from them, and "had heard the voice of the Lord speaking [to him] in very word" (Jacob 7:5). He also speaks of what he calls "a perfect knowledge" of Christ (Jacob 4:12). He does not define exactly what a perfect knowledge is, but the context suggests to me that he is saying there is more to the gospel than merely learning doctrines and principles. Important as these are, we have the opportunity to go even further and receive a perfect knowledge of Christ. Here is the passage: "And now, beloved, marvel not that I tell you these things: for why not speak of the atonement of Christ, and attain to a perfect knowledge of him, as to attain to the knowledge of a resurrection and the world to come?" (Jacob 4:12).

What is a perfect knowledge over and beyond knowing the written concepts and the principles and having a testimony? I think it is being an eyewitness to the Redeemer. Who would know this better than Jacob?

CONCLUSION

Jacob is one of the greatest doctrinal teachers and theologians of the Book of Mormon, and thus of all scripture. He demonstrates a philosophical grasp of the gospel and offers unique and valuable insights into important doctrinal matters. Father Lehi was of a similar disposition. It is no coincidence that among all of Lehi's blessings to his sons, the blessing he gave to Jacob is the most doctrinal (see 2 Nephi 2). The content of that blessing has captured the attention of most Book of Mormon students because of its statements about the Creation, the Fall, Adam's condition before and after the Fall, man's agency, and the idea of opposition in all things. While the blessing is in the words of Lehi, I find it significant that it was to the youthful Jacob that he said these things. The blessing fits his mind and spirituality.

I have not included every detail about Jacob but have brought together enough to demonstrate the nature of the man. There is a tone in his teachings and writings that reveals the heart of a "just and holy" man (Alma 3:6) who was close to the Lord. He was a special witness of the Lord Jesus Christ, a man with a perfect knowledge of Christ, a man who knew Christ. He was a diligent advocate and teacher, a prophet, theologian, historian, father, and man of God.

NOTES

1. George A. Reynolds, *A Dictionary of the Book of Mormon* (Salt Lake City: Parry, 1891), 156–57.

2. Robert J. Matthews, *Who's Who in the Book of Mormon,* 3d ed. (Provo, Utah: Brigham Young University, 1969), 25, 82.

3. C. Terry Warner, "Jacob," *Ensign,* October 1976, 24–30.

4. Joseph Smith, *Teachings of the Prophet Joseph Smith,* comp. Joseph Fielding Smith (Salt Lake City: Deseret Book, 1976), 319.

5. See Joseph Fielding Smith, *Doctrines of Salvation,* comp. Bruce R. McConkie (Salt Lake City: Bookcraft, 1956), 3:91–94; Bruce R. McConkie, *Mormon Doctrine,* 1st ed. (Salt Lake City: Bookcraft, 1958), 598–99.

6. "Oh Say, What Is Truth?" *Hymns* (Salt Lake City: The Church of Jesus Christ of Latter-day Saints, 1985), no. 272.

12

King Benjamin: In the Service of Your God

Susan Easton Black

Many years ago Moses declared to gathered Israel, "Love the Lord your God, and . . . serve him with all your heart and with all your soul" (Deuteronomy 11:13). Since this declaration, many rulers of the house of Israel have vacillated in their love of and service to the Lord. Yet there was one Israelite king who obediently lived this ancient command. His name was Benjamin, king over the land of Zarahemla in ancient America in the second century B.C. Unfortunately, we know little about King Benjamin's reign except the last part, which is recorded in the book of Mosiah. That part radiates with the brightness, hope, and love of a righteous Christian king. His example is an ensign to rulers and a beacon to all disciples of Christ. My purpose in this paper is to share understanding and insight into the significance King Benjamin placed on the mysteries of God and service and to show how these concepts are interrelated.

King Benjamin, like prophets before him, wanted his people to share in the knowledge of revealed truth that he had obtained by prophecy, revelation, and the ministration of an angel. His love for his people had grown as he defended them against both external and

---

Susan Easton Black is a professor of Church history and doctrine at Brigham Young University.

internal forces of destruction. Near the end of his life, King Benjamin wanted to give his people one last sermon, "that [he] might go down in peace, and [his] immortal spirit may join the choirs above in singing the praises of a just God" (see Mosiah 2:28, 30).

In an outpouring of love, this elderly king desired to share with his people his most precious pearl, the great mysteries that he had extracted from eternal realms. He did not merely inform subordinate heads of the government so they, in turn, could disseminate the mysteries. Rather he considered his revelation, prophecy, and visit by an angel so precious that he wanted to personally tell everyone his message at the same time. All were invited to come to the heart of the kingdom, the city of Zarahemla, to hear it.

Mosiah, Benjamin's oldest son, gathered the people so they could hear their prophetic king. King Benjamin stated that the purpose of this gathering was for him to "proclaim unto this my people out of mine own mouth that thou [Mosiah] art a king and a ruler over this people, whom the Lord our God hath given us. And moreover, I shall give this people a name, that thereby they may be distinguished above all the people which the Lord God hath brought out of the land of Jerusalem" (Mosiah 1:10–11).

The place for gathering was not the king's residence, his palace, or government offices. It was the temple, the house of the Lord. The time was appointed and a nation responded.

The people of Zarahemla and the people of Mosiah all gathered at the temple. Their cultural distinction, readily apparent by name usage alone, had existed since Mosiah I (King Benjamin's father) and his followers first discovered the people of Zarahemla. These "people of Zarahemla" were the inhabitants of Zarahemla who traced their heritage to Mulek, the son of Zedekiah, while the "people of Mosiah" (Mosiah 1:10) were the descendants of those who followed Mosiah I when he escaped from a wicked Nephite culture and found Zarahemla. Benjamin desired to unite these two distinct peoples with one name and one purpose, with a name that would "never . . . be blotted out, except it be through transgression" (Mosiah 1:12). He knew this would bring them abundant joy and rejoicing throughout time and all eternity.

BENJAMIN'S SPEECH COMBINES MYSTERIES OF GOD WITH SERVICE TO HUMANITY

Benjamin delivered his long-awaited message in a series of three orations on different topics. The first is contained in Mosiah 2:9–41, the second in Mosiah 3:1–27, and the third in Mosiah 4:4–30. These three topics were separate and distinct from each other and echoed the three areas of service that King Benjamin had performed in his reign. In the first section, Benjamin spoke as a king reporting his royal stewardship, recalling how he had provided them temporal and spiritual peace. For his second topic he spoke as a prophet, once again teaching his people how to avoid spiritual chaos and unrest. In this phase of his speech he spoke the words of an angel, words that emphasized Christ's service to others, including a portrayal of Christ's atoning sacrifice. For his third and final topic, the prophet Benjamin spoke of how service can extend the knowledge of the glory, truth, and justice of God beyond a spiritual awakening. Thus Benjamin fulfilled his final act of service by bringing his people spiritual salvation.

The common element in each section was the hope-filled message of service to God through service to humanity. The first two messages were examples of service from Benjamin's and Christ's lives. The third message was a discourse on how the people could retain a remission of their sins by implementing these examples of service.

BENJAMIN'S EXAMPLE OF SERVICE

After a lifetime of service, King Benjamin's final act of service was to help his people understand and live in abiding love. To illustrate abiding love he used an example that all the people recognized—himself and his own actions. He reminded them first of his actions in the realm of civil government during times of peace, not of his earlier military role in the beginning of his reign. He pointed out his caring and responsible civil actions, such as not allowing murder, plundering, stealing, adultery, or confinement in dungeons (see Mosiah 2:13). He had not used harsh disciplinary measures or tyrannical or arbitrary means to stop depredations in his kingdom. Instead he had emphasized obedience to the commandments of God and avoidance of wickedness. He had governed his people through this Christian approach and through his own frugality and simplicity in living. As he spoke, remembering the implementation of these governing principles, he humbly stated, "I have only been in the service of God" (Mosiah 2:16).

Following this gospel-based review of his royal stewardship, King Benjamin proclaimed to his people, "I can answer [with] a clear conscience before God this day" (Mosiah 2:15). Service for Benjamin had become a sign of pure love. By establishing a civil government based on the commandments of God, King Benjamin manifested his love to his subjects. He had clearly embarked "in the service of God" as he began his reign "and had serve[d] him with all [his] heart, might, mind and strength" (D&C 4:2). He now stood on a tower at the end of that reign, blameless before God and before his people.

King Benjamin did not review his royal service "to boast" (Mosiah 2:16). He stated, "I tell you these things that ye may learn wisdom," which he defined by saying, "When ye are in the service of your fellow beings ye are only in the service of your God" (Mosiah 2:17). Like Jesus Christ in His ministry, King Benjamin gave selfless service. Benjamin knew by revelation and experience the great mystery that Christ would later teach during His earthly ministry: "Inasmuch as ye have done it unto one of the least of these my brethren, ye have done it unto me" (Matthew 25:40).

King Benjamin also knew his own life was merely a type and shadow of Christ. He knew each person listening must turn his or her own heart, might, mind, and strength to God. Like the prophets before him, Benjamin realized that "in every work that [one] began in the service of the house of God, and in the law, and in the commandments, to seek his God, he did it with all his heart" (2 Chronicles 31:21). With a humble appeal, he pled with his people, "If I, whom ye call your king, do labor to serve you, then ought not ye to labor to serve one another? . . . If I . . . do merit any thanks from you, O how you ought to thank your heavenly King!" (Mosiah 2:18–19).

King Benjamin taught that the combination of service and gratitude was higher than sacrificing the firstlings of the flocks. It was to "render all the thanks and praise which your whole soul has power to possess" (Mosiah 2:20). Yet, even if you achieved this height of gratitude, "ye would be unprofitable servants" (Mosiah 2:21). What the Lord required of His sons and His daughters was that they keep the commandments. If they kept the commandments, they would be blessed. These blessings included prosperity in the land and protection from enemies (see Mosiah 2:31).

CHRIST'S EXAMPLE OF SERVICE

After commenting on his own service, Benjamin began to prophesy, saying, "I have things to tell you concerning that which is to come" (Mosiah 3:1). The prophetic message he expressed during the second phase of his speech was made known to him by an angel. Because of his prayers and personal righteousness, the angel told Benjamin what the shepherds were to learn over 120 years later: "I am come to declare unto you the glad tidings of great joy" (Mosiah 3:3; see also Luke 2:10). These glad tidings were of the birth of Jesus in Bethlehem and His ministry among the Jews.

Christ's ministry had not been revealed to Benjamin as a series of mere verbal sermons, preachings, or admonitions; rather, it was revealed as a continuous series of examples of service. These acts included "healing the sick, raising the dead, causing the lame to walk, the blind to receive their sight, and the deaf to hear, and curing all manner of diseases" (Mosiah 3:5).

After these scenes, Benjamin was shown Christ's greatest service—the Atonement: "And lo, he shall suffer temptations, and pain of body, hunger, thirst, and fatigue, even more than man can suffer, except it be unto death; for behold, blood cometh from every pore, so great shall be his anguish for the wickedness and the abominations of his people" (Mosiah 3:7).

The atoning sacrifice had been symbolically declared by earlier prophets (see Isaiah 53:6; Moses 5:7). Yet only when the prophet Benjamin spoke of Mary and the Atonement, death, and the

Resurrection of Christ did an entire nation hear the glorious good news in fulness and in power. Previous prophets alluded to the same message, but their people were "stiffnecked" (Mosiah 3:14; see also Exodus 32:9; Isaiah 48:4). Of necessity, types and shadows replaced clear revealed light, and the law of Moses replaced the fulness of the joyous news of the Redemption. But for the people gathered to hear Benjamin the prophet, there was no symbolic replacement, no delaying substitution, no alternative name. There was "no other name given nor any other way nor means whereby salvation [could] come unto the children of men, only in and through the name of Christ, the Lord Omnipotent" (Mosiah 3:17).

King Benjamin delivered his message in plainness because those gathered had come prepared to learn of Christ. They had before them a benevolent prophet whose example had taught them preparatory to their receiving these angelic words. They had listened and had already begun to put off the natural man and become Saints. They had learned from his actions and words the need to demonstrate in their sacrificial offerings a spirit of rejoicing and thanksgiving to God. They were becoming like children, "submissive, meek, humble, patient, full of love, willing to submit to all things which the Lord [saw] fit to inflict upon [them]" (Mosiah 3:19).

In solemn unity they cried, "O have mercy, and apply the atoning blood of Christ that we may receive forgiveness of our sins, and our hearts may be purified" (Mosiah 4:2). They further pled, "We believe in Jesus Christ, the Son of God, who created heaven and earth, and all things; who shall come down among the children of men" (Mosiah 4:2).

RETAINING A REMISSION OF SINS THROUGH SERVICE

In an attitude of loving tenderness, King Benjamin expressed his knowledge that what his people now felt was a beginning. It was an awakening, not a fulfillment. His people had been in spiritual darkness and in a state of slumber. Just as the angel told Benjamin to "awake," Benjamin now called upon his people to "awake" (Mosiah 3:2; 4:5).

They were to arise from slumbering in the types and shadows of the law of Moses to find the gospel of Christ and Christian service.

Benjamin recognized that his people had tasted of the goodness, power, wisdom, love, and glory of God. Obtaining a remission of sins had brought "exceedingly great joy in [their] souls," proclaimed Benjamin (Mosiah 4:11). Yet to this noble prophet, remembrance and retention of this joy was vital as well. There is a marked difference between having a taste of food and enjoying a continuing feast. King Benjamin desired that his people feast spiritually on and endure in the word of God. This feasting and enduring comes by remembering and retaining the knowledge of the greatness of God and your own nothingness. It is renewed "even in the depths of humility, [by] calling on the name of the Lord daily, and standing steadfastly in the faith of that which is to come" (Mosiah 4:11). As the climax of his third message, Benjamin promised in surety, "If ye do this ye shall always rejoice, and be filled with the love of God, and always retain a remission of your sins" (Mosiah 4:12). In other words, they would not just taste but feast as they grew in the knowledge of glory, truth, and justice.

He promised them that this glory or love would produce peaceful coexistence in the kingdom and that this unity would be lasting because it would be upheld and sustained by righteousness. A righteous people would have no desire "to injure one another," but would desire "to render to every man according to that which is his due" (Mosiah 4:13). That which was due to every man, woman, and child, according to the prophet Benjamin, was Christlike service.

Benjamin taught that service should commence with family members. Husbands, wives, sons, and daughters were to give and receive Christian service. The prophet Benjamin focused on specific service needed by children:

"And ye will not suffer your children that they go hungry, or naked; neither will ye suffer that they transgress the laws of God, and fight and quarrel one with another, and serve the devil, who is the master of sin, or who is the evil spirit which hath been spoken of by our fathers, he being an enemy to all righteousness.

"But ye will teach them to walk in the ways of truth and soberness;

ye will teach them to love one another, and to serve one another" (Mosiah 4:14–15).

Through the specific service outlined for parents to give to their children, the great eternal mystery of peace and happiness passes from one generation to another.

With service within the family as a foundation, the Lord counseled that service be extended to those outside the family who stand in need of succor. The Prophet Joseph Smith stated, "A man filled with the love of God, is not content with blessing his family alone, but ranges through the whole world, anxious to bless the whole human race."[1] The "whole human race" includes those who "stand in need of your succor" or substance, the beggar, and even "the man [who] has brought upon himself his misery" (Mosiah 4:16–17). For in actuality, all are beggars unto the Lord.

Therefore, "impart of the substance that ye have one to another" (Mosiah 4:21). If you are poor as to earthly means, Benjamin counseled, "Say in your hearts that: I give not because I have not, but if I had I would give" (Mosiah 4:24). It is apparent that Benjamin was appealing to the gathered people to give Christlike service and develop a consecrated Zion society. Each person present was to emulate more than a type and shadow of a benevolent king; each was to emulate the Savior in his earthly ministry. Benjamin commanded the people, "Impart of your substance to the poor, every man according to that which he hath, such as feeding the hungry, clothing the naked, visiting the sick and administering to their relief, both spiritually and temporally, according to their wants" (Mosiah 4:26). As they administered their charitable service, they were to do so "in wisdom and order; for it is not requisite that a man should run faster than he has strength" (Mosiah 4:27).

REACTION OF THE NATION TO BENJAMIN'S SPEECH

When King Benjamin finished his speech, he desired to know whether his people believed the words he had spoken. Did they believe the great mysteries he had shared? The people cried with one voice, saying,

"Yea, we believe all the words which thou hast spoken unto us" (Mosiah 5:2). They had followed the admonition of King Benjamin and had opened their ears that they might hear, their hearts that they might understand, and their minds that they might accept the mysteries of God.

Through the confirmation of the Holy Ghost they attested to the truthfulness of Benjamin's words. Because of their receptivity, each had experienced a mighty change of heart. All who read or heard Benjamin's words were changed. "We have no more disposition to do evil, but to do good continually," proclaimed the people (Mosiah 5:2). They "could prophecy of all things" if it were expedient (Mosiah 5:3).

A nation changed. All of the people, excepting their little children, expressed their commitment and willingness to enter into a covenant. They had partaken of the "infinite goodness of God, and the manifestations of his Spirit" and were willing to make a binding promise between themselves and God (Mosiah 5:3). This covenant was "to do his will, and to be obedient to his commandments in all things that he shall command [them], all the remainder of [their] days" (Mosiah 5:5). Benjamin achieved his desire to unite his people in purpose by uniting them in Christian service.

Because they were united in purpose, they could now be united in name. They would be known throughout the land and throughout centuries to come as the children of Christ (see Mosiah 5:7). This name would distinguish them from all other people. It would be a sign to the Lamanites, the Zoramites, and every other "-ite" that this people in 124 B.C. served the Lord and kept His commandments.

In conclusion, Benjamin warned that transgression was the only way to lose the bonding name. Benjamin did not want his people to be divided again. He counseled, "Be steadfast and immovable, always abounding in good works, that Christ, the Lord God Omnipotent, may seal you his, that you may be brought to heaven, that ye may have everlasting salvation and eternal life" (Mosiah 5:15).

CONCLUSION

As the speech ended, the names of all the people were recorded, and a church of Christ was established in Zarahemla. This scene of becoming a covenant people, to be known as the children of Christ, would be repeated again and again through the centuries that followed. In our dispensation the Lord, through holy prophets, has again organized a covenant people known as the children of Christ.

We are privileged to read the abridged words of King Benjamin, which are some of the most divine and glorious ever uttered by a prophet. The truths revealed by this ancient sovereign-prophet illuminate the path leading to God. Our responsibility, as we read these words and listen to modern prophets, parallels the responsibility of Christians in 124 B.C. We, too, are to "succor the weak, lift up the hands which hang down, and strengthen the feeble knees" (D&C 81:5). We, too, are to "be anxiously engaged in a good cause, and do many things of [our] own free will, and bring to pass much righteousness" (D&C 58:27). Service is our covenant obligation as members of Christ's church in this dispensation.

Nothing is more exalting to the soul than selfless service. For as Benjamin expressed it, "When ye are in the service of your fellow beings ye are only in the service of your God" (Mosiah 2:17). The person who renders anonymous, loving service may be unknown to us, but the gift and the giver are known to God. As this service is rendered we should remember the Savior's counsel, "Do not your alms before men, to be seen of them" (Matthew 6:1). Instead, we must be careful that we "let not [our] left hand know what [our] right hand doeth" (Matthew 6:3). And when our service eases the burden of another, we must "tell no man" (Matthew 8:4).

Christlike service has overtones of the Atonement. By giving service we are promised that we can retain "remission of [our] sins from day to day" (Mosiah 4:26). As all are in need of our service, all may benefit by it. Only when we lift another's burden will God lift our own cares. It is a holy paradox. The disciples who stagger and even fall because their burdens are too heavy can lighten their burdens by carrying the weight of another's burden. By so doing their hearts will be lighter, their lives brighter, and their souls greater. Hopefully, we look upward as we move forward in service to God and to humanity.

"Then shall the King say unto them on his right hand, Come, ye blessed of my Father, inherit the kingdom prepared for you from the foundation of the world:

"For I was an hungred, and ye gave me meat: I was thirsty, and ye gave me drink: I was a stranger, and ye took me in:

"Naked, and ye clothed me: I was sick, and ye visited me: I was in prison, and ye came unto me. . . .

"Verily I say unto you, Inasmuch as ye have done it unto one of the least of these my brethren, ye have done it unto me" (Matthew 25:34–36, 40).

NOTE

1. Joseph Smith, *Teachings of the Prophet Joseph Smith,* comp. Joseph Fielding Smith (Salt Lake City: Deseret Book, 1976), 174.

13

The Natural Man: An Enemy to God

Robert L. Millet

President Ezra Taft Benson observed: "Just as a man does not really desire food until he is hungry, so he does not desire the salvation of Christ until he knows why he needs Christ. No one adequately and properly knows why he needs Christ until he understands and accepts the doctrine of the Fall and its effect upon all mankind. And no other book in the world explains this vital doctrine nearly as well as the Book of Mormon."[1]

Indeed, serious and careful study of the Fall in the Book of Mormon can drive people to their knees, bringing them to acknowledge their own weaknesses and thus their need for the Lord's redemption. The Atonement is necessary because of the Fall, and unless people sense the effects of Eden—both cosmically and personally—they cannot comprehend the impact of Gethsemane and Calvary. In this article I will attend primarily to a doctrinal message about humanity that was delivered to King Benjamin by an angel of God. At the same time, I will consider related passages in the Book of Mormon that bear upon and amplify this timeless truth—that the natural man is an enemy to God and a foe to all righteousness.

Robert L. Millet is the Richard L. Evans Professor of Religious Understanding and former dean of Religious Education at Brigham Young University.

I am indebted to my colleague, H. Curtis Wright, emeritus professor of library science at Brigham Young University, for his assistance with many of the concepts developed in this paper. Throughout I use the scriptural phrase "natural man" to refer to both men and women.

THE SETTING

Benjamin the prophet-king had warred a good warfare, had finished his course, and was prepared to render an accounting of his earthly stewardship to his people and to God. In the strength of God, he had led his people to victory over their enemies. In the company of holy and just men, he had confounded false prophets and teachers, spoken the word of truth with power and authority, perpetuated the record of Nephi, and established peace in the land of Zarahemla (see Omni 1:25; Words of Mormon 1:12–18). His garments were clean, and his conscience was void of offense.

King Benjamin called his oldest son, Mosiah, to succeed him and asked him to summon the people to a large conference at the temple (1) to announce his retirement and the appointment of Mosiah to serve in his stead, (2) to account to his people concerning his reign and ministry, and (3) to give to them a name, "that thereby they may be distinguished above all the people which the Lord God hath brought out of the land of Jerusalem; . . . a name that never shall be blotted out, except it be through transgression" (Mosiah 1:11–12). His sermon, contained in Mosiah 2, is one of the most eloquent and profound in all of holy writ, a timely treatise not for slothful servants, but a dispensation of the "mysteries of God" (Mosiah 2:9) to some of the most "diligent people" whom God had led out of Jerusalem (Mosiah 1:11). It is also a timeless message to those in any age who have kept the commandments of God or who strive to do so. It points the way to the Master by unfolding in plainness and clarity the doctrines of the Fall of man and the Atonement of Christ. It sets forth the proper foundation—a theological foundation—for service, for Christian compassion, and for kindness so that human works become the Lord's works—enduring testimonies of that Lord whose they are.

THE DOCTRINE OF THE FALL

The gospel or plan of salvation is designed, according to President Brigham Young, for "the redemption of fallen beings."[2] The existence of a plan of deliverance indicates that there must be something from which we need to be delivered. This is a hard doctrine, one that strikes at the heart of man-made religions and suggests the need for revealed religion. People too often attempt to temper the doctrine of the Fall, to soften its effects. Yet the Fall is a companion doctrine to the Atonement. In fact, there are no serious or extended treatments of the Atonement in the Book of Mormon that are not somehow connected, either directly or by obvious implication with the Fall.

We know that because Adam and Eve transgressed by partaking of the forbidden fruit they were cast from the Garden of Eden and from the presence of the Lord, which is spiritual death. As a result came blood, sweat, toil, opposition, bodily decay, and finally physical death. Elder Orson F. Whitney taught that the Fall was "a step forward—a step in the eternal arch of human progress."[3]

Even though the Fall was a vital part of the great plan of the Eternal God—as much a foreordained act as Christ's intercession—our state, including our relationship to and contact with God, changed dramatically. Early in the Nephite record, Lehi "spake concerning the prophets, how great a number had testified of . . . [the] Redeemer of the world. Wherefore, all mankind were in a lost and in a fallen state, and ever would be save they should rely on this Redeemer" (1 Nephi 10:5–6). Again, the coming of the Messiah presupposes the need for redemption.

Joseph Smith wrote to John Wentworth, "We believe that men will be punished for their own sins, and not for Adam's transgression" (Articles of Faith 1:2). The Lord affirms this proclamation in His statement to Adam: "I have forgiven thee thy transgression in the Garden of Eden" (Moses 6:53). This declaration must, however, be understood in the proper doctrinal context. Although God forgave our first parents their transgression, although there is no original sin entailed upon Adam and Eve's children, and although "the Son of God hath atoned for original guilt, wherein the sins of the parents cannot be answered upon the heads of the children" (Moses 6:54), we must not conclude that all is well.

To say that we are not condemned by the Fall of Adam is not to say that we are unaffected by it. Jehovah explained to Adam, "Inasmuch as thy children are conceived in sin, even so when they begin to grow up, sin conceiveth in their hearts, and they taste the bitter, that they may know to prize the good" (Moses 6:55). We do not believe, with Calvin, in the moral depravity of humanity. We do not believe, with Luther, that human beings, because of intrinsic carnality and depravity, do not even have the power to choose good over evil. And we do not believe that children are born in sin, that they inherit the so-called sin of Adam, either by sexual union or by birth. Rather, children are *conceived* in sin, meaning first, that they are conceived into a world of sin, and second, that conception is the vehicle by which the *effects* of the Fall (not the original guilt, which God has forgiven) are transmitted to Adam and Eve's posterity. To be sure, there is no sin in sexual union within the bonds of marriage, nor is conception itself sinful. Rather, through conception the flesh originates; through the process of becoming mortal one inherits the effects of the fall of Adam—both physical and spiritual.

To say that we are not punished for the transgression of Adam is not to say that we are not subject to or affected by it. In fact, Lehi taught Jacob that in the beginning God "gave commandment that all men must repent; for he showed unto all men that they were lost, because of the transgression of their parents" (2 Nephi 2:21; see also Alma 22:14). Thus we all need to repent, since we all have the propensity to sin because we inherited Adam and Eve's fallen nature. "We know that thou art holy," the brother of Jared confessed to the Almighty, "and dwellest in the heavens, and that we are unworthy before thee; *because of the fall our natures have become evil continually;* nevertheless, O Lord, thou hast given us a commandment that we must call upon thee, that from thee we may receive according to our desires" (Ether 3:2; emphasis added).

Again, conception, which clothes us in the flesh, is the mechanism of transmission, the means by which Adam and Eve's fallen nature (both physical and spiritual death) is transferred from generation to generation. The propensity for and susceptibility to sin are implanted in our nature at conception, just as death is. Both death and sin are present only as potentialities at conception, and therefore neither is fully evident at birth. Death and sin do, however, become actual parts of our nature as we grow up. Sin comes spontaneously, just as death does. In the case of little children, the results of this fallen nature (sinful actions and dispositions) are held in abeyance by virtue of the Atonement until they reach the age of accountability. When children reach the age of accountability, however, they become subject to spiritual death and must thereafter repent and come unto Christ by covenant and through the ordinances of the gospel.

The teachings of modern apostles and prophets confirm the testimony of ancient Book of Mormon prophets. Elder Bruce R. McConkie summarized the effects of the Fall as follows:

"Adam fell. We know that this fall came because of transgression, and that Adam broke the law of God, became mortal, and was thus subject to sin and disease and all the ills of mortality. We know that the effects of his fall passed upon all his posterity; *all inherited a fallen state,* a state of mortality, a state in which spiritual and temporal death prevail. In this state all men sin. *All are lost. All are fallen.* All are cut off from the presence of God. . . . Such a way of life is inherent in this mortal existence. . . .

"Death entered the world by means of Adam's fall—death of two kinds, temporal and spiritual. Temporal death passes upon all men when they depart this mortal life. It is then that the eternal spirit steps out of its earthly tenement, to take up an abode in a realm where spirits are assigned, to await the day of their resurrection. *Spiritual death passes upon all men when they become accountable for their sins. Being thus subject to sin they die spiritually;* they die as pertaining to the things of the Spirit; they die as pertaining to the things of righteousness; they are cast out of the presence of God. It is of such men that the scriptures speak when they say that the natural man is an enemy to God."[4]

"I have learned in my travels," the Prophet Joseph Smith observed, "that man is treacherous and selfish, but few excepted."[5] "Men have been ever prone to apostacy," President John Taylor pointed out. "Our fallen nature is at enmity with a godly life."[6]

THE NATURAL MAN

In setting forth the doctrine of atonement, King Benjamin taught the lesson that is the focus of this paper: "The natural man is an enemy to God," he said, "and has been from the fall of Adam, and will be, forever and ever, unless he yields to the enticings of the Holy Spirit, and putteth off the natural man and becometh a saint through the atonement of Christ the Lord" (Mosiah 3:19). What is king Benjamin saying about humanity? What is the natural man, and how may he be characterized?

Simply stated, natural men and women are unregenerated beings who remain in their fallen condition, living without God and godliness in the world. They are unredeemed creatures without comfort, beings who live by their own light. On the one hand, natural men and women may be people bent on lechery and lasciviousness; they may love Satan more than God, and therefore they are "carnal, sensual, and devilish" (Moses 5:13). After having preached to and pleaded with his son Corianton, and after having taught him that "wickedness never was happiness," (Alma 41:10), Alma said, "And now, my son, all men that are in a state of nature, or I would say, in a carnal state, are in the gall of bitterness and in the bonds of iniquity." Now note how such persons are enemies to God: "They are without God in the world, and they have gone contrary to the nature of God; therefore, they are in a state contrary to the nature of happiness" (Alma 41:11).

In the same vein, Abinadi warned the priests of Noah of that day wherein natural men and women—in this case the vile and wicked—would receive their just rewards:

"And then shall the wicked be cast out, and they shall have cause to howl, and weep, and wail, and gnash their teeth; and this because they would not hearken unto the voice of the Lord; therefore the Lord redeemeth them not.

"For they are carnal and devilish, and the devil has power over them; yea, even that old serpent that did beguile our first parents, which was the cause of their fall" (Mosiah 16:2–3).

And then Abinadi explained how the Fall opened the way for people to reject the Spirit and choose sin: "Which [Fall] was the cause of all mankind becoming carnal, sensual, devilish, knowing evil from good, subjecting themselves to the devil. Thus all mankind were lost; and behold, they would have been endlessly lost were it not that God redeemed his people from their lost and fallen state" (Mosiah 16:3–4).

At this point we might be prone to sit back, let out a sigh of relief, and offer gratitude to God that because of the atoning work of Christ, the battle is over. But Abinadi continued his warning: "But remember that he that persists in his own carnal nature, and goes on in the ways of sin and rebellion against God, remaineth in his fallen state and the devil hath all power over him. Therefore he is as though there was no redemption made, being an enemy to God; and also is the devil an enemy to God" (Mosiah 16:5). Sons of perdition experience this exclusion to its fullest at the time of the Judgment, while all others except celestial candidates will experience much of it. We should here attend carefully to the fact that the phrase "persists in his own carnal nature" implies that individuals, in spite of the Atonement, have such a nature in which to persist. Further, "*remaineth* in his fallen state" does not simply mean *get into* a fallen state through sin. It is true that the scriptures affirm that one becomes "carnal, sensual, and devilish" through loving Satan more than God, through willful disobedience to the commandments (Moses 5:13; 6:49; emphasis added). But to be a fallen being is not necessarily to be a carnal, sensual, and devilish being. One becomes fallen by coming into mortality; a fallen person becomes carnal, sensual, and devilish by defying the truth and sinning against it.

On the other hand, natural men and women need not be what we would call degenerate. They may well be moral and upright men and women, bent upon goodness and benevolence. However, they operate in and are acclimated to the present fallen world. Such persons do not enjoy the enlivening powers of the Holy Ghost: they have not received the revealed witness of the truth, and they have not enjoyed the sanctifying powers of the blood of Christ. Although their behavior is proper and appropriate according to societal standards, these natural men and women have not hearkened sufficiently to the Light of Christ to be led to the covenant gospel (see Mosiah 16:2; see also D&C 84:45–48). "The whole world lieth in sin," the Savior declared in a modern revelation, "and groaneth under darkness and under the bondage of sin.

"And by this you may know they are under the bondage of sin, because they come not unto me" (D&C 84:49–50).

More specifically, with regard to those outside the restored gospel, the Lord states: "There are none that doeth good except those who are ready to receive the fulness of my gospel, which I have sent forth unto this generation" (D&C 35:12).

And what of the members of The Church of Jesus Christ of Latter-day Saints? Are any of us natural men or women? We certainly qualify for that title if we are guilty of gross wickedness, if we have sinned against gospel light and have not thoroughly repented. And yes, we are relatively guilty too if we persist in a nature which leads us to exist in twilight when we might bask in the light of the Son. In 1867 President Brigham Young declared to the people of the Church: "There is no doubt, if a person lives according to the revelations given to God's people, he may have the Spirit of the Lord to signify to him His will, and to guide and to direct him in the discharge of his duties, in his temporal as well as his spiritual exercises. I am satisfied, however, that in this respect, we live far beneath our privileges."[7] Members of the Church who refuse to climb toward greater spiritual heights, who have no inclination to further anchor themselves in the truth, who have become satisfied with their present spiritual state—these are they who are natural men and women, persons generally of goodwill who do not understand that through their smugness and complacency they are aiding and abetting the cause of Satan. "Fallen man," C. S. Lewis perceptively observed, "is not simply an imperfect creature who needs improvement: he is a rebel who must lay down his arms."[8]

What are some broad characteristics of natural men and women? Consider the following:

1. *They are unable or unwilling to perceive spiritual realities.* Paul explained that "the natural man receiveth not the things of the Spirit

of God: for they are foolishness unto him: neither can he know them, because they are spiritually discerned" (1 Corinthians 2:14). In exulting over the Lord's infinite mercy—His willingness to snatch His children from evil and forgive their sins—Ammon said: "What natural man is there that knoweth these things? I say unto you, there is none that knoweth these things, save it be the penitent" (Alma 26:21). Similarly, a modern revelation teaches, "No man has seen God at any time in the flesh, except quickened by the Spirit of God. Neither can any natural man abide the presence of God, neither after the carnal mind" (D&C 67:11–12; see also Moses 1:11).

"How difficult it is to teach the natural man," Brigham Young declared, "who comprehends nothing more than that which he sees with the natural eye!" President Young went on to say: "How hard it is for him to believe! How difficult would be the task to make the philosopher, who, for many years, has argued himself into the belief that his spirit is no more after his body sleeps in the grave, believe that his intelligence came from eternity, and is as eternal, in its nature, as the elements, or as the Gods. Such doctrine by him would be considered vanity and foolishness, it would be entirely beyond his comprehension. It is difficult, indeed, to remove an opinion or belief into which he has argued himself from the mind of the natural man. Talk to him about angels, heavens, God, immortality, and eternal lives, and it is like sounding brass, or a tinkling cymbal to his ears; it has no music to him; there is nothing in it that charms his senses, soothes his feelings, attracts his attention, or engages his affections, in the least; to him it is all vanity."[9]

2. *They are fiercely independent.* Joseph Smith taught that "all men are naturally disposed to walk in their own paths as they are pointed out by their own fingers, and are not willing to consider and walk in the path which is pointed out by another, saying, This is the way, walk ye in it, although he should be an unerring director, and the Lord his God sent him."[10] Seeking to be independent, natural men and women ironically end up conforming to the trends of the day. Natural men and women, at least those who have "the carnal mind," are "not subject to the law of God" (Romans 8:7) but rather are subject to their own

whims, passions, and desires. C. S. Lewis remarked that "until you have given up yourself to [the Lord] you will not have a real self. Sameness is to be found most among the most 'natural' men, not among those who surrender to Christ. How monotonously alike all the great tyrants and conquerors have been: how gloriously different are the saints."[11]

Samuel the Lamanite expressed the tragic end of those whose natural view of reality causes them to spend their days climbing the wrong ladder: "But behold, your days of probation are past; ye have procrastinated the day of your salvation until it is everlastingly too late, and your destruction is made sure; yea, for ye have sought all the days of your lives for that which ye could not obtain; and ye have sought for happiness in doing iniquity, which thing is contrary to the nature of that righteousness which is in our great and Eternal Head" (Helaman 13:38).

In the words of a Protestant counselor: "Fallen man has taken command of his own life, determined above all else to prove that he's adequate for the job. And like the teen who feels rich until he starts paying for his own car insurance, we remain confident of our ability to manage life until we face the reality of our own soul. . . . To put it simply, people want to run their own lives. Fallen man is both terrified of vulnerability and committed to maintaining independence. . . . The most natural thing for us to do is to develop strategies for finding life that reflect our commitment to depending on our own resources."[12]

3. *They are proud, overly competitive, reactionary, and externally driven.* Natural men and women—be they the irreverent and ungodly or the well-meaning but spiritually unregenerate—are preoccupied with self and obsessed with personal aggrandizement. Their lives are keyed to the rewards of this ephemeral sphere; their values derive solely from pragmatism and utility. They take their cues from the world and the worldly. "The central feature of pride," as President Ezra Taft Benson warned the Latter-day Saints, "is enmity—enmity toward God and enmity toward our fellowmen." The look of natural men and women is neither up (to God) nor over (to their fellow humans), except as the horizontal glance allows them to maintain a distance from others. "Pride is essentially competitive in nature," President Benson explained.

"We pit our will against God's. When we direct our pride toward God, it is in the spirit of 'my will and not thine be done.' . . . The proud cannot accept the authority of God giving direction to their lives. . . . The proud wish God would agree with them. They aren't interested in changing their opinions to agree with God's." With regard to other people, the proud "are tempted daily to elevate [themselves] above others and diminish them. . . . In the words of C. S. Lewis: 'Pride gets no pleasure out of having something, only out of having more of it than the next man.'" In short, "Pride is the universal sin, the great vice. . . . [It] is the great stumbling block to Zion."[13]

4. *They yield themselves to the harsh and the crude.* The Spirit of the Lord has a calming and quieting influence upon those who cultivate it and enjoy its fruits. As a sanctifier, the Holy Ghost "expands, and purifies all the natural passions and affections. . . . It inspires virtue, kindness, goodness, tenderness, gentleness and charity."[14] On the other hand, as President Spencer W. Kimball declared, the natural man—the person who lives without this divine refinement—"is the 'earthy man' who has allowed rude animal passions to overshadow his spiritual inclinations."[15]

FREQUENT REACTIONS TO THE DOCTRINE

As I indicated earlier, the doctrine of the natural man is a hard doctrine, one that is not only misunderstood but also frequently denied. Reactions to the idea that the natural man is an enemy to God are numerous. Some of these we will now consider.

1. *We all enjoy the Light of Christ.* One rejoinder to this doctrine is that every person that comes into the world is endowed by God with the Light of Christ. Although it is true that the Light of Christ is a gift and endowment from God, this is a doctrine that requires some explanation, for it is necessary to distinguish between two aspects of the Light of Christ. On the one hand, there is the natural or physical light or law by which the sun, moon, and stars operate—the light by which we see and the means by which human, animal, and plant life abound (see D&C 88:6–13, 50). On the other hand, there is what might be called a redemptive dimension of the Light of Christ, a light that we

must receive, a voice to which we must hearken before we are led to the higher light of the Holy Ghost and are thereby redeemed from our fallen state. Because we have our agency, we can choose to accept or reject this light. Whether such redemptive light takes the form of reason or judgment or conscience, we must exercise some degree of faith to enjoy its benefits. Thus, although it is true that the Spirit gives light to all of us, it only spiritually enlightens and redeems those of us who hearken to it (see D&C 84:42–50).

2. *The spirit of humankind is good.* Those who contend that humans are basically good, that their inherent inclination is to choose righteousness, enjoy quoting a statement made by Brigham Young in which he seems to take quite a different view of who and what the natural man is: "It is fully proved in all the revelations that God has ever given to mankind that they naturally love and admire righteousness, justice and truth more than they do evil. It is, however, universally received by professors of religion as a Scriptural doctrine that man is naturally opposed to God. This is not so. Paul says, in his Epistle to the Corinthians, 'But the natural man receiveth not the things of God,' but I say it is the unnatural 'man that receiveth not the things of God.' . . . That which was, is, and will continue to endure is more natural than that which will pass away and be no more. The natural man is of God."[16] There is no question, in light of the belief in human depravity held by so many in the nineteenth century, that the doctrines of the Restoration were a refreshing breeze in a dry and arid spiritual climate. The revelation that God had forgiven Adam and Eve of their transgression, as well as the corollary principle that little children who die before the time of accountability are saved, served to set the Latter-day Saints apart from much of the Christian world and certainly painted a more positive and optimistic picture of human nature. The scriptures teach that we lived before we came here, that we are all the sons and daughters of God, and that our spirits literally inherited from our exalted Sire the capacity to become like Him (see Abraham 3:22–23; D&C 76, 58–59). These are all true doctrines. When understood they can do much to lift our sights toward the glorious and the ennobling."

Such beliefs, however, do not invalidate the burden of scripture—

there was a fall, and the Fall takes a measured and meaningful toll upon earth's inhabitants. Obviously President Young used the phrase "natural man" differently from the way that Paul or King Benjamin used it. His reference is to the spirit of man, the willing and striving eternal agent which is a child of God. His point is a good one: human beings can choose good as well as evil and can, through the proper exercise of their God-given agency, stand as spiritual beings before the Almighty. And yet our spirits can be and are influenced by our physical bodies, inasmuch as the latter are subject to our present fallen state. President Brigham Young also taught:

"Now, I want to tell you that [Satan] does not hold any power over man, only so far as the body overcomes the spirit that is in a man, through yielding to the spirit of evil. The spirit that the Lord puts into a tabernacle of flesh, is under the dictation of the Lord Almighty; but the spirit and body are united in order that the spirit may have a tabernacle, and be exalted; and the spirit is influenced by the body, and the body by the spirit.

"In the first place the spirit is pure, and under the special control and influence of the Lord, but the body is of the earth, and is subject to the power of the devil, and is under the mighty influence of that fallen nature that is on the earth. If the spirit yields to the body, the devil then has power to overcome both the body and spirit of that man."[17]

On another occasion, President Young taught that "there are no persons without evil passions to embitter their lives. Mankind are revengeful, passionate, hateful, and devilish in their dispositions. This we inherit through the fall, and the grace of God is designed to enable us to overcome it."[18]

3. *Little children are innocent.* Too often, Latter-day Saints become concerned and confused about the scriptural statement that children are conceived in sin (see Moses 6:55) and ask, "Are children pure?" The answer to this question is always a resounding "Yes!" No one disputes that. The real issue is why children are pure. Two possibilities suggest themselves: (1) the Greek or humanistic response is that children are pure because human nature is pure, prone toward the good; while (2) the Christian gospel response is that children are pure because of the

Atonement, because Jesus Christ declared them so. To paraphrase the words of Lehi, children are redeemed because of the righteousness of our Redeemer (see 2 Nephi 2:3). Benjamin, declaring the words of the angel, said, "And even if it were possible that little children could sin they could not be saved." That is, if Christ required children to be responsible for those actions or deeds which are ostensibly wrong and sinful, they could not be saved, had there been no atonement. "But I say unto you," Benjamin explains, "they are blessed; for behold, as in Adam, or by nature, they fall, even so the blood of Christ atoneth for their sins" (Mosiah 3:16).

The revelations state that little children "cannot sin, for power is not given unto Satan to tempt little children, until they begin to become accountable before me" (D&C 29:47). All of us know of deeds performed by little children that may only be described as evil. I am aware of a seven-year-old who in an act of rage killed his brother. The act of murder is a heinous sin. But in this case the child's action is not counted as sin. Why? Because, in the words of God, "Little children are redeemed from the foundation of the world through mine Only Begotten" (D&C 29:46). Christ explained that "the curse of Adam is taken from [children] in me, that it hath no power over them" (Moroni 8:8). Little children are subject to the effects of the Fall, just as all of us are; they are not, however, held accountable for their actions. In summary, little children are saved without any preconditions—without faith, repentance, or baptism. Their innocence is decreed and declared by and through the tender mercies of an all-loving Lord. Children are innocent because of the Atonement, not because there is no sin in their nature.

4. *Joseph Smith taught that we are gods in embryo.* Some people believe that Joseph Smith and the Latter-day Saints progressed or evolved beyond the doctrine of the Fall, that the message of the Book of Mormon was later quietly but surely superseded by the purer pronouncements in the King Follett Sermon. To me such views are groundless and misleading. It was in 1841 that the Prophet made his now-famous statement about the correctness and power of the Book of Mormon.[19] Only the night before the Prophet's martyrdom, "Hyrum

Smith read and commented upon extracts from the Book of Mormon, on the imprisonments and deliverance of the servants of God for the Gospel's sake. Joseph bore a powerful testimony to the guards of the divine authenticity of the Book of Mormon, the restoration of the Gospel, the administration of angels, and that the kingdom of God was again established upon the earth."[20] That scene in Carthage certainly bespeaks more than sentimental attachment on the part of the Prophet to the scriptural record—and to the doctrines it put forward—that had come to light through his instrumentality almost two decades earlier. The fact is, on some occasions Joseph Smith spoke of the nobility of humankind, and on some occasions he spoke of the carnality of humankind.[21] To conclude that the Prophet taught only of humankind's nobility—or, for that matter, that he taught only of humankind's ignobility—is to misrepresent his broader theological view.[22]

PUTTING OFF THE NATURAL MAN

During his speech at the temple, King Benjamin explained that "men drink damnation to their own souls except they humble themselves and become as little children, and believe that salvation was, and is, and is to come, in and through the atoning blood of Christ, the Lord Omnipotent. "For the natural man is an enemy to God, and has been from the fall of Adam, and will be, forever and ever, unless he yields to the enticings of the Holy Spirit, and putteth off the natural man and becometh a saint through the atonement of Christ the Lord, and becometh as a child, submissive, meek, humble, patient, full of love, willing to submit to all things which the Lord seeth fit to inflict upon him, even as a child doth submit to his father" (Mosiah 3:18–19).

We do not put off the natural man by living longer. We do not change our natures by simply attending meetings and being involved in the work of the Church. The Church is a divine organization. It administers the saving gospel. The transformation from the natural state to the spiritual state, however, is accomplished only through the mediation and Atonement of Jesus Christ, through the power of the Holy Ghost. No one goes from death to life without that enabling power we call the grace of God. Programs to develop self-control, plans to modify human behavior, and schemes directed toward the shaping of more appropriate actions have fallen and will forever fall far short of the mark which Christ has set. These programs are at best deficient and at worst perverse. In the language of President Ezra Taft Benson: "The Lord works from the inside out. The world works from the outside in. The world would take people out of the slums. Christ takes the slums out of people, and then they take themselves out of the slums. The world would mold men by changing their environment. Christ changes men, who then change their environment. The world would shape human behavior, but Christ can change human nature."[23]

Those who are born again or born from above—who die as to the things of unrighteousness and begin to live again as pertaining to the things of the Spirit—are like little children, clean and pure. Through the atoning blood of Christ they have had their sins remitted and have entered the realm of divine experience. Putting off the natural man involves putting on Christ. As Paul counseled the Saints in his day, those who put off the "old man" are "renewed in the spirit of [their] mind." They "put on the new man, which after God is created in righteousness and true holiness" (Ephesians 4:22–24), and "which is renewed in knowledge after the image of him that created him" (Colossians 3:10).

This renovation of the natural man may be dramatic and rapid for some. Such was the case with Enos (see Enos 1:1–8) and with the people of King Benjamin who underwent a "mighty change," such that they had "no more disposition to do evil, but to do good continually" (Mosiah 5:2). It may be like the experiences of Alma the Younger or Paul, both of whom were redirected and reoriented through the ministry of heavenly beings (see Mosiah 27; Alma 36; Acts 9). As to the miraculous conversion of King Lamoni—and thus of the unspeakable power of Christ to forge new creatures—the Nephite record attests: "King Lamoni was under the power of God; [Ammon] knew that the dark veil of unbelief was being cast away from his mind, and the light which did light up his mind, which was the light of the glory of God, which was a marvelous light of his goodness—yea, this light had infused such joy into his soul, the cloud of darkness having been dispelled, and that the light of everlasting life was lit up in his soul, yea, he knew that this had overcome his natural frame, and he was carried away in God" (Alma 19:6).

"But we must be cautious," President Benson has warned us, "as we discuss these remarkable examples. Though they are real and powerful, they are the exception more than the rule. For every Paul, for every Enos, and for every King Lamoni, there are hundreds and thousands of people who find the process of repentance much more subtle, much more imperceptible. Day by day they move closer to the Lord, little realizing they are building a godlike life."[24]

Those who have put off the natural man—what Paul called the "works of the flesh" (Galatians 5:19)—begin to enjoy what he also called the "fruit of the Spirit," namely "love, joy, peace, longsuffering, gentleness, goodness, faith, meekness, temperance"; they begin to "walk in the Spirit" (Galatians 5:22–23, 25). As King Benjamin explained, they are humble and submissive, eager to know and carry out the will of the Savior, eager to have their own wishes swallowed up in a higher will (see Mosiah 3:19). Surely the highest and grandest fruit of the Spirit is love—what the scriptures call charity, the "pure love of Christ" (Moroni 7:47).

"And again, I remember," Moroni stated humbly to his Master, "that thou hast said that thou hast loved the world, even unto the laying down of thy life for the world. . . .

"And now I know that this love which thou hast had for the children of men is charity; wherefore, except men shall have charity they cannot inherit that place which thou hast prepared in the mansions of thy Father" (Ether 12:33–34).

This charity is more than an emotion, higher than a sweet feeling, more transcendent than an effort to perform good deeds. It is literally a fruit of the Spirit, a heavenly endowment that can only be granted and bestowed by an all-loving God. The true followers of Christ come to love as He loves because they have become as He is. In short, they have become saints, members of the household of faith who seek the way of holiness and have enjoyed the sublime sanctifying powers of the Holy Ghost.

CONCLUSION

We shall spend all our days seeking to subdue the flesh and put off the natural man; this is the challenge of mortality. "Will sin be perfectly destroyed?" Brigham Young asked. "No, it will not, for it is not so designed in the economy of Heaven. . . . Do not suppose that we shall ever in the flesh be free from temptations to sin. Some suppose that they can in the flesh be sanctified body and spirit and become so pure that they will never again feel the effects of the power of the adversary of truth. Were it possible for a person to attain to this degree of perfection in the flesh, he could not die neither remain in a world where sin predominates. Sin has entered into the world, and death by sin. I think we shall more or less feel the effects of sin so long as we live, and finally have to pass the ordeals of death."[25] Zion is built "in process of time" (Moses 7:21); it is only by patience and long-suffering that the Saints of the Most High become a holy people.

There is great virtue in truth and great power in the proclamation of the truth. President Ezra Taft Benson has repeatedly warned the Saints of the condemnation, scourge, and judgment that rest upon the Church because of our near neglect of the Book of Mormon (see D&C 84:54–61). He has, however, reminded us that the condemnation can be lifted through serious study and consistent application of the teachings and patterns for living provided in that sacred volume. "I am deeply concerned," he once said, "about what we are doing to teach the Saints at all levels the gospel of Jesus Christ as completely and authoritatively as do the Book of Mormon and Doctrine and Covenants. By this I mean teaching the 'great plan of the Eternal God,' to use the words of Amulek (Alma 34:9).

"Are we using the messages and the method of teaching found in the Book of Mormon and other scriptures of the Restoration to teach this great plan of the Eternal God? . . .

"The Book of Mormon Saints knew that the plan of redemption must start with the account of the fall of Adam. In the words of Moroni, 'By Adam came the fall of man. And because of the fall of man came Jesus Christ, . . . and because of Jesus Christ came the redemption of man' (Mormon 9:12).

"We all need to take a careful inventory of our performance and also the performance of those over whom we preside to be sure that we are teaching the 'great plan of the Eternal God' to the Saints.

"Are we accepting and teaching what the revelations tell us about the Creation, Adam and the fall of man, and redemption from that fall through the atonement of Christ?"[26]

As stated earlier, just as we do not desire food until we are hungry, so the living waters can bless our lives only to the degree to which we acknowledge our fallen condition, seek diligently to put off the natural man, and receive deliverance from sin through repentance. "It requires all the atonement of Christ," Brigham Young noted, "the mercy of the Father, the pity of angels and the grace of the Lord Jesus Christ to be with us always, and then to do the very best we possibly can, to get rid of this sin within us, so that we may escape from this world into the celestial kingdom."[27]

In the words of C. S. Lewis, the animation and renovation of human character "is precisely what Christianity is about. This world is a great sculptor's shop. We are the statues and there is a rumor going round the shop that some of us are some day going to come to life."[28] When we do so, as individuals and as a people, to quote a modern prophet, "a new day will break and Zion will be redeemed."[29]

NOTES

1. Ezra Taft Benson, *A Witness and a Warning* (Salt Lake City: Deseret Book, 1988), 33.

2. Brigham Young, in *Journal of Discourses* (London: Latter-day Saints' Book Depot, 1854–97), 1:1; hereafter cited as *JD*.

3. Orson F. Whitney, in Conference Report, April 1908, 90.

4. Bruce R. McConkie, *The Promised Messiah* (Salt Lake City: Deseret Book, 1978), 244, 349–50; emphasis added.

5. Joseph Smith, *Teachings of the Prophet Joseph Smith,* comp. Joseph Fielding Smith (Salt Lake City: Deseret Book, 1976), 30.

6. John Taylor, *Mediation and Atonement* (Salt Lake City: Deseret News, 1892), 197.

7. Brigham Young, in *JD,* 12:104.

8. C. S. Lewis, *Mere Christianity* (New York: Macmillan, 1960), 59.

9. Brigham Young, in *JD,* 1:2.

10. Smith, *Teachings,* 26–27.

11. Lewis, *Mere Christianity,* 190.

12. Larry Crabb, *Inside Out* (Colorado Springs: NavPress, 1988), 15–16, 54.

13. Ezra Taft Benson, "Beware of Pride," *Ensign,* May 1989, 4, 6.

14. Parley P. Pratt, *Key to the Science of Theology* (Salt Lake City: Deseret Book, 1970), 61.

15. Spencer W. Kimball, "Ocean Currents and Family Influences," *Ensign,* November 1974, 112.

16. Brigham Young, in *JD,* 9:305.

17. Brigham Young, in *JD,* 2:255–56; see also Smith, *Teachings,* 181, 187, 189, 226.

18. Brigham Young, in *JD,* 8:160.

19. See Smith, *Teachings,* 194.

20. Joseph Smith, *History of the Church of Jesus Christ of Latter-day Saints,* ed. B. H. Roberts, 2d ed., rev. (Salt Lake City: Deseret Book, 1957), 6:600.

21. For the latter perspective, see Smith, *Teachings,* 26–27, 30, 196, 249, 252, 258, 303, 315, 328.

22. For a more detailed discussion of this matter, see Robert L. Millet, "Joseph Smith and Modern Mormonism: Orthodoxy, Neoorthodoxy, Tension, and Tradition," *BYU Studies* 29, no. 3 (summer 1989): 49–68.

23. Ezra Taft Benson, "Born of God," *Ensign,* November 1985, 6.

24. Ezra Taft Benson, "A Mighty Change of Heart," *Ensign,* October 1989, 2–5.

25. Brigham Young, in *JD,* 10:173.

26. Benson, *A Witness and a Warning,* 32–33.

27. Brigham Young, in *JD,* 11:39.

28. Lewis, *Mere Christianity,* 140.

29. Benson, *A Witness and a Warning,* 66.

14

Abinadi's Commentary on Isaiah

Monte S. Nyman

About 150 B.C. a group of Nephites living in the land of Lehi-Nephi fell into bondage to their Lamanite neighbors. Previously the Lord had raised up a prophet named Abinadi who called the Nephites to repentance, but "they were wroth with him, and sought to take away his life; but the Lord delivered him out of their hands" (Mosiah 11:26). Two years later, Abinadi returned and prophesied of their impending bondage to the Lamanites and of the fiery fate of Noah, their king. Abinadi was carried before the king and cast into prison until he could be tried before a council of the king's priests. In questioning Abinadi, the priests attempted to "find something" with which they could accuse him and either imprison or execute him. To their astonishment, he boldly confounded them in all their words (see Mosiah 12:1–19).

One of the priests asked Abinadi the meaning of a passage from Isaiah, one of the greatest prophets of the Old Testament (see Mosiah 12:20–24; compare Isaiah 52:7–10). Since the priest obviously did not understand the Isaiah text, he seemed to assume Abinadi wouldn't understand it either because Isaiah was not generally understood by the people of Nephi (see 2 Nephi 25:1) and was not understood particularly by

---

Monte S. Nyman is an emeritus professor of ancient scripture at Brigham Young University.

those in a state of spiritual decline. But Abinadi was a prophet of the Lord "filled with the spirit of prophecy"; he chastised the priests for their lack of understanding and accused them of perverting the ways of the Lord and not applying their hearts to understanding. Then he asked them what they taught their people (see Mosiah 12:25–27). To their answer, "We teach the law of Moses," he queried further, "Why do ye not keep it?" Another question probed still deeper: "Doth salvation come by the law of Moses?" (Mosiah 12:28–31). To their answer that it did, Abinadi skillfully refuted their false preaching and showed how the law of Moses was a type and shadow of Jesus Christ (see Mosiah 13:27–31). He then declared that Moses and all of the prophets who had ever prophesied had testified that Jesus Christ would come into the world in the form of a man and that he would bring to pass the resurrection of the dead (see Mosiah 13:33–35). As evidence that all the prophets had testified of Christ, Abinadi quoted and commented on what is now Isaiah 53 in the King James Bible.

ABINADI'S COMMENTARY ON ISAIAH 53

Isaiah 53 is a well-known prophecy among Christians and Jews. Christians generally interpret it as a prophecy of the life and suffering of Jesus Christ. The Jewish interpretation is that Isaiah is describing the suffering of the entire nation of Israel, not a specific person. Abinadi's commentary sustains the Christian interpretation with details not found in the writings of other Christians. Abinadi's commentary on Isaiah 53, although sometimes confusing to Church members, amplifies the beautiful message of Isaiah. Abinadi's great doctrinal insights and explanations of the true role of Jesus Christ are textual proofs that "Jesus is the Christ, the Eternal God" (Book of Mormon, title page).

After discussing the great truths of Isaiah 53, Abinadi returned to the original question raised by King Noah's priest—the meaning of the text of Isaiah 52:7–10. His answer is also a commentary on that passage. But before he interpreted those verses, Abinadi explained the messiahship of Jesus Christ and His gospel as the message of peace. Only then would the priests be prepared to understand this passage of Isaiah. In the analysis that follows, I will first quote Isaiah's words as written in Mosiah, and then I will add relevant phrases from Abinadi's commentary and other interpretative helps from the New Testament and modern revelation. I will then draw conclusions from the collective commentaries.

Mosiah 14:1: "Yea, even doth not Isaiah say: Who hath believed our report, and to whom is the arm of the Lord revealed?" (compare Isaiah 53:1).

Although Abinadi does not comment directly on this verse, the context in which he quotes it makes his interpretation clear. He had just declared that all of the prophets since the world began testified of Christ. To support this statement, he said, "Yea, even doth not Isaiah say" and proceeded to quote the entirety of Isaiah 53. Clearly Abinadi understands this passage not to be a prophecy of suffering Israel, but a prophecy of Jesus Christ, of whom all the prophets have testified. And yet, the people were receptive neither to Isaiah's prophecies of Christ, nor to Abinadi's, nor to those of the other prophets. It was the hard hearts of the people and their lack of understanding of the law that brought Isaiah to cry, "Who hath believed our report?"

Other scriptures support Abinadi's interpretation. For example, Jacob, the brother of Nephi, had prophesied "that none of the prophets have written, nor prophesied, save they have spoken concerning this Christ" (Jacob 7:11; see also 4:4–6). The Savior Himself, when He ministered in the flesh, showed how the law of Moses, the Prophets, and the Psalms (the three divisions of the Hebrew Bible), had all foretold of Him (see Luke 24:27, 44). Paul's epistle to the Romans confirmed that many of the people would not accept the testimony of the ancient prophets. He said, "But they have not all obeyed the gospel" (Romans 10:16), quoting the first phrase of Isaiah 53:1 to support his statement. Thus, both the Book of Mormon and the Bible give us the correct meaning of Isaiah's words "who hath believed our report?"

Abinadi does not comment on the last half of Isaiah 53:1, "and to whom is the arm of the Lord revealed?" However, John interprets the many miracles that Jesus did among the Jews during His sojourn in the flesh as a fulfillment of Isaiah's words that the arm of the Lord would be revealed (see John 12:37–38). The performance of miracles exhibited His power as the Son of God. Thus the people rejected the written testimony of their Redeemer as well as the physical evidence provided by His manifestations of miracles. Although both testimonies were rejected, the two types of witnesses established the divinity of the Messiah.

Mosiah 14:2: "For he shall grow up before him as a tender plant, and as a root out of dry ground; he hath no form nor comeliness; and when we shall see him there is no beauty that we should desire him" (compare Isaiah 53:2).

This verse gives only a vague picture of Christ and His nature on earth. However, Abinadi teaches quite specifically about Christ and His nature. In Mosiah 15:1–4 Abinadi comments on the nature of Christ as both the Father and the Son:

"I would that ye should understand that God himself shall come down among the children of men, and shall redeem his people.

"And because he dwelleth in flesh he shall be called the Son of God, and having subjected the flesh to the will of the Father, being the Father and the Son—

"The Father, because he was conceived by the power of God; and the Son, because of the flesh; thus becoming the Father and Son—

"And they are one God, yea, the very Eternal Father of heaven and of earth" (Mosiah 15:1–4).

Jesus Christ attained godhood in the premortal life (see Joseph Smith Translation, John 1:1–2). He was the God of Abraham, Isaac, and Jacob and the leader of the children of Israel out of Egypt (see 1 Nephi 19:10; 1 Corinthians 10:1–4). Jesus' coming among humankind begins with His birth and childhood. Isaiah had previously foretold the Redeemer's birth (Isaiah 7:14; 9:6), but in Isaiah 53 he describes His childhood. When studied in its context, Abinadi's commentary provides a beautiful explanation of the life, the nature, and the roles of our Lord and Savior as He came "down among the children of men" (Mosiah 15:1).

Abinadi's specific commentary in Mosiah 15:2 is difficult to understand on a first or even a second reading: "And because he dwelleth in flesh he shall be called the Son of God, and having subjected the flesh to the will of the Father, being the Father and the Son" (Mosiah 15:2). This verse refers to Jesus' mortal ministry, when He would come to earth as a mortal and be called the Son of God; however, He would subject Himself while in His mortal tabernacle to do the will of His Father in Heaven. The will of the Father was that Christ "be lifted up upon the cross; and after that [he] had been lifted up upon the cross, that [he] might draw all men unto [him], that as [he had] been lifted up by men even so should men be lifted up by the Father, to stand before [him], to be judged of their works, whether they be good or whether they be evil" (3 Nephi 27:14). In other words, the Father's will was for Christ to come and atone for all humankind. Thus, while He would live upon the earth as the Son of God, He would carry out the will of the Father and through divine investiture of authority would represent the Father. Therefore, He would be the Father and the Son while living upon the earth.

The above explanation by Abinadi qualifies as a commentary on the first phrase of Isaiah 53:2: "For he shall grow up before him as a tender plant, and as a root out of dry ground." By substituting nouns for pronouns, we get a clearer picture: "For [Christ] shall grow up before [Elohim] as a tender plant." A tender plant is one that must be given special care by the gardener. It may need to be covered at night to protect it from frost, uncovered during the day to enable it to absorb the light and sunshine, and watered at frequent or regular hours. In like manner, the Father cared for His Son throughout His early childhood.

Luke records that "the child [Jesus] grew, and waxed strong in spirit, filled with wisdom: and the grace of God was upon him" (Luke 2:40). At age 12, He went with His parents on their annual passover trek to the temple. Upon their return, Jesus tarried behind—unknown to His parents. Missing Him at the end of the first day's journey, they spent three days searching for Him and found Him conversing with the learned doctors of Judaism (see Luke 2:41–48). In response to His mother's mild chastisement, He responded, "How is it that ye sought me? wist ye not that I must be about my Father's business? And they understood not the saying which he spake unto them" (Luke 2:49–50). Even His mother seems not to have known the extent to which His

Heavenly Father had tutored Him. He had indeed been cared for by the Father as a tender plant.

The phrase "root out of dry ground" may be interpreted as Christ growing up in apostate Judaism. In Revelation 22:16, Christ identifies Himself as "the root and the offspring of David."

Both Mary, His mother, and Joseph, His stepfather, were descendants of David and of the lineage of Judah (see Matthew 1:1–17; Luke 3:23–38). Judah, as a nation, was spiritually barren and could not give Him the nurturing He needed to prepare Him for His ministry; that nurturing was given to Him instead by His Father. His nurturing was perfect and prepared Christ for His ministry in due time. Joseph Smith taught that Jesus was prepared for His ministry long before He was thirty years of age but waited to begin His ministry until the Father directed Him: "When still a boy He had all the intelligence necessary to enable Him to rule and govern the kingdom of the Jews, and could reason with the wisest and most profound doctors of law and divinity, and make their theories and practice to appear like folly compared with the wisdom He possessed; but He was a boy only, and lacked physical strength even to defend His own person; and was subject to cold, to hunger and to death."[1]

Being thus prepared, He carried out the will of the Father when the time came for Him to fulfill His ministry.

Having referred to the ministry of Jesus, Abinadi comments on the nature of the Son of God during mortality that would enable Him to finalize His ministry by bringing about the Resurrection. Christ is "the Father, because he was conceived by the power of God; and the Son, because of the flesh; thus becoming the Father and Son" (Mosiah 15:3). Because He was conceived by an immortal being, His immortal Father in Heaven, Jesus had immortality as a part of His own nature. Because He was born of a mortal woman, He was also part mortal. Being mortal He was subject to death and had power to lay down His life; being immortal He had power to break the bands of death, or take up His life. This He clearly taught to the Jews during His earthly ministry:

"Therefore doth my Father love me, because I lay down my life, that I might take it again.

"No man taketh it from me, but I lay it down of myself. I have power to lay it down, and I have power to take it again. This commandment have I received of my Father" (John 10:17–18).

Possessing the power of the Father enabled Him to overcome the grave and bring about the Resurrection. Through His dual nature He was the Father and Son, being immortal as well as mortal.

Abinadi's explanation of Christ's nature seems to be a commentary on the latter part of Isaiah 53:2: "He hath no form nor comeliness; and when we shall see him there is no beauty that we should desire him" (Mosiah 14:2). That Jesus had "no form nor comeliness" is the prophet Isaiah's way of saying that He looked like a normal Jewish boy and was not distinctive in His looks because He was the Son of God. People in Nazareth did not look upon Him as different from His brothers and sisters or other children in the community. They referred to Him as "the carpenter's son" (Matthew 13:54–56) or "the son of Joseph whose father and mother we know" (John 6:42). His having "no beauty that we should desire him" is not an indication of ugliness or plainness but is poetic parallelism, a repetition of the same thought in the second line. It was another expression of the fact that He looked like any other child growing up in Nazareth. Abinadi's commentary explains how this was possible: Christ was both mortal and the divine Son of God.

After describing the dual nature of the mortal Messiah, Abinadi adds one more dimension to his description of the Savior: "And they are one God, yea, the very Eternal Father of heaven and of earth" (Mosiah 15:4). Verse 4 is a summation of the two previous verses. The one God referred to is Jesus Christ. The plural "they" refers to the dual roles in His ministry and to His dual nature as the Father and the Son. He is the Son of God, but by divine investiture of authority He represents the Father in His ministry; having immortality and mortality in His nature He has power over life and death. Thus He has all power in heaven and in earth. He is the divine Son of God with all the attributes of His Father to make the Atonement and bring about the

Resurrection. His is the role of the Father and the Son, and He is thus one God.[2]

Abinadi's statement that Christ is "the very Eternal Father of heaven and of earth" (Mosiah 15:4) undoubtedly refers to the creative power of Christ as the Father of this earth and of other earths in the heavens. That Christ created this and other worlds is repeatedly taught in the New Testament (see John 1:3, 10; Colossians 1:16; Hebrews 1:2). It is also confirmed in modern scripture (see D&C 14:9; 76:24; 93:10; Moses 1:31–33). A diagram of Abinadi's teaching in Mosiah 15:2–4 would be thus:

TABLE 1. SUMMARY OF ABINADI'S COMMENTARY ON ISAIAH 53:2–4

A. How Christ Is Both the Father and the Son

	The Father	*The Son*
Christ's ministry provides the Atonement.	He is the Father because He does the will of the Father (Mosiah 15:2).	He is the Son because He dwelt in the flesh (Mosiah 15:2).
Christ's nature provides the Resurrection.	He was immortal because He was conceived by the power of God (Mosiah 15:3).	He was mortal because He was born of a mortal mother with the power to lay down His life (Mosiah 15:3).

B. Christ's Dual Nature

Christ created the heaven and earth.	He is one God—Jesus Christ (Mosiah 15:4).

The prophet Abinadi had masterfully shown the apostate priests the role of Christ as the Father by divine investiture of authority and the divine nature that would enable Him to atone for the sins of humankind and provide for their resurrection. In addition, he testified that Christ was the Father as the Creator of heaven and earth.

The supposedly complex definition of Jesus Christ given by Abinadi is really quite simple and beautiful when seen in the light of Abinadi's commentary on Isaiah, which is supported by modern revelation. In a revelation to Joseph Smith that was at least in part originally of the record of John, the Lord proclaimed: "And that I am in the Father, and the Father in me, and the Father and I are one—The Father because he gave me of his fulness, and the Son because I was in the world and made flesh my tabernacle, and dwelt among the sons of men" (D&C 93:3–4). This shows that John, as well as Abinadi, and certainly all of the prophets, knew and appreciated the role of Jesus Christ.

Other Book of Mormon prophets also understood and taught the position of Christ as fulfilling the role of the Father as well as the Son. Nephi, son of Lehi, taught that "there is a God, and he is Christ, and he cometh in the fulness of his own time" (2 Nephi 11:7). Amulek taught the repentant lawyer Zeezrom that there is only one God who is the Son of God and that "he is the very Eternal Father of heaven and of earth, and all things which in them are; he is the beginning and the end, the first and last" (Alma 11:39; see also 26–40).

In the meridian of time as Nephi prayed on behalf of his people concerning the coming of the sign of Christ's birth as prophesied by Samuel the Lamanite, the voice of the Lord came to Nephi saying that the sign would be given that night and that on the morrow He would come into the world to fulfill what the prophets had spoken and made known from the foundation of the world. He further testified that He would come "to do the will, both of the Father and of the Son—of the Father because of me, and of the Son because of my flesh" (3 Nephi 1:13–14). And as a last example, hundreds of years before the Nephite prophets taught these truths, the Lord appeared to the brother of Jared and identified Himself as "he who was prepared from the foundation of the world to redeem [his] people. Behold, I am Jesus Christ. I am the Father and the Son. In me shall all mankind have life, and that eternally, even they who shall believe on my name" (Ether 3:14). Thus we see that this eternal truth of Christ's true position was taught throughout the history of the Nephites and among the Jaredites as well. Hopefully, as we understand the role of Jesus Christ as the Father and the Son as taught in the Book of Mormon, we will also appreciate more fully the subtitle of the Book of Mormon, "Another Testament of Jesus Christ."

A further verification of Christ's various roles as the Father was given in "A Doctrinal Exposition by the First Presidency and the Twelve" on 30 June 1916. On this occasion, the Brethren gave detailed information and scriptural evidence about the four uses of the term *Father* that appear in the scriptures. Their exposition is really the key to understanding Mosiah 15. Because of the length and detail of this exposition, I will just outline its four major points here.[3]

1. Father as literal parent (see Hebrews 12:9; Ether 3:14)
2. Father as Creator (see Mosiah 15:4; Alma 11:38–39; Ether 4:7)
3. Jesus Christ, the Father of those who abide in His gospel (see John 17:6–12, 20–24; D&C 9:1; 25:1; 34:3; 121:7)
4. Jesus Christ, the Father by divine investiture of authority (see John 14:28; Revelation 22:8–9; D&C 93:21)

All the scriptural uses of the term *Father* thus refer to Jesus Christ, except our being the spirit offspring of our Father in Heaven. The title page of the Book of Mormon declares that a major purpose of the book is "the convincing of the Jew and Gentile that Jesus is the Christ, the Eternal God" (see also 2 Nephi 26:12–13). Understanding Abinadi's commentary on Isaiah helps fulfill this major purpose.

Mosiah 14:3–5: "He is despised and rejected of men; a man of sorrows, and acquainted with grief; and we hid as it were our faces from him; he was despised, and we esteemed him not.

"Surely he has borne our griefs, and carried our sorrows; yet we did esteem him stricken, smitten of God, and afflicted.

"But he was wounded for our transgressions, he was bruised for our iniquities; the chastisement of our peace was upon him; and with his stripes we are healed" (compare Isaiah 53:3–5).

Abinadi gives but one verse of commentary: "And thus the flesh becoming subject to the Spirit, or the Son to the Father, being one

God, suffereth temptation, and yieldeth not to the temptation, but suffereth himself to be mocked, and scourged, and cast out, and disowned by his people" (Mosiah 15:5). Here Abinadi explains Isaiah's prophecy of Christ's ministry. Not only would Christ be rejected and humiliated, but He would also be tempted. However, He would not yield to temptation. This comment by Abinadi helps us better understand the Savior's ministry and also the perfect example He set as part of the overall Atonement for humankind. As He commanded the Nephites, we are also to be the manner of beings that He was in His ministry (see 3 Nephi 27:27). We must be "willing to submit to all things which the Lord seeth fit to inflict upon [us], even as a child doth submit to his father" (Mosiah 3:19), or, as Abinadi says, to submit our flesh to the Spirit as the Son had to the Father.

The writings of the New Testament apostles also support Abinadi's commentary. Matthew paraphrased Isaiah 53:4—"Himself took our infirmities, and bare our sicknesses"—to show its fulfillment in Jesus' casting out devils and healing the sick in Capernaum (see Matthew 8:16–17). Paul taught the Hebrews that Jesus "was in all points tempted like as we are, yet without sin" (Hebrews 4:15). And Peter quotes or paraphrases parts of Isaiah 53:4–5 and equates it with Jesus' being on the cross: "Who his own self bare our sins in his own body on the tree, that we, being dead to sins, should live unto righteousness: by whose stripes ye were healed" (1 Peter 2:24). While His mission culminated on the cross, His entire life and particularly His ministry was one of temptation: being mocked, scourged, cast out, and disowned by His people. Mark records that Jesus taught His disciples "that the Son of man must suffer many things, and be rejected of the elders, and of the chief priests, and scribes, and be killed" (Mark 8:31). With the support of these scriptures, we may conclude that Abinadi gave us a briefer but very accurate commentary of the Savior's ministry.

Mosiah 14:6: "All we like sheep have gone astray; we have turned every one to his own way; and the Lord hath laid on him the iniquities of us all" (compare Isaiah 53:6).

Abinadi explains the relationship between Christ and the Father after He had completed His ministry: "Having ascended into heaven, having the bowels of mercy; being filled with compassion towards the children of men; standing betwixt them and justice; having broken the bands of death, taken upon himself their iniquity and their transgressions, having redeemed them, and satisfied the demands of justice" (Mosiah 15:9). This commentary sheds further light on the role of Jesus Christ as the Father and the Son. Having suffered for all humankind's sins, Jesus Christ fulfilled the demands of justice in His role as the Father. His compassion to those who repent illustrates His role as the Son as His mercy satisfies the demands of justice. While the New Testament tells us that the Atonement was accomplished, we must turn to the Book of Mormon to enlarge our understanding of the roles of mercy and justice. Further sections of the Book of Mormon, such as Amulek's testimony to the apostate Zoramites (see Alma 34:15–16) and Alma's instructions to his wayward son Corianton (see Alma 42), are also most enlightening on these principles of mercy and justice. An analysis of these references will be left to another time.

Mosiah 14:7: Isaiah prophesies of Jesus' being judged before Pilate and Herod: "He was oppressed, and he was afflicted, yet he opened not his mouth: he is brought as a lamb to the slaughter, and as a sheep before her shearers is dumb so he openeth not his mouth" (compare Isaiah 53:7).

Abinadi's commentary on this verse is little more than a repetition of Isaiah: "And after all this, after working many mighty miracles among the children of men, he shall be led, yea, even as Isaiah said, as a sheep before the shearer is dumb, so he opened not his mouth" (Mosiah 15:6). The New Testament records Jesus' appearance before Pilate and Herod. While Jesus did answer Pilate, He did so only sparingly, and on one occasion He gave him no answer (see John 19:9). When Pilate sent Him to Herod, Jesus answered Him not a word. Herod could only retaliate by mocking Him (see Luke 23:8–11). Peter described the trials this way: "Who, when he was reviled, reviled not again; when he suffered, he threatened not; but committed himself to him that judgeth righteously" (1 Peter 2:23). Isaiah's prophecy was fulfilled.

Mosiah 14:8: "He was taken from prison and from judgment: and who shall declare his generation? for he was cut off out of the land of the living: for the transgressions of my people was he stricken" (compare Isaiah 53:8).

In his commentary, Abinadi elaborates on the death of the Savior, speaking of the Resurrection following the Crucifixion and then answering Isaiah's question: "Who shall declare his generation?" (see Mosiah 15:7–13). Abinadi first comments on the Savior's crucifixion and death, "Yea, even so he shall be led, crucified, and slain, the flesh becoming subject even unto death, the will of the Son being swallowed up in the will of the Father" (Mosiah 15:7), and then concludes, "And thus God breaketh the bands of death, having gained the victory over death; giving the Son power to make intercession for the children of men" (Mosiah 15:8). Today we find the concept of breaking the bands of death and gaining a victory over death in Paul's first epistle to the Corinthians; however, Paul is quoting what "is written" (1 Corinthians 15:54–55). Where was it written? Some have supposed it to be a quotation from Hosea 13:14, but if so, the Hosea text has been greatly modified. It seems more logical that this quote is a part of the plain and precious parts that have been lost from the Bible (see 1 Nephi 13:23–29). Nonetheless, that the Resurrection of Christ would break the bands of death and gain victory over the grave was known to the Old Testament prophets. Abinadi would probably not have coined a phrase so close to what Paul was reading from the Hebrew Bible. Of course the Spirit could have dictated the same words, but it seems most logical that both Paul and Abinadi were quoting from an earlier text.

After speaking of the Resurrection and Atonement of Christ (see Mosiah 15:8–9), Abinadi answers the question posed by Isaiah: "And now I say unto you, who shall declare his generation?": "Behold, I say unto you, that when his soul has been made an offering for sin he shall see his seed. And now what say ye? And who shall be his seed?" (Mosiah 15:10). Abinadi combines his answer to "who shall declare his generation" with Isaiah's declaration that when Christ made "his soul an offering for sin he shall see his seed." The question and the declaration go hand in hand. Those who are spiritually begotten of Christ through being born again are adopted as His sons and daughters (see

Galatians 4:1–7; Romans 8:14–17; Mosiah 5:7). Thus, the adopted, born-again sons and daughters of Jesus Christ will declare the message of the gospel that Jesus Christ was sent to the earth to redeem all humankind. Following His death, Christ's apostles and others were to take this message to all the world (see Mark 16:15). Abinadi explains at some length that these messengers will be the prophets and those who have accepted and lived their message:

"Behold I say unto you, that whosoever has heard the words of the prophets, yea, all the holy prophets who have prophesied concerning the coming of the Lord—I say unto you, that all those who have hearkened unto their words, and believed that the Lord would redeem his people, and have looked forward to that day for a remission of their sins, I say unto you, that these are his seed, or they are the heirs of the kingdom of God.

"For these are they whose sins he has borne; these are they for whom he has died, to redeem them from their transgressions. And now, are they not his seed?

"Yea, and are not the prophets, every one that has opened his mouth to prophesy, that has not fallen into transgression, I mean all the holy prophets ever since the world began? I say unto you that they are his seed" (Mosiah 15:11–13).

Although Isaiah's prophecy continues, Abinadi has laid the groundwork and returns to the original question about the meaning of Isaiah 52:7, posed by Noah's apostate priest.

ABINADI'S RESPONSE TO THE PRIESTS

Mosiah 12:21: "How beautiful upon the mountains are the feet of him that bringeth good tidings; that publisheth peace; that bringeth good tidings of good; that publisheth salvation; that saith unto Zion, Thy God reigneth" (compare Isaiah 52:7).

Abinadi's commentary on this verse constitutes the rest of Mosiah 15. Because of Abinadi's extensive discussion of Isaiah 53, King Noah's priests are prepared to understand not only the meaning of the verse in question but also the Plan of Salvation. Abinadi's commentary begins with an interpretation of Isaiah 52:7 and ends with a call to repentance.

Abinadi had already established the idea that the seed of Christ are those spiritually begotten of Him as their Father of eternal life. He now states that these same servants are the publishers of peace, and how beautiful upon the mountains were their feet and the feet of those who are now and who will yet publish peace (see Mosiah 15:14–17). True peace comes only from the gospel, so those who travel (upon their feet) to preach the gospel upon the mountains of the earth are beautiful in the eyes of the people who accept their message.

This verse also refers to the founder of that peace—Jesus Christ. Without Him there would be no peace. In Abinadi's words:

"And behold, I say unto you, this is not all. For O how beautiful upon the mountains are the feet of him that bringeth good tidings, that is the founder of peace, yea, even the Lord, who has redeemed his people; yea, him who has granted salvation unto his people;

"For were it not for the redemption which he hath made for his people, which was prepared from the foundation of the world, I say unto you, were it not for this, all mankind must have perished" (Mosiah 15:18–19).

Christ broke the bands of death, and as the Son of God He reigns and has power over the dead that He may bring about their resurrection. The first resurrection includes those who "have been, and who are, and who shall be, even until the resurrection of Christ" (Mosiah 15:21). It includes the prophets and those who believed in their words and kept the commandments. They will dwell with Christ, who redeemed them, and have eternal life (see Mosiah 15:22–23). The first resurrection also includes those who died in ignorance before Christ came, not having had salvation declared to them (see Mosiah 15:24). Although Abinadi does not expound upon this group, Peter and modern revelation qualify their salvation upon the condition of their accepting the gospel in the spirit world (see 1 Peter 3:18; 4:5–6; D&C 137:7–9). Abinadi also announces that little children shall have eternal life (see Mosiah 15:25; see also D&C 137:10).

Abinadi closes his commentary on Isaiah 52:7 with a warning to those who rebel against Christ and die in their sins, those who have known the commandments and would not keep them. These ought to tremble and fear, for salvation does not come to such, and justice will claim them instead of mercy (see Mosiah 15:26–27).

Mosiah 12:22–24: "Thy watchmen shall lift up the voice; with the voice together shall they sing: for they shall see eye to eye when the Lord shall bring again Zion;

"Break forth into joy; sing together ye waste places of Jerusalem; for the Lord hath comforted his people, he hath redeemed Jerusalem;

"The Lord hath made bare his holy arm in the eyes of all the nations; and all the ends of the earth shall see the salvation of our God" (compare Isaiah 52:8–10).

Abinadi's commentary paraphrases Isaiah's words: "And now I say unto you that the time shall come that the salvation of the Lord shall be declared to every nation, kindred, tongue, and people" (Mosiah 15:28). Abinadi prefaced and followed his commentary on this verse with a paraphrase of Isaiah 52:10, which states that the salvation of the Lord shall be declared to every nation, kindred, tongue, and people (see Mosiah 15:28–16:1). Isaiah's declaration that salvation would come when the Lord would bring again (gather) Zion and when the Lord comforted (gathered) His people in Jerusalem designates the two major gathering places of the latter days. It also sheds light upon the reference to the mountains where peace is published, or, in other words, where the gospel will be taught. Both Zion and Jerusalem are designated, in scripture, as the tops of the mountains (see Isaiah 40:9; 1 Nephi 19:13; 2 Nephi 12:2; D&C 133:12–13). While the gospel will eventually be taught to all peoples, the major centers of administering the gospel will be from Zion (the Americas) and Jerusalem. The people who accept the gospel shall see eye to eye and confess that God's judgments are just because they will understand the gospel taught by the prophets and the missionaries.

Abinadi proceeds to warn those who have become wicked, carnal, sensual, and devilish because of the Fall (see Mosiah 16:2–5). He speaks of Christ as though He had already come (see Mosiah 16:6) and then either quotes or paraphrases the lost scripture concerning Christ's breaking the bands of death (see Mosiah 16:7–8). He comments further on

Christ as the light and life of the world and on the power of the Resurrection and Judgment that is to come (see Mosiah 16:9–12).

Abinadi concludes his comments with a warning to Noah's wicked priests:

"And now, ought ye not to tremble and repent of your sins, and remember that only in and through Christ ye can be saved?

"Therefore, if ye teach the law of Moses, also teach that it is a shadow of those things which are to come—

"Teach them that redemption cometh through Christ the Lord, who is the very Eternal Father" (Mosiah 16:13–15).

The priests did not hearken to Abinadi's warning; rather, they put him to death because he would not recall the words he had taught about God (see Mosiah 17:1–13). Sometime after Abinadi's death, Limhi, the king of a group of Nephites in bondage to the Lamanites, also witnessed that Abinadi was martyred for his testimony of Christ:

"And a prophet of the Lord have they slain; yea, a chosen man of God, who told them of their wickedness and abominations, and prophesied of many things which are to come, yea, even the coming of Christ.

"And because he said unto them that Christ was the God, the Father of all things, and said that he should take upon him the image of man, and it should be the image after which man was created in the beginning; or in other words, he said that man was created after the image of God, and that God should come down among the children of men, and take upon him flesh and blood, and go forth upon the face of the earth—

"And now, because he said this, they did put him to death; and many more things did they do which brought down the wrath of God upon them" (Mosiah 7:26–28).

Thus, Abinadi was killed because he taught the truth about Christ as the God of the Nephites. The Prophet Joseph Smith was also killed because he taught the same concept of Christ and the Godhead. As members of the Church and true disciples of Jesus Christ, we have the responsibility of taking this great truth to the world. We can do this through the message given in the Book of Mormon.

APPENDIX A

TABLE 2. ABINADI'S COMMENTARY ON ISAIAH

Abinadi speaks in . . .	*Commenting on . . .*	*Other commentary*
Mosiah 14:1	Isaiah 53:1	Romans 10:16; John 12:37–38
Mosiah 15:2	Isaiah 53:2a	Luke 2:40–50
Mosiah 15:3	Isaiah 53:2b	Revelation 22:16; Matthew 13:55–56; John 6:42
Mosiah 15:4	Isaiah 53:2	
Mosiah 15:5	Isaiah 53:3–5	3 Nephi 27:27; Mosiah 3:19; Matthew 8:16–17; Hebrews 4:15; 1 Peter 2:24; Mark 8:31
Mosiah 15:9	Isaiah 53:6	Alma 34:15–16; 42
Mosiah 15:6	Isaiah 53:7	
Mosiah 15:7–8	Isaiah 53:8	1 Corinthians 15:54–55; Mosiah 5:7
Mosiah 15:11–13	Isaiah 53:10b	
Mosiah 15:14–27	Isaiah 52:7	1 Peter 3:18–20; 4:5–6; D&C 137:7–10
Mosiah 15:28–16:1	Isaiah 52:8–10	
Mosiah 16:2–12	Lost scripture?	
Mosiah 16:13–15	Conclusion	

APPENDIX B

Isaiah 53:9: "And he made his grave with the wicked, and with the rich in his death; because he had done no violence, neither was any deceit in his mouth" (compare Mosiah 14:9).

Abinadi does not comment on this verse from Isaiah. Did the priests understand it? Jesus was crucified between two thieves (see Matthew 27:38; Mark 15:27; Luke 23:32–33; John 19:18). He was buried in the tomb of a rich man, Joseph of Arimathaea (see Matthew 27:57–60; Mark 15:42–46; Luke 23:50–53; John 19:38–42). Isaiah's announcement that He had done "*no evil*" (Mosiah 14:9; emphasis added) is the only word change between the text of the King James Bible and the Book of Mormon. The King James Version records, "He had done no violence" (Isaiah 53:9). "No evil" is consistent with Abinadi's earlier declaration that He yielded not to temptation (see Mosiah 15:5). No "deceit in his mouth" proclaims that He spoke truth at all times. Peter slightly varies the same Isaiah passage: "Neither was *guile* found in his mouth" (1 Peter 2:22; emphasis added). The message is clear: there was no reason or basis that justified His crucifixion. However, His death was not only foreknown but was foreordained (see 1 Peter 1:20; Ether 3:14). Isaiah understood this clearly.

Isaiah 53:10: "Yet it pleased the Lord to bruise him; he hath put him to grief: when thou shalt make his soul an offering for sin, he shall see his seed, he shall prolong his days, and the pleasure of the Lord shall prosper in his hand" (compare Mosiah 14:10).

The wording of the opening phrase of this verse may have two meanings depending on the interpretation of the word *Lord,* as capitalized in the Book of Mormon text. In the King James text, the word is all in capital letters, LORD. Some would interpret this to mean Jehovah, and others would interpret it to refer to Elohim. Since there are no original manuscripts, the correct interpretation can be determined only by the context. Through the years, scribes have altered the word for God back and forth to fit their own understanding.[4] If the person referred to as Lord is Elohim, then the phrase would read that it pleased Elohim to bruise Christ or allow Him to suffer affliction and grief as a part of the Atonement. This interpretation was nicely summarized by John in his Gospel: "For God so loved the world, that he gave his only begotten Son, that whosoever believeth in him should not perish, but have everlasting life" (John 3:16).

If the word *Lord* is interpreted to refer to Jehovah, then it would read that it pleased Jehovah to bruise Christ. Since Jehovah is the Old Testament name for Christ, this may sound like an impossible interpretation. However, it could be interpreted to say that Christ was willing to suffer to bring about the Atonement. This interpretation is sustained in modern revelation. In a revelation to Orson Pratt, Jesus Christ identified Himself as He "who so loved the world that he gave his own life, that as many as would believe might become the sons of God" (D&C 34:1–3). Perhaps both interpretations are valid. Certainly Elohim was the author of the Plan of Salvation that provided for a Savior (see Moses 4:1–2; Abraham 3:27–28), and, as revealed to Orson Pratt, Christ did make a freewill offering.

The offering of Christ's soul for sin was done in the Garden of Gethsemane. There He suffered as a God "temptations, and pain of body, hunger, thirst, and fatigue, even more than man can suffer, except it be unto death; for behold, blood cometh from every pore, so great shall be his anguish for the wickedness and the abominations of his people" (Mosiah 3:7; see also 2 Nephi 9:20–21; Alma 7:11; Luke 22:44). As He paid this all-encompassing price for sin, He apparently had a panoramic view of all the world's experiences, past, present, and future and, in some way beyond our comprehension, He placed Himself in the position of every inhabitant of the earth, that He might satisfy the demands of justice for the punishment of every broken law of humankind. He was able to prolong His days, at least in a figurative sense, that He might pass through this agonizing ordeal for the entire period of the earth's habitation by mortal beings, from Adam to the final scene. With the payment of this eternal debt, the pleasure (will) of the Lord (Jehovah or Christ) and Lord (Elohim) was fulfilled, and Christ prospered by fulfilling the mission of His atonement. With the sacrifice of His soul and the end of His mortal life, Christ's seed became responsible for prolonging His days in another way, that of carrying on His mission. His seed, as stated above, are the prophets and teachers of the gospel and all who accept the gospel message (see Mosiah 15:10–13).

Isaiah 53:11: "He shall see of the travail of his soul, and shall be satisfied: by his knowledge shall my righteous servant justify many; for he shall bear their iniquities" (compare Mosiah 14:11).

An understanding of verse 11 comes by substituting nouns for the pronouns. From the context of the verse, it is clear that Elohim shall see the travail of Jesus Christ's soul and shall be satisfied. Jesus suffered in Gethsemane and had "taken upon himself [the people's] iniquity and their transgressions, having redeemed them, and satisfied the demands of justice" (Mosiah 15:9). Jesus' knowledge of the sins of all humankind (see 2 Nephi 9:20) and His sinlessness—a "righteous servant"—enabled Him to make an eternal sacrifice. Many people will thus be able to justify themselves and obtain salvation because Jesus paid for their sins. Some have interpreted the servant's justifying of "many" as evidence that Jesus, in His foreknowledge, only suffered for those who He knew would repent. This interpretation is not consistent with Jacob's declaration that Jesus "suffereth the pains of all men, yea, the pains of every living creature, both men, women, and children, who belong to the family of Adam" (2 Nephi 9:21); or with Jacob and Amulek's pronouncement that the Atonement must be "an infinite atonement" (2 Nephi 9:7), or "an infinite and eternal sacrifice" (Alma 34:10). Samuel the Lamanite taught that the Atonement brought humankind back into the presence of God (see Helaman 14:17). However, Jacob taught that only those who repent, are baptized, and have perfect faith in the Holy One of Israel will be saved—and if not they will be damned (see 2 Nephi 9:23–24). Therefore, although Jesus paid for the sins of all humankind, not all will meet the criteria for obtaining those blessings in their lives (see D&C 19:16–19). Those who do meet the criteria will be part of the fulfillment of Isaiah's further prophecy, which follows:

Isaiah 53:12: "Therefore will I divide him a portion with the great, and he shall divide the spoil with the strong; because he hath poured out his soul unto death: and he was numbered with the transgressors; and he bare the sin of many, and made intercession for the transgressors" (compare Mosiah 14:12).

The context shows that Elohim, or the Father, is still speaking in this verse. Because Jesus had fulfilled His role as the Redeemer of humankind, He "ascended into heaven" (Mosiah 15:9) and took His position on the right hand of the Father in the council of the Gods (see D&C 20:24). In turn, Jesus was willing to divide His blessings, or spoils—a term referring to what was obtained after winning a battle—with those who accept and remain strong in the gospel. He taught this principle to His disciples at the end of His ministry: "Ye are they which have continued with me in my temptations. And I appoint unto you a kingdom, as my Father hath appointed unto me; That ye may eat and drink at my table in my kingdom, and sit on thrones judging the twelve tribes of Israel" (Luke 22:28–30).

Jesus was able to do this because He had poured out His soul unto death, or had freely given His life that "I might take it again. No man taketh it from me, but I lay it down of myself" (John 10:17–18). In accomplishing this momentous task He was numbered with the transgressors, or suffered the most degrading of deaths at that time. Prior to His death He had gone to Gethsemane and there, as Isaiah foretold, borne the sins of those who repented and also paid for those who ignorantly sinned. As explained earlier, Christ paid for the sins of all humankind, both the repentant and unrepentant, but the context of Isaiah describes only those who benefitted from the Atonement by repenting of their sins. Having completed his prophecy of Christ's suffering, Isaiah returned to prophesy of the gathering of Israel (see Isaiah 54), the subject he had left to insert this inspiring and now well-known prophecy of Christ's mission.

NOTES

1. Joseph Smith, *Teachings of the Prophet Joseph Smith,* comp. Joseph Fielding Smith (Salt Lake City: Deseret Book, 1976), 392.

2. It should be kept in mind that Abinadi is not instructing prospective members of the Church. He is accusing, chastising, and refuting a group of apostate priests who claim to be scriptural authorities. Recall his words to them earlier:

"And now Abinadi said unto them: Are you priests, and pretend to teach this people, and to understand the spirit of prophesying, and yet desire to know of me what these things mean?

"I say unto you, wo be unto you for perverting the ways of the Lord! For if ye understand these things ye have not taught them; therefore, ye have perverted the ways of the Lord" (Mosiah 12:25–26).

3. James R. Clark, comp., *Messages of the First Presidency* (Salt Lake City: Bookcraft, 1965), 5:26–34; see also James E. Talmage, *Articles of Faith* (Salt Lake City: Deseret Book, 1981), appendix 2, 466–73.

4. Illustrations of the variant use of the word may be seen in a comparison of the almost identical Psalms 14 and 53, or in Psalm 110 and Matthew's quotation of it in Matthew 22:44. It seems apparent that scribes have pondered and altered these quotations to fit their private interpretations of the text.

15

Alma's Conversion: Reminiscences in His Sermons

S. Kent Brown

The sermons of Alma deserve at least a fraction of the centuries-long attention that the epistles of the Apostle Paul have received. Alma's recorded sermons, whether formal or spontaneous, weave a tapestry of complex and variegated colors, of rich imagery, and yet of a bold and simple unity that holds in tight focus the unspeakable blessings of accepting the Atonement of Jesus Christ. This chapter looks at only one of the colorful strands woven into Alma's sermons, that of reminiscences of his conversion experience: the three days during which he was completely unconscious, after the unexpected appearance of the angel of the Lord to him and several friends (see Mosiah 27; Alma 36). To be sure, students of the Book of Mormon have long recognized that Alma's life-changing, three-day experience stood at the foundation of all that he did and said for the rest of his life. But unlike Moses and Isaiah, who almost never referred to their life-changing experiences, Alma's memory of that remarkable ordeal was present with him to the point that all his sermons are infused with allusions to it.

The passage that describes Alma's conversion experience in most detail, beginning with the appearance of the angel and recounting

S. Kent Brown is a professor of ancient scripture and director of ancient studies at Brigham Young University.

events of the next three days, is chapter 36 of his book. Importantly, we have a second narration of the angel's words and the resulting impact on Alma in chapter 27 of the book of Mosiah. Moreover, this same passage records some of the words that Alma spoke immediately following his experience (see Mosiah 27:24–31). Because the angel's utterance is important for our study, and because by his own admission Alma did not hear all that the angel said—"the angel spake more things unto me, which were heard by my brethren, but I did not hear them; . . . I fell to the earth and I did hear no more" (Alma 36:11)—I shall borrow from the account in Mosiah 27 to fill in the picture.

ALMA'S CONVERSION STORY: ALMA 36

Alma's personal recollection, recounted to his oldest son, Helaman, exhibits a number of features that appear in Alma's later sermons and extemporaneous addresses. Let me briefly summarize Alma 36 since it forms a principal key to understanding a pattern of reminiscences in Alma's sermons and sermonettes. One significant element consists of his emphasis on God's deliverance of His people, whether they be the children of Israel from Egypt, Lehi's family from Jerusalem, or others (see Alma 36:2, 28–29). A second element, which borrows language from the first, is Alma's stress on God's deliverance of the individual soul from the bondage of sin (see Alma 36:17–18). A third ingredient, related to the second, consists of a set of expressions that describe Alma's own troubled and sinful state before he received forgiveness of his sins. In this instance, he describes himself as "racked with eternal torment," "tormented with the pains of hell" and "encircled about by the everlasting chains of death" (Alma 36:12–13, 18). Associated directly with his torment, and evidently a part of it, was his feeling of "inexpressible horror" at the thought of standing "in the presence of my God, to be judged of my deeds" (Alma 36:14–15). A fourth component turns out to be the exact reversal of the third: indescribable joy and enlightenment at receiving forgiveness of sins through Jesus' atonement (see Alma 36:19–21). A fifth feature is his persistent description of his experience as being "born of God," a phrase that is distinctive to Alma among Book of Mormon authors (see Mosiah 27:25, 28; Alma

5:14; 36:5, 23–24, 26; 38:6) just as Alma is unique among Book of Mormon writers in using the phrases, "born of the Spirit" and "born again" (see Mosiah 27:24–25; Alma 5:49; 7:14). A sixth element arises from his actions as a preacher of salvation, which followed his extraordinary experience, bringing others to taste "as I have tasted" and to see "eye to eye as I have seen" (see Alma 36:26).

SERMON IN ZARAHEMLA: ALMA 5

The initial test of whether these observations had an impact on Alma's preaching comes in his first recorded sermon (Alma 5), a long and carefully articulated address delivered, presumably over a period of time and on various occasions, to "the people in the church which was established in the city of Zarahemla" (Alma 5:2), possibly consisting of seven or more congregations (see Mosiah 25:23). As one might expect, most of the elements listed above are present in the opening segment of Alma's discourse. After establishing his divine authority for preaching (see Alma 5:3), he noted that the Exodus-like deliverances of his immediate ancestors were illustrations of God's "mercy and long-suffering" and that it was important to remember these divine acts (Alma 5:4–6). On this note, he next asked his hearers, "Have ye sufficiently retained in remembrance that [God] has delivered their souls from hell?" (Alma 5:6). In framing this question, Alma effectively shifted the focus of his listeners from the Exodus and other such events to the Atonement by borrowing the language of the former to describe the latter. Specifically, Alma's use of the verb *deliver* in this context formed a firm bridge between his reference to the Exodus and his recounting of the blessings that flow from accepting the Atonement, a discussion of which immediately follows (see Alma 5:7–27).

As a further illustration of a pattern of reminiscences in this sermon, Alma's vocabulary in his discourse on the Atonement exhibits clear ties to his account of the aftermath of his encounter with the angel in Alma 36. There he spoke initially of being "racked with eternal torment" and "tormented with the pains of hell" at the memory of his sins (Alma 36:12–13), and being "encircled about by the everlasting chains of death" (Alma 36:18). Because the "thought of coming into the presence of my God did rack my soul with inexpressible horror," Alma had wished to "become extinct both soul and body, that I might not be brought to stand in the presence of my God, to be judged of my deeds" (Alma 36:14–15). Then, as he described his feelings of receiving a remission of sins, he spoke in opposite terms of the "joy, and . . . marvelous light I did behold," as well as of a vision of "God sitting upon his throne, surrounded with numberless concourses of angels, in the attitude of singing and praising their God." Alma exclaimed, "My soul did long to be there" (Alma 36:20, 22). Moreover, he talked of being "born of God" and wanting to share the joy and happiness he had received (Alma 36:23–24). Importantly, the early part of his Zarahemla speech follows a similar pattern. After noting God's deliverance of His people, the children of Israel, Alma described the ancestors of his hearers as being "encircled about by the bands of death, and the chains of hell, and an everlasting destruction did await them" (Alma 5:7). In counterbalance, he next affirmed that these forebears were not destroyed or lost; rather, the "bands of death" and "chains of hell . . . were loosed, and their souls did expand, and they did sing redeeming love" (Alma 5:8–10). Then speaking of his father, Alma noted that that there had been "a mighty change wrought in his heart" (Alma 5:12), as there had been in his own and he asked the congregation whether they themselves had been "born of God" (Alma 5:14), a phrase that he had used to describe himself. His mentioning the "song of redeeming love" (Alma 5: 9, 26) seems to be tied to the vision of God and His angels that he had seen and heard at the end of his three days of torment. That he had wanted to join in the singing is evidence of this change (see Alma 36:22).

SERMON IN GIDEON: ALMA 7

Alma's next recorded sermon appears in chapter 7. It is much shorter and less formal. He delivered it in the land of Gideon, which was apparently settled by the faithful people from the colony of Limhi whom he had known as a child. Because the sermon is chiefly an address to faithful friends, a clear patterning of reminiscences does not emerge as it does in the first section of the Zarahemla sermon. Even though the tone throughout Alma 7 is generally warm and informal, certain elements do exhibit formal language which, in Alma's words, came at the behest of the Spirit. For instance, the phrases "the Spirit hath said this much unto me" (Alma 7:9) and "for the Spirit saith" (Alma 7:14) clearly set out the authority and necessity for Alma's commanding words in verses 9 and 14 through 16. However, elements that echo Alma's experience do appear. For example, when speaking of the necessity of repenting he said that one must "be born again" (Alma 7:14), a phrase that uniquely characterizes Alma's messages elsewhere. Further, he said that the Lamb of God is "mighty to save" (Alma 7:14), a phrase that recalls similar language describing God's redeeming power manifested in the Exodus of the children of Israel (see Exodus 32:11; Deuteronomy 4:37; 7:8; 9:26). In another place, he spoke of looking forward "for the remission of your sins . . . which is to come" (Alma 7:6), possibly a recollection of his own remission of sins (see Alma 36:19–21).

SERMON IN AMMONIHAH: ALMA 9–13

Alma's third recorded sermon, which occupies most of chapter 9, was delivered under contentious conditions in the city of Ammonihah. In an effort to postpone arrest (see Alma 9:7), he opened his address by scolding his listeners for not remembering "that our father, Lehi, was brought out of Jerusalem by the hand of God" (Alma 9:9). The same point is made twice in Alma 9:22. The description of the Son of God as one who will be "quick to hear the cries of his people" (Alma 9:26) also exhibits ties to the Exodus of the Israelites from Egypt: God heard the cries of the children of Israel (see Exodus 3:7, 9; see also Exodus 6:5). That Alma raised the issue of remembering "the captivity of [their] fathers" illustrates that Alma was obedient to the angel's command that he remember it (see Mosiah 27:16) and that he felt it important to observe this instruction in his preaching (see Alma 36:2, 28–29). His subsequent reference to "a state of endless misery and woe" for the unrepentant, and his warning that God "will utterly destroy you from off the face of the earth" (Alma 9:11–12) both recall the misery that Alma felt and the destruction that he feared during his three-day ordeal (see Alma 36:11–16). Moreover, the reason for warning the people of Ammonihah of impending divine annihilation was the same as the angel's reason for threatening Alma and his brethren with destruction: so that they would no longer lead others astray, a notion also at home in the Exodus (see Deuteronomy 20:17–18). The words of the angel to Alma were: "If thou wilt of thyself be destroyed, seek no more to destroy the church of God" (Alma 36:9, 11). To the people of Ammonihah Alma said in turn, "If ye persist in your wickedness . . . ye shall be visited with utter destruction. . . . For [God] will not suffer you that ye shall live in your iniquities, to destroy his people" (Alma 9:18–19).

In contrast, God's wondrous power to deliver was not only apparent in the orchestrated escapes of His people in the past but also in "the salvation of their souls" which comes about "according to the power and deliverance of Jesus Christ" (Alma 9:28). Once again, the focus on terms such as *power* and *deliverance* recollects Exodus-like events while at the same time describing the most marvelous of all deliverances, the Atonement of Jesus Christ. Finally, Alma's reference to the Final Judgment recalls another element in his description of his three-day ordeal. To the people of the city he issued this warning: "I say unto you, that it shall be more tolerable for [the Lamanites] in the day of judgment than for you, if ye remain in your sins" (Alma 9:15). The sense is clear. For the people of Ammonihah, the Judgment would be terrible. On this matter, Alma could speak with poignant feeling. When he had been forced into a harried contemplation of his own sins, Alma came to wish that he "could be banished and become extinct both soul and body, that I might not be brought to stand in the presence of my God, to be judged of my deeds" (Alma 36:15).

On the same day that Alma was obliged to deliver his sermon under contentious conditions to the people of Ammonihah (see Alma 9), he spontaneously responded to questions raised by several persons (Alma 12–13), including Zeezrom, a lawyer and skilled speaker who had openly opposed the preaching of Alma and his companion Amulek (see Alma 10:31). While no real pattern of reminiscences emerges from Alma's extemporaneous words, three elements that can be tied to Alma's three-day conversion experience are readily identifiable. One has to do with the prophetic function of angels, clearly recalling the role of the angel of the Lord who confronted Alma and his companions. In an apparent effort to assure his listeners that divine powers were then declaring repentance and salvation among his own people, Alma observed that "the voice of the Lord, by the mouth of angels, doth declare [salvation] unto all nations; . . . wherefore they [the angels] have come unto us" (Alma 13:22). Further, "angels are declaring [salvation] unto many at this time in our land" (Alma 13:24). Why? Because, said Alma, "at the time of [the Messiah's] coming" His arrival will "be made known unto just and holy men, by the mouth of angels" (Alma 13:24–26).

The second element deals with a notion that one might expect from Alma when one considers the character of his audience in Ammonihah: the terrible, eternal fate that awaits those unrepentant individuals who do not accept Jesus' Atonement. On this topic, Alma speaks of the wicked coming to be "bound down by the chains of hell" (Alma 13:30; see also Alma 12:17), echoing the description of his nightmarish vision of being "encircled about by the everlasting chains of death" (Alma 36:18; see also Moses 7:26–27). To the people of Ammonihah, Alma had a good deal to say about such chains. By his words the devil, or adversary, seeks to "encircle you about with his chains, that he might chain you down to everlasting destruction" (Alma 12:6). Alma then spelled out what he meant by the word *chains.* Speaking of those who harden their hearts, he proclaimed that they consequently receive "the lesser portion of the word until they know nothing concerning [God's] mysteries; and then they are taken captive by the devil, and led by his will down to destruction." This situation, Alma disclosed, "is what is meant by the chains of hell" (Alma 12:10–11).

Closely related to this second element is a third that concerns the scene at the judgment bar of God. Of his own torment, Alma said that the thought of standing before God "did rack my soul with inexpressible horror" and brought him to wish that he "could be banished and become extinct both soul and body" (Alma 36:14–15). To the people of Ammonihah, Alma made a similar point: "If we have hardened our hearts against the word, . . . then will our state be awful. . . . And in this awful state we shall not dare to look up to our God" (Alma 12:13–14). Moreover, sharing Alma's one-time desire to become extinct, those who persist in their sins "would fain be glad if [they] could command the rocks and the mountains to fall upon [them] to hide [them] from his presence" (Alma 12:14). In addition, those who come thus to the judgment bar of God will do so with "everlasting shame" (Alma 12:15).

As a capstone to this spontaneous address, Alma pled with his audience from the memory of the fearful experience through which he had suffered. Near the end he besought them, "Now, my brethren, I wish from the *inmost part of my heart,* yea, with *great anxiety even unto pain,* that ye would hearken unto my words, and cast off your sins, and not procrastinate the day of your repentance" (Alma 13:27; emphasis added). Because of his own ordeal, he knew better than most about the terrible consequences facing those who reject the message of salvation. In the case of the people of Ammonihah, Alma's dire prophecies were fulfilled when an invading Lamanite army destroyed the city and all of its inhabitants in a single day (see Alma 16:1–3, 9–11).

ALMA'S SOLILOQUY: ALMA 29

Alma's soliloquy in chapter 29 also exhibits reminiscences of his three-day experience. First, he wishes that he were an angel and, like the angel of the Lord who confronted him, he wishes he could "go forth and speak . . . with a voice to shake the earth, . . . as with the voice of thunder" (Alma 29:1–2). The descriptions of the appearance of the angel of the Lord to Alma and his friends are compelling. In his own words, Alma recounted: "God sent his holy angel to stop us by the way. And behold, he spake unto us, as it were the voice of thunder, and the whole earth did tremble beneath our feet" (Alma 36:6–7).

The account from other witnesses says that "the angel of the Lord appeared unto them; . . . and he spake as it were with a voice of thunder, which caused the earth to shake upon which they stood" (Mosiah 27:11). The similarities cannot be missed. They combine mention of the angel with reference to his thundering voice and the resulting earthquake.

The reference to the captivity of Alma's forebears forms a second tie. In his soliloquy Alma says:

"I also remember the captivity of my fathers; for I surely do know that the Lord did deliver them out of bondage. . . .

"Yea, I have always remembered the captivity of my fathers; and that same God who delivered them out of the hands of the Egyptians did deliver them out of bondage" (Alma 29:11–12).

At this point, we recall the angel's instructions to Alma: "Go, and remember the captivity of thy fathers . . . for they were in bondage, and [God] has delivered them" (Mosiah 27:16).

Alma's service as a divine instrument in bringing others to God comprises a third connection. In his soliloquy Alma declared:

"This is my glory, that perhaps I may be an instrument in the hands of God to bring some soul to repentance; and this is my joy.

"And behold, when I see many of my brethren truly penitent, and coming to the Lord their God, then is my soul filled with joy" (Alma 29:9–10).

Similarly, in his personal recounting Alma told his son Helaman that from the time of his three-day ordeal until that moment, "I have labored without ceasing, that I might bring souls unto repentance; that I might bring them to taste of the exceeding joy of which I did taste" (Alma 36:24). He continued by speaking metaphorically of his success in his missionary endeavors as if it were fruit of agricultural labors:

"The Lord doth give me exceedingly great joy in the fruit of my labors;

"For because of the word which he has imparted unto me, behold, many have been born of God, and have tasted as I have tasted, and have seen eye to eye as I have seen" (Alma 36:25–26; see also Alma 29:13–15).

A fourth component, related to the third, may form the most direct reference to Alma's three-day trial. In the soliloquy he expressed gratitude for those who had come to the Lord through his efforts in the following words: "When I see many of my brethren truly penitent, and coming to the Lord their God, then is my soul filled with joy" (Alma 29:10). Significantly, the next lines form the direct link to Alma's experience with the powers of Jesus' Atonement: "Then do I remember what the Lord has done for me, yea, even that he hath heard my prayer" (Alma 29:10). In my view, we have the words of this very prayer in Alma's comments to Helaman. Alma says that during his three-day ordeal he recalled his father's prophecies about the coming of Jesus Christ. Afterwards, he says,

"I cried within my heart: O Jesus, thou Son of God, have mercy on me, who am in the gall of bitterness, and am encircled about by the everlasting chains of death.

"And now, behold, when I thought this, I could remember my pains no more; yea, I was harrowed up by the memory of my sins no more" (Alma 36:18–19).

Because of that unforgettable moment when he received forgiveness of sins from God, Alma said fervently and gratefully, "I remember [God's] merciful arm which he extended towards me" (Alma 29:10).

The next two ties are less firm; however, they are worth mentioning. The first has to do with Alma's guilt. From his description of his reaction to his sins, it is clear that he did not see himself as a blameless person before God. For instance, he said that in his three-day experience, "I saw that I had rebelled against my God, and that I had not kept his holy commandments" (Alma 36:13). In discussing who is blameworthy before God and who is not, Alma gave the following in his dissertation, a clear characterization of his own situation when confronted by the angel of the Lord:

"He that knoweth good and evil, to him it is given according to his desires, whether he desireth good or evil, life or death, joy or remorse of conscience" (Alma 29:5). Alma had certainly experienced "remorse of conscience." He said:

"My soul was harrowed up to the greatest degree and racked with all my sins.

"Yea, I did remember all my sins and iniquities, for which I was tormented with the pains of hell" (Alma 36:12–13).

The second extra component deals with a hint of Alma's state during the three days that he was unable to respond physically but was fully conscious mentally. In the soliloquy in chapter 29 he spoke of his joy at the accomplishments of his friends, the sons of Mosiah, during their ministries among the Lamanites. And he hinted that the joy that he felt at such moments almost overcame him: "Now, when I think of the success of these my brethren my soul is carried away, even to the separation of it from the body, as it were, so great is my joy" (Alma 29:16). Perhaps Alma was thinking of his own ecstatic experience when he wrote these words.

THE TRIAL OF KORIHOR: ALMA 30

While we can read a substantial amount of what Alma said during the trial of Korihor (see Alma 30), because of the nature of the legal interchange we would normally expect to find nothing linked to Alma's three-day ordeal. But one matter reaches back to that experience: the idea that one soul perishes so that others may live.[1] To illustrate, when the angel of the Lord scolded Alma and his friends, the angel specifically said to Alma: "If thou wilt of thyself be destroyed, seek no more to destroy the church of God" (Alma 36:9). This thought led Alma not only to be "racked with eternal torment" because of all his "sins and iniquities" (Alma 36:12–13) but apparently to conclude that he "had murdered many of [God's] children, or rather led them away unto destruction" (Alma 36:14). In the case of Korihor, Alma tried to warn him simply to repent and not to seek a sign from God.

"I am grieved," said Alma to Korihor, "that ye will still resist the spirit of the truth, that thy soul may be destroyed.

"But behold, it is better that thy soul should be lost than that thou shouldst be the means of bringing many souls down to destruction" (Alma 30:46–47).

Clearly, Alma had once faced the possibility that his own life might have been taken to preserve others; and his own experience of coming face to face with this reality seems to underlie his appeal to Korihor not to "resist the spirit of the truth" (Alma 30:46).

SERMON TO ZORAMITES: ALMA 32–33

About 75 B.C., before the Zoramite people convinced the Lamanites to oppose Nephite interests—an act which led to war in the following year (see Alma 35:10–13)—Alma and his missionary companions had tried to preach to the Zoramites (see Alma 31:1–7). Even though Alma spoke frequently and to various groups in his missionary activity among these people, only one of his discourses to an audience of the poorer class is preserved (see Alma 32–33). In this address Alma touched on several points that link to his three-day experience. One of the most prominent of these points concerns his affirmation that God "imparteth his word by angels unto men, yea, not only men but women also" (Alma 32:23). Part of Alma's testimony consisted of his knowledge that his missionary companion, Amulek, had been visited and taught by an angel (see Alma 10:7–10). The mention of women in Alma 32:23 seems important. Depending on who the subject is in Alma 10:11—it is either Alma or the angel—the angel may have also appeared to others of Amulek's household, including "my women, and my children" (Alma 10:11). Alma had received many angelic visitations (see Alma 8:14); however, the first and most important visitation occurred when he and the sons of Mosiah were confronted by the angel of the Lord (see Mosiah 27:11; Alma 36:5–6). Thus he was a personal witness that angels were imparting the word of God to his fellow beings.

A second feature is Alma's discussion of the virtues of humility, where he contrasts being compelled to be humble with the humility that some seek without compulsion. His audience, who were from the poorer classes of the Zoramite people and who had been cast out of their synagogues (see Alma 32:5), certainly invited such a comparison because of their circumstances. Nevertheless, in a real sense Alma had been compelled himself to become humble by the angel of the Lord. Thus, Alma spoke out of his own experience when he made the following observation:

"Because ye are compelled to be humble blessed are ye; for a man sometimes, if he is compelled to be humble, seeketh repentance. . . .

"And now . . . do ye not suppose that they are more blessed who truly humble themselves because of the word?

"Yea, he that truly humbleth himself, and repenteth of his sins, and endureth to the end, the same shall be blessed—yea, *much more blessed* than they who are compelled to be humble because of their exceeding poverty" (Alma 32:13–15; emphasis added).

Alma concluded his discussion by saying: "Blessed are they who humble themselves without being compelled to be humble; . . . yea, without being brought to know the word, or even compelled to know, before they will believe" (Alma 32:16). While there may exist other reminiscences to Alma's three-day experience in this discourse, they are more difficult to demonstrate. Two come to mind. The first has to do with Alma's metaphorical use of the verb *taste* in the sense of tasting light (see Alma 32:35) and tasting joy (see Alma 36:24, 26). The second possible tie would link the concern for those who seek "a sign from heaven" (Alma 32:17) and the fact that Alma was given a clear heavenly sign in the person of the angel of the Lord who appeared to him.

COUNSEL TO HIS SONS: ALMA 38–42

In his counsel to his second son Shiblon, Alma spoke briefly and directly of his experience. After mentioning that during his ordeal he had been "born of God" (Alma 38:6), Alma related the following:

"The Lord in his great mercy sent his angel to declare unto me that I must stop the work of destruction among his people. . . .

"And it came to pass that I was three days and three nights in the most bitter pain and anguish of soul; and never, until I did cry out unto the Lord Jesus Christ for mercy, did I receive a remission of my sins. But behold, I did cry unto him and I did find peace to my soul" (Alma 38:7–8).

Another connection exists between Alma's words to Shiblon and those to Helaman. It consists of the tie between Exodus terminology and that used in reference to the Atonement. As I have already noted, the verb *deliver* regularly describes the Lord's actions on behalf of both the Hebrew slaves in Egypt and the Nephite peoples who found themselves in grave circumstances. When he complimented his second son on his patience in the face of persecution, Alma affirmed: "Thou knowest that the Lord did deliver thee" (Alma 38:4). He then continued by saying, "Now my son, Shiblon, I would that ye should remember, that as much as ye shall put your trust in God even so much ye shall be delivered out of your trials, and your troubles, and your afflictions, and ye shall be lifted up at the last day" (Alma 38:5).

The clear connection between God's power to deliver and the Resurrection is not to be missed. In Alma's extended counsel to his third and youngest son, Corianton (see Alma 39–42), there are only a few references to Alma's three-day ordeal, such as, "Is it not as easy at this time for the Lord to send his angel to declare these glad tidings unto us as unto our children, or as after the time of his coming?" (Alma 39:19). Apparently, the appearance of the angel of the Lord to Alma was in the back of his mind when he discussed God's interest in informing His children in advance about the coming of the Messiah. A second point of contact is Alma's urgent plea that his children not lead others astray. He declared that the "Spirit of the Lord" had directed him to command his children "to do good, lest they lead away the hearts of many people to destruction" (Alma 39:12). Likewise, the angel of the Lord had earlier commanded Alma to "seek no more to destroy the church of God" (Alma 36:9), effectively accusing Alma of leading others astray and leading Alma to accuse himself in very serious terms: "I had murdered many of [God's] children, or rather led them away unto destruction" (Alma 36:14).

A third feature in Alma's instructions to Corianton is his description of the fearful condition of the wicked. In his review of the "state of the soul between death and the resurrection" (Alma 40:11), Alma said of the wicked:

"These shall be cast out into outer darkness; there shall be weeping, and wailing, and gnashing of teeth, and this because of their own iniquity. . . .

"Now this is the state of the souls of the wicked, yea, in darkness, and a state of awful, fearful looking for the fiery indignation of the wrath of God upon them" (Alma 40:13–14).

Alma further characterized this period as "that endless night of darkness" (Alma 41:7) and the inheritance of the wicked as "an awful death" that is tantamount to drinking "the dregs of a bitter cup" (Alma 40:26). An unrepentant Corianton's evil acts, Alma certified, "will stand as a testimony against you at the last day" (Alma 39:8). Such words, of course, recall Alma's own horror at the thought of seeing God at the judgment bar: "So great had been my iniquities, that the very thought of coming into the presence of my God did rack my soul with inexpressible horror" (Alma 36:14).

SUMMARY

Virtually every one of Alma's recorded sermons, whether it was a formal discourse or a spontaneous address, is characterized by the recollection of one or more features of his three-day conversion experience. The exceptions are his long prayer offered just before he and his companions began their work among the people of Zoram (see Alma 31:26–35) and his final words to his son Helaman which included his dire prophecy about the eventual extinction of their people (see Alma 45:2–14). Perhaps the element most frequently alluded to is the appearance of the angel of the Lord. Further, Alma frequently referred to the captivity and deliverance of earlier generations, whether the Israelite slaves or his Nephite forebears, the memory of which was specifically enjoined on him by the angel. An important connection, not made as often, concerned the association of Exodus-like deliverances with the power of deliverance manifested in Jesus' atonement. In quite a different vein, Alma repeatedly mentioned the fate of the wicked in terrifying language and imagery that he similarly used to describe his own horror at facing God at the Final Judgment. In addition, almost as a counterbalance, he also regularly noted the unspeakable joy and light that believers would experience if they would accept Jesus' redemption. A final ingredient is his testimony of what happened as a result of his determination and actions to bring others to accept Jesus' atonement—to be "born of God," to taste "as I have tasted," and to see "eye to eye as I have seen" (Alma 36:26).

NOTE

1. The justification is first laid out in Nephi's dramatic encounter with the drunken Laban (see 1 Nephi 4:11–13). Compare Caiaphas' maxim about the need for Jesus' death (see John 11:50; 18:14) that bears the sense of political expediency. The underlying principle can be seen in 2 Samuel 20:20–22 and in Jonah 1:12–15. For similar Jewish formulations of the idea, see those cited by Hermann L. Strack and Paul Billerbeck, *Kommentar zum Neuen Testament aus Talmud und Midrasch* (Munich: C. H. Beck, 1924), 2:545–46. Most of these instances deal with political reasons for one to die instead of many. Legal and religious grounds are not spelled out.

16

THE CONCEPT OF HELL

Larry E. Dahl

What is taught in the Book of Mormon about hell? How is the word *hell* used, and what other terms or phrases are employed to describe or mean the same thing? Is hell a temporary or a permanent condition? When is "that awful crisis," spoken of by Amulek, "the night of darkness wherein there can be no labor performed," when the devil "doth seal" as his those who have procrastinated their repentance? (see Alma 34:33–35). What is meant by the phrases "die in their sins" (Moroni 10:26) and "die in their wickedness" (1 Nephi 15:33), and what does that portend for the future? Is the hell or "outer darkness" described by Alma to which the "wicked" are assigned at mortal death permanent or temporary? (see Alma 40:13). These last three questions really become one question: Is mortal death the great watershed of spiritual opportunity, or can one receive the gospel, repent, and improve while in the postmortal spirit world between death and the resurrection? This paper will examine the contents of the Book of Mormon relating to these queries. I acknowledge that the interpretation of Alma 34:32 herein differs somewhat from the traditional explanation, but I believe the interpretation derives from the text itself and

Larry E. Dahl is an emeritus professor of Church history and doctrine at Brigham Young University.

is consistent with all else taught on the subject in the Book of Mormon.

USE OF WORDS AND TERMS MEANING HELL

The word *hell* appears sixty-two times in the text of the Book of Mormon. Thirty-three times it stands alone, without modifiers or explanation of what it means, as in, "And thus we see the end of him who perverteth the ways of the Lord; and thus we see that the devil will not support his children at the last day, but doth speedily drag them down to hell" (Alma 30:60). Twenty-nine times the word *hell* is used with descriptive modifiers, for example, "depths of hell" (1 Nephi 12:16), "hell which hath no end" (1 Nephi 14:3), "awful hell" (1 Nephi 15:29, 35; Alma 19:29; 54:7), "sleep of hell" (2 Nephi 1:13), "gates of hell" (2 Nephi 4:32; 3 Nephi 11:39–40; 18:13), "pains of hell" (Jacob 3:11; Alma 14:6; 26:13; 36:13), "chains of hell" (Alma 5:7, 9–10; 12:11; 13:30; 26:14), "child of hell" (Alma 11:23; 54:11), "powers of hell" (Alma 48:17), "everlasting hell" (Helaman 6:28), "hell fire" (3 Nephi 12:22; Mormon 8:17), and "endless hell" (Moroni 8:13).

Numerous times in the Book of Mormon other terms or phrases are used to mean *hell,* and these terms add to our understanding of what hell really is. For example, note Nephi's explanation, which he received from an angel, of the river of filthy water in his and his father's visions of the tree of life:

"And they said unto me: What meaneth the river of water which our father saw?

"And I said unto them that the water which my father saw was filthiness; and so much was his mind swallowed up in other things that he beheld not the filthiness of the water.

"And I said unto them that it was an awful gulf, which separated the wicked from the tree of life, and also from the saints of God.

"And I said unto them that it was a representation of that awful hell, which the angel said unto me was prepared for the wicked.

"And I said unto them that our father also saw that the justice of God did also divide the wicked from the righteous; and the brightness thereof was like unto the brightness of a flaming fire, which ascendeth up unto God forever and ever, and hath no end" (1 Nephi 15:26–30; see also 12:16–18).

Hell is equated here with the "river," "an awful gulf," and the "justice of God," which separated the wicked from the righteous and from the tree of life. This equation can help us better understand the Savior's parable of the rich man and Lazarus, recorded in Luke 16:19–31. What was the "great gulf fixed" that separated the rich man from Abraham and Lazarus? Nephi's explanation of "an awful gulf" or "the justice of God" seems to fit well. Why couldn't Abraham or Lazarus go and relieve the rich man's suffering? Probably for the same reason the five wise virgins couldn't share their oil with the five foolish virgins in another parable Jesus told. One person simply cannot endow another with spiritual maturity nor erase the inevitable consequences of an errant life. Only God can make a person spiritually whole, and His justice requires that it be done in a prescribed way. Each person creates his own "awful gulf," and each person must traverse the path to wholeness himself, voluntarily and completely yielding to the will of God and exercising faith in Jesus Christ and in His infinite atonement. Neither Abraham nor Lazarus nor wise virgins can do it for others.

Other terms or phrases used in the Book of Mormon to refer to hell are "eternal gulf of misery and woe" (2 Nephi 1:13), "kingdom of the devil" (2 Nephi 2:29; 28:19; Alma 41:4), "spiritual death" (2 Nephi 9:12), "awful monster" (2 Nephi 9:10), "lake of fire and brimstone" (2 Nephi 9:19, 26; 28:23), "misery and endless torment" (Mosiah 3:25; Moroni 8:21), "awful chains" (2 Nephi 28:22), "everlasting chains of death" (Alma 36:18), "slumber of death" (Jacob 3:11), "deep sleep" (Alma 5:7), "second death" (Alma 13:30), "place of filthiness" (1 Nephi 15:34), "endless night of darkness" (Alma 41:7), "misery which never dies" (Mormon 8:38), and "dregs of a bitter cup" (Alma 40:26).

HELL IS PERMANENT FOR SOME

Several of these terms appear to say that hell is a permanent condition. And for some people it is. Jacob, Nephi, King Benjamin, an angel speaking to Benjamin, Amulek, Alma, and Samuel the Lamanite all testified of a permanent hell and the qualifications for being consigned to it. In the following Book of Mormon quotations from these seven individuals, three points stand out: the permanency of the hell spoken of, the thoughts and feelings of those in hell, and the thoughts, feelings, and actions that bring us to hell, or bring hell to us. The testimonies of these prophets (and an angel) are foundational in understanding what the Book of Mormon teaches about hell and are important as a context for interpreting Alma 34 and 40, where some of the key doctrines relating to hell are found.

Jacob explained that at the Resurrection and Final Judgment, "we shall have a perfect knowledge of all our guilt, and our uncleanness, and our nakedness; and the righteous shall have a perfect knowledge of their enjoyment, and their righteousness, being clothed with purity, yea, even with the robe of righteousness. . . . They who are righteous shall be righteous still, and they who are filthy shall be filthy still; wherefore, they who are filthy are the devil and his angels; and they shall go away into everlasting fire, prepared for them; and their torment is as a lake of fire and brimstone, whose flame ascendeth up forever and ever and has no end" (2 Nephi 9:14, 16).

Nephi warned that anger against the truth and also carnal security inspired of the devil can lead to an endless hell:

"For behold, at that day shall he rage in the hearts of the children of men, and stir them up to anger against that which is good.

"And others will he pacify, and lull them away into carnal security, that they will say: All is well in Zion; yea, Zion prospereth, all is well—and thus the devil cheateth their souls, and leadeth them away carefully down to hell.

"And behold, others he flattereth away, and telleth them there is no hell; and he saith unto them: I am no devil, for there is none—and thus he whispereth in their ears, until he grasps them with his awful chains, from whence there is no deliverance.

" . . . And all that have been seized therewith must stand before the throne of God, and be judged according to their works, from whence they must go into the place prepared for them, even a lake of fire and brimstone, which is endless torment" (2 Nephi 28:20–23).

King Benjamin explained that open rebellion against God after we have known the truth brings "never-ending torment":

"And now, I say unto you, my brethren, that after ye have known and have been taught all these things, if ye should transgress and go contrary to that which has been spoken, that ye do withdraw yourselves from the Spirit of the Lord, that it may have no place in you to guide you in wisdom's paths that ye may be blessed, prospered, and preserved—

"I say unto you, that the man that doeth this, the same cometh out in open rebellion against God; therefore he listeth to obey the evil spirit, and becometh an enemy to all righteousness; therefore, the Lord has no place in him, for he dwelleth not in unholy temples.

"Therefore if that man repenteth not, and remaineth and dieth an enemy to God, the demands of divine justice do awaken his immortal soul to a lively sense of his own guilt, which doth cause him to shrink from the presence of the Lord, and doth fill his breast with guilt, and pain, and anguish, which is like an unquenchable fire, whose flame ascendeth up forever and ever.

"And now I say unto you, that mercy hath no claim on that man; therefore his final doom is to endure a never-ending torment" (Mosiah 2:36–39).

An angel further instructed King Benjamin that mercy can have no claim on those who are found to still be "evil" at the final judgment day:

"And now I have spoken the words which the Lord God hath commanded me.

"And thus saith the Lord: They shall stand as a bright testimony against this people, at the judgment day; whereof they shall be judged, every man according to his works, whether they be good, or whether they be evil.

"And if they be evil they are consigned to an awful view of their own guilt and abominations, which doth cause them to shrink from the presence of the Lord into a state of misery and endless torment, from whence they can no more return; therefore they have drunk damnation to their own souls.

"Therefore, they have drunk out of the cup of the wrath of God, which justice could no more deny unto them than it could deny that Adam should fall because of his partaking of the forbidden fruit; therefore, mercy could have claim on them no more forever.

"And their torment is as a lake of fire and brimstone, whose flames are unquenchable, and whose smoke ascendeth up forever and ever. Thus hath the Lord commanded me" (Mosiah 3:23–27).

Amulek testified that Christ will redeem "those who believe on his name; and . . . none else. "Therefore the wicked remain as though there had been no redemption made, except it be the loosing of the bands of death; for behold, the day cometh that all shall rise from the dead and stand before God, and be judged according to their works" (Alma 11:40–41).

Those found still classed among the wicked are redeemed from death but not from hell.

Alma echoed Amulek's teaching on the matter and explained what constitutes the second death pronounced upon the wicked at the bar of God:

"And Amulek hath spoken plainly concerning death, and being raised from this mortality to a state of immortality, and being brought before the bar of God, to be judged according to our works.

"Then if our hearts have been hardened, yea, if we have hardened our hearts against the word, insomuch that it has not been found in us, then will our state be awful, for then we shall be condemned.

"For our words will condemn us, yea, all our works will condemn us; we shall not be found spotless; and our thoughts will also condemn us; and in this awful state we shall not dare to look up to our God; and we would fain be glad if we could command the rocks and the mountains to fall upon us to hide us from his presence.

"But this cannot be; we must come forth and stand before him in his glory, and in his power, and in his might, majesty, and dominion, and acknowledge to our everlasting shame that all his judgments are just; that he is just in all his works, and that he is merciful unto the children of men, and that he has all power to save every man that believeth on his name and bringeth forth fruit meet for repentance.

"And now behold, I say unto you then cometh a death, even a second death, which is a spiritual death; then is a time that whosoever dieth in his sins, as to a temporal death, shall also die a spiritual death; yea, he shall die as to things pertaining unto righteousness.

"Then is the time when their torments shall be as a lake of fire and brimstone, whose flame ascendeth up forever and ever; and then is the time that they shall be chained down to an everlasting destruction, according to the power and captivity of Satan, he having subjected them according to his will.

"Then, I say unto you, they shall be as though there had been no redemption made; for they cannot be redeemed according to God's justice; and they cannot die, seeing there is no more corruption" (Alma 12:12–18).

Samuel, the Lamanite prophet, added his witness that those who are found unrepentant at the bar of God suffer a second death, a spiritual death:

"But behold, the resurrection of Christ redeemeth mankind, yea, even all mankind, and bringeth them back into the presence of the Lord.

"Yea, and it bringeth to pass the condition of repentance, that whosoever repenteth the same is not hewn down and cast into the fire; but whosoever repenteth not is hewn down and cast into the fire; and there cometh upon them again a spiritual death, yea, a second death, for they are cut off again as to things pertaining to righteousness" (Helaman 14:17–18).

HELL IS TEMPORARY FOR MOST

Clearly the Book of Mormon teaches of a permanent hell for the devil and his angels and for those who, at the final judgment day, are found to be "wicked" or "filthy still"—rebellious, defiant, incorrigible enemies of God, having chosen to follow Satan rather than Christ. Just as clearly, however, the Book of Mormon affirms that for all the rest of mankind who suffer the pains, chains, or sleep of hell, it is a temporary sojourn. The possibility of escaping hell is inherent in Father Lehi's plea to his sons, "Awake; awake from a deep sleep, yea, even from the sleep of hell, and shake off the awful chains by which ye are bound, which are the chains which bind the children of men, that they are carried away captive down to the eternal gulf of misery and woe" (2 Nephi 1:13). Similarly, Jacob encouraged his brethren to "shake off the chains of him that would bind [them] fast" (2 Nephi 9:45). Just how can one "awake" from the "sleep of hell" and "shake off" binding chains? Alma explained that it can be done through faith in the Atonement of Jesus Christ, repentance, and spiritual rebirth. Speaking to members of the Church at Zarahemla concerning their fathers who were liberated from spiritual captivity, Alma declared:

"And moreover, have ye sufficiently retained in remembrance that he has delivered their souls from hell?

"Behold, he changed their hearts; yea, he awakened them out of a deep sleep, and they awoke unto God. Behold, they were in the midst of darkness; nevertheless, their souls were illuminated by the light of the everlasting word; yea, they were encircled about by the bands of death, and the chains of hell, and an everlasting destruction did await them.

"And now I ask of you, my brethren, were they destroyed? Behold, I say unto you, Nay, they were not.

"And again I ask, were the bands of death broken, and the chains of hell which encircled them about, were they loosed? I say unto you, Yea, they were loosed, and their souls did expand, and they did sing redeeming love. And I say unto you that they are saved.

"And now I ask of you on what conditions are they saved? Yea, what grounds had they to hope for salvation? What is the cause of their being loosed from the bands of death, yea, and also the chains of hell?

"Behold, I can tell you—did not my father Alma believe in the words which were delivered by the mouth of Abinadi? And was he not a holy prophet? Did he not speak the words of God, and my father Alma believe them?

"And according to his faith there was a mighty change wrought in his heart. Behold I say unto you that this is all true.

"And behold, he preached the word unto your fathers, and a mighty change was also wrought in their hearts, and they humbled themselves and put their trust in the true and living God. And behold, they were faithful until the end; therefore they were saved.

"And now behold, I ask of you, my brethren of the church, have ye spiritually been born of God? Have ye received his image in your countenances? Have ye experienced this mighty change in your hearts?

"Do ye exercise faith in the redemption of him who created you? . . .

" . . . For there can no man be saved except his garments are washed white; yea, his garments must be purified until they are cleansed from all stain, through the blood of him of whom it has been spoken by our fathers, who should come to redeem his people from their sins" (Alma 5:6–15, 21).

Alma was probably as well qualified as any mortal to explain the awfulness of hell and the process and joy of being released therefrom. He vividly recounted his escape from hell to his son Helaman:

"I was racked with eternal torment, for my soul was harrowed up to the greatest degree and racked with all my sins.

"Yea, I did remember all my sins and iniquities, for which I was tormented with the pains of hell; yea, I saw that I had rebelled against my God, and that I had not kept his holy commandments.

"Yea, and I had murdered many of his children, or rather led them away unto destruction; yea, and in fine so great had been my iniquities, that the very thought of coming into the presence of my God did rack my soul with inexpressible horror.

"Oh, thought I, that I could be banished and become extinct both soul and body, that I might not be brought to stand in the presence of my God, to be judged of my deeds.

"And now, for three days and for three nights was I racked, even with the pains of a damned soul.

"And it came to pass that as I was thus racked with torment, while I was harrowed up by the memory of my many sins, behold, I remembered also to have heard my father prophesy unto the people concerning the coming of one Jesus Christ, a Son of God, to atone for the sins of the world.

"Now, as my mind caught hold upon this thought, I cried within my heart: O Jesus, thou Son of God, have mercy on me, who am in the gall of bitterness, and am encircled about by the everlasting chains of death.

"And now, behold, when I thought this, I could remember my pains no more; yea, I was harrowed up by the memory of my sins no more.

"And oh, what joy, and what marvelous light I did behold; yea, my soul was filled with joy as exceeding as was my pain!

"Yea, I say unto you, my son, that there could be nothing so exquisite and so bitter as were my pains. Yea, and again I say unto you, my son, that on the other hand, there can be nothing so exquisite and sweet as was my joy" (Alma 36:12–21).

THE POSTMORTAL SPIRIT WORLD

Plainly, then, those living on the earth who are chained and tormented with the pains of hell can escape their current and future suffering by yielding their hearts and lives to the Savior. But what about those who die and go into the spirit world not yet reconciled to God, not yet righteous, not yet spiritually reborn, not yet having their garments washed white in the blood of the Lamb? And what about those who have been born again, cleansed, and numbered among the righteous but who later falter and are yet struggling through spiritual adolescence or even spiritual indolence? Does hell await them in the spirit world? If so, can they, like those on earth, shake loose from the chains of hell, or must they be forever damned with the devil and his angels? What does the Book of Mormon say about this issue?

The Book of Mormon contains little information about what happens in the spirit world between death and the Resurrection. And what information is provided leaves many questions unanswered. Alma "inquired diligently of God" (Alma 40:3) concerning the matter and shared with his son Corianton what he learned:

"Now, concerning the state of the soul between death and the resurrection—Behold, it has been made known unto me by an angel, that the spirits of all men, as soon as they are departed from this mortal body, yea, the spirits of all men, whether they be good or evil, are taken home to that God who gave them life.

"And then shall it come to pass, that the spirits of those who are righteous are received into a state of happiness, which is called paradise, a state of rest, a state of peace, where they shall rest from all their troubles and from all care, and sorrow.

"And then shall it come to pass, that the spirits of the wicked, yea, who are evil—for behold, they have no part nor portion of the Spirit of the Lord; for behold, they chose evil works rather than good; therefore the spirit of the devil did enter into them, and take possession of their house—and these shall be cast out into outer darkness; there shall be weeping, and wailing, and gnashing of teeth, and this because of their own iniquity, being led captive by the will of the devil.

"Now this is the state of the souls of the wicked, yea, in darkness, and a state of awful, fearful looking for the fiery indignation of the wrath of God upon them; thus they remain in this state, as well as the righteous in paradise, until the time of their resurrection" (Alma 40:11–14).

Alma spoke of only two groups: the "righteous" and the "wicked." We are left to wonder what level of righteousness is required for "paradise" and what level of wickedness consigns one to "outer darkness." Alma did not talk about any change in the status of either group as they await the Resurrection. He did say that at the Resurrection the principle of "restoration" will be realized with each group—the "righteous shin[ing] forth in the kingdom of God," and the wicked being "cast out," experiencing "an awful death, . . . for they die as to things pertaining to things of righteousness" (Alma 40:24–26). He explained that the wicked cannot inherit the kingdom of God, "for they are unclean, and no unclean thing can inherit the kingdom of God" (Alma 40:26).

If Alma was being consistent in his use of the word *wicked* throughout the chapter, then it appears that those designated wicked, both in the spirit world awaiting resurrection and at the time of the Resurrection, are sons of perdition. They qualified for that designation in mortality by choosing "evil works rather than good," thereby separating themselves from the Spirit of the Lord, and permitting "the spirit of the devil [to] enter into them, and take possession of their house [i.e., body]" (Alma 40:13). The righteous, on the other hand, experience happiness, peace, and rest in the spirit world, and at the Resurrection they will "shine forth in the kingdom of God" (Alma 40:25). Because there is such a wide variation in the works of individuals, a natural question is whether they all receive the same level of happiness and rest in the spirit world and the same level of blessings in the kingdom of God after the Resurrection. On this matter the Book of Mormon is silent, except for the concept that at the Resurrection all people will be "judged of their works" (1 Nephi 15:32; 2 Nephi 9:44; see also Mosiah 3:24; Alma 41:3). It might be argued on that basis that in "paradise" and in the "kingdom of God," as opposed to "outer darkness" and the "kingdom of the devil," there are rewards commensurate with various levels of works or righteousness. But again, the Book of Mormon is not explicit on the matter.

THE NIGHT OF DARKNESS

Amulek also spoke of things pertaining to death, repentance, and the final state of the wicked. He taught:

"For behold, this life is the time for men to prepare to meet God; yea, behold the day of this life is the day for men to perform their labors.

"And now, as I said unto you before, as ye have had so many witnesses, therefore, I beseech of you that ye do not procrastinate the day of your repentance until the end; for after this day of life, which is given us to prepare for eternity, behold, if we do not improve our time while in this life, then cometh the night of darkness wherein there can be no labor performed.

"Ye cannot say, when ye are brought to that awful crisis, that I will repent, that I will return to my God. Nay, ye cannot say this; for that same spirit which doth possess your bodies at the time that ye go out of this life, that same spirit will have power to possess your body in that eternal world.

"For behold, if ye have procrastinated the day of your repentance even until death, behold, ye have become subjected to the spirit of the devil, and he doth seal you his; therefore, the Spirit of the Lord hath withdrawn from you, and hath no place in you, and the devil hath all power over you; and this is the final state of the wicked" (Alma 34:32–35).

These verses are often interpreted to mean that we must repent before mortal death or we face a "night of darkness wherein there can be no labor performed," leaving little hope for change in the postmortal spirit world. Verse 34—which talks about the "same spirit" that possesses our bodies at death having power to possess our bodies "in that eternal world," or in the Resurrection—is advanced as added evidence that changes in our nature will not likely occur between death and resurrection. Why? Because, the reasoning goes, although we receive, lay down, and receive again our physical bodies, our spirits are "us" (attitudes, desires, habits, our very nature) through premortal life, mortality, the postmortal spirit world, and on into the Resurrection. If we are not interested in the gospel in one phase of our existence, changing arenas will not necessarily change our nature. We are basically the "same spirit" passing from one phase of eternity to another. The *possibility* of change is allowed; the *probability* of change is not so sure.

Undoubtedly, we ought to repent now and not procrastinate, because indeed ultimately there comes a "night of darkness wherein there can be no labor performed" (Alma 34:33). But was Amulek saying that the night of darkness for everyone is mortal death? If we accept the proposition that the night of darkness for all mankind is indeed mortal death, then the sense of Alma 34:34–35 seems to be that anyone who has procrastinated repentance until then becomes sealed to the devil in eternity. That idea is not in harmony with what we know from Doctrine and Covenants 76 and 138, which allows for even the telestially wicked and rebellious on earth to be redeemed from hell and the devil at the end of the Millennium.

Simply changing our residence from mortality to the spirit world will not change our nature. That is good doctrine. But is that what Amulek was trying to convey in these verses? A careful examination of Amulek's sermon, comparing it with Alma's discourse in Alma 40 discussed above, suggests another possible view of Amulek's intent. First, consider the matter in verse 34 of "that same spirit" (singular) possessing "bodies" (plural) at the time of death and again in the Resurrection.

What is "that same spirit"? Does it mean an individual's spirit, or does it refer to the "spirit of the devil," which is the thrust of verse 35? With that question in mind, consider those two verses again:

"Ye cannot say, when ye are brought to that awful crisis, that I will repent, that I will return to my God. Nay, ye cannot say this; for *that same spirit* which doth possess your bodies at the time that ye go out of this life, *that same spirit will have power* to possess your body in that eternal world.

"For behold, if ye have procrastinated the day of your repentance even until death, behold, ye have become subjected to *the spirit of the devil,* and he doth seal you his; therefore, the Spirit of the Lord hath withdrawn from you, and hath no place in you, and *the devil hath all power over you,* and this is the final state of the wicked" (Alma 34:34–35; emphasis added).

If Amulek was indeed referring to the "spirit of the devil" as "that same spirit" which has power to possess the same bodies in the Resurrection that it possessed at mortal death, we understand better the meaning of "awful crisis" and "the night of darkness wherein there can be no labor performed." It would mean the devil has sealed them as his,[1] and there is no labor that they can perform to escape. Alma later used almost the same words as Amulek to describe the condition of the "wicked" who are cast into outer darkness in the spirit world and are later resurrected to a second or spiritual death. He explained, "And then shall it come to pass, that the spirits of the wicked, yea, who are evil—for behold, they have no part nor portion of the Spirit of the Lord; for behold, they chose evil works rather than good; therefore the spirit of the devil did enter into them, and take possession of their house—and these shall be cast out into outer darkness; there shall be weeping, and wailing, and gnashing of teeth, and this because of their own iniquity, being led captive by the will of the devil" (Alma 40:13). It seems clear that Alma and Amulek were "reading from the same page" on this matter. And that should not surprise us, inasmuch as Amulek was tutored for "many days" by Alma and by an angel before he "began to preach and to prophesy unto the people" (Alma 8:27, 32; 10:10).

I have suggested that the Book of Mormon does not address the issue of a temporary hell in the postmortal spirit world from which one can escape at the Resurrection and Final Judgment. Why, it may be asked, is such a doctrine not made clear in the Book of Mormon, when it is made clear in the Doctrine and Covenants (see D&C 76:81–89, 100–112; 138) and alluded to in the Pearl of Great Price (see Moses 7:36–39)? We do not know why. Neither the Lord nor His prophets have given an explanation. What are the possibilities?

Some argue that the Book of Mormon reflects Joseph Smith's early notions of things and that he only later came to a more complete understanding. I do not accept this argument because it rejects considerable evidence of the Book of Mormon's veracity as well as the Prophet's testimony that the Book of Mormon is a translation of an ancient document and was translated by the gift and power of God. There may be some merit, however, in the following ideas:

First, there is ample evidence that the Lord took an active interest and role in what was recorded and what was selected to be preserved for our day (see 1 Nephi 9:1–6; Words of Mormon 1:1–11; 3 Nephi 23:1–14). Not even a hundredth part of what was said and done was recorded, and we have only a brief abridgment of that (see Jacob 3:13; Words of Mormon 1:5; Helaman 3:14; 3 Nephi 5:8; 26:6; Ether 15:33).

Second, some "greater things" were deliberately withheld as a trial of faith, with the promise that if people would believe what was written, "greater things [would] be made manifest unto them" (3 Nephi 26:9–12).

Third, it may be that in their public preaching[2] the Lord forbade the Book of Mormon prophets from spelling out the particulars of escaping hell in the spirit world and the promise of various levels of rewards for those who are redeemed from hell and the devil. Perhaps the spiritual maturity (or lack thereof) of their audiences (see 1 Nephi 18:20; Enos 1:23; Helaman 12:1–6) called for the either-or approach that is so common in the Book of Mormon—people are designated either righteous or wicked (see Alma 40:12–13); they are either saved or damned (see 2 Nephi 9:23–24); they can choose Christ or Satan, liberty and eternal life or captivity and death (see 2 Nephi 2:27); they are raised to endless happiness or endless misery (see Alma 41:4–5).

Preaching in such terms may be expedient to get people's attention, to get them thinking about the consequences of their choices. That possibility is supported by the Lord's explanation of why the terms "endless torment" and "eternal damnation" are used. He said, "wherefore it is more express than other scriptures, that it might work upon the hearts of the children of men, altogether for my name's glory" (D&C 19:7). Once a person begins his spiritual journey by receiving milk, he is gradually prepared to receive and digest meat.

Fourth, Nephi learned that assignments to record different portions of the Lord's message for mankind are given to various prophets, the entire message to come forth in the Lord's due time. Nephi was not to write some of the things that were reserved for John to write (see 1 Nephi 14:18–30). For the complete answer we may well have to wait until "that day when the Lord shall come" and "he shall reveal all things" (D&C 101:32).

CONCLUSION

The Book of Mormon teaches that hell is real. It is guilt and pain and anguish and torment, an inexpressible horror, which is like an unquenchable fire. It is despair. It is weeping and wailing and gnashing of teeth. Sadly, for some that condition is forever. For most, however, hell is a temporary condition. By virtue of Christ's atonement mankind can be freed from hell by yielding their hearts to God and coming unto Christ. Eventually, all except the devil and his angels and those who have dwelt in mortality and become sons of perdition will be redeemed from hell.

The Book of Mormon speaks of only two groups who inhabit the postmortal spirit world: the righteous, who exist in a state of happiness called paradise; and the wicked, who are consigned to outer darkness—the wicked being those who have been captivated by the devil and who will be resurrected to an endless hell. The Book of Mormon does not speak of levels in paradise or in the postresurrection kingdom of God, but it does say that each will be resurrected and returned to the presence of God to be judged "according to his works." If individuals are to be judged according to their works, of necessity there will be levels of rewards, because their works are so varied.

The Book of Mormon warns against procrastinating the day of repentance, affirming that there will come an "awful crisis" (Alma 34:34), a "night of darkness wherein there can be no labor performed" (Alma 34:33). Another possible approach to the "awful crisis," a "night of darkness wherein there can be no labor performed," is that when death comes, nothing can be done *in mortality* to change the attitudes and behavior exhibited before death; we cannot change what we have done, and now, in the spirit world, must face the inevitable consequences of that behavior. We must experience hell at the appropriate level and for as long as it takes to make things right. Justice cannot be robbed nor destroyed, but it can be appeased, satisfied, even overpowered, by mercy through the Atonement of Jesus Christ and an individual's repentance and obedience (see Alma 34; 42). The Book of Mormon teaches that for sons of perdition that night of darkness comes at mortal death. It does not say that mortal death is the night of darkness for *everyone.*

Although its teachings about hell are not as complete as those set forth in latter-day revelation, what the Book of Mormon teaches is in harmony with those revelations. The Book of Mormon, carefully read, inspires a longing to avoid the pains of hell, even temporarily, and teaches its readers how to do that.

It seems fitting to conclude with a typical Book of Mormon exhortation that mankind choose liberty and eternal life rather than captivity and death. This plea is part of Father Lehi's farewell testimony:

"Wherefore, men are free according to the flesh; and all things are given them which are expedient unto man. And they are free to choose liberty and eternal life, through the great Mediator of all men, or to choose captivity and death, according to the captivity and power of the devil; for he seeketh that all men might be miserable like unto himself.

"And now, my sons, I would that ye should look to the great Mediator, and hearken unto his great commandments; and be faithful unto his words, and choose eternal life, according to the will of his Holy Spirit;

"And not choose eternal death, according to the will of the flesh and the evil which is therein, which giveth the spirit of the devil power to captivate, to bring you down to hell, that he may reign over you in his own kingdom" (2 Nephi 2:27–29).

NOTES

1. This also seems to be the sense of those passages in the Book of Mormon that speak of people who "die in their sins" (see 2 Nephi 9:38–39; Jacob 6:6–10; Mosiah 2:38–39; Mosiah 15:26; Alma 12:16; Moroni 10:26).

2. I suggest that the prophets themselves understood the Plan of Salvation and the redemptive opportunities in the postmortal spirit world. These men saw the Savior (see 2 Nephi 11:3; Mormon 1:15; Ether 9:21–22; 12:39). They were instructed by both the Father and the Son (see 2 Nephi 31:10–12, 14–15), which is interesting in light of what the Prophet Joseph Smith taught about the privileges of those who make their calling and election sure, and receive the Second Comforter (see Joseph Smith, *Teachings of the Prophet Joseph Smith,* comp. Joseph Fielding Smith [Salt Lake City: Deseret Book, 1938], 150–51). The gospel has been the same from the beginning, and those who come unto Christ according to the pattern Nephi calls the "doctrine of Christ" (2 Nephi 31:21) are taught that gospel by the Holy Ghost. Surely the Book of Mormon prophets knew the gospel Plan of Salvation. In all dispensations, however, prophets may only dispense to others that which is expedient, that which the Lord "seeth fit that they should have" (Alma 29:8), "according to the heed and diligence which they give unto him" (Alma 12:9).

17

Types and Shadows of Deliverance in the Book of Mormon

M. Catherine Thomas

Grasping the Lord's outstretched hand requires reaching into the unknown for the unseen. The Lord provided the Book of Mormon to assist the humble seeker to bridge that gap. In the Book of Mormon the Lord often identifies His empowering grace with the words *deliver* or *deliverance.* The Book of Mormon also frequently deals with types of deliverance; that is, with examples or instances of deliverance. This sacred scripture presents a series of dilemmas, which are types of the troubles that men and women face in all dispensations: being lost, hungry, enslaved, in danger, or possessed by such painful emotions as anger, guilt, depression, and fear.

Deliverance from such trouble is a major theme of the Book of Mormon. A computer count shows that the words derived from *deliver* occur more than two hundred times in the 531 pages of the Book of Mormon, signifying the importance of the principle.[1] Thus we repeatedly learn that God will provide some deliverance from trouble if we will but turn to Him. The Book of Mormon speaks to all ages, and its principles apply to people everywhere. No one can ever have a dilemma that the Lord cannot turn into some form of deliverance. The purpose

---

M. Catherine Thomas is a former associate professor of ancient scripture at Brigham Young University.

of this essay is not only to heighten our sensitivity to deliverance in the Book of Mormon and thereby increase our faith in the accessibility of Christ's help but also to point out the principles by which deliverance is obtained.

All Book of Mormon accounts of deliverance ultimately point the reader's mind to the greatest deliverance of all, the redemption of mankind from physical and spiritual death by the Lord Jesus Christ. The object of all the deliverances is to bring that which is miserable, scattered, alienated, and spiritually dead back into living oneness with Christ: deliverance is a function of the power of at-one-ment in Jesus Christ. Jacob explained:

"And because of the way of *deliverance* of our God, the Holy One of Israel, this death, of which I have spoken, which is the temporal, shall *deliver* up its dead;

" . . . Which spiritual death is hell.

" . . . O the greatness of the mercy of our God, the Holy One of Israel! For he *delivereth* his saints from that awful monster the devil, and death, and hell, and that lake of fire and brimstone, which is endless torment" (2 Nephi 9:11–12, 19; all italics here and hereafter are the author's emphasis).

DELIVERANCE AS A THEME OF THE BOOK OF MORMON

We find the theme of deliverance in the first chapter of the Book of Mormon: "Behold, I, Nephi, will show unto you that the tender mercies of the Lord are over all those whom he hath chosen, because of their faith, to make them mighty even unto the power of *deliverance*" (1 Nephi 1:20).

Clearly *deliverance* is a key word as Nephi, under the Lord's inspiration, set it up as an important theme of the entire Book of Mormon. Following are some random samples of the use of *deliverance* in the Book of Mormon: Nephi explained to his fearful brothers, "The Lord is able to *deliver* us, even as our fathers, and to destroy Laban, even as the Egyptians" (1 Nephi 4:3); Alma rebuked the unbelief of the people of Ammonihah: "Have ye forgotten so soon how many times he *delivered* our fathers out of the hands of their enemies, and preserved them from being destroyed, even by the hands of their own brethren?" (Alma 9:10); and Alma also taught his son Helaman, "I would that ye should do as I have done, in remembering the captivity of our fathers; for they were in bondage, and none could *deliver* them except it was the God of Abraham, and the God of Isaac, and the God of Jacob; and he surely did *deliver* them in their afflictions" (Alma 36:2).

Helaman wrote of his experiences with his two thousand stripling warriors: "We did pour out our souls in prayer to God, that he would strengthen us and *deliver* us out of the hands of our enemies. . . . Yea, and it came to pass that the Lord our God did visit us with assurances that he would *deliver* us; yea, insomuch that he did speak peace to our souls, and did grant unto us great faith, and did cause us that we should hope for our *deliverance* in him" (Alma 58:10–11).

A systematic survey of the fifteen books of the Book of Mormon suggests how well the idea of deliverance is spread through its pages. Such a wide distribution demonstrates that Nephi, Jacob, and Mormon used *deliverance* as one of the organizing principles of the Book of Mormon.

First Nephi. "And I, Nephi, beheld that the Gentiles that had gone out of captivity were *delivered* by the power of God out of the hands of all other nations" (1 Nephi 13:19).

Second Nephi. "O house of Israel, is my hand shortened at all that it cannot redeem, or have I no power to *deliver?*" (2 Nephi 7:2).

Jacob. The prophet Jacob teaches the concept of deliverance but does not use the word in his own book; however, the word does appear in 2 Nephi 6:17 ("For the Mighty God shall *deliver* his covenant people") and 2 Nephi 9:10–13, both of which are Jacob's writings.

Enos and Jarom. Neither Enos's twenty-seven verses nor Jarom's fifteen verses include this sense of the word *deliver.* Nevertheless, Enos 1:15 conveys the concept of deliverance: "Whatsoever thing ye shall ask in faith, believing that ye shall receive in the name of Christ, ye shall receive it."

Omni. "Wherefore, the Lord did visit them in great judgment;

nevertheless, he did spare the righteous that they should not perish, but did *deliver* them out of the hands of their enemies" (Omni 1:7).

Words of Mormon. The eighteen verses of the Words of Mormon teach the concept but do not use the word *deliver* in our sense.

Mosiah. "Put your trust in him, and serve him with all diligence of mind, [and] if ye do this, he will, according to his own will and pleasure, *deliver* you out of bondage" (Mosiah 7:33).

Alma. "God would make it known unto them whither they should go to defend themselves against their enemies, and by so doing, the Lord would *deliver* them; and this was the faith of Moroni, and his heart did glory in it" (Alma 48:16).

Helaman. "O, how could you have forgotten your God in the very day that he has *delivered* you?" (Helaman 7:20).

Third Nephi. "As the Lord liveth, except ye repent of all your iniquities, and cry unto the Lord, ye will in nowise be *delivered* out of the hands of those Gadianton robbers" (3 Nephi 3:15).

Fourth Nephi. The forty-nine verses of 4 Nephi do not use the term *deliverance.*

Mormon. The Lord said, "And thrice have I *delivered* them out of the hands of their enemies, and they have repented not of their sins" (Mormon 3:13).

Ether. The book of Ether expresses the concept of deliverance: "Therefore when they were encompassed about by many waters they did cry unto the Lord, and he did bring them forth again upon the top of the waters" (Ether 6:7), but does not use the term *deliverance.*

Moroni. Moroni does not use *deliverance* in our sense.

In all, we find that eight of the fifteen books employ the word *deliverance* in the sense of divine power working for mortals. The shorter books are generally the ones that lack it. Most of the longer books possess many instances of the use of *deliverance.*

GROUP DELIVERANCE

The Book of Mormon provides many examples and types of deliverance that range from saving an entire nation, as in the often-evoked story of the exodus of the children of Israel out of Egypt,[2] to the individual deliverance that Nephi pleaded for (see 2 Nephi 4:27–33). First, we will consider some examples of the deliverance of groups of people.

Helaman 5 describes the fearful cloud of darkness that descended upon the Lamanites who had imprisoned the brothers Nephi and Lehi. The Lamanites cried out, "What shall we do, that this cloud of darkness may be removed from overshadowing us?" The inspired Aminadab instructed: "You must repent, and cry unto the voice, even until ye shall have faith in Christ, . . . and when ye shall do this, the cloud of darkness shall be removed from overshadowing you" (Helaman 5:40–41). Of course, the cloud represented their spiritual darkness which they could not perceive until God showed them that their spiritual darkness was like this cloud of physical darkness. When the cloud was removed, a holy fire encircled every soul, and then they were able to sense the sweetness of spiritual fire and the joy of having been delivered from their darkness by the light and love of Jesus Christ.

A second example appears in King Mosiah's observation, following the miraculous escape of King Limhi's people, that "were it not for the interposition of their all-wise Creator, and this because of their sincere repentance, they must unavoidably remain in bondage until now. But behold, he did *deliver* them because they did humble themselves before him; and because they cried mightily unto him he did *deliver* them out of bondage; and thus doth the Lord work with his power in all cases among the children of men, extending the arm of mercy towards them that put their trust in him" (Mosiah 29:19–20).

Not only does this passage mention deliverance by divine power but, like the passage in Helaman 5, it also explains how deliverance is obtained: "And thus doth the Lord work with his power in all cases among the children of men, extending the arm of mercy towards them that put their trust in him" (Mosiah 29:20). Thus it would appear that repentance, humility, and crying mightily to the Lord are taught repeatedly as the means by which one gains access to divine deliverance "in all cases."

JOURNEYS

One important means by which the Book of Mormon makes divine deliverance understandable to us is through accounts of journeys, such as the classic example alluded to by prophets throughout the Book of Mormon: the Exodus of the children of Israel out of Egypt. These prophets used the Exodus as the prototype of deliverance, usually for the purpose of bringing the people to repentance through remembrance of God's miraculous deliverance in the past. Wherever the Exodus appears in the Book of Mormon, it appears within the larger concept of deliverance.

For example, Nephi urged his brothers to help build the boat. He recounted the Exodus to enlist their confidence and cooperation (see 1 Nephi 17:23–31). He reminded them that on the Israelite journey, God fed His people manna (see 1 Nephi 17:28), that He caused water to come from the rock (see 1 Nephi 17:29), that He provided light and direction, and that He did "all things for them which were expedient for man to receive" (1 Nephi 17:30).[3] Nephi compared the Exodus to the journey on which the Nephites were about to embark. He told his brothers that on this journey, too, God would be their light (see 1 Nephi 17:13), would make their food sweet (see 1 Nephi 17:12), and would provide every necessary thing for the journey—if they would keep his commandments. The Lord promised, Nephi explained further, that "after ye have arrived in the promised land, ye shall know that I, the Lord, am God; and that I, the Lord, did deliver you from destruction; yea, that I did bring you out of the land of Jerusalem" (1 Nephi 17:14). One reason for requiring people to undertake journeys in the Book of Mormon is to make it possible for them to have experiences that drive them to their extremity, at which point they discover the delivering power of God.

All major journeys in the Book of Mormon are allegorical as well as actual, reflecting not only the different kinds of the Lord's deliverances but also the principles on which the deliverances depend. All these journeys typify every person's sojourn on earth and the tasks that each is given to accomplish. Only God has the overview of the journey, and only God knows what will be needed along the way. He offers everything each person needs to succeed in the quest. As the Book of Mormon amply illustrates, however, people must often be persuaded to receive Christ's divine deliverance for their earthly journeys.

The destination of each divinely guided journey is a promised land where spiritual enlargement will be possible. The land prepared by God is "a land which is choice above all other lands" (1 Nephi 2:20; Ether 1:42). And, as the journeys represent the individual's sojourn on earth, so the destinations represent the kingdom of heaven, or reentering the presence of God. Again, the journeys represented in the Book of Mormon typify everyone's earthly sojourn and his or her need for divine help at every juncture.

Four examples will suffice to illustrate the principles underlying deliverance on journeys:

1. Lehi's journey to the New World.
2. Alma the Elder's journey from the land of Nephi across the wilderness to the land of Zarahemla.
3. The trek of King Limhi and Ammon to Zarahemla.
4. The Jaredite voyage to the choice land.

The first example is Lehi's journey. On their way to a promised land, Lehi and his family began a seemingly impossible trip through dangerous wilderness and across a terrifying ocean. Alma provided the allegorical interpretation of this journey and emphasized both the necessity as well as the ease of consulting the Lord in all our affairs (Alma 37:38–47). In the book of Alma we learn the name of Lehi's ball or director, Liahona, which signifies a compass (Alma 37:38). Because constant revelation is a difficult spiritual reality for people to grasp, the Lord designed the palpable Liahona not only to help Lehi's family find their way to the promised land but also to teach the principles on which revelation depends, illustrating how individuals actually go forward depending on God as though they were holding a Liahona in their hands. Nephi explained how his family made the compass work:

"And it came to pass that I, Nephi, beheld the pointers which were in the ball, that they did work according to the faith and diligence and heed which we did give unto them.

"And there was also written upon them a new writing, which was plain to be read, which did give us understanding concerning the ways of the Lord; and it was written and changed from time to time, according to the faith and diligence which we gave unto it. And thus we see that by small means the Lord can bring about great things" (1 Nephi 16:28–29).

Alma explained further: "And it did work for them according to their faith in God; therefore, if they had faith to believe that God could cause that those spindles should point the way they should go, behold, it was done; therefore they had this miracle, and also many other miracles wrought by the power of God, day by day.

"Nevertheless, because those miracles were worked by small means it did show unto them marvelous works. They were slothful, and forgot to exercise their faith and diligence and then those marvelous works ceased, and they did not progress in their journey;

"Therefore, they tarried in the wilderness, or did not travel a direct course, and were afflicted with hunger and thirst, because of their transgressions" (Alma 37:40–42).

We learn at least four simple but profound principles here that teach us how to go to the Lord for help:

1. If they just *believed* that the ball would deliver them, it did. Simple belief connects the believer with the powers of heaven.

2. Not only did their belief make the ball work but they also received many other miracles, even day by day.

3. Although the means were small, the works were marvelous. As a ship is worked by a small helm (see D&C 123:16), so the powers of divine deliverance are engaged by small means on earth; that is, by belief, humility, humble petitioning of the Lord, obedience, and persistence.

4. When the travelers grew lazy and neglected to ask, divine deliverance ceased, and they became hungry, thirsty, and lost. Perhaps it is not the mysterious nature of revelation and divine grace that keeps us from pursuing heavenly help but the energy that the Lord may require of us—the faith, the diligence, and the heeding.

Alma explained the symbolism of the Liahona's delivering power: "I would that ye should understand that these things are not without a shadow; for as our fathers were slothful to give heed to this compass (now these things were temporal) they did not prosper; even so it is with things which are spiritual.

"For behold, it is as easy to give heed to the word of Christ, which will point to you a straight course to eternal bliss, as it was for our fathers to give heed to this compass, which would point unto them a straight course to the promised land.

"And now I say, is there not a type in this thing? For just as surely as this director did bring our fathers, by following its course, to the promised land, shall the words of Christ, if we follow their course, carry us beyond this vale of sorrow into a far better land of promise" (Alma 37:43–45).

The Lord provides physical symbols of spiritual realities to help the reader understand unseen spiritual powers. The tools of deliverance are interesting in themselves: the Liahona, the plates of brass, the sword of Laban, fire, clouds, boats, and shining stones. Each instrument of deliverance represents the unseen but real, accessible spiritual power in the Savior.

The second and third examples of journeys, both recorded in Mosiah, illustrate again the *conditions* on which divine deliverance is granted. God provides deliverance in response to the preparation and righteousness of the people. For example, in the case of Alma's group in Helam, the people escaped during broad daylight as the enemy miraculously slept, in contrast to the more natural escape of Limhi's community, which took place under cover of night while drunken Lamanites slept (see Mosiah 22–24). Clearly some deliverances happen miraculously, whereas others occur more naturally and progress more slowly. In the case of Limhi's group, the people needed more time to repent of Abinadi's martyrdom before they were ready for deliverance, and so the Lord took more time: "The Lord was slow to hear their cry because of their iniquities; nevertheless the Lord did hear their cries, and began to soften the hearts of the Lamanites that they began to ease their burdens; yet the Lord did not see fit to *deliver* them out of bondage" (Mosiah 21:15).

Alma's group, on the other hand, had believed on Alma's words alone, had left their property, and had risked their lives to be baptized; therefore, they were prepared to exercise more faith and to accept miraculous deliverance:

"Alma and his people did not raise their voices to the Lord their God, but did pour out their hearts to him; and he did know the thoughts of their hearts.

"And it came to pass that the voice of the Lord came to them in their afflictions, saying: Lift up your heads and be of good comfort, for I know of the covenant which ye have made unto me; and I will covenant with my people and *deliver* them out of bondage.

" . . . That ye may know of a surety that I, the Lord God, do visit my people in their afflictions.

" . . . And they did submit cheerfully and with patience to all the will of the Lord.

"And it came to pass that so great was their faith and their patience that the voice of the Lord came unto them again, saying: Be of good comfort, for on the morrow I will *deliver* you out of bondage" (Mosiah 24:12–16).

The Lord suits the type of deliverance to the spiritual needs of the groups involved.

The fourth example is the Jaredite journey across the ocean. This journey provides another example of physical and spiritual deliverance. Tangible instruments of deliverance abound here. Moroni recorded that when the Jaredites crossed the great deep in their watertight vessels, the Lord "caused that there should be a furious wind blow upon the face of the waters, towards the promised land. . . .

" . . . Many times [they were] buried in the depths of the sea, because of the mountain waves which broke upon them, and also the great and terrible tempests which were caused by the fierceness of the wind. . . .

" . . . When they were encompassed about by many waters they did cry unto the Lord, and he did bring them forth again upon the top of the waters. . . .

" . . . They were driven forth; and no monster of the sea could break them, . . . and they did have light continually, whether it was above the water or under the water" (Ether 6:5–7, 10).

The recurrent motif of light in these journeys, and in this case from shining stones, draws our attention. During the Exodus, Jehovah led the children of Israel by a pillar of fire. The Lord had earlier told the brother of Jared, "For behold, I am the Father, I am the *light,* and the life, and the truth of the world" (Ether 4:12). In the course of the terrifying journey, these Jaredites could see the light from the stones and understand that it represented the unseen but very powerful love of Jesus Christ. The journey through the deep also recalls the Savior's teaching about the winds and rains that beat vainly upon the invincible man or woman of Christ (see Matthew 7:24–25).

PERSONAL DELIVERANCE

The Book of Mormon offers help from personal trouble. Nephi, angry and in despair, gave us a good description of depression:

"O wretched man that I am! Yea, my heart sorroweth because of my flesh; my soul grieveth because of mine iniquities.

"I am encompassed about, because of the temptations and the sins which do easily beset me.

"And when I desire to rejoice, my heart groaneth because of my sins" (2 Nephi 4:17–19).

But as Nephi's heart turned to many evidences in his own life of the Lord's love and intervention, he rebuked himself for his despair because he remembered the principle of deliverance. Nephi's is perhaps the most sublime expression in scripture of faith in the Savior's power to deliver:

"Awake, my soul! No longer droop in sin. Rejoice, O my heart, and give place no more for the enemy of my soul.

"Do not anger again because of mine enemies. Do not slacken my strength because of mine afflictions.

"Rejoice, O my heart, and cry unto the Lord, and say: O Lord, I will praise thee forever; yea, my soul will rejoice in thee, my God, and the rock of my salvation.

"O Lord, wilt thou redeem my soul? Wilt thou *deliver* me out of the hands of mine enemies? Wilt thou make me that I may shake at the appearance of sin? . . .

"Yea, I know that God will give liberally to him that asketh. Yea, my God will give me, if I ask not amiss; therefore I will lift up my voice unto thee; yea, I will cry unto thee, my God, the rock of my righteousness. Behold, my voice shall forever ascend up unto thee, my rock and mine everlasting God" (2 Nephi 4:28–31, 35).

Moroni taught that despair comes of iniquity (see Moroni 10:22). By *iniquity* he seems to mean lack of faith in the deliverance offered by the Savior. He stated, "Christ truly said . . . : If ye have faith ye can do all things which are expedient unto me" (Moroni 10:23). That is, because there is a Savior, there are solutions to seemingly unsolvable problems.

The life of Alma the Younger demonstrates several examples of individual deliverance. He declared that he was "supported under trials and troubles of every kind, yea, and in all manner of afflictions; . . . and I do put my trust in him, and he will still *deliver* me" (Alma 36:27). Alma gave the benefit of his belief and experience to his son: "I would that ye should remember, that as much as ye shall put your trust in God even so much ye shall be *delivered* out of your trials, and your troubles, and your afflictions, and ye shall be lifted up at the last day" (Alma 38:5). Although in the following passage he did not use the word *deliverance,* he clearly described a release from his own personal hell:

"For three days and for three nights was I racked, even with the pains of a damned soul.

" . . . I was thus racked with torment. . . .

" . . . I cried within my heart: O Jesus, thou Son of God, have mercy on me, who am in the gall of bitterness, and am encircled about by the everlasting chains of death.

"And now, behold, when I thought this, I could remember my pains no more; yea, I was harrowed up by the memory of my sins no more.

"And oh, what joy, and what marvelous light I did behold; yea, my soul was filled with joy as exceeding as was my pain!" (Alma 36:16–20).

Later, as a more mature missionary, Alma viewed the abysmal apostasy of the Zoramites and exclaimed: "O Lord, my heart is exceedingly sorrowful; wilt thou comfort my soul in Christ. . . . O Lord, wilt thou comfort my soul, and give unto me success." Then, speaking for his companions he said: "Yea, wilt thou comfort their souls in Christ" (Alma 31:31–32). "And the Lord provided for them that they should hunger not, neither should they thirst; yea, and he also gave them strength, that they should suffer no manner of afflictions, save it were swallowed up in the joy of Christ" (Alma 31:38). Thus Alma impressed us with the point that divine deliverance is readily available to those who will come to the Lord.

All the dilemmas illustrated in the Book of Mormon contain dangerous elements uncontrollable by mortals, so that when deliverance comes, no one will be confused about the One from whom it comes. Life's path is strewn with seemingly unsolvable dilemmas so that people will be driven to God for help. The Lord's methods may be based on the principle that the greater the trouble, the more likely one will turn to Him for help. We are reminded that the only way that God can teach how faith works is through experience, some of it necessarily very dangerous. When the hand of God is revealed in the midst of a seemingly unsolvable situation, one's confidence in the presence of God gains strength.

The principles of misery and happiness operate in each sphere along the path to salvation. A person can experience spiritual death, misery, sorrow, and suffering here as well as hereafter. One can experience oneness, joy, consolation, and peace here as well as hereafter. All these experiences are governed by spiritual principles. Oneness with Christ produces spiritual life and happiness here, now, and forever. Neglect of the spiritual principles embraced by the Atonement causes many of the miseries of spiritual death here and hereafter. The consequences of obedience to or neglect of these principles may differ in intensity between this mortal estate and the next life but not in their essential quality. Only obedience to Christ's atonement delivers us from the negative end of the spectrum of experience, whatever estate we inhabit.

After considering only a sampling of the deliverances described in the Book of Mormon, and having noted their prevalence, I suggest that the book's authors and editors, under divine direction, used the term *deliverance* as one of the organizing principles for the entire Book of

Mormon. Therefore, if the Book of Mormon is really about deliverance, it is also about Christ's atonement.

Because deliverance is a major function of the Savior's atoning sacrifice, the illustrations of deliverance serve as metaphors for such other synonyms of *atonement* as *redemption* and *salvation.* Therefore, every instance of deliverance is also an instance of redemption, salvation, or at-one-ment. I conclude that the Book of Mormon was provided, at least in part, to illustrate how grace and atonement actually work in the lives of those who come to Christ. Obviously Limhi and his people trekking across a wilderness some two thousand years ago may mean little to the reader until he realizes that Limhi's journey is analogous to his own life journey. Thereafter, a person will read the Book of Mormon differently as he or she grasps the insight that humility, prayer, and obedience can draw down divine deliverance in the midst of one's own wilderness trials. The Book of Mormon is a handbook of principles for traveling one's earthly path by the divine enabling power of the Lord Jesus Christ. The Book of Mormon, quick and powerful, the living word of God, is designed so that the reader who approaches it with humility can use it for personal revelation; that is, as a personal Liahona. The Book of Mormon is itself a tool of deliverance. Nephi made the same point with this instruction: "Wherefore, I said unto you, feast upon the words of Christ; for behold, the words of Christ will *tell you all things what ye should do*" (2 Nephi 32:3).

We have seen that the instances of deliverance throughout the Book of Mormon can infuse the reader with hope for deliverance from his or her own troubles, instruct one in how to go to the Lord for help, and fill the soul with faith in the eternal constancy and accessibility of the great Deliverer.

NOTES

1. This figure also includes a few instances of *deliver* to mean "to hand over" as in "the Lord will deliver Laban into your hands" (1 Nephi 3:29) or "I did deliver the plates unto my brother Chemish" (Omni 1:8). Obviously synonyms

like *save* and *preserve* might be studied in combination with *deliverance.* My objective here is not a word study but a demonstration of how the Lord used one word to make clearer the abstract principle of God's grace.

2. See S. Kent Brown, "The Exodus Pattern in the Book of Mormon," *BYU Studies* 30, no. 3 (summer 1990): 111–26, for discussion of Exodus language used in the Book of Mormon.

3. The word *expedient* is interesting, suggesting that God must take care not to provide too much deliverance so that individuals have sufficient experience with the forces that govern the natural world.

18

Faith unto Repentance

Brent L. Top

In every dispensation, from Adam to the present day, the Lord's anointed prophets have been under a divine mandate to "preach nothing save it were repentance and faith on the Lord" (Mosiah 18:20). The central message of the gospel of Jesus Christ is and has always been that through the Atonement of the Lamb of God, the scarlet sins of man can become "white as snow" (Isaiah 1:18). Without a knowledge and acceptance of what the scriptures generally, and the Book of Mormon specifically, teach about the doctrine of repentance, one may seek through self-justification to make repentance easier than it really is or through doctrinal distortion to make it more difficult than it needs to be.

DOCTRINAL DEFICIENCIES OF "CHECKLIST" REPENTANCE

When we view repentance as a mere checklist of steps that must be taken for every sin ever committed, we fall prey to the spiritual pitfalls and doctrinal deficiencies of such a simplistic and superficial approach. Several deficiencies, each with potential pitfalls, are evident.

Brent L. Top is an endowed professor of moral education and a professor of Church history and doctrine at Brigham Young University.

First, without the understanding that repentance is a fruit of faith, a person may go through a repentance checklist and feel satisfied he has met all the requirements for repentance but not realize his efforts have not been efficacious. Checklist repentance undertaken without faith in the Redeemer may produce results similar to those described by the prophet Isaiah: "It shall be unto them, even as unto a hungry man which dreameth, and behold he eateth but he awaketh and his soul is empty; or like unto a thirsty man which dreameth, and behold he drinketh but he awaketh and behold he is faint, and his soul hath appetite" (2 Nephi 27:3).

Second, a mechanical approach to repentance may prevent the repentant sinner from ever "catching up." Seeking to apply some arbitrary checklist for every sin committed is like taking two steps backward for each step forward. Because we continually make mistakes and sin, it becomes impossible to conscientiously go through this process for every sin. An overemphasis on the mechanics of repentance may leave one so discouraged, thinking it impossible to fully repent for every sin, that he may give up in despair and sink deeper into the quicksands of sin.

A third deficiency in this approach to repentance is that for some sins and situations there may not be any way to complete the checklist. The "Rs of Repentance" (such as restitution) may not apply. President Spencer W. Kimball wrote, "There are some sins for which no adequate restitution can be made, and others for which only partial restitution is possible."[1]

The final and most important doctrinal fallacy in the concept of checklist repentance is that by concentrating on our outward actions we tend to emphasize our efforts and ignore the cleansing power of Christ. This approach to repentance makes it appear as though a remission of sins is something obtained primarily by mortal effort. Such a view minimizes the miraculous Atonement of Jesus Christ and the grace of God that makes a remission of sins possible. If we focus all of our attention and efforts on the steps we must take to repent, we tend to overlook what He did to make repentance possible. A humanistic or mechanical approach to repentance promotes "pseudo self-reliance."

Relying only upon our own efforts robs us of the repentance-enabling power of Christ. Thus the worst danger of this superficial view of repentance is that it causes an unwitting but crucial oversight of the most important "R" of repentance—Redeemer.

FAITH IN CHRIST AS THE FOUNDATION OF ALL TRUE REPENTANCE

The Book of Mormon is replete with examples and teachings on faith in the Lord as the empowering ingredient in repentance. The prophet Enos learned firsthand from the Lord the central role of faith in true repentance. In Enos's account of his "wrestle" before God, which led him to a remission of sins, we do not see him going methodically through some series of steps to repent. We see him pondering the words of eternal life, pleading with the Lord to satisfy his spiritual hunger:

"And my soul hungered; and I kneeled down before my Maker, and I cried unto him in mighty prayer and supplication for mine own soul; and all the day long did I cry unto him; yea, and when the night came I did still raise my voice high that it reached the heavens.

"And there came a voice unto me, saying: Enos, thy sins are forgiven thee, and thou shalt be blessed.

"And I, Enos, knew that God could not lie; wherefore, my guilt was swept away.

"And I said: Lord, how is it done?

"And he said unto me: *Because of thy faith in Christ . . . thy faith hath made thee whole*" (Enos 1:4–8; emphasis added).

The Lord simply stated that it was faith in Christ that had brought about Enos's remission of sins, and not his outward actions of repentance, as important as they were. Enos learned what Nephi had taught earlier—that a remission of sins and ultimate salvation cannot be obtained merely by righteous deeds but rather through "unshaken faith in [Christ], relying wholly upon the merits of him who is mighty to save" (2 Nephi 31:19). "True repentance is based on and flows from faith in the Lord Jesus Christ," declared President Ezra Taft Benson. "There is no other way."[2]

When we rely "wholly upon the merits" of Christ, we will submit to the designated requirements of repentance as a natural consequence of faith instead of an adherence to a checklist. Our actions and attitudes of penitence become evidence of our faith and not a substitute for it.

The prophet Amulek also taught that it is the "great and last sacrifice" of Jesus Christ that gives power and efficacy to the doctrine of repentance. He emphatically declared that faith must precede repentance for the cleansing mercy of the Messiah to be enjoyed:

"And behold, this is the whole meaning of the law, every whit pointing to that great and last sacrifice; and that great and last sacrifice will be the Son of God, yea, infinite and eternal.

"And thus he shall bring salvation to all those who shall believe on his name; this being the intent of this last sacrifice, to bring about the bowels of mercy, which overpowereth justice, and bringeth about means unto men that they may have *faith unto repentance.*

"And thus mercy can satisfy the demands of justice, and encircles them in the arms of safety, while he that exercises no *faith unto repentance* is exposed to the whole law of the demands of justice; therefore only unto him that has *faith unto repentance* is brought about the great and eternal plan of redemption.

"Therefore may God grant unto you, my brethren, that ye may begin to exercise your *faith unto repentance,* that ye begin to call upon his holy name, that he would have mercy upon you;

"Yea, cry unto him for mercy; for he is mighty to save" (Alma 34:14–18; emphasis added).

Perhaps no scriptural example better illustrates Amulek's teaching of "faith unto repentance" and the need to "cry unto [God] for mercy" than the Book of Mormon account of Alma the Younger's dramatic conversion. Alma was a sinner who was "racked with torment" and "harrowed up by the memory of [his] many sins," who pleaded with the Lord to do something for him that he could not do for himself. Again, we do not see Alma mechanically going through a series of steps to repentance. In fact, there is no scriptural evidence that he had previously performed any of the actions traditionally taught as sequential steps to forgiveness. The record reveals, however, that Alma's miraculous change from a life of sin to a life of service and spirituality resulted from his "faith unto repentance":

"And it came to pass that as I was thus racked with torment, while I was harrowed up by the memory of my many sins, behold, I remembered also to have heard my father prophesy unto the people concerning the coming of one Jesus Christ, a Son of God, to atone for the sins of the world.

"Now, as my mind caught hold upon this thought, I cried within my heart: O Jesus, thou Son of God, have mercy on me, who am in the gall of bitterness, and am encircled about by the everlasting chains of death.

"And now, behold, when I thought this, I could remember my pains no more; yea, I was harrowed up by the memory of my sins no more.

"And oh, what joy, and what marvelous light I did behold; yea, my soul was filled with joy as exceeding as was my pain!" (Alma 36:17–20).

Merciful relief was extended to Alma because of his newly exercised faith in the atonement of Christ. Alma's subsequent abandonment of sinful practices, his restitution for past mistakes, and his life of continued commitment to the kingdom of God grew out of his faith in the cleansing power of Christ's atonement. Another scriptural example also affirms this principle. Nephi saw in vision the Savior's twelve apostles, who "*because of their faith in the Lamb of God* their garments are made white in his blood. . . . These are made white in the blood of the Lamb, *because of their faith in him*" (1 Nephi 12:8–11; emphasis added). The cleansing of our garments comes to us, as it did to Enos, Alma, and the ancient apostles, not because of our own righteous acts but "because of the righteousness of thy Redeemer" (2 Nephi 2:3)—because of His infinite atonement.

Indeed, faith in the Lord Jesus Christ as the first principle of the gospel and repentance as the second, along with all other principles and ordinances of the gospel, have their foundation in the Savior's atoning sacrifice. Truly, then, repentance stems only from faith in the redemptive and cleansing power of the blood of the Lamb of God. Elder

Orson Pratt taught, "The first effect of true faith is a sincere, true, and thorough repentance of all sins. Faith is the starting point—the foundation and cause of our repentance."[3]

Without the merciful Atonement, there could be no forgiveness of our sins. And without unwavering faith in that Atonement, there can be neither repentance nor saving works of righteousness. Thus, paraphrasing Nephi's familiar teaching, it is by grace that we receive a remission of our sins, after all we can do (see 2 Nephi 25:23).

While there really is no set recipe or checklist of steps that must be taken in every case of repentance, we must still do "all we can do." The Lord has specified that "all we can do" begins with unshaken faith in Christ. Other than this, the Book of Mormon (and the other standard works) gives no list of "Rs" of repentance. It does, however, provide doctrinal teachings and examples of how "faith unto repentance" leads one, both by inward attitudes and outward actions, to fulfill the Lord's stated requirements of repentance revealed in our day. "By this ye may know if a man repenteth of his sins—behold, he will confess them and forsake them" (D&C 58:43).

CONFESSING SIN: INWARD ATTITUDES AND OUTWARD ACTIONS

Speaking of the Nephite Church, Moroni wrote that "they were strict to observe that there should be no iniquity among them; . . . and if they repented not, and confessed not, their names were blotted out, and they were not numbered among the people of Christ" (Moroni 6:7). The Book of Mormon confirms the concept taught in both the Old and New Testaments, as well as in modern revelation, that confession is an integral part of true repentance; whether it be private, personal confession of sins, or a more public confession to the church, such as Moroni described. The act of verbal confession serves as an outward reminder of what should be happening inside the soul of man. Confession is like a mirror in which one can examine himself spiritually and recognize his need for the cleansing power of Christ. The Apostle Paul spoke of confession that involves both the heart and mouth (see Romans 10:10). Similarly, the Book of Mormon teaches that true repentance, born of faith in Christ, yields an action of confession coming from the mouth that mirrors an attitude of confession born in the heart.

"A Broken Heart and a Contrite Spirit"

True repentance that leads to confession is, as Paul said, born of a "godly sorrow" (see 2 Corinthians 7:9–10). Godly sorrow is the indicator of true faith in Christ and the only genuine motivation for bringing forth "fruit meet for repentance" (Alma 12:15). The Book of Mormon describes the attitude of "godly sorrow" as "a broken heart and a contrite spirit" (2 Nephi 2:7; see also 3 Nephi 9:19–20; 3 Nephi 12:19; Ether 4:15; Moroni 6:2). Both terms can be used interchangeably in describing the concept of God's sorrow—feeling the sorrow for our sins that God would have us feel in order to bring about our repentance and submission to His will.

Godly sorrow—the broken heart and contrite spirit—is much more than remorse or regret over having sinned. Mormon observed anguish in his own people and described it as "the sorrowing of the damned" (Mormon 2:12–14). It was a sorrow born of sins and circumstances that did not produce "faith unto repentance." Many may be remorseful for past actions and regret the consequences that have befallen them but do nothing to change, to come unto Christ and partake of His mercy and to comply with the requirements of the gospel. A "broken heart and contrite spirit" is an attitude that always leads to a commitment to change. Alma spoke of this kind of motivational sorrow for sin when he declared to Corianton, "Let your sins trouble you, with that trouble which shall bring you down unto repentance" (Alma 42:29). "The sorrow that is acceptable in the sight of God, is that which leads to true repentance, or reformation of conduct," wrote Elder Orson Pratt. "This kind of sorrow will lead us to obey every commandment of God; it will make us humble and childlike in our dispositions; it will impart unto us meekness and lowliness of mind; it will cause our hearts to be broken and our spirits to be contrite; it will cause us to watch, with great carefulness, every word, thought, and deed; it will call up our past dealings with mankind, and we will feel most anxious to make restitution to all whom we may have, in any way, injured . . . these and many other good things are the results of a Godly sorrow for sin. This is repentance not in word, but in deed: this is the sorrow with which the heavens are pleased."[4]

When the Book of Mormon describes a "broken heart and contrite spirit" it implies considerably more than just a repentant attitude. We gain a better understanding of the relationship of a "broken heart and contrite spirit" to confession and repentance by examining Book of Mormon statements concerning two important elements of godly sorrow.

An "awful awareness" of our unworthiness before God. Before sinners can exercise "faith unto repentance" and obtain a remission of sins, they must experience something akin to what King Benjamin described as "an awful view of their own guilt and abominations, which doth cause them to shrink from the presence of the Lord" (Mosiah 3:25). That stark realization of guilt, King Benjamin declared, awakens "you to a sense of your nothingness, and your worthless and fallen state" (Mosiah 4:5). It thus produces a total dependence upon the Lord and a humility of soul that permits the seeds of repentance to take root. This "awful awareness" must include a self-inflicted stripping away of all rationalization and self-justification. There is no room in a broken heart and contrite spirit for making feeble excuses or blaming others for our sins. "Do not endeavor to excuse yourself in the least point because of your sins," Alma counseled Corianton, "but do you let the justice of God, and his mercy, and his long-suffering have full sway in your heart; and let it bring you down to the dust in humility" (Alma 42:30). Accompanying this "awful awareness" of unworthiness before the Lord is the yearning to be cleansed and to stand approved. It is much more than mere recognition of sin. It is a sackcloth-and-ashes humility that promotes spiritual growth and leads one to a condition described by President David O. McKay as a "change of nature befitting heaven."[5]

Willing submission and surrender to God's will. The Book of Mormon also teaches that one most important indicator of contrition is a willingness to submit to whatever the Lord requires of us in order to obtain a remission of sins. Not only did King Benjamin teach his people about the necessity of an "awful awareness" of their sinful state, but he also taught them that their faith in Christ would lead them to voluntarily surrender to the Lord. Overcoming the natural man and obtaining a remission of sins required that "they humble themselves and become as little children" (Mosiah 3:18). A person who has faith in the Lord and desires to be forgiven of sin is willing to do whatever is necessary. He yields his own will "to the enticings of the Holy Spirit, and putteth off the natural man and becometh a saint through the atonement of Christ the Lord, and becometh as a child, submissive, meek, humble, patient, full of love, willing to submit to all things which the Lord seeth fit to inflict upon him" (Mosiah 3:19). Helaman, speaking of church members in his day, described how such submission, born of faith, leads to "the purifying and the sanctification of their hearts, which sanctification cometh because of their yielding their hearts unto God" (Helaman 3:35).

In contrast to the people of King Benjamin and Helaman, some desire repentance whose hearts are not yet broken and whose spirits are less than contrite. Such persons may become selectively submissive. They desire to repent on their own terms rather than on the Lord's. They wish to make repentance easy, pain-free, and convenient. In reality the process is difficult and demanding and may require humiliation, public embarrassment, pain, restrictions, or inconvenience. Lehi warned such people that Christ offered "himself a sacrifice for sin, to answer the ends of the law, unto all those who have a broken heart and a contrite spirit; and unto *none else* can the ends of the law be answered" (2 Nephi 2:7; emphasis added). "There can be no conditions attached to unconditional surrender to God," wrote Elder Neal A. Maxwell. "Unconditional surrender means we cannot keep our obsessions, possessions, or cheering constituencies . . . Every obsession or preoccupation must give way in total submission."[6]

If we truly possess the proper attitude of confession, as taught in the Book of Mormon, our hearts will be broken with a piercing sorrow for sin and an "awful awareness" of our unworthiness and total dependence upon the mercy of the Savior. Our spirits will be contrite—filled with desire to submit to God's will and to learn from Him what we must do to obtain a remission of our sins.

"If He Confess His Sins before Thee and Me . . . I Will Forgive Him"

To confess without a proper repentant attitude is merely to take another ineffectual step in the checklist of repentance. Confession is a natural response to faith and godly sorrow. When our hearts are broken and our spirits contrite, the desire to set things right will lead us to follow the Spirit and turn away from groping for the letter of the law.

One contribution of the Book of Mormon to an understanding of the doctrine of repentance is its confirmation of the role of confession to the Lord and to proper priesthood leaders. The Lord instructed Alma that "whosoever transgresseth against me, him shall ye judge according to the sins which he has committed; and if he confess his sins before *thee* and *me,* and repenteth in the sincerity of his heart, him shall *ye* forgive, and I will forgive him also" (Mosiah 26:29; emphasis added). From Alma's account we learn that there are two types of confession and two types of forgiveness. In this dispensation the Lord has reaffirmed this important principle (see D&C 59:12). Elder Bruce R. McConkie explained the significance of these two types of confession: "There are thus two confessions and two sources of forgiveness. A sinner must always confess all sins, great and small, to the Lord; in addition, any sins involving moral turpitude and any serious sins for which a person might be disfellowshipped or excommunicated must also be confessed to the Lord's agent, who in most instances is the bishop. The bishop is empowered to forgive sins as far as the church is concerned, meaning that he can choose to retain the repentant person in full fellowship and not impose court penalties upon him. Ultimate forgiveness in all instances and for all sins comes from the Lord and from the Lord only."[7]

The Lord does not require confession as a part of repentance to humiliate, embarrass, or cause one to feel punished by a vindictive God. Neither is confession a mere disclosure of deeds. It is, rather, an opportunity to covenant with the Lord that we are turning away from sin and will make the necessary adjustments in our lives. Confession without a solemn commitment to change does not guarantee any enduring effects. When we understand how "faith unto repentance" and confession are related, we recognize that confession is provided by a merciful and loving Savior to impart the inspired counsel, comfort, and direction that is only available from the Lord and His authorized servants. When we "cast our burdens upon the Lord" through complete confession and a commitment to forsake sin, we are in a position to be taught by the Master. His guidance far surpasses any emotional lift or well-meant advice from mere mortals. "And if men come unto me I will show unto them their weakness. . . . And my grace is sufficient for all men that humble themselves before me; for if they humble themselves before me, and have faith in me, then will I make weak things become strong unto them" (Ether 12:27). The spiritual motivation to confess, characterized in the Book of Mormon as "willful submission to the Lord," will prompt the transgressor to approach the Lord and the proper priesthood leader, as necessary, in humble confession to receive His counsel and support. Under such conditions, the necessary *action* of confession as taught by Alma, as a fruit of the *attitude* of confession, as taught by King Benjamin, becomes a blessing rather than a burden.

FORSAKING SIN

The Book of Mormon illustrates and confirms what is plainly taught in other scriptures, both ancient and modern, that confession must be accompanied by the forsaking of sin. Forsaking sin is all too often misunderstood to mean that one merely stops committing the particular sin of which he is repenting. The abandonment of that sin is necessary and is certainly one element of forsaking, but to view the scriptural concept of forsaking sin only by this narrow definition may rob us of a complete perspective of the true nature of repentance. The Book of Mormon teaches that forsaking requires the abandonment of sinfulness in every aspect of our lives and character. Without this broader application, forsaking is fragmented, and real, enduring change eludes us. One cannot merely forsake a specific sin or sinful situation and cling tenaciously to other sins. It is not just the stopping of a sinful practice that is required. What is needed is a change in one's disposition and desire for sin.

The Book of Mormon gives numerous examples of how forsaking sin, in the truest sense, brings about a total transformation of one's life. King Lamoni's father understood forsaking sin to be an element of genuine repentance when he declared: "I will give away *all my sins* to know thee . . . and be saved at the last day" (Alma 22:18; emphasis added). His forsaking of sin was not selective but rather a total surrender. This comprehensive view of forsaking sin was articulated by President Joseph F. Smith: "True repentance is not only sorrow for sins, and humble penitence and contrition before God, but it involves the necessity of turning away from them, *a discontinuance of all evil practices and deeds,* a thorough reformation of life, a vital change from evil to good, from vice to virtue, from darkness to light."[8]

Forsaking sin and confessing sin each require a change of attitude and behavior. It is not just the abandonment of an action—it is the changing of one's entire being. Alma described this mortal metamorphosis as a "mighty change in your hearts," which causes a person to "sing the song of redeeming love" (see Alma 5:14, 26). Such forsaking, as an indicator of true repentance, involves a mighty change of one's heart—one's desires and deeds—and a mighty change of direction and devotion.

A "Mighty Change" of Heart

The Lord has promised that if we will indeed abandon our wicked deeds and desires, He will perform a great miracle in our behalf that will bring about a newness of attitude, character, and being. He has promised to create in us "a new heart and a new spirit" (Ezekiel 18:31). The Lamanite prophet Samuel held up the works of the repentant and faithful Lamanites as an example to the wicked Nephites of the miracle of a new heart that occurs through "faith unto repentance." He explained that his Lamanite brethren had been "led to believe the holy scriptures, yea, the prophecies of the holy prophets, which are written, which leadeth them to faith on the Lord, and unto repentance, *which faith and repentance bringeth a change of heart unto them*" (Helaman 15:7; emphasis added). This mighty change of behavior, thoughts, attitudes, and desires comes as a merciful gift of grace—"after all we can do" (2 Nephi 25:23). When we have demonstrated our faith, repentant determination, and renewed devotion, then the indispensable grace of God is what brings about a remission of sins.

True repentance, as taught in the Book of Mormon, is a demanding process, and once we have committed ourselves to it, there can be no hesitation. We must not attempt to straddle the line of demarcation between good and evil. We cannot, figuratively speaking, have one hand reaching for the fruit of the "tree of life" while continuing to dance and dine in the "great and spacious building," for it requires both hands and our whole heart and soul to cling to the rod of iron (see 1 Nephi 11:8–36). The examples of individuals in the Book of Mormon who were transformed through their "faith unto repentance" make it clear that we must do all that we can as mortals to become totally "new creatures."

A "Mighty Change" of Direction and Devotion

Forsaking sin involves not only a turning *from* evil practices but also a turning *to* God in greater righteousness and service. Just as Paul taught King Agrippa that repentance means to "turn to God, and do works meet for repentance" (Acts 26:20), so the Book of Mormon teaches that repentance requires actions that demonstrate renewed love for God and increased commitment to a life of righteousness. The resulting "works meet for repentance" are naturally two-directional—we cannot demonstrate greater love and worship of God without also gaining an intensified desire to serve and bless the lives of others. Alma taught that the covenants associated with baptism for the remission of sins require devotion on our part to both God and our fellowmen (see Mosiah 18:8–10).

Increased devotion to God. Alma taught his people at the waters of Mormon that the covenant of baptism for the remission of sins involves a commitment, or solemn promise, to God "that ye will serve him and keep his commandments" (Mosiah 18:10). Writing to his son Moroni, Mormon taught that "fulfilling the commandments [of God] bringeth remission of sins" (Moroni 8:25). King Benjamin taught his people that for them to *obtain* and *retain* a remission of their sins, they must continue "calling on the name of the Lord daily, and standing steadfastly in the faith," and "grow[ing] in the knowledge of the glory of him that created [them]" (Mosiah 4:11–12). King Benjamin further pointed out that our renewed devotion toward God would also affect our relationships with our fellowmen. "And ye will not have a mind to injure one another," he declared, "but to live peaceably, and to render to every man according to that which is his due" (Mosiah 4:13).

Increased love and service to our fellowmen. Alma taught that if we truly desire to have the heavy burden of sin lifted from our weary shoulders, we must be "willing to bear one another's burdens" and be "willing to mourn with those that mourn; yea, and comfort those that stand in need of comfort" (Mosiah 18:8–9). King Benjamin declared, "When ye are in the service of your fellow beings ye are only in the service of your God" (Mosiah 2:17). In all of the standard works, there is perhaps no more profound example of how service and love of others flow naturally out of true repentance than the story of the sons of Mosiah. Before their remarkable conversion these young men were, according to the scriptural record, "the very vilest of sinners" (Mosiah 28:4). Because of the sincerity of their repentance and the intensity of their faith in and gratitude for the Atonement of Christ, they were later "zealously striving to repair all the injuries which they had done to the church, confessing all their sins, and publishing all the things which they had seen, and explaining the prophecies and the scriptures to all who desired to hear them.

"And thus they were instruments in the hands of God in bringing many to the knowledge of the truth. . . .

"Now they were desirous that salvation should be declared to every creature" (Mosiah 27:35–36; 28:3; see also Helaman 5:17).

The subsequent lives of righteousness and service of the sons of Mosiah are evidence that true repentance prompted them to make a spiritual restitution for their sins. While it is true that we can in no way, of ourselves, repay the Savior, make full restitution for our sins, or overcome our sinfulness by our efforts alone, we can show our appreciation for His sacrifice by making a spiritual restitution through a lifelong devotion to God and to our fellowmen. Although we will continue to be "unprofitable servants" (Mosiah 2:21), if we truly have "faith unto repentance," we will strive to follow the example of the sons of Mosiah, who spent their lives "zealously striving to repair all the injuries" caused by their sins.

"I HAVE REPENTED OF MY SINS; . . . BEHOLD I AM BORN OF THE SPIRIT"

The Book of Mormon constantly reminds us that repentance is inextricably linked with faith in Christ and that forgiveness of sins comes as a gift of God's grace to man only upon condition of "faith unto repentance." Even though we may diligently work to confess and forsake our sins, we cannot of ourselves attain the "mighty change of heart." Our own efforts, however noble, if not by-products of faith in the Savior, will produce only an incomplete or temporary change of life. President Benson wrote that many in the world "demonstrate great willpower and self-discipline in overcoming bad habits and weaknesses of the flesh. Yet at the same time they give no thought to the Master, sometimes even openly rejecting Him. Such changes of behavior, even if in a positive direction, do not constitute true repentance."[9]

Like those spoken of by President Benson, we often struggle mightily, even with the best of intentions, trying to overcome our carnal ways through our own efforts. We may feel overwhelmed, frustrated, and hopeless, unable to change when we rely solely on our puny human willpower. We can never achieve a remission of sins in that way. The spiritual rebirth that purges sin from our soul, of which the Book of Mormon repeatedly speaks, comes only as gift of the Spirit—made possible only through the Atonement of Jesus Christ. Alma declared, "I have repented of my sins, and have been redeemed of the Lord; behold I am born of the Spirit" (Mosiah 27:24). The Book of Mormon shows us the means whereby we, after we have done "all we can do," may know that we have been "born of the Spirit" and have received a forgiveness of our sins. The words and lives of Enos, King Benjamin, Alma, Helaman, Lamoni, and others, provide us with valuable insights into what one feels and does when he is cleansed by the atoning blood of Christ.

Peace of Conscience

One most significant indicator of forgiveness, described in the Book of Mormon, is found in Enos's declaration upon hearing the Lord assure him that his sins were forgiven: "My guilt was swept away" (Enos 1:6). Approximately four centuries after Enos, King Benjamin's people experienced similar feelings after their prayer of penitence (see Mosiah 4:2). The scriptural record recounts the miraculous spiritual rebirth that effected a remission of their sins and was accompanied by a "peace of conscience, because of the exceeding faith which they had in Jesus Christ" (Mosiah 4:3).

Unfortunately, some people have mistakenly equated a "peace of conscience" with an elimination of the memory of sins. They feel that they are not forgiven as long as they continue to remember their past misdeeds. The Book of Mormon helps to dispel this myth and to clarify what is meant by a "peace of conscience." It is obvious from Alma's record that he could vividly remember his sins as he counseled his sons a generation later. He described his relief upon receiving a remission of his sins: "I could remember my pains no more; . . . I was harrowed up by the memory of my sins no more" (Alma 36:19). Although he could continue to remember his sins and even the pain that he had suffered, his conscience was no longer tortured by guilt.

Joy and Divine Love

Another indicator of forgiveness of sins often cited in Book of Mormon conversion experiences is that of an overwhelming feeling of joy and love. "And oh, what joy, and what marvelous light I did behold," declared Alma, "yea, my soul was filled with joy as exceeding as was my pain!" (Alma 36:20). The miraculous conversion of King Lamoni and his wife also resulted in the feeling of joy and love that accompanies forgiveness and spiritual rebirth. As the queen arose from her overpowering spiritual experience, she declared: "O blessed Jesus, who has saved me from an awful hell!" (Alma 19:29). The record continues: "And when she had said this, she clasped her hands, being filled with joy" (Alma 19:30). The people of King Benjamin experienced something similar when they penitently petitioned God for His mercy and forgiveness. The scriptures record that "the Spirit of the Lord came upon them, and they were filled with joy, having received a remission of their sins" (Mosiah 4:3).

Although we may not be so totally overcome by the Spirit that we fall to the earth in a spiritual trance, like Lamoni and his wife (see Alma 19:13, 18), we can feel "exquisite joy" like Alma and Benjamin's people. Associated with this increased sense of joy is also an intensified awareness of divine love. Alma characterized that feeling as a desire to "sing the song of redeeming love" (Alma 5:26).

No Desire for Sin

Another important testament of the spiritual transformation that brings with it forgiveness of sins is a "mighty change" in our disposition and desires. King Benjamin's people experienced this fruit of repentance and joyfully declared: "The Spirit of the Lord Omnipotent . . . has wrought a mighty change in us, or in our hearts, that we have no more disposition to do evil, but to do good continually" (Mosiah 5:2). King Lamoni, his wife, and all those who were converted through Ammon's ministrations to the king also testified "that their hearts had been changed; that they had no more desire to do evil" (Alma 19:33). Similarly, Alma spoke of high priests whose "garments were washed white through the blood of the Lamb" and who subsequently "could not look upon sin save it were with abhorrence" (Alma 13:11–12).

We, like these ancient Book of Mormon people, can determine to a degree when we have been forgiven and to what extent we have been spiritually reborn by examining our disposition toward evil and our desires "to do good continually." This condition does not mean that we never again succumb to temptation, but it does mean that sinfulness becomes repugnant to us and that we desire righteousness and seek to do good.

Love for Our Fellowmen

When we are forgiven of our sins and feel an intensified love and appreciation for the Lord, a natural outgrowth of those feelings is a desire that our fellowmen also experience the goodness and mercy of

God. In Lehi's dream, after he had partaken of the fruit of the tree of life, which filled his soul with inexpressible joy, he declared, "I began to be desirous that my family should partake of it also" (1 Nephi 8:12). Enos also exemplified this attitude when, after the Lord had assured him that his sins were forgiven, his compassion and concern extended beyond himself to his brethren the Nephites, and even to his enemies the Lamanites (see Enos 1:9–13). We see this fruit of forgiveness in the declaration of Alma: "I have labored without ceasing, that I might bring souls unto repentance; that I might bring them to taste of the exceeding joy of which I did taste; that they might also be born of God, and be filled with the Holy Ghost" (Alma 36:24). If we desire to know whether our repentance is accepted of the Lord, we should take spiritual inventory of our feelings of concern for others and our involvement in compassionate service.

Increased Spiritual Understanding

King Benjamin's people witnessed that accompanying the remission of their sins came "the manifestations of his Spirit" and "great views of that which is to come" (Mosiah 5:3). When we are truly penitent, we are prepared to have the Holy Ghost teach and testify to us of the "mysteries of God" (Alma 26:22). Thus another fruit of forgiveness, as seen in the Book of Mormon, is renewed guidance by the Holy Ghost, a greater understanding and yearning for spiritual things, and an increased spiritual discernment of the things of God.

God's Image Engraven upon Our Countenances

Speaking to the Church in Zarahemla, Alma posed a simple, yet significant, question to the Saints regarding the level of their spiritual transformation: "Have ye received [God's] image in your countenances?" (Alma 5:14). Perhaps Alma was referring to the literal, visible change that comes upon a person whose sins are forgiven and whose countenance is illuminated by the Spirit of the Lord, but he was probably also alluding to the inward transformation of the whole being. By "countenance" Alma probably meant our whole being: our bearing, manner, behavior, and appearance. In other words, do our actions "image" or reflect those of the Savior?[10]

BECOMING A "NEW CREATURE" IN CHRIST: EVENT OR PROCESS?

Most examples in the Book of Mormon of women and men whose sins were forgiven and who experienced spiritual rebirth involve dramatic or almost sensational events. Enos, Alma the Younger, King Lamoni and his wife, and King Benjamin's people all underwent a sudden change of heart during a singular event or experience. But what about us? Will each of us experience this cleansing spiritual regeneration in the same manner? Elder McConkie answered: "A person may get converted in a moment, miraculously. . . . But that is not the way it happens to most people. With most people, conversion [and the accompanying remission of sins] is a process; and it goes step by step, degree by degree, level by level, from a lower state to a higher, from grace to grace, until the time that the individual is wholly turned to the cause of righteousness. Now this means that an individual overcomes one sin today and another sin tomorrow. He perfects his life in one field now, and in another field later on. And the process goes on until it is complete, until we become, literally, as the Book of Mormon says, saints of God instead of natural men."[11]

Even in the Book of Mormon, most of the people who exercised faith, repented of their sins, and kept the commandments received a remission of their sins through a gradual process rather than a singular event (see Helaman 3:35, Moroni 8:25–26).

President Benson counseled us not to become discouraged by expecting the sensational or by comparing our experiences with those of others. "We must be careful, as we seek to become more and more godlike, that we do not become discouraged and lose hope. Becoming Christlike is a lifetime pursuit and very often involves growth and change that is slow, almost imperceptible."[12]

Through Book of Mormon and other ancient and modern prophets, the Lord continues to extend an invitation to all mankind to come unto Him, the Physician of men's souls, and be healed spiritually. All who desire to be clean, to have the heavy burden of sin lifted, and to once again feel God's divine approbation may receive the miracle of forgiveness if they will but approach the Savior with "faith unto repentance." "Come unto Christ, who is the Holy One of Israel," wrote Amaleki as he closed the book of Omni, "and partake of his salvation, and the power of his redemption. Yea, come unto him, and offer your whole souls as an offering unto him, and continue in fasting and praying, and endure to the end; and as the Lord liveth ye will be saved" (Omni 1:26). Alma, who spoke not only as a prophet but also from his own miraculous experience, often reiterated the Lord's injunction to repent and partake of the blessings of forgiveness:

"Behold, he sendeth an invitation unto all men, for the arms of mercy are extended towards them, and he saith: Repent, and I will receive you.

"Yea, he saith: Come unto me and ye shall partake of the fruit of the tree of life; yea, ye shall eat and drink of the bread and the waters of life freely" (Alma 5:33–34).

And finally, Alma gives us this promise, which epitomizes the central message of the Book of Mormon: "Therefore, whosoever repenteth, and hardeneth not his heart, he shall have claim on mercy through mine Only Begotten Son, unto a remission of his sins; and these shall enter into my rest" (Alma 12:34).

NOTES

1. Spencer W. Kimball, *The Miracle of Forgiveness* (Salt Lake City: Bookcraft, 1969), 194.

2. Ezra Taft Benson, *The Teachings of Ezra Taft Benson* (Salt Lake City: Bookcraft, 1988), 71.

3. Orson Pratt, "True Faith," *A Series of Pamphlets by Orson Pratt* (Liverpool: Franklin D. Richards, 1852), 5–6; in *A Compilation Containing the Lectures on Faith,* comp. N. B. Lundwall (Salt Lake City: N. B. Lundwall, 1940), 76–77.

4. Orson Pratt, "True Repentance," *A Series of Pamphlets by Orson Pratt*

(Liverpool: Franklin D. Richards, 1852), 30–31; republished in *Orson Pratt: Writings of an Apostle* (Salt Lake City: Mormon Heritage Publishers, 1976).

5. David O. McKay, *Gospel Ideals* (Salt Lake City: Improvement Era, 1953), 13.

6. Neal A. Maxwell, *"Not My Will, but Thine"* (Salt Lake City: Bookcraft, 1988), 92–93.

7. Bruce R. McConkie, *A New Witness for the Articles of Faith* (Salt Lake City: Deseret Book, 1985), 236.

8. Joseph F. Smith, *Gospel Doctrine* (Salt Lake City: Deseret Book, 1939), 100.

9. Benson, *Teachings,* 71.

10. For a more extensive discussion of this interpretation of Alma 5:14 and the meanings of such words as "image," "engraven," and "countenance," see Andrew F. Skinner, "Alma's 'Pure Testimony,'" in *Studies in Scripture, volume 7, 1 Nephi to Alma 29,* ed. Kent P. Jackson (Salt Lake City: Deseret Book, 1987), 301.

11. Bruce R. McConkie, address at Brigham Young University First Stake Conference, 11 February 1968; in Brent L. Top, *"Though Your Sins Be As Scarlet"* (Salt Lake City: Bookcraft, 1989), 122.

12. Benson, *Teachings,* 72.

19

Ten Testimonies of Jesus Christ from the Book of Mormon

John W. Welch

One very important function of the Book of Mormon: Another Testament of Jesus Christ is to convey to the modern world powerful testimonies of the divine mission and essential attributes of Jesus Christ, "to the convincing of the Jew and Gentile that Jesus is the Christ, the Eternal God" (title page). The Book of Mormon is a convincing witness for Jesus Christ because its writers freely shared their personal testimonies of Him and communicated their individual feelings and thoughts about His attributes and functions. By examining and comparing the many personal testimonies of Jesus Christ that are found in the Book of Mormon, we can see that they are both similar and different: while agreeing in their basic truths and doctrines, they differ in their emphasis and style. Most interestingly, the attributes of Jesus Christ emphasized by the various prophets in the Nephite records are often the attributes with which each prophet especially identified because of his own spiritual experiences, callings, and individual circumstances.[1]

Jesus was personally known to many people in the Book of Mormon. He appeared to several, including Lehi (see 1 Nephi 1:9),

---

John W. Welch is a professor of law at Brigham Young University and editor-in-chief of BYU Studies.

Nephi (see 2 Nephi 11:2), Jacob (see 2 Nephi 2:4; 11:3), Lamoni (see Alma 19:13), Mormon (see Mormon 1:15), the brother of Jared (see Ether 3:14), and Moroni (see Ether 12:39), as well as to the multitude and disciples in 3 Nephi. Others, such as Benjamin, Alma, Amulek, and Samuel the Lamanite, saw an "angel of the Lord" (Mosiah 4:1; Mosiah 27:11; Alma 10:7; Helaman 13:7), which may be a euphemism for seeing the Lord Himself (for example, it is difficult to distinguish between the "angel of the Lord" and Jehovah in Genesis 16:7–11; 22:11–15; Exodus 3:2; and Judges 2:1–4).[2] Thus, their teachings and testimonies of Jesus are based on firsthand knowledge and acquaintance.

All Book of Mormon prophets taught "more or less" (Mosiah 13:33; see also Jacob 4:5) the same "word" of belief in Jesus Christ (see chart 1).[3] In visions, public speeches, and personal statements they typically declared (1) that Jesus is the Son of God, (2) who would come down to earth to live as a mortal, (3) to heal the sick, cast out devils, and suffer physically and spiritually, (4) to take upon Himself the sins of the world and redeem His people, (5) to be put to death by crucifixion and rise from the dead, (6) to bring to pass the resurrection of all mankind, and (7) to judge all people in the last day according to their works (see chart 2).

For example, when Alma invited the Zoramite poor to plant that seed of faith in their hearts, the specific "word" that he wanted them to plant (see Alma 33:23) appears to epitomize the basic Nephite testimony embracing these seven points. Alma urged the people to "[1] believe in the Son of God, [2] that he will come to redeem his people, and [3] that he shall suffer and die [4] to atone for their sins; and [5] that he shall rise again from the dead, [6] which shall bring to pass the resurrection, [7] that all men shall stand before him to be judged at the last and judgment day, according to their works" (Alma 33:22).

The prophets of the Book of Mormon regularly referred to these points when they testified of Christ. Accordingly, on another occasion, Alma essentially rehearsed the same seven points in the city of Gideon and expressly identified them as the "testimony which is in me" (Alma 7:13). Indeed, it is reasonable to assume that Alma's "word" of faith in

Chart 1

Consistent Elements in Nephite Declarations of Faith

Speaker	Reference	Believe in the Son of God	He will come to redeem his people	He shall suffer and die	He will atone for their sins	He shall rise again from the dead	He will bring to pass the resurrection	He shall judge all men
Nephi	1 Nephi 11:31–33		✓	✓	✓			
Nephi	1 Nephi 19:9–10		✓	✓	✓	✓	✓	
Jacob	2 Nephi 9:5–15	✓	✓	✓	✓	✓	✓	✓
Nephi	2 Nephi 25:12–13	✓	✓	✓	✓	✓	✓	
Benjamin	Mosiah 3:5–10	✓	✓	✓	✓	✓		✓
Abinadi	Mosiah 15:5–9, 20; 16:10	✓	✓	✓	✓	✓	✓	✓
Amulek	Alma 11:39–41	✓	✓		✓		✓	✓
Alma	Alma 33:22	✓	✓	✓	✓	✓	✓	✓
Moroni	Mormon 9:1–14	✓	✓	✓	✓		✓	✓

Chart 2

Nephite Declaration of Faith

1 We "believe in the Son of God,
2 that he will come to redeem his people,
3 and that he shall suffer and die
4 to atone for their sins;
5 and that he shall rise again from the dead,
6 which shall bring to pass the resurrection,
7 that all men shall stand before him,
to be judged"

—Alma 33:22

Christ represented a standard Nephite testimony that was regularly used in Alma's day.

No doubt these points of testimony were distilled from the words of the Nephite prophets who had preceded Alma. All seven elements can be found scattered throughout the writings of Nephi (see 1 Nephi 11:31–33; 19:9–10; 2 Nephi 25:12–13), Jacob (see 2 Nephi 9:5–15), Abinadi (see Mosiah 15:5–9), and King Benjamin (see Mosiah 3:5–10). It appears that Alma molded them into a concise statement of belief that was especially useful in the newly established churches in the land of Zarahemla over which he presided. This observation is corroborated by the fact that Amulek's testimony is quite similar to Alma's:

"Yea, [1] he is the very Eternal Father of heaven and of earth, and all things which in them are; he is the beginning and the end, the first and the last; and [2] he shall come into the world to redeem his people; and [4] he shall take upon him the transgressions of those who believe on his name; and these are they that shall have eternal life, and salvation cometh to none else. Therefore the wicked remain as though there had been no redemption made, except it be the loosing of the bands of death; for behold, [6] the day cometh that all shall rise from the dead and stand before God, and [7] be judged according to their works" (Alma 11:39–41).

This basic pattern persisted to the end of Nephite civilization, as is reflected in one of Moroni's last testimonies of Christ:

"And because of the fall of man [2] came Jesus Christ, [1] even the Father and the Son; and [4] because of Jesus Christ came the redemption of man. And because of the redemption of man, which came by Jesus Christ, they are brought back into the presence of the Lord; yea, this is wherein all men are redeemed, [3] because the death of Christ [6] bringeth to pass the resurrection, which bringeth to pass a redemption from an endless sleep, from which sleep all men shall be awakened by the power of God when the trump shall sound; and they shall come forth, both small and great, and [7] all shall stand before his bar, being redeemed and loosed from this eternal band of death, which death is a temporal death. And then cometh the judgment of the Holy One upon them" (Mormon 9:12–14).

CHART 3

Names Used for Christ by Major Book of Mormon Authors

	Lehi	Nephi	Jacob	Abinadi	Benjamin	Alma	Amulek	Samuel	Mormon	Moroni
A Messiah	2	1								
A Son of God						**1**				
All-Powerful Creator			**1**							
Beloved Son		**1**								
Christ		40	12	8	12	12	8	2	43	46
Christ Jesus						**1**				
Christ the Lord				1	1					
Christ the Son							1		1	1
Creator			3		1	1		1		
Eternal Father		2		2			2		1	5
Eternal God		2	1				2			1
Father		18	3	5	2		1	1	13	22
Father of Heaven and Earth		1		1	1		1	1		
Father and Son				**1**						
First-Fruits	**1**									
God	41	135	87	44	57	201	29	9	76	72
God of Abr., Isaac, Jacob		1				2				1
Good Shepherd						**7**				
Great Creator			**3**							
Great and Eternal Head								**1**		
Great Mediator	**2**									
Great and True Shepherd								**1**		
Heavenly King					**1**					
His Son Jesus Christ									**1**	
Holy Being										**1**
Holy Child									**1**	
Holy Messiah	**2**									
Holy One	1	1	1			2			1	1
Holy One of Israel	2	14	17							
Holy One of Jacob		**1**								
Jehovah										**1**
Jesus		4	2						9	6
Jesus Christ		4			3	3	1	1	7	17
King of Heaven			1			1				

Chart 3
CONTINUED

	Lehi	Nephi	Jacob	Abinadi	Benjamin	Alma	Amulek	Samuel	Mormon	Moroni
Lamb		29				1	1			1
Lamb of God	1	31				1				2
Lord	64	175	46	49	32	54	29	47	53	54
Lord God	8	38	18		6	8	1	1	1	1
Lord God Almighty	1	1	1							
Lord God of Hosts		**2**								
Lord God Omnipotent					**2**					
Lord of Hosts		9	7					3		
Lord Jesus										**1**
Lord Jesus Christ					1	3		1	3	2
Lord Omnipotent					**4**					
Maker			**2**							
Messiah	13	12	2	1						
Mighty God			**1**							
Mighty One of Israel		**1**								
Mighty One of Jacob		1	1							
Only Begotten of the Father		1				2	1			
Only Begotten Son			2			3				
Prophet	**1**									
Redeemer	5	12	3			3		1	2	
Savior	1	4	1		1				4	1
Shepherd		2				11		1	1	
Son		8		6		12	1		2	8
Son of the Eternal Father		**2**								
Son of the Everlasting God		**1**								
Son of the Most High God		**1**								
Son of Righteousness		**1**								
The Christ		**1**								
The Son of God	2	5		1	2	10	8	3	3	3
The Very Christ		1							1	
The Very God									**1**	
True Messiah	2	1								
Very God of Israel		**1**								
Totals										
References to Christ	148	565	215	119	126	339	86	74	224	247
Names used unique to author	4	10	4	1	3	3	0	2	3	3
Different names used by author	17	38	22	11	15	20	14	15	20	21
Percent names unique to author	24	26	18	9	20	15	0	13	15	14

Building upon this foundational testimony of Christ, each Book of Mormon prophet distinctively accented certain attributes of Jesus Christ. Judging simply from the names and titles they used in referring to the Lord, we can see that each Book of Mormon prophet related to and testified of Jesus in his own individual way, revealing to us things about Jesus Christ and also about the prophets who knew Him (see chart 3).

It should not surprise us to find that Jesus Christ meant (and means) different things to different people according to their personal circumstances and perspectives. As is well known, the New Testament testimonies of Christ reflect a variety of views about Jesus. No single account is likely to do justice even to a small portion of what Jesus said, did, was, is, and will be. To each of us, Christ is both the same and different. He is the same eternal God who came down to earth to atone for the sins of all mankind and to make the Resurrection possible, but He is also ever new and different, since our own experiences cause us to emphasize and cherish different things about Him, even at different times in our lives.

The testimonies of Jesus in the Book of Mormon display this same true-to-life reality. Distinct personal profiles emerge when the words of the following ten Book of Mormon prophets are identified and compared. Moreover, in many cases, the attributes and functions of Jesus Christ emphasized by each Book of Mormon prophet correspond closely with the personal circumstances and experiences of these prophets.[4]

LEHI

From the visions and revelations he received, Lehi knew the tender mercies of the promised Messiah. The surviving words of Lehi contain some fifteen different titles that refer to this God, the One he saw descending out of the midst of heaven (see 1 Nephi 1:9). Except for five common Israelite terms infrequently used by Lehi ("God," "Lord," "Lord God Almighty," "Holy One," and "Holy One of Israel"), all of Lehi's designations cluster around the redemptive and mediating functions of this Messiah. Lehi most often calls Him "a Messiah," "the Messiah," "the true Messiah," "the holy Messiah," "this Redeemer," "their Redeemer," or "thy Redeemer." In addition Lehi learned from the angel that this Redeemer would be called "the Lamb of God." Lehi's messianic terminology manifests greater variation than that of any other Book of Mormon prophet, and Lehi is the only one ever to call the Lord "a Savior" (1 Nephi 10:4), "a prophet" (1 Nephi 10:4), "the great Mediator" (2 Nephi 2:27–28), or "firstfruits unto God" (2 Nephi 2:9).

These points take on added meaning in the context of Lehi's personal experiences. To Lehi, who fled from Jerusalem and the lands of his inheritance, the Messiah would be, above all, a Messiah and a Redeemer who would come to restore the fallen, the lost, and the displaced. He would restore them to the lands of their inheritance. He alone is seen as the "great Mediator" who makes it possible for all people to choose between good and evil (2 Nephi 2:26–28) and thereby be redeemed and live again.

Lehi emphasized God's mercy to all mankind (see 1 Nephi 1:14). Of all Book of Mormon prophets, he spoke especially of the "multitude of his tender mercies" (1 Nephi 8:8; see also 1:20), of His "infinite goodness" (2 Nephi 1:10), and of the "arms of his love" (2 Nephi 1:15). That emphasis goes hand-in-hand with the fact that Lehi had prayed mightily and wept bitterly over the wickedness of his people and the stubbornness of his eldest sons. But he never gave up hope. He remained extraordinarily patient, loving, and merciful toward his neighbors who had violently rejected him and toward Laman and Lemuel, even after he knew that they would never partake of the fruit of the tree of life (see 1 Nephi 8:37) and had conspired to kill him (see 1 Nephi 17:44).

Lehi's orientation toward the Redeemer was markedly universal. Since he had read plainly in the heavenly book "of the coming of a Messiah, and also the redemption of *the world*" (1 Nephi 1:19; emphasis added), Lehi knew that God would redeem not only a lost and fallen Israel but the entire world—certainly a bold and unpopular doctrine in most Jewish circles in Lehi's day. Lehi spoke emphatically about the Messiah who would come to redeem "all mankind" (1 Nephi 10:6; see also 2 Nephi 10; 2:27), and make intercession "for all the children of men" (2 Nephi 2:9–10).

Unlike most other Book of Mormon prophets (who also served as kings, judges, and military leaders), Lehi was exclusively a prophet. He stood firmly in the tradition of Israelite prophecy. Hence Lehi was readily and uniquely inclined to identify Jesus as "a prophet" (1 Nephi 10:4; see also Deuteronomy 18:15: "God will raise up unto thee a Prophet" like unto Moses) and to make special mention of the fact that another prophet would prepare the way of the Lord before His coming (see 1 Nephi 10:8; see also Isaiah 40:3). Lehi's strong Israelite roots are also apparent in his reference to the Lord as the "firstfruits" that typically belonged to God.[5]

Lehi knew many things about the coming Messiah, but not everything. The name of Christ, for example, was apparently first revealed to Jacob after Lehi's death (see 2 Nephi 10:3), and it was Nephi who disclosed later yet that the Messiah's "name shall be Jesus Christ, the Son of God" (2 Nephi 25:19).[6]

NEPHI

Nephi followed his father in using the names of "Messiah," "Redeemer," and "Savior," but he introduced several other terms and concepts as he sought and obtained greater understanding of his father's visions. The names that Nephi used for Christ reflect this elaboration.

Most notable among these names are those that reflect the sonship of Christ. On twenty occasions, Nephi identified Jesus as "the Son of God," "the only begotten Son," "the only begotten of the Father," "the Son of the everlasting God," "the Son of the Eternal Father," "the Son of the Living God," "the Son of the Most High God," "the Son of Righteousness," "the Son," or the "beloved Son." Only Alma the Younger approaches the wide variety of filial designations for Jesus used by Nephi. That may somehow subtly reflect the fact that both Nephi and Alma had deep and significant relationships with their fathers: Nephi strived to know exactly the things that his father had seen (see 1 Nephi 14:29) and to be a righteous successor to Lehi; Alma spent the years after his conversion remembering the bondage and deliverance of his father and labored "without ceasing" to undo the damage he had done as a young man to his father's ministry (see Alma 36:24, 29).

Nephi (who himself knew what it meant to be persecuted for righteousness' sake, both by those at Jerusalem and by his own brothers) referred sixty times in his writings to Jesus Christ as "the Lamb" or "the Lamb of God" (as the angel called Him), befitting the divine offering of His sacrifice.[7] After Nephi's time, however, the phrase "Lamb of God" rarely appears in the Book of Mormon (perhaps sheep were less common in the New World).

For years, Nephi tried to teach his brothers and his people to walk in the paths of obedience. Nephi and his brother Jacob also experienced the harrowing episodes of being led through an uncharted desert and across an endless expanse of ocean by the Liahona. From those experiences Nephi knew the necessity of staying on the Lord's strait and narrow path. For Nephi and Jacob, the images of Christ as the keeper of the only gate that leads to eternal life (see 2 Nephi 9:41; 33:9) and as the example that people must follow (see 2 Nephi 31:10) were distinctively vivid metaphors.

Likewise, as ruler and teacher of his people, Nephi emphasized the rulership of Christ, the only true God who would ever come. Nephi particularly saw Christ as the ultimate source of life and law, the only one in whom the law would be fulfilled (see 2 Nephi 25:16–18, 25–27).

JACOB

Jacob was called as a young man to serve the Lord as a priest: Lehi set him apart and blessed him to spend all his days in God's service (see 2 Nephi 2:3), and Nephi consecrated him to be a priest (see 2 Nephi 5:26). Jacob officiated in delivering the great covenant speech around the time of Nephi's coronation (see 2 Nephi 6–10); he spoke to his people from the temple (see Jacob 2–4); and he and his lineage had the sacred obligation of keeping the religious records on the small plates of Nephi. To a remarkable degree, Jacob's priestly functions are reflected in the testimony that he bears of Christ.

As mentioned above, Jacob introduced the word *Christ* (or its Hebrew equivalent) into broad Nephite usage. That word in Greek or Hebrew derives from a word whose meanings include "anointed." To the extent that he himself was a "consecrated" priest, who both proclaimed the eternal gospel of Christ and performed atoning sacrifices in the temple of Nephi pursuant to the law of Moses (see 2 Nephi 5:10, 16), Jacob would have identified personally with the fact that Jesus was anointed to perform His holy and eternal atoning mission.

Indeed, Jacob is the first in the Book of Mormon to expound on the Atonement of Christ. He told how Christ would suffer and die for all mankind so they might become subject to Him through His "infinite atonement," which overcomes the Fall and brings resurrection and incorruptibility (see 2 Nephi 9:5–14). He spoke repeatedly of such things as uncleanness, guilt, robes of righteousness (see 2 Nephi 9:14), flesh being consumed by fire (see 2 Nephi 9:16), shaking one's garments (see 2 Nephi 9:44), and fatness (see 2 Nephi 9:51). Whatever else these words might mean, they evoke priestly images of temple sacrifice and ritual (for example, the forbidden fat belonged to the Lord; see Leviticus 7:3–31). Jacob thus saw Christ in connection with traditional atonement imagery drawn from Israelite temple practices.

Jacob also saw fit to refer to Christ as the "great Creator" (three times: 2 Nephi 9:5, 6; Jacob 3:7), "the all-powerful Creator" (Jacob 2:5), and the "Maker" (twice: 2 Nephi 9:40; Jacob 2:6). He has more to say about Christ as Creator than any other Book of Mormon prophet, and in this connection it is significant that the Creation account was an integral part of typical ancient temple worship.[8]

The purpose of temple sacrifice in ancient Israel was to purify the people. The objective of their temple service was to become "holy men unto me" (Exodus 22:31), "for I the Lord, which sanctify you, am holy" (Leviticus 21:8). Indeed the main body of laws of priestly sacrifice in Israel came to be known as the Holiness Code. That is consistent with the fact that Jacob, of all Book of Mormon prophets, strongly prefers to call Christ "the Holy One of Israel" (seventeen times) or simply "the Holy One" (once). Lehi and Nephi account for the other fourteen times the designation "Holy One of Israel" appears; but after the time of the small plates, this title drops out of Nephite usage—perhaps because the temple service declined in prominence as people knew that its sacrifice merely typified the only meaningful sacrifice—Christ's—or perhaps because the Nephites, over time, became less inclined to identify personally with a remote and by then unfamiliar land of Israel.

Jacob also designated Christ the "King of heaven" (2 Nephi 10:14; see also Isaiah 6:5). Coming around the time of Nephi's coronation, this reference stands as a solemn reminder of Nephi's reluctance to become king (see 2 Nephi 5:18), for God is truly the only king in Israel. From the fact that immoral lawbreakers were not punished by the kings, I infer that Jacob was at odds with the kings and the rising aristocracy in the city of Nephi much of his life (see Jacob 1:15–16), and thus we may see an indication of antimonarchical leanings in his eagerness to recognize Christ as King. The only other Book of Mormon prophet to call Jesus "the King of heaven" was Alma in his speech delivered in the city of Zarahemla (Alma 5:50) as the first chief judge in that city where kings had ruled for many generations and in which king-men would fight for several ensuing decades to reinstate the institution of kingship, Alma had his own reasons, much like Jacob's, for promoting the idea that Jesus alone was King.

ABINADI

Abinadi stands out as a lone prophetic voice, singularly and courageously decrying the perversions of King Noah and his priests. After spending two years as a fugitive, Abinadi returned to the city of Nephi by himself to deliver his prophetic warnings and condemnations. He was alone in his preaching, alone in his tenacious rebuttal against Noah's court, and alone in the flames of martyrdom. He suffered, an innocent victim who had done no evil, although four different legal allegations were leveled against him.[9]

The attributes of Christ featured by Abinadi correlate readily with these experiences of Abinadi. Primarily, Abinadi depicted Christ as one who would innocently suffer, alone, to redeem His people. Three times Abinadi emphatically asserted that God Himself would bear the iniquities of His people: "Were it not for the atonement, which God himself shall make" (Mosiah 13:28); "God himself should come down among the children of men" (Mosiah 13:34); and "God himself shall come down among the children of men, and shall redeem his people" (Mosiah 15:1). That major point of emphasis for Abinadi was also a new formulation. No other Book of Mormon prophet before Abinadi had used those exact words (and only Alma does so after him; see Alma 42:15). So unequivocal was Abinadi's formulation that the priests of Noah found it the basis of their blasphemy charge: "For thou hast said that God *himself* should come down among the children of men" (Mosiah 17:8; emphasis added). Just as Abinadi himself went down alone into the pit of certain martyrdom that awaited him in Noah's court, so God Himself would come into the world.

Except for Alma's attempt, no defenders or companions came forward to assist or rescue Abinadi. Likewise, Abinadi made no mention of any apostles, disciples, or others who might come to the aid of the suffering Messiah. Indeed, little room is left for God the Father to figure into Abinadi's soteriology. Abinadi strongly emphasized the fatherhood and sonship of Christ, seeing Christ as the "very Eternal Father of heaven and of earth" (Mosiah 15:4). Interestingly, the words of Abinadi contain the word "Father" exactly eight times, "Son" eight times, and "Christ" eight times, as if to signal Christ's fatherhood and sonship equally. While God the Father is clearly present in Abinadi's theology,[10] the realities of Christ's atonement were such that in the final hour God the Father was effectively not there, for Jesus had to bear the suffering alone. Perhaps to emphasize the loneliness of that task, Abinadi saw Christ both as Father and Son: the Atonement was not to be a team effort.

The dominant feature of Abinadi's teaching is about the Redemption and that it will come through suffering (the words *redeem* or *redemption* appear nineteen times in Abinadi's words). Despite God's mighty power, He will be "oppressed" and "afflicted" (Mosiah 13:35). Abinadi drew those words from the prophecies of Isaiah that the servant would be "despised and rejected of men; a man of sorrows, and acquainted with grief," "afflicted," "wounded for our transgressions," "oppressed, and he was afflicted" (Isaiah 53:3–7; Mosiah 14:3–7). As Isaiah prophesied, "he hath poured out his soul unto death" (Isaiah 53:12; Mosiah 14:12), and "so he shall be led, crucified, and slain, the flesh becoming subject even unto death" (Mosiah 15:7). Of all Book of Mormon prophets, Abinadi was similarly called upon to surrender his will to God, even unto death by fire.

Abinadi used noticeably simple nomenclature for Christ: he called Him "the Messiah," "Christ," "Father," "Son," and all the rest simply "Lord." There is no literary embellishment or flourish in Abinadi's speech. That stylistic feature enhances the simplicity and directness of his message, and it also implements the plainness of Isaiah's vision: "He hath no form nor comeliness; and when we shall see him, there is no beauty that we should desire him" (Isaiah 53:2; Mosiah 14:2). Similarly, no artifice or adornment, no tendency toward the ornate embellishments of Noah's edifices, was suited to the plain and forthright style of the prophet Abinadi.

BENJAMIN

Around 124 B.C. King Benjamin received from the angel of the Lord a succinct explanation of the atoning mission of Christ (see Mosiah 3:2–27). Those words became the centerpiece of Benjamin's speech, during which he announced to his people that his son Mosiah was their new king (see Mosiah 1:10; Mosiah 2:30) and gave the people a new name that distinguished them above all people (see Mosiah 1:11).

On a day when the newly appointed king normally received his new coronation name and titles, Benjamin solemnly disclosed for the first time an extended name of Jesus Christ and gave it to the entire multitude by way of covenant. The new name testified that the Savior would be called "Jesus Christ, the Son of God, the Father of heaven and earth, the Creator of all things from the beginning" (Mosiah 3:8). The people's use of this name in their response (see Mosiah 4:2) and its subsequent reappearance in the record (see Helaman 14:12) suggest that this extended name had sacred, perhaps ceremonial significance among the Nephites.[11]

Benjamin's speech, which was delivered at the temple in

Zarahemla, where blood sacrifices were routinely performed under the law of Moses (see Mosiah 2:3), emphasized more than any other aspect of Christ's ministry the atoning functions of His blood. Four times Benjamin mentioned the "blood" of Christ in connection with the Atonement (see Mosiah 3:11, 15, 16, 18), and the people answered him, saying, "Apply the atoning blood of Christ" (Mosiah 4:2). Other Book of Mormon prophets had previously spoken and would later speak of having their garments washed white in the blood of the Lamb, but no prophet gave such clear information about the atoning work of Christ's blood itself or placed such central attention on the fact that Christ's blood actually would be spilt. Benjamin alone described Jesus' bloody sweat coming from every pore in anguish for His people (see Mosiah 3:7).[12]

Interestingly, Benjamin linked the atoning blood of Christ with the full range of atonement concepts under the law of Moses; he assured the people that Christ's blood atones for the sins of all those who humble themselves and repent and for the sins of those "who have fallen by the transgression of Adam, who have died not knowing the will of God concerning them, or who have ignorantly sinned" (Mosiah 3:11). The need under the law of Moses to atone even for sins committed in ignorance is stated in Numbers 15:27–29, and such iniquities were of particular interest on the Day of Atonement, when the scapegoat carried away "all their iniquities" (Leviticus 16:22).

Indeed, so holy was the Day of Atonement in the Jewish tradition that on this day—and on this day alone—could the name of God, YHWH, be pronounced. Exactly ten times during the traditional Yom Kippur service in Israel would the priest utter this name out loud, and each time upon hearing the name the Israelites would fall prostrate to the ground.[13] Thus, it is noteworthy that in Benjamin's speech, the exalted name *Lord God* appears ten times (five as "Lord God," four as "Lord God Omnipotent," and one as "Lord Omnipotent"). Seven of these utterances are in the words of the angel to Benjamin (see Mosiah 3:5, 13, 14, 17, 18, 21, 23); the other three are in the words of Benjamin (see Mosiah 2:30, 41; 5:15), occurring at important ceremonial breaking points in the speech.

In addition to the atoning dimensions of Christ's blood that were of special notice to Benjamin, the Lord's kingship was prominent in Benjamin's testimony of Jesus. That is not surprising, since Benjamin was a strong, benevolent king. Benjamin referred favorably to the Lord as the "heavenly King," who was righteously represented by the earthly king (Mosiah 2:19), and uniquely spoke five times of the Lord's being "omnipotent" (Mosiah 3:5, 17, 18, 21; 5:15). Consistent with Benjamin's personal interests and circumstances in life, he was the only Book of Mormon writer ever to use the word "omnipotent."

ALMA THE YOUNGER

Alma, the judicial and religious defender of the freedom of belief (ca. 100–73 B.C.), taught faith in Jesus Christ, the Master of personal conversion. Alma had tasted the transforming joy that came when he called upon the name of Jesus Christ for mercy (see Alma 36:18–21; Mosiah 27:24), and in his subsequent sermons Alma described how the "image of God" might be "engraven upon your countenances" (Alma 5:19) and how the word of Christ is to be planted in each convert's soul, where if nourished it would spring up as an everlasting tree of life (see Alma 32:28–40; 33:22–23). Indelibly changed by his own overwhelmingly joyous conversion and rescue as he stood at the brink of God's destroying judgment, Alma personally knew of the mercy of God (which he mentions more than sixteen times), of the deliverance of God (more than twelve times), of God's "plan of redemption" (eight times), of the joy of conversion (more than twenty times), and of the inevitability that God will judge all people (more than ten times).

As chief judge, Alma was particularly interested in God's justice. He gave the only discourse on the relationship of justice and mercy (see Alma 42) as well as the most complete description of the evidence that the divine judge will assess in making that judgment: "Our words will condemn us, yea, all our works will condemn us; we shall not be found spotless; and our thoughts will also condemn us" (Alma 12:14). Alma was also the only writer in scripture to attribute to God the quality of "equity" (three times; see Alma 9:26; 10:21; 13:9).

After leaving his political, judicial, and military posts as the head of the Nephite state, Alma devoted himself to testifying of Christ. Alma found that only by "bearing down in pure testimony" could he hope to "pull down, by the word of God, all the pride and craftiness and all the contentions which were among his people" (Alma 4:19). Alma tried to appeal to all segments of Nephite society—to the faithful in Gideon, to the apostates in Ammonihah, to the inconstant in Zarahemla, and to the poor in Antionum—and his use of terminology reflects his broad orientation. Alma used a wide range of names for Christ: names that speak of Jesus Christ christologically, personally, or redemptively; phrases that reflect His sonship, divinity, rulership, and deliverances of Israel; titles that acknowledge Him as the Creator who remembers all His creations and as the good Shepherd who leads His people.

The only category of names that Alma seems to have avoided are names that speak of Jesus' fatherhood. Perhaps Alma avoided such references because the traditional Nephite designation of Jesus as "the Father *of heaven and of earth,*" i.e., the Creator, (2 Nephi 25:12; emphasis added; see also 1 Nephi 22:9; Mosiah 3:8; Alma 11:39; Helaman 14:12; 16:18) had been made a subject of manipulation and rhetorical controversy by Alma's opponents (see Alma 11:38).

AMULEK

Amulek, one of Alma the Younger's most celebrated converts, was a wealthy man who had acquired prestige and riches by his own industry. He was the master of a large household (see Alma 10:11), and after his conversion he was proud of his illustrious Nephite lineage (see Alma 10:3–4). He was evidently quite literate, perhaps providing many of the books (which would have been costly) that were burned when the women and children of the faithful were incinerated in Ammonihah. I assume that some of Amulek's own family (see Alma 10:11) were among those who "had been taught to believe in the word of God" and who were accordingly martyred (Alma 14:8), and he was undoubtedly a close friend of many of the other martyrs and of the men with whom he was cast out.[14] Amulek saw the awful annihilation of the apostate city of Ammonihah, and he lost all of his valuable earthly possessions as the city was destroyed by the sword, burnt by fire, and reduced to a heap.

Notwithstanding these developments, and perhaps because of them, Amulek turned more ardently than any other Book of Mormon prophet to superlative descriptions of the infinite scope of the Atonement of Jesus Christ. Nothing else would ever be commensurate with the "great and last sacrifice" that would be "infinite and eternal" (Alma 34:14). No form of human revenge or avenging would ever bring back the lives that were lost in the atrocity of Ammonihah.

Amulek's testimony of Christ shines in the light of his background and experiences. He is the only one ever to refer to the Atonement of Jesus Christ as the "great and last sacrifice" (five times). For Amulek it is the magnitude of the Atonement that is impressive. Not once does he mention the suffering of Christ, for mortal suffering, no matter how extreme, is still of finite duration. Amulek, therefore, made no attempt to explain or depict the mechanics of the great, last, infinite, and eternal sacrifice to "atone for the sins of the world" (Alma 34:8; see also 11:40). To Amulek, who himself had been exposed to terrible risks of harm and torture, it was especially pertinent to describe the Atonement as encircling people "in the arms of *safety*" (Alma 34:16; emphasis added), a phrase unique to him in all of scripture.

Coming unto Christ, in Amulek's admonition, requires faith and patience (see Alma 34:3). Amulek had learned patience, suffering many days in prison in Ammonihah. He also emphasized the urgency of repentance, singularly urging people not to procrastinate the day of their repentance (see Alma 34:35), for he had seen the fate of his fellow citizens in Ammonihah who had failed to repent in time. When Amulek spoke of the certainty that the unrepentant "must unavoidably perish" (Alma 34:9) and face "that awful crisis" (Alma 34:34), for God will not dwell "in unholy temples" (Alma 34:36), he testified from spiritual knowledge and actual experience.

Having seen the consequences of excessive greed and materialism, it is also not surprising that Amulek, formerly a very wealthy man, would tell even the poorest of the Zoramites that if they wanted God to have mercy on them and to hear their prayers, they must not "turn away the needy, and the naked, and visit . . . the sick and afflicted, and impart of [their] substance . . . to those who stand in need" (Alma

34:28). Amulek is the only person in scripture ever to use the word "charitable" (Alma 34:29). He knows that without repentance and charity "all are hardened; . . . and must perish except it be through the atonement which it is expedient should be made" (Alma 34:9).

Amulek's favorite and most distinctive name of Christ is "the Son," or "the Son of God" (eight occurrences). He also used the name "Christ" (eight times), "the Lamb" (once), and "the very Eternal Father of heaven and of earth, and all things which in them are" (once: Alma 11:39). But above all, for Amulek, Jesus was "the Son of God." Depicting Christ in His familial relationship with the Father may have been especially tender to Amulek, to whom lineage and family were especially sensitive and important and whose own sons might have been among those children who perished in the fire in Ammonihah.

SAMUEL THE LAMANITE

About 30 B.C. many Lamanites were converted to Christ when the walls of a prison were destroyed, God's light shone, and His voice spoke out of an enveloping cloud of darkness (see Helaman 5:33–43). Twenty-five years later an important Lamanite prophet named Samuel appeared on the walls of Zarahemla and foretold that even more significant signs of light would appear at the time of Jesus' birth and that massive destructions and darkness would be seen at His death (see Helaman 14:2–27). It is unknown whether Samuel had been present to witness in person the awesome manifestation of God's power when the prison walls had collapsed and the faces of Nephi and Lehi had shone out of the darkness and the voice of God had spoken from heaven, but even if he only knew those events secondhand, they were powerful events in the collective lives of the Lamanites, who knew from that experience that God could easily do the same again to the wicked at the time of His crucifixion. Accordingly, the thrust of Samuel's prophecies of destruction and darkness were vivified by the earlier events at the prison destroyed by God in the land of Nephi.

Consistent with his prediction of cursed destruction for the wicked, Samuel was one of the few Book of Mormon prophets to call Jesus the "Lord of Hosts." Outside of numerous occurrences of this phrase in passages in the Book of Mormon that are quoted from Isaiah and Malachi, only Nephi, Jacob, and Samuel used this title. They usually did so in condemning or cursing the wicked: "A curse shall come upon the land, saith the Lord of Hosts, . . . then shall ye weep and howl in that day, saith the Lord of Hosts" (Helaman 13:17, 32). This title speaks of the Lord as the Head of the hosts (soldiers). "This name certainly contains the affirmation that Yahweh is the true head of Israel's armies, . . . it [also] affirms his universal rulership that encompasses every force or army, heavenly, cosmic and earthly."[15] Thus Samuel, who dominantly spoke of Jesus Christ in His role as a warrior engaged in mortal conflict with the forces of evil, also uniquely referred to Him as the "great and Eternal Head" (Helaman 13:38).

MORMON

In addition to being a prophet, Mormon was a father, commander-in-chief of the Nephite armies, record keeper, and abridger. He was an extremely young appointee, being charged with keeping records at the age of ten and commanding the armies at the age of sixteen. He learned by sad experience that his direct action had failed. His personal leadership was unsuccessful because of the awful conditions of the Nephites at his time. Mormon chose to withdraw and to work indirectly, as an "idle witness" and as a record keeper, hoping that by preserving the word of God he might indirectly teach and do some good.

Perhaps consistent with these experiences, Mormon's testimony of Christ is most often an indirect one. He used the term "Christ" thirty-three times; all but seven of these are found in prepositional phrases, such as "the light of Christ," "alive in Christ," "the gift of Christ," "the atonement of Christ," "the words of Christ," and so on. Mormon seems to focus more on the indirect manifestations and attributes of Christ than on the person of Christ Himself. When he used the name "Jesus Christ," a favorite expression with his son Moroni, Mormon uniformly augmented the personal name of Jesus Christ with the more formal title "Lord Jesus Christ" (Moroni 7:2; 8:2; 9:26). Once, in 3 Nephi 5:1, Mormon spoke of Jesus as the Redeemer and Savior, in connection with the redemption of the promised land of the Israelites (see 3 Nephi 5:20, 26), but otherwise, names and titles for Jesus are almost nonexistent in Mormon's original writings.

Mormon had a great love for children, perhaps owing in part to having been recognized as a chosen and worthy child at a very young age. Thus he alone referred to Jesus as the "Holy Child, Jesus" (Moroni 8:3) and saw the Redemption of Christ most powerfully efficacious in the salvation of little children (see Moroni 8:8).

MORONI

It is hard to imagine that Moroni's life circumstances were very pleasant. His young childhood saw the inexorable deterioration of society around him and his family. His father, Mormon, must have spent most of his time tediously preparing what he knew would be the final testimony of his collapsing world. Moroni's young manhood was spent in war, as he led a division of ten thousand into a hopeless slaughter. His last thirty-six years were spent wandering, alone and hunted like an animal for his refusal to deny Christ. He was the keeper of the words of Christ and the preserver of the most sacred prayers of Jesus, which Moroni included in the record only after he knew that those words would be safe from the hands of apostates and infidels. During those lonely years of wandering, Jesus Christ appeared to Moroni in plain humility, speaking with him face to face in Moroni's own language (see Ether 12:39).

Moroni's testimony of Christ, like the testimonies of his predecessors, mirrors the conditions that surrounded him. He saw the only good in the world existing in Christ; he affirmed that all that is good does not deny Christ (see Moroni 10:6), just as he had staunchly refused to deny Christ even at the peril of his life. Moroni repeatedly beckoned his readers to come unto Christ and deny ungodliness, which was rampant in the world he had known. By contrast, holiness was a main attribute of Christ mentioned by Moroni (see Mormon 9:3–5), Jesus being identified as a "holy Being" (Mormon 9:3) and as the "Holy One" (Mormon 9:14).

Moroni used very few titles for Christ that reflect Jesus' position or official station (such as "Lord," "Lord God," or "Father of heaven and earth"). Moroni's texts never use such titles as "Redeemer" or "Savior," and they scantly mention such words as "Lord," "Father and Son," or "Lamb." More distinctly than any other Book of Mormon writer, Moroni used the two-part name of "Jesus Christ" (sixteen times), the name that figures especially in the sacrament prayers and priesthood ordinances, which Moroni treasured and preserved. Moreover, Moroni showed his own acquaintance with Jesus, calling Him by the simple name of "Jesus" alone (eight times), far more than any other Book of Mormon prophet. This intimacy bespeaks the fact that Moroni had indeed walked many years with Jesus as his only companion, evidently on a first-name basis.

Moroni's last exhortations were for people to come unto Christ and be perfected (or finished) in Him (see Moroni 10:32–33). As the finisher of the Nephite records, Moroni identified clearly with the role of Christ as the finisher of human righteousness: "Yea, come unto Christ, and be perfected in him, . . . that by his grace ye may be perfect in Christ" (Moroni 10:32).

Finally, Moroni concluded the plates of Mormon, looking forward to the time when all people will meet Him "before the pleasing bar of the great Jehovah, the Eternal Judge of both quick and dead" (Moroni 10:34). This text is the only one in which a Book of Mormon prophet used the name "Jehovah."[16] Assuming that the word "Jehovah" in Moroni 10:34 is a literal translation of the ancient Hebrew *tetragrammaton* (the protected holy name of God), it appears that he finally felt safe in writing this name as a concluding seal, knowing that no one else in his lifetime would see the record and, in reading it, misuse that sacred name.

Through the spiritual experiences of its writers—many of whom were eyewitnesses of Christ's glory—we can see that the Book of Mormon communicates clear, personal knowledge of Jesus Christ. The Book of Mormon is an intimate scripture: Its purpose is to bring individuals to Christ. It exhorts each reader, personally, to "come unto Christ, and lay hold upon every good gift" (Moroni 10:30). Individual readers can identify vividly with the testimonies of Christ found in the Book of Mormon largely because those testimonies themselves are projections of eternal realities through the personal lenses of noble characters.

Arising out of the ten testimonies examined above, several concluding observations can be made:

1. These testimonies are true to life. They are corroborated by the credentials of authentic personal experience and complex individual diversity. They make sense historically, and they emerge distinctly even from widely scattered primary sources within individual authors.

2. The testimonies become linguistically more definite as time progresses. Lehi at first spoke of Jesus being "*a* Messiah," "*a* prophet," "*a* Savior" (1 Nephi 10:4; emphasis added) or "*this* Redeemer" (1 Nephi 10:5; emphasis added), but this designation soon crystallized in Nephi's abridgment as "*the* Messiah" (1 Nephi 10:7, 9–10; emphasis added).[17] It is also evident that Lehi was not explicit at first about the meaning of the "redemption" of this Messiah. Was it to be a spiritual redemption in the next life, or a physical redemption of the land now or later? This question was raised at least twice by Laman and Lemuel (see 1 Nephi 15:31; 22:1) and finally answered by Nephi: it would be both (see 1 Nephi 22:3).

3. The record often indicates when and how important details about Christ were revealed. The name of "Christ," for example, was told to Jacob by an angel; the name of "Jesus Christ" was revealed to Nephi; the extended name, "Jesus Christ, the Son of God, the Father of heaven and earth, the Creator of all things from the beginning," was first given to the people by King Benjamin to distinguish them above all people led by the Lord. Nephite knowledge of Christ, like all other facets of revealed knowledge, grew "line upon line" (2 Nephi 28:30).

4. As times and conditions changed, some words used in describing Christ dropped out of the Nephite texts, whereas others became more frequent in usage. Words such as "Messiah," "Lamb of God," and "Holy One of Israel" were used often by Lehi, Nephi, and Jacob but rarely by later Book of Mormon writers. The earlier writers tend to connect the Lord more with Israel than do the later authors.

5. The earlier Book of Mormon writers use greater variety in their names for Christ than do the later writers. In the early texts, more forms of expression were used and greater variety exists in their formulations. Of the sixty-seven names researched in this study, Lehi used

fifteen, Nephi used thirty-two, and Jacob, nineteen. Nephite religious speech was evidently more varied in the earlier generations when the revelations were new. As Nephite religious practices and culture became more established, standardized forms and conventions of discourse evidently prevailed.

6. Significantly different names for Christ are used by the various writers of the Book of Mormon. Of the sixty-seven names, thirty-seven are used by only one of the ten prophets under examination. That is further evidence of the multiple authorship of the ancient records underlying the Book of Mormon.

7. The names used for Christ in the Book of Mormon are important conveyors of meaning, content, and power. Names in antiquity typically conveyed meaning. They bespoke the character, individuality, and qualities of the person.[18] Knowing and personally taking upon oneself the name of God was a sacred and vital function in ancient Israel and in the Book of Mormon: In the Old Testament, Jehovah said, "And they shall put my name upon the children of Israel; and I will bless them" (Numbers 6:27), and in the Book of Mormon King Benjamin proclaims, "There is no other name given whereby salvation cometh" (Mosiah 5:8). From the profiles left in their written words, it is evident that these prophets bore the name of Christ personally upon their hearts and souls.

As Joseph Smith and Sidney Rigdon saw the glory of the Lord Jesus Christ, they exclaimed, "And now, after the many testimonies which have been given of him, this is the testimony, last of all, which we give of him: That he lives!" (D&C 76:22). Well does their modern testimony mention that *many* testimonies have been given of Him.

NOTES

1. The thesis of this article was first presented in my entry entitled "Jesus Christ in the Book of Mormon" in the *Encyclopedia of Mormonism* (New York: Macmillan, 1992), 2:748–50. The charts are reproduced from John W. Welch and J. Gregory Welch, *Charting the Book of Mormon* (Provo, Utah: FARMS, 1999).

2. On "the angel of the Lord" as a manifestation of Jehovah Himself, see

Gerhard Kittel, *Theological Dictionary of the New Testament* (Grand Rapids, Mich.: Eerdmans, 1964), 1:77–78.

3. See Robert J. Matthews, "What the Book of Mormon Tells Us about Jesus Christ," in *The Book of Mormon: The Keystone Scripture,* ed. Paul R. Cheesman (Provo, Utah: Religious Studies Center, Brigham Young University, 1988), 21–43, and "The Atonement of Jesus Christ: 2 Nephi 9," in *The Book of Mormon: Second Nephi, The Doctrinal Structure,* ed. Monte S. Nyman and Charles D. Tate Jr. (Provo, Utah: Religious Studies Center, Brigham Young University, 1989), 177–99; Robert L. Millet, "Another Testament of Jesus Christ," in *The Book of Mormon: First Nephi, The Doctrinal Foundation,* ed. Monte S. Nyman and Charles D. Tate Jr. (Provo, Utah: Religious Studies Center, Brigham Young University, 1988), 161–75; see also Joseph Fielding McConkie, "The Testimony of Christ through the Ages," in *The Book of Mormon: Jacob through Words of Mormon, To Learn with Joy,* ed. Monte S. Nyman and Charles D. Tate Jr. (Provo, Utah: Religious Studies Center, Brigham Young University, 1990), 157–73.

4. In analyzing these individual testimonies of Christ, I have tried to examine all the names and titles used by each prophet to refer to Christ, as well as the attributes and functions of Christ that they mention. The resulting profiles, of course, are not absolute; they only reflect the words that have survived in the Nephite record and are not necessarily indicative of all the words ever spoken. I have considered three factors to be especially significant in sketching these possible profiles: (1) unique phrases, (2) frequently repeated words or phrases, and (3) points that are given the greatest emphasis in the messages of each prophet. Each profile could easily be developed further.

5. On the "firstfruits" in Israelite sacrificial law, see Exodus 13:1–13; 23:19; Leviticus 2:12, 14; 23:17, 20; Nehemiah 10:35.

6. Jacob's word *Christ* (the English translation being based on the Greek word *christos,* meaning "anointed") took an important step by focusing on the role of the Messiah as the holy, anointed one. Nephi's word *Jesus,* like the name *Joshua* (which derives from the Hebrew root *yashac,* meaning "to deliver, rescue, or save"), added emphasis to the Messiah's role as Savior, a *mosiah* (see Isaiah 49:26); see John Sawyer, "What Was a *mosiac?*" *Vetus Testamentum* 15 (1965): 475–86; see FARMS Update, April 1989. I count 2 Nephi 10:3 as the first appearance of the word *Christ* in the Book of Mormon, since the name *Jesus Christ* that appears in the manuscripts and 1830 edition of 1 Nephi 12:18 was deleted by Joseph Smith in the 1837 edition.

7. This name implicitly assumes familiarity with such images as the dumb

sheep before the slaughterer (see Isaiah 53:7) or the substituted ram in the sacrifice of Isaac (see Genesis 22).

8. See John M. Lundquist, "The Common Temple Ideology of the Ancient Near East," in *The Temple in Antiquity*, ed. Truman G. Madsen (Provo, Utah: Religious Studies Center, Brigham Young University, 1984), 59–71; Stephen D. Ricks, "Liturgy and Cosmogony" (Provo, Utah: FARMS, 1981).

9. He was indicted with the crimes of false prophecy, bearing false witness, blasphemy, and reviling or lying about the king.

10. God the Father is implicit in the passage "he shall grow up *before him* as a tender plant" (Mosiah 14:2; emphasis added) and explicit in Abinadi's statement about Christ "having subjected the flesh to the will of the Father" (Mosiah 15:2; see also 15:5).

11. When the multitude fell down upon the ground, overcome in awe by the fear of the Lord, they repeated back to the king essentially the words of this name: "We believe in Jesus Christ, the Son of God, who created heaven and earth, and all things" (Mosiah 4:2; see also 5:15). This name was uttered once again by Samuel the Lamanite. As he cursed the people of Zarahemla (the same city in which Benjamin had given this name more than a century earlier), Samuel told them "of the coming of Jesus Christ, the Son of God, the Father of heaven and of earth, the Creator of all things from the beginning" (Helaman 14:12). One may suspect that Samuel evoked the wrath of the people in Zarahemla not only by prophesying their doom but also by openly reminding them of their neglect of this most sacred and holy name.

12. For evidence of this as an authentic part of the earliest Christian accounts of Jesus' passion, see Bruce M. Metzger, *A Textual Commentary on the Greek New Testament* (London: United Bible Societies, 1971), 177.

13. See Babylonian Talmud, Yoma 187. The number ten is a symbolic number, representing completeness and perfection.

14. The believing men were driven out, not killed (see Alma 14:7; 15:1), and all their property was undoubtedly lost, confiscated, or forsaken (see Alma 15:16). That Amulek's family were believers seems likely, since he mentions having women, children, father, kinsfolk, and friends in Alma 10:4 and 10:11, but Alma 15:16 says only that he was rejected by his friends, father, and kindred. I assume that the word "kindred" in Alma 15:16 does not encompass the women and children, although the phrase "all my kindred" in Alma 10:11 may.

15. R. Laird Harris, ed., *Theological Wordbook of the Old Testament* (Chicago: Moody, 1980), 750–51.

16. It appears only one other time, in 2 Nephi 22:2, a passage quoted from Isaiah.

17. Compare also the early christological words (quoted from Zenos) that speak only of "*thy* Son" (Alma 33:11, 13, 16; emphasis added), with Alma's subsequent understanding of these words to mean "*the* Son" (Alma 33:14, 17; emphasis added).

18. See Truman G. Madsen, "'Putting on the Names': A Jewish-Christian Legacy," and Bruce H. Porter and Stephen D. Ricks, "Names in Antiquity: Old, New, and Hidden," in *By Study and Also by Faith,* ed. John M. Lundquist and Stephen D. Ricks (Salt Lake City: Deseret Book and FARMS, 1990), 1:461, 474, 502.

— 20 —

THE FIRST COMING OF THE LORD TO THE JEWS: A BOOK OF MORMON PERSPECTIVE

Richard D. Draper

Speaking prophetically, Alma told the Saints at Gideon that "there be many things to come; and behold, there is one thing which is of more importance than they all—for behold, the time is not far distant that the Redeemer liveth and cometh among his people" (Alma 7:7). Alma was not the only Book of Mormon prophet who knew of things to come. But he knew, as he reminded his hearers, that there was one future event more important than any other: the coming of the Savior to the earth.

Their prophecies included some very specific items, some stated more clearly than most found in the Bible. For instance, the Nephite prophets knew from the time God called Lehi to His work that the Savior would come six hundred years in the future; they knew that His mother would be named Mary and that she would dwell in Nazareth; and they also knew that He would not appear unto them as a mortal man. There were additional details that God revealed to them concerning the Lord's first coming—details that He wanted them to understand. Their understanding of the mortal Messiah and His mission came solely from God. As a result, the Book of Mormon emphasizes what the Father

Richard D. Draper is a professor of ancient scripture and serves as managing director of the Religious Studies Center at Brigham Young University.

felt was important about Jesus' first coming. By bringing all these prophetic elements together, we can get a clear picture of the essentials. The purpose of this paper is to bring together those items, that we might better understand what the Father wants to emphasize concerning the Lord's first coming. For the sake of space, this paper will be limited to revealed information about the Savior's ministry among the Jews.

Though this study is about the Lord's first coming, it also has something to say about the foreknowledge of God and how God uses that foreknowledge to further His work. The Book of Mormon shows us that God knows the future down to the smallest details, such as the names by which His mortal children shall be known and where they shall reside. It also shows us that God willingly reveals details of the future to His prophets and through them to His other children. He does this that all might be prepared to take full advantage of that which is to come.

The Book of Mormon also shows us that not all respond favorably to the faith that prophecy demands. Many, especially among the Nephite intellectuals, found the doctrine impossible to believe. Sherem took Jacob to task for perverting the way of truth by promoting the "worship of a being which ye say shall come many hundred years hence." He assured Jacob that "this is blasphemy; for no man knoweth of such things; for he cannot tell of things to come" (Jacob 7:7). Korihor preached "unto the people against the prophecies which had been spoken by the prophets, concerning the coming of Christ" (Alma 30:6). He boldly asked, "Why do ye look for a Christ? For no man can know of anything which is to come" (Alma 30:13). The prophetic witness of the first coming of the Lord proves both of these men wrong. In the book's witness of the first coming of the Savior, we see just how much righteous men and women knew about the future.

THE LITERAL SON OF GOD

One of the strongest messages that comes through the pages of the Book of Mormon is that the Messiah would be the Son of God. Alma testified that "he shall be born of Mary, . . . who shall be overshadowed and conceive by the power of the Holy Ghost, and bring forth a son, yea, even the Son of God" (Alma 7:10). An angel assured Nephi that Mary was "the mother of the Son of God, after the manner of the flesh" (1 Nephi 11:18). That is a striking statement. The great Jehovah, the Creator of heaven and earth, would enter the world just as any other baby. Though His conception might be miraculous, His birth would not be. Like us, He would in the natural way take upon Himself flesh and blood and go forth among the children of men (see Mosiah 7:26–27). How apropos, if homey, is King Benjamin's statement that the Redeemer would "dwell in a tabernacle of clay" (Mosiah 3:5).

However, we must be careful not to make the mortal Savior too much like ourselves. The Book of Mormon testifies that He was something special, something unique. Though He might dwell in a tabernacle of clay, He would come "with power" and "go forth amongst men, working mighty miracles" (Mosiah 3:5). He would have the power to do His mighty works as a direct result of being the "Only Begotten of the Father" (2 Nephi 25:12). Never in the history of this telestial world would there be another born as Son of Elohim. His conception and birth allowed Him to retain His station as God. Abinadi avowed that "God himself shall come down among the children of men, and take upon him the form of man, and go forth in mighty power" (Mosiah 13:34). It is of note that Abinadi does not say that Jesus will be a man but rather He would have man's form, through which He would be able to manifest His "mighty power."

Alma elaborated on this point, saying that the Redeemer would "take upon him the image of man, and it should be the image after which man was created in the beginning; or in other words, he said that man was created after the image of God, and that God should come down among the children of men" (Mosiah 7:27). The point is that Jesus stood apart from all others born of mortal women, even though we look like Him and He lived like us. It was because He was different that He could fulfill His mission, for "he shall suffer temptations, and pain of body, hunger, thirst, and fatigue, even more than *man* can suffer, except it be unto death; for behold, blood cometh from every pore, so great shall be his anguish for the wickedness and the abominations of his people" (Mosiah 3:7; emphasis added). Two important points come out of this scripture. First, it separates the Savior from the class of beings called "man." He endured what no "man" could endure in terms of spiritual and physical suffering. Second, His godly abilities allowed His body to withstand the physical anguish the Atonement required.

When teaching the Zoramites, Amulek also stressed that Jesus was something other than man. Explaining the need for a great and last sacrifice, he said that it would "*not [be] a sacrifice of man,* neither of beast, neither of any manner of fowl; for it shall *not be a human sacrifice;* but . . . infinite and eternal" (Alma 34:10; emphasis added). His testimony, like those of Abinadi and Benjamin, seems startling. How could the Savior, born after the manner of the flesh, be considered anything other than human? But Amulek is making an important point. He expands Abinadi's division of mortals into two categories by distinguishing whether or not they are infinite and eternal. If one is not infinite and eternal, then one is man; if one is infinite and eternal, then one is not man. Jesus was the Son of God and consequently even as a mortal was infinite and eternal. Thus, He carried with Him attributes no other mortal ever carried. Thus, Amulek could affirm that the "great and last sacrifice will be the Son of God, yea, infinite and eternal" (Alma 34:14).

BOTH THE FATHER AND THE SON

The Savior was unique in two other ways. First, He was the "Only Begotten of God." No other would ever be born in the flesh as God's child. Second, as a mortal He was the Eternal Father. Therefore, He was at the same time the Son of God and the Eternal Father. Benjamin testified that He would "be called Jesus Christ, the Son of God, the Father of heaven and earth" (Mosiah 3:8). Nephi quoted Isaiah saying that "unto us a child is born, . . . and his name shall be called, . . . The Mighty God, The Everlasting Father" (2 Nephi 19:6).

Abinadi, in an extremely difficult passage, explained this dual characteristic. He noted that "God himself shall come down among the children of men" (Mosiah 15:1) and that He would come as "the Father and the Son" (Mosiah 15:2). What gave Him the power to be the Father? Abinadi said it was because "he was conceived by the power of God" (Mosiah 15:3). Just what Abinadi meant by that phrase is puzzling, but it seems clear that the Savior's power as Father came as a direct result of something He inherited from God. What made Him the Son? The act by which God gave Him "the flesh" (Mosiah 15:2–3). Thus, Abinadi observed, He became "the Father and the Son" (Mosiah 15:3). The prophet went on to testify that "they are one God, yea, the very Eternal Father of heaven and earth" (Mosiah 15:4), and that Jesus, even though He came in the dual role of Son and Father, would be that "one God, [who] suffereth temptation, and yieldeth not to temptation, but suffereth himself to be mocked, and scourged, and cast out, and disowned by his people" (Mosiah 15:5). All this stresses the point that the Savior, even as a mortal, was unlike anyone else.

However, we should not get the idea from all this that the Savior could not relate to us. The testimony of the Book of Mormon explicitly states otherwise. Just because He was God and the Son of God, He was not, as Abinadi testified, shielded from temptation or pain or sorrow. Alma knew that the Savior would "go forth, suffering pains and afflictions and temptations of every kind; and this that the word might be fulfilled which saith he will take upon him the pains and the sicknesses of his people" (Alma 7:11). Indeed, He would "take upon him their infirmities" (Alma 7:12). There was a divine reason why: "that his bowels may be filled with mercy, according to the flesh, that he may know according to the flesh how to succor his people" (Alma 7:12). Therefore, as "the Spirit knoweth all things," the flesh also needed to know. Consequently, the mortal Christ would suffer "according to the flesh" (Alma 12:13)—and, remember, He would suffer even more than man can suffer without dying.

Someone once pointed out a myth that many believe. According to the myth, good people know little of temptation because only bad people are ever really touched by it. Nothing could be further from the truth. What does a person know about the seductive force or unrelenting pressure of temptation if he never resists? Only those who hold out against temptation ever really feel its depth and power. Christ never yielded. Therefore, He not only sympathizes with those who must struggle against it; He also empathizes. Thus, He could ascend "into heaven having the bowels of mercy; being filled with compassion towards the children of men" (Mosiah 15:9).

Before that ascension, He had first to come to earth and fulfill His mission. The Nephite prophets were well aware that the Lord would come six hundred years after Lehi left Jerusalem, but they did not keep their dating system based on this prophecy. Instead, they followed a more traditional method of keeping track of years according to the reign of kings and judges. As a result, we don't know if the general population knew that the exact year of the Lord's first coming had been revealed. That uncertainty changed with the preaching of Samuel the Lamanite. He told them the Lord would come in five years and gave the people a very specific sign by which they would know that the Lord had indeed come. There would be "one day and a night and a day, as if it were one day and there were no night" (Helaman 14:4). In addition, "there shall a new star arise, such an one as ye never have beheld" (Helaman 14:5). By this they would know that the Son of God had come "to redeem all those who believe on his name" (Helaman 14:2).

HIS EARLY MINISTRY

In addition to knowing when He would be born, they also knew it would be some time before He would start His actual ministry. During that period "the Spirit of the Lord shall rest upon him, the spirit of wisdom and understanding, the spirit of counsel and might, the spirit of knowledge and of the fear of the Lord; and shall make him of quick understanding in the fear of the Lord" (2 Nephi 21:2–3). Then, after He had matured, He would go forth.

Before the ministry, He would have to take care of a very important matter: His baptism. The Father, through the amount of detail He revealed about this event, underscored its importance. Nephi taught that John the Baptist would play the principal role in the ordinance. Though John is never mentioned by name, his status is. Lehi called him "a prophet who should come before the Messiah, to prepare the way of the Lord" (1 Nephi 10:7) and knew that he would "baptize in Bethabara, beyond Jordan" (1 Nephi 10:9). Nephi also saw "the prophet who should prepare the way before" the Lord (1 Nephi 11:27).

They knew that he would come out of the wilderness and tell the people to make straight the path of the Lord. He would testify that one stands "among you whom ye know not; and he is mightier than I, whose shoe's latchet I am not worthy to unloose" (1 Nephi 10:8). The mission of John the Baptist would also include an additional witness. "And after he had baptized the Messiah with water," Lehi taught, "he should behold and bear record that he had baptized the Lamb of God" (1 Nephi 10:10).

Concerning Jesus Himself, Nephi predicted that "after he was baptized, . . . the Holy Ghost [would] come down and abide upon him in the form of a dove" (1 Nephi 11:27). The dove came as a sign that the Savior had been "obedient unto him [the Father] in keeping his commandments" (2 Nephi 31:7–8). It also showed that the power of the Holy Ghost comes only after one has entered into the water (see 2 Nephi 31:12).

Nephi helps us understand why the Father revealed so much detail about the Savior's baptism. He shows us two points in particular. The first has to do with the condescension of God. The term denotes the act of voluntarily laying aside privilege, rank, or dignity. In vision, Nephi saw the Savior do this. "The angel said to me again: Look and behold the condescension of God! And I looked and beheld the Redeemer of the world, of whom my father had spoken. . . . And the Lamb of God went forth and was baptized [by a man]" (1 Nephi 11:26–27). He who was holy and the Redeemer of humankind condescended to be baptized by a man who, though one of the greatest born of woman, was not worthy to untie His sandal straps.

The second deals with the Savior's need to fulfill all righteousness. The Lord had done all that had been required of Him up to the point He was about to start His ministry, which includes living for thirty years in a state of holiness. But He could not stop now. He had to continue until He had done all that the Father required. At this point, the Father required that Jesus show "unto the children of men that, according to the flesh he humbleth himself before the Father, and witnesseth unto the Father that he would be obedient unto him in keeping his commandments" (2 Nephi 31:7). Further, He had to show "the children of men the straitness of the path, and the narrowness of the gate, by which they should enter, he having set the example before them" (2 Nephi 31:9). Indeed, He did show the way, for if the Savior was holy and still had to fulfill the Father's will by being baptized, "how much more need have we, being unholy, to be baptized" (2 Nephi 31:5).

"MINISTERING UNTO THE PEOPLE"

Once the Savior had met that requirement, He was ready to move on to the next phase of His mission. That phase was to go "forth ministering unto the people, in power and great glory" (1 Nephi 11:28). Abinadi testified He would "go forth in mighty power upon the face of the earth" (Mosiah 13:34). The power would be manifest, among other ways, through miracles. The prophets were well aware of the breadth of those miracles, which would include "healing the sick, raising the dead, causing the lame to walk, the blind to receive their sight, and the deaf to hear, and curing all manner of diseases. And he shall cast out devils, or the evil spirits which dwell in the hearts of the children of men" (Mosiah 3:5–6). As Nephi saw, these miracles were not few and far between. "I beheld multitudes of people who were sick, and who were afflicted with all manner of diseases, and with devils and unclean spirits. . . . And they were healed by the power of the Lamb of God; and the devils and the unclean spirits were cast out" (1 Nephi 11:31).

As a result of these deeds, "multitudes were gathered together to hear him" (1 Nephi 11:28). Among these Nephi saw "many fall down at his feet and worship him" (1 Nephi 11:24). Twelve of these would be called to His service. Nephi knew, by angelic testimony, that their title would be "apostle" (1 Nephi 11:34) and that, someday, they would "judge the twelve tribes of Israel" (1 Nephi 12:9). Before that day, they would assist the Lord in His ministry. One of their main functions would be to "bear record" of the Lamb of God (see 1 Nephi 13:24).

The Book of Mormon prophets knew that the Savior would devote most of His time to teaching the people. His message would carry the pure "word of God" (1 Nephi 11:25). Through it, those who would hear would be brought to "the love of God" (1 Nephi 11:25). Such love, as Nephi understood, "sheddeth itself abroad in the hearts of the children of men; wherefore, it is the most desirable above all things" (1 Nephi 11:22). Indeed, it is "the most joyous to the soul" (1 Nephi 11:23).

THE ATONEMENT: POWER TO REDEEM

His teachings and His miracles were the foundations to the Lord's central work. "A prophet would the Lord God raise up among the Jews," Lehi testified, "even a Messiah, or, in other words, a Savior of the world" (1 Nephi 10:4). This Messiah, he went on to say, would also be the "Redeemer of the world" (1 Nephi 10:5). The two tasks, redemption and salvation—though closely related—are not identical. Redemption carries the idea of paying the price necessary to bring a person or people out of bondage. Salvation, on the other hand, goes beyond merely freeing them. It carries with it the idea of assuring them further existence in which they can enjoy security and happiness.

The Savior's power to redeem grew out of the Atonement. It was through the Atonement that He paid the necessary price to save humankind. Jacob assured his people that "redemption cometh in and through the Holy Messiah; for he is full of grace and truth. Behold, he offereth himself a sacrifice for sin, to answer the ends of the law, unto all those who have a broken heart and a contrite spirit" (2 Nephi 2:6–7). He paid the price of Himself. "His blood atoneth for the sins of those who have fallen by the transgression of Adam," King Benjamin taught. It covered those "who have died not knowing the will of God concerning them, or who have ignorantly sinned" (Mosiah 3:11). This sentence gives us a feel for the breadth of the Savior's redeeming power. However, its full force would not come upon all people, only those who met the proper criteria. "He shall come into the world to redeem his people," Amulek taught, "and he shall take upon him the transgressions of those who believe on his name" (Alma 11:40). It is true that there is a universal aspect of the Redemption: "Because of the intercession for all, all men come unto God; wherefore, they stand . . . to be judged of him according to the truth and holiness which is in him" (2 Nephi 2:10). Thus, some aspects of the Savior's atonement benefit everyone.

However, that is not the whole story. As Nephi, the son of Helaman, testified, Jesus "hath power given unto him . . . to redeem them from their sins because of repentance" (Helaman 5:11). The Nephites understood that the Savior paid the price to redeem us from the Fall; however, it would be up to each individual to accept the Redemption and the freedom it brought. Repentance is the means God has provided by which we may show our acceptance. Seeing repentance in this way allows us to focus on its positive aspects. So often we see it as the burden we pay to have our sins remitted. The truth of the matter is that Christ has given us a gift: redemption. It is freely given, but we must accept it. We do that by repenting. When we accept the Lord's gift, He forgives our sins. Samuel the Lamanite said, "Repent of all your sins, that thereby ye may have a remission of them through his merits" (Helaman 14:13).

That redemption opens the way for full salvation through which the individual can secure eternal life and joy. Benjamin testified that the Lord "cometh unto his own, that salvation might come unto the children of men even through faith on his name" (Mosiah 3:9). It is of note that God designed the Savior's mission to the Jews as the means of taking salvation to all His children. The Father sent Jesus specifically to the Jews, but the objective was not Jewish salvation alone. What happened to the Savior while He was with the Jews would open the way for the salvation of all people. In Benjamin's seemingly simple statement, we see that God made the wicked among the Jews, like He made Assyria or Babylon, instruments in bringing about His will.

The Book of Mormon shows that the Savior designed the teachings, acts, signs, and miracles of His ministry to promote faith in Him so He could save the people. The Book of Mormon prophets knew that "there is no other . . . means whereby man can be saved, only through the atoning blood of Jesus Christ" (Helaman 5:9). But people had to have faith in that blood or they would not do what was required of them to be saved. Amulek explained why it was necessary for sinners to accept the Lord, forsake their sins, and become clean. It was because the Lord "cannot save them in their sins; for I cannot deny his word, and he hath said that no unclean thing can inherit the kingdom of heaven; therefore, how can ye be saved except ye inherit the kingdom of heaven? Therefore, ye cannot be saved in your sins" (Alma 11:37). The Lord's power operated only to save people from their sins. That meant that they had to forsake their sins through faith and repentance.

"SLAIN FOR THE SINS OF THE WORLD"

Through His teachings, signs, miracles, and loving kindness, the Lord sought to create that faith by which He could save the people. But "even after all this," taught King Benjamin, "they shall consider him a man, and say that he hath a devil" (Mosiah 3:9). Among the multitudes that came to hear Him, there were many who would turn away and "cast him out from among them" (1 Nephi 11:28). Eventually, the prophets saw, the Jews' fear and hatred would turn murderous. Nephi saw in vision that "the Son of the everlasting God was judged of the world" (1 Nephi 11:32). The irony is amazing. The righteous God and judge of all would be judged by the world. But their judgment would not be righteous. "And the world, because of their iniquity, shall judge him to be a thing of naught; wherefore they scourge him, and he suffereth it; and they smite him, and he suffereth it. Yea, they spit upon him, and he suffereth it, because of His loving kindness and his long-suffering towards the children of men" (1 Nephi 19:9). Benjamin said these people, unyielding to His loving kindness, "shall scourge him, and shall crucify him" (Mosiah 3:9). In this way, "he was lifted up upon the cross and slain for the sins of the world" (1 Nephi 11:33).

He was slain not only for the sins of the world but also because of them. People do not seem to realize that sin is blinding. But sin cannot blind in and of itself. Rather, it is the instrument whereby people blind themselves. Having done so, a Jewish mob moved against their God, and He "yieldeth himself, according to the words of the angel, as a man, into the hands of wicked men, to be lifted up" (1 Nephi 19:10).

The use of the word *wicked* is arresting. It points to much more than simply not measuring up to a spiritual standard. The word describes a conscious and deliberate opposition to and violation of moral law. Though many of the Lord's initial followers may have inadvertently blinded themselves with sin, the Book of Mormon makes it clear that the Jewish leadership knew what they were doing. Therefore, its prophets could say that the Messiah will "come among the Jews, among those who are the more wicked part of the world; and they shall crucify him—for thus it behooveth our God, and there is none other nation on earth that would crucify their God. For should the mighty miracles be wrought among other nations they would repent, and know that he be their God. But because of priestcrafts and iniquities, they at Jerusalem will stiffen their necks against him, that he be crucified" (2 Nephi 10:3–5).

Due to their murderous hatred, they would do more than just crucify Him. They would first put Him through tremendous humiliation and torture. He saw it coming and said, "I gave my back to the smiter, and my cheeks to them that plucked off the hair. I hid not my face from the shame of spitting" (2 Nephi 7:6). Further, He would not fight them. "He shall be led, yea, even as Isaiah said, as a sheep before the shearer is dumb, so he opened not his mouth" (Mosiah 15:6). So wicked men judged the God of judgment, shamed Him, humiliated Him, and then crucified Him.

The Book of Mormon, however, shows that the situation is not as black as it appears. At least two positive things came out of it. The first was for the Lord Himself, who at the time "when his soul has been made an offering for sin he shall see his seed" (Mosiah 15:10). Just when He would see His seed Abinadi does not make clear. Could it have been during the agony of Gethsemane or on the cross? Or was it after, as He ministered to the spirit world or, later, to people on two continents? The text is not clear. But Abinadi knew who it was the Lord would see. It was those who "looked forward to that day for a remission of their sins, . . . or they [who] are the heirs of the kingdom of God" (Mosiah 15:11). The Savior would see these, and His soul would rejoice.

The second item was that all the suffering and torture worked to God's end: "Christ shall come among the children of men, to take upon him the transgressions of his people, and that he shall atone for the sins of the world" (Alma 34:8). His mission was twofold. First, He would take upon Him the transgressions of His people. In that way He would pay the debt of sin and redeem them from death and hell. In addition,

He would save them by making an atonement on their behalf. The word *atonement* carries with it the idea of reconciliation. An atonement is needed when two estranged parties must come together for the benefit of either or both. Alma taught that due to sin people suffer both temporal and spiritual death. As a result of this, when they die physically, their souls are "miserable, being cut off from the presence of the Lord" (Alma 42:11). The only way to reclaim them from their fallen state is to reconcile them to God. But justice had claim on them, due to sin, and demanded their separation from God. The Savior gave His blood and thus redeemed them from sin and also freed them from justice, but on a condition that they accept His mercy. However, He would not force anyone to live according to the *law* of mercy.

JUSTICE AND MERCY

Two points need to be understood. First, the Savior's death allowed the *law* of mercy to operate within the bounds of the *law* of justice. Second, Jesus did not die to move His people from law to lawlessness. His death made it possible for them to live according to the law of mercy rather than the law of justice. Those who chose mercy still lived according to the law and therefore, the Savior could reconcile them to the Father. The means by which they could choose to come under the law of mercy was repentance. So, Alma explains, "The plan of mercy could not be brought about except an atonement should be made; therefore God himself atoneth for the sins of the world, to bring about the plan of mercy, to appease the demands of justice" (Alma 42:15). In doing so, Jesus made it possible for us to return to the Father. Of all the prophecies dealing with the first coming, the Lord's mission as Savior and Redeemer is central.

The Book of Mormon prophets told their people that they would know when Jesus made that atonement. Nephi explained that there would be "three days of darkness, which should be a sign given of his death unto those who should inhabit the isles of the sea, more especially given unto those who are of the house of Israel" (1 Nephi 19:10). But the event would be signaled by far more severe conditions than mere darkness. Indeed, "the rocks of the earth must rend; and because of the groanings of the earth, many of the kings of the isles of the sea shall be wrought upon by the Spirit of God, to exclaim: The God of nature suffers" (1 Nephi 19:12).

RESURRECTION

His suffering and death would not be the last events defining His first coming to the Jews. He still had to be resurrected and ascend in order to prepare for His second coming. Therefore, "after he is laid in a sepulchre for the space of three days he shall rise from the dead, with healing in his wings" (2 Nephi 25:13; see also 1 Nephi 19:10). It is of note that the Lord's healing ministry would continue even into the Resurrection. It would focus on healing the breach between man and God. Through the power of the Resurrection, the Father "breaketh the bands of death, having gained the victory over death; giving the Son power to make intercession for the children of men" (Mosiah 15:8). "Behold, the resurrection of Christ redeemeth mankind, yea, even all mankind, and bringeth them back into the presence of the Lord. Yea, and it bringeth to pass the condition of repentance, that whosoever repenteth the same is not hewn down and cast into the fire," for "there cometh upon them again a spiritual death, yea, a second death, for they are cut off again as to things pertaining to righteousness" (Helaman 14:17–18).

With the Resurrection and reconciliation made, the Savior's first coming to the Jews met all its objectives, and He departed from these people, never to return until He would come to them again in the last days.

An observation in closing: most of what the Book of Mormon teaches about the Lord's first coming is laid out in the books of Nephi. God had already revealed the essential elements of His Son's mission before Lehi ever left the Old World. Therefore, the righteous Nephites had a clear picture of the Savior's mortal mission from the beginning. Later prophets generally did little more than confirm what was already known. The point is that God saw fit to reveal all the essentials about His Son's mortal ministry early so that the Nephite people, far removed from the place of the first coming of the Lord, could still be prepared for and take advantage of what He offered.

21

The Doctrine of a Covenant People

Joseph Fielding McConkie

According to holy writ, whenever the Lord has a people whom He acknowledges as His own, that acknowledgment comes in the form of a covenant. In our day we hear much about "making a commitment for Christ." But it is covenants of which we speak, not commitments. The word *commitments* is not found in the scriptures. The word *covenants* is found a multitude of times. A commitment is a personal pledge and may be quite serious, while a covenant is a two-way promise. God is its author and is the guarantor of its terms. Angels are its witnesses. It is, in the realms of spiritual things, a legal and binding agreement between God and the individual.

It is the concept of a covenant that binds all the books of the Bible and all the generations of faithful Saints together. The two divisions of the Bible, the Old Testament and New Testament, could have been more properly denominated the Old Covenant and New Covenant. The Bible story is like the popular historical novels of our day in which the saga of a family is traced from generation to generation. In order to study the Bible we divide its books into chapters and verses. We rarely get the whole thing pieced back together so that we see it as the epic

---

Joseph Fielding McConkie is a professor of ancient scripture at Brigham Young University.

family saga that it is. In so doing, we could be compared to people so busy collecting pebbles on the beach that they fail to see the ocean.

One problem with this kind of Bible study is that all too often those who are busily collecting scriptural pebbles are doing so primarily to have something to throw at those whose interpretation differs from their own. Meanwhile they lose sight of the book's most plain and precious parts. Among the precious things lost is the concept of the eternal family unit. Forgotten is the fact that salvation is a family affair, that God made covenants with our ancient fathers, and that those covenants center in blessings that were also promised to us. We become theological and spiritual orphans. We are, in the words of Malachi, left without "root nor branch" (Malachi 4:1). We suppose we can have salvation independent of family responsibilities. The whole thing is akin to going through life without really knowing our parents or families.

The readers of the Book of Mormon, if they have a Bible background, will immediately be aware that it purports to be a continuation of the Bible story. It is a part of the same great family saga. Perhaps we have been insensitive to how tightly the visit and teachings of the Savior as recorded in 3 Nephi fit with the biblical account.

DEFINITIONS

Before we analyze that story, it will be helpful for us to briefly define some key words and phrases. We will define terms as the Book of Mormon writers used them.

Jew. Lehi, a descendant of Joseph through Manasseh (see Alma 10:3), considered himself a Jew because he was a citizen of the kingdom of Judah. He was a Jewish national. Thus, the Book of Mormon writers speak of themselves and their posterity as descendants of the Jews (see 2 Nephi 30:4; D&C 19:27).

Gentile. As used in the Bible the word *Gentile* means "nation"—i.e., a collective body. It is used in a similar manner in the Book of Mormon. As a Jew is a Jewish national, so a Gentile is a citizen of a Gentile nation. Thus Joseph Smith, a pure-blooded Israelite, is referred to as a Gentile, and the gospel, it is prophesied, will be restored in a Gentile nation. Any nation that does not have prophets at its head, revelation as its constitution, and the Messiah as its king, is a Gentile nation.

Remnant of Jacob. The remnant of Jacob is the twelve tribes collectively. A remnant of Jacob could be any of the various scattered parts of Jacob's family. For instance, Lehi's descendants are a remnant of Jacob.

Times of the Gentiles. The phrase *times of the Gentiles* refers to the period between the destruction of the kingdom of Israel after the earthly ministry of Christ and the reestablishment of that nation with Christ as its king in the Millennium. At the beginning of the Millennium, all Gentile or man-made governments will be superseded by the law of the gospel with Christ as king.

Redemption of Jerusalem. To be redeemed is to be freed from the dominion and power of Satan. Jerusalem will be redeemed when the law of the gospel again becomes the law of its citizens. Christ will be their king, and the citizens of that kingdom will have taken upon themselves His name in the waters of baptism and will again be a covenant people.

Salvation of our God. The phrase *salvation of our God,* which is commonly found in prophetic descriptions of the winding up scene of earth's history, refers to the ultimate triumph of Christ. The word *salvation* used in the Bible is a translation of the Hebrew word *yeshooaw* and could also have been translated "deliverance" or "victory." To see the salvation of our God is to see the triumph of Christ over all His enemies. It will include the gathering of all the tribes of Israel into one fold with the Lord's sanctuary in their midst.

With this background we turn to the account of Christ's visit to the Nephites as recorded in 3 Nephi. In doing so, it is a panoramic view that we seek, not the pebbles on the beach. Our interest is to see the relationship Christ establishes between the doctrine of covenants and the promise of salvation.

A VOICE TO THOSE IN DARKNESS

Twice during that terrible night of darkness that attested to the death of Christ in the Old World, the voice of the Redeemer spoke to those in the New World. I do not think I overstate the matter in suggesting that the world has never known a more dramatic teaching moment. The audible voice of the Lord had been heard speaking from the heavens before, but never to such an extensive and numerous audience. May I suggest that we have not given sufficient attention to what was said on those two occasions. We will begin this study at that point.

First came a voice of warning: "Wo, wo, wo unto this people; wo unto the inhabitants of the whole earth except they shall repent; for the devil laugheth, and his angels rejoice, because of the slain of the fair sons and daughters of my people; and it is because of their iniquity and abominations that they are fallen!" (3 Nephi 9:2). Note the language used to describe those who had been slain. They were the "fair sons and daughters of [Christ's] people"—the seed of those with whom He had covenanted.

The recitation of the destruction of great cities followed: Zarahemla, Moroni, Moronihah, Gilgal, Onihah, Mocum, Jerusalem, Gadiandi, Gadiomnah, Jacob, Gimgimno, Jacobugath, Laman, Josh, Gad, and Kishkumen. Their destruction came because there were no righteous among them and because they had soiled themselves with the blood of the Lord's prophets and Saints. Then came the testimony: "I am Jesus Christ the Son of God. . . . I came unto my own, and my own received me not" (3 Nephi 9:15–16). Of those who had received Him He said, "Them have I given to become the sons of God; and even so will I to as many as shall believe on my name, for behold, by me redemption cometh, and in me is the law of Moses fulfilled" (3 Nephi 9:17).

The Mosaic dispensation had now ended. The old covenant had been fulfilled. Thus the instruction: "Ye shall offer up unto me no more the shedding of blood; yea, your sacrifices and your burnt offerings shall be done away, for I will accept none of your sacrifices and your burnt offerings" (3 Nephi 9:19). Foreshadowing the new order or covenant, He said: "Ye shall offer for a sacrifice unto me a broken heart and a contrite spirit. And whoso cometh unto me with a broken heart and a contrite spirit, him will I baptize with fire and with the Holy Ghost" (3 Nephi 9:20). So great was the astonishment caused by this most unique communication from heaven that there was silence in the land for the space of many hours. Even the wailing over the loss of kindred and loved ones ceased.

A second time, from the midst of the darkness, the voice of the Lord was heard:

"O ye people of these great cities which have fallen, who are descendants of Jacob, yea, who are of the house of Israel, how oft have I gathered you as a hen gathereth her chickens under her wings, and have nourished you.

"And again, how oft would I have gathered you as a hen gathereth her chickens under her wings, yea, O ye people of the house of Israel, who have fallen; yea, O ye people of the house of Israel, ye that dwell at Jerusalem, as ye that have fallen; yea, how oft would I have gathered you as a hen gathereth her chickens, and ye would not.

"O ye house of Israel whom I have spared, how oft will I gather you as a hen gathereth her chickens under her wings, if ye will repent and return unto me with full purpose of heart.

"But if not, O house of Israel, the places of your dwellings shall become desolate until the time of the fulfilling of the covenant to your fathers" (3 Nephi 10:4–7).

This lament is familiar to the New Testament reader though this is an expanded version of it. It has meaning only in the context of the covenant made to the fathers. It certifies the speaker as the Messiah. No one else has power to gather Israel, and no one else is under covenant to do so. The burden of the message is that because of their family ties and because their fathers were the children of Jacob, they were gathered and nourished. Had other branches of the family been equally willing, they too would have been gathered and blessed in a like manner. The refrain then switches from a past to a future tense with a rhetorical question—"How oft will I gather you" if you will repent and return to me? Then the warning, a very believable warning, to those to whom the Lord spoke: If you refuse spiritual fidelity, if you are not my children according to the terms of the covenant, if you have no claim to an inheritance either temporally or spiritually, your dwelling places will be desolate, a desolation which will continue "until ye have received from the hand of the Lord a just recompense for all your sins" (Joseph Smith Translation,

Luke 13:36). Following these words, the weeping and howling for those who had been lost again filled the darkness of the night.

Mormon, who is writing the account of these things, observes at this point that Jacob had prophesied concerning a remnant of Joseph. He asks, "Are not we a remnant of the seed of Joseph? And these things which testify of us, are they not written upon the plates of brass?" (3 Nephi 10:17).

CHRIST'S APPEARANCE AT THE TEMPLE

The third occasion in which a voice from heaven was heard in 3 Nephi was that of the Father introducing His Son to those assembled at the temple in the land Bountiful. In my judgment, the best reading of the text places this a year later (see 3 Nephi 8:5; 10:18). A group of about 2,500 people—men, women, and children—were assembled "conversing about this Jesus Christ, of whom the sign had been given concerning his death" (3 Nephi 11:2; see also 17:25). They were there as families. The nature of temple worship either anciently or in our own dispensation is not such that we would normally expect a family congregation of this size to be present. I wonder if this was not a meeting being held for the purpose of commemorating the events of the terrible night of darkness.

The unannounced and unanticipated appearance of Christ fits the pattern of Malachi's prophecy that the messenger of the covenant would "suddenly come to his temple" (Malachi 3:1). In so saying, I am not suggesting that this constitutes the fulfillment of that prophecy, only that it fits the pattern, a pattern that I anticipate would have been duplicated in Christ's visits among the other scattered remnants of Israel.

The voice from heaven attested that the glorious being descending from heaven was His Beloved Son and all were commanded to hear Him. The heavenly visitor announced Himself to be the Christ, the light and life of the world. The multitude fell to the earth in a reverent awe. They were then invited to come forth, each in turn, to feel the prints in His hands and in His feet that they might know that this was indeed the "God of Israel, and the God of the whole earth, and [that he had] been slain for the sins of the world" (3 Nephi 11:14).

CALLING THE TWELVE TO HEAD THE NEW DISPENSATION

Following this matchless experience in which each of those present became special witnesses of the reality of Christ's suffering and triumph over death, Nephi was called and given the authority to baptize. Eleven others were also called and given the same authority. Instructions then followed relative to the manner in which that ordinance was to be performed. All capable of repentance were to be baptized (see 3 Nephi 11:21–27).

The reader of the Book of Mormon will be aware that the ordinance of baptism was not new to the nation of the Nephites. Easily the greatest discourse on the subject in holy writ was penned by Nephi, the son of Lehi, nearly six hundred years earlier (see 2 Nephi 31). Why then would a second baptism be necessary? The text does not answer this question. It is obvious, however, that the old covenant, namely the law of Moses, had come to an end. This was a new day, and a new order of things was now being introduced. The appearance of Christ, with His renewal of authority, formally constituted a new gospel dispensation among the Nephites. It was a time of new beginnings, and all were invited to claim anew their birthright in the household of faith.

Thus, the twelve disciples were called to stand at the head of the new covenant or dispensation. Again the Old World pattern was followed. Their number is significant and that significance would not have been lost on either the twelve or the multitude. The action is both symbolic and prophetic. Elder Bruce R. McConkie observed: "As there are twelve tribes in Israel, so there are twelve apostles for all Israel and the world; as Jehovah gave his saving truths to the twelve sons of Jacob and their seed, throughout their generations, so Jesus is placing in the hands of his twelve friends the saving truths and powers for their day; and as the names of the twelve tribes of Israel are written on the twelve gates of the Holy Jerusalem, which shall descend from God out of heaven, so are the names of the twelve apostles of the Lamb written on the twelve foundations of the walls of that celestial city."[1]

Calling a quorum of twelve would also have been understood as a prophecy of an ultimate day when all twelve tribes of Israel would again be united as one nation under their true Messiah. As long as we have twelve apostles, the promise exists that Israel will be gathered and the promises made to the fathers will be fulfilled.[2]

It would be difficult to overstate the importance of the Quorum of the Twelve in the destiny of the Church and kingdom of God. We have it in the mouths of three witnesses—the organizations instituted by Christ in Palestine, among the Nephites, and in our own dispensation. In each instance the foundation of the Church is the Quorum of Twelve Apostles.

There are always those would-be leaders and self-ordained prophets who break with the order instituted by the Savior. Their claim is predictable enough—the Brethren are in a state of apostasy, while they just happen to be the "one mighty and strong" (D&C 85:7), who will, according to prophecy (Isaiah is usually the source), enter the scene just in time to save us all. What ought not be lost on us is that such claims violate the covenant made to the fathers in both a symbolic and a literal sense. The Twelve have the authority to perform the ordinance of baptism whereby all others become heirs of the covenant of salvation. True ministers always come with the ordinances of salvation. They are always covenant spokesmen.

The New World version of the sermon at the temple in Bountiful identifies the first beatitude, the one upon which all the others rest, as the sustaining of the Twelve. The second is the covenant of baptism by the authority given to the Twelve. The revelations of our dispensation build on this pattern—the following language from the Doctrine and Covenants:

"The Twelve shall be my disciples, and they shall take upon them my name; and the Twelve are they who shall desire to take upon them my name with full purpose of heart.

"And if they desire to take upon them my name with full purpose of heart, they are called to go into all the world to preach my gospel unto every creature.

"And they are they who are ordained of me to baptize in my name, according to that which is written;

"And you have that which is written before you [having reference to the very things we are reading in 3 Nephi]; wherefore, you must perform it according to the words which are written" (D&C 18:27–30).

This places the remainder of Christ's discourse to the Nephites in the context of covenant worthiness.

Some have tripped over the fact that those called in the New World were referred to as disciples rather than apostles. Note that in the revelation just cited, the emphasis is similar to that in the Book of Mormon. It centers on the idea of "the Twelve" rather than on that of disciples or apostles.

A Dictionary of Christ and the Gospels observes: "They were twelve, and were accordingly known as 'the Twelve.' It is doubtful whether it is proper to supply such a substantive as 'disciples' or 'apostles.' There is authority in the [New Testament] for the use of both of these phrases, but it does not follow that the name first given to this inmost circle of our Lord's adherents was 'the twelve disciples' rather than 'the Twelve.'"[3] Joseph Smith assured us, however, that those in the New World were apostles in the full sense of the word. He taught that the order on this continent was the same, the offices the same, the priesthood the same, the ordinances the same, and the gifts and powers the same as were enjoyed on the Eastern continent.[4]

The Old World version of this sermon has been interpreted as an ethical discourse by a great teacher in the community. The Book of Mormon counterpart makes it plain that these are the words of the Messiah spelling out the great doctrines of the kingdom or the conditions of the covenant. This stands as a classical illustration of the plain and precious things that have been taken from the Bible.

In the New World beatitudes, those who "give heed" to the words of the Twelve and are baptized by their authority are promised that they will receive the companionship of the Holy Ghost. More blessed still, we are told, are those who will accept the testimony of the apostles without having seen Christ. These too are promised a remission of sins and the companionship of the Holy Ghost after their baptism (see 3 Nephi 12:1–2). The doctrine of baptism and sustaining the Twelve places what follows in the context of a covenant between Christ and those who bear His name.

THE COVENANT SERMON

All who have so covenanted are charged with being the salt of the earth. The symbolism and imagery of this metaphor are poignant. Salt, we assume, would have been used among the Nephites, as it was in the Old World, to preserve the meat used in the sacrificial offerings and also as a purifying agent. Such is the role of the covenant people. They are to preserve and purify all that is acceptable to the Lord. Salt loses its savor only through mixture and contamination; so it is with Israel: they lose their chosen role by compromising their actions or their faith. In so doing, they break the terms of their covenant and are, in the words of the Master, "good for nothing, but to be cast out and to be trodden under foot of men" (3 Nephi 12:13).

Further emphasizing the idea of a new day and a new covenant, the Savior said:

"Therefore those things which were of old time, which were under the law, in me are all fulfilled.

"Old things are done away, and all things have become new" (3 Nephi 12:46–47).

Notwithstanding this statement, some were still unclear as to the fulfillment of the law of Moses, and the Savior said to them:

"Marvel not that I said unto you that old things had passed away, and that all things had become new.

"Behold, I say unto you that the law is fulfilled that was given unto Moses.

"Behold, I am he that gave the law, and I am he who covenanted with my people Israel; therefore, the law in me is fulfilled, for I have come to fulfill the law; therefore it hath an end" (3 Nephi 15:3–5).

Then comes the assurance:

"I do not destroy the prophets, for as many as have not been fulfilled in me, verily I say unto you, shall all be fulfilled.

"And because I said unto you that old things have passed away, I do not destroy that which hath been spoken concerning things which are to come.

"For behold, the covenant which I have made with my people is not all fulfilled; but the law which was given unto Moses hath an end in me.

"Behold, I am the law, and the light. Look unto me, and endure to the end, and ye shall live; for unto him that endureth to the end will I give eternal life.

"Behold, I have given unto you the commandments; therefore keep my commandments. And this is the law and the prophets, for they truly testified of me" (3 Nephi 15:6–10).

Turning His attention again to the Twelve, Jesus said: "Ye are my disciples; and ye are a light unto this people, who are a remnant of the house of Joseph.

"And behold, this is the land of your inheritance; and the Father hath given it unto you" (3 Nephi 15:12–13).

OTHER SHEEP

At this point in His discourse Christ linked those of the New World with their counterparts in the Old: "Ye are they of whom I said: Other sheep I have which are not of this fold; them also I must bring, and they shall hear my voice; and there shall be one fold, and one shepherd" (3 Nephi 15:21). The Savior explained that people in the Old World had not understood what He meant when He spoke of "other sheep." Their failure to understand, He said, was the result of "stiffneckedness," "unbelief," and "iniquity" (3 Nephi 15:18–19). This is an instructive note explaining why so many are not able to understand the words of the Savior today. As to those in the Old World, the Savior indicated that if they were to ask, having made the proper spiritual preparations to receive, they could obtain by the Holy Ghost a knowledge of the lost remnants of their family. In either case, the Nephites were commanded to make a record of those sayings that they might go forth to the believing among the Gentiles in a future day (see 3 Nephi 16:4).

Those of the Old World supposed that Christ was referring to the Gentiles in His reference to "other sheep." This indicates that they did not fully understand the implications of the Abrahamic covenant. In the divine economy of things, those of Israel were to be accorded the privilege of His personal appearance while others were to obtain their assurance of saving truths by and through the Holy Ghost. This favored status, Christ said, came by the will of the Father (see 3 Nephi

15:15–24). This is a strong and not particularly popular doctrine. Singularly of the synoptic writers, Matthew is virtually alone in referring to it. This accords with the idea that he was writing to those of his own lineage who knew the scriptural promises. John also makes some references to Israel's favored status in the verses that surround the "other sheep" text. Let us briefly consider the words of both men.

In recording the commission given to the Twelve, Matthew notes that they were directed to limit their preaching and healing ministry to Israel (see Matthew 10:5–6). Both he and Mark record the occasion when the Savior cast a devil out of a Gentile girl because of the faith of her mother. Matthew's language, however, is more emphatic in emphasizing the status of Israel. Matthew has the woman addressing Jesus as both "Lord" and the "Son of David" (Matthew 15:22). Mark records neither. Matthew also recounts that Jesus turned a deaf ear to her plea for help until the Twelve encouraged Him to hear her. He then took the teaching moment, stating, "I am not sent but unto the lost sheep of the house of Israel" (Matthew 15:24). Again she pleaded for His help and He responded, "It is not meet to take the children's bread, and to cast it to dogs [to share it with Gentiles]" (Matthew 15:26). Undaunted, the Gentile woman responded: "Truth, Lord: yet the dogs eat of the crumbs which fall from their masters' table. Then Jesus answered and said unto her, O woman, great is thy faith: be it unto thee even as thou wilt. And her daughter was made whole from that very hour" (Matthew 15:27–28).

Initially, Jesus declined not only to heal the woman's daughter, but even to give courteous response to her for no reason other than that she was a Gentile. Though perhaps less dramatic, the feel of these words recorded by John in the context of the "other sheep" discourse carry much the same spirit:

"Ye believe not, because ye are not of my sheep, as I said unto you.

"My sheep hear my voice, and I know them, and they follow me:

"And I give unto them eternal life; and they shall never perish, neither shall any man pluck them out of my hand.

"My Father, which gave them me, is greater than all; and no man is able to pluck them out of my Father's hand" (John 10:26–29).

A knowledge of worthiness in the premortal existence is essential to understanding such actions. Independent of such understanding, God becomes capricious and grossly unjust. But, when this concept is understood we see Him as both just and wise. Just as whatever degree of intelligence one obtained in the first estate is so much the advantage in mortal probation, likewise the first to be gathered or brought into the gospel fold are those prepared to listen, those born with faith and a propensity to be obedient, those whom He can send forth to declare the saving truths of the gospel to all the nations of the earth. These are the spirits that God promised Abraham would be born as his seed.[5]

THE COVENANT MEAL AND THE SACRAMENT

What we have traditionally supposed to be the ordinance of sacrament is recorded in both chapters 18 and 20 of 3 Nephi. A careful reading suggests that something more is taking place. First, the purpose of the sacrament is the renewal of the covenant of baptism. Earlier in the day's activities the Savior had called the Twelve and commissioned them to baptize, or rebaptize as the case might be, all who sought membership in the Church and kingdom of God. At this point, however, none of them had been baptized. The Twelve were baptized between Christ's first and second visits, but there is no indication that anyone else was. The other baptisms would have to wait until after the three-day ministry of the Savior. Second, it should also be noted that the administration of the sacrament preceded Christ's formal conferral of authority on the newly called Twelve.

The third peculiarity of these two sacrament services is the emphasis given to the fact that all present made a meal of the bread and wine. This is particularly clear in the first instance. Following Christ's breaking and blessing the bread, we read: "And when they [the Twelve] had eaten and were filled, he commanded that they should give unto the multitude. And when the multitude had eaten and were filled" (3 Nephi 18:4–5). In like manner, following His administering of the wine, we read that after the Twelve were "filled," they "gave unto the multitude, and they did drink, and they were filled" (3 Nephi 18:9).

When I have asked classes what the implications of this are, they have been quick to respond that it means that the multitude were filled with the Spirit. Yet they had already heard the audible voice of God introduce His Son from heaven, witnessed the descent of the Son of Man, heard Him testify of His divine Sonship, witnessed the appearance of angels and a circling flame of fire, witnessed mass healings, and had their children blessed. To suppose that they had not yet been filled with the Spirit is inconceivable.

In the instance of the first sacrament service, the Savior sent the Twelve to get bread and wine. In the second instance He miraculously provided it. This second instance is obviously a New World counterpart of His feeding of the multitude in the Old World. The number present on this occasion is unknown but was far in excess of the 2,500 who had been in attendance the previous day.

It should also be noted that there would have been a need for physical nourishment, if not for the adults, then certainly for the children. Consider the time it would take for approximately 2,500 people to personally handle and feel the wounds in His hands and His feet. For each of them to have shared ten seconds with the Savior would have consumed nearly seven hours.

In the context of the covenant traditions of Israel, it seems a natural thing to suppose that this was a covenant meal after the pattern of the one recorded in Exodus 24 where Moses, Aaron, Nadab, Abihu, and the seventy princes or elders of Israel went up on the side of Sinai (symbolically the holy place) and there saw God and "did eat and drink" (Exodus 24:11). This text is almost universally understood as referring to the eating of a covenant meal by the representatives of Israel in the presence of God on the holy mountain.[6] One commentary notes: "By means of the meal, Yahweh takes the whole community, represented by the clan elders, into his family. The meal is the assurance and support given by the superior, Yahweh, to the inferior, Israel."[7] The idea of two parties eating and drinking together to formally ratify a covenant is common to both the Bible and the customs of the ancient Near East.[8] To eat together was to be bound together by mutual obligation.[9] The meal was a seal of the alliance whereby "the weaker is taken into the family of the stronger," who provides the meal.[10]

The Old Testament and the Book of Mormon occasions have obvious similarities. The place of the meal in both cases is the temple or the holy mount, which represents the temple. Both meals are in the presence of the God of Israel. The occasion in both instances is the introduction of a new gospel dispensation. Symbolically, both represent a ratifying seal of the covenant the people have made.

After the three-day ministry in the Americas, it appears that the more traditional sacrament observance became the order of the day. Indeed, we read that Christ continued to appear to His disciples on many occasions to break bread and bless it for them (see 3 Nephi 26:13).

THE DAY OF THE GENTILES

Perhaps no part of Christ's instruction to the Nephites, relative to the promises of the covenant and the events of the last days, has been more misunderstood than those things He said relative to the days of the Gentiles. This section will attempt to unravel that misunderstanding.

Taking the meridian of time as a starting point, the gospel was preached first to the Jews and thereafter to the Gentiles. In our dispensation, the dispensation of the fulness of times, the gospel was, according to prophecy, brought forth by Gentiles who in turn will take it to all the nations of the earth. After the Gentiles have had ample opportunity to receive it and then turn on it in wickedness, it will be taken from them and given back to its original stewards. Thus, the first shall be last and the last first (see 1 Nephi 13:42).

When we speak of the day of the Gentiles being fulfilled, we are speaking of that time when "the consumption decreed" will make "a full end of all nations" (D&C 87:6) and a messianic kingdom will be established in their stead. Thus, the day of the Gentile will end—its power, authority, and influence will be no more. With the millennial kingdom established, the great work of the gathering of all the tribes of Israel will continue until Jacob's sons enjoy that glory and power of which King David's and King Solomon's days were but a type and shadow (see 3 Nephi 21:13–18; 22).

Three times the Savior refers to the words of Micah relative to the remnant of Jacob, who are to be "among the Gentiles in the midst of many people as a lion among the beasts of the forest, as a young lion among the flocks of sheep: who, if he go through, both treadeth down, and teareth in pieces, and none can deliver" (Micah 5:8; see also 3 Nephi 16:15; 20:16; 21:12). Interpretations of this are plentiful. Typically, they center in a censuring labor of the Lamanites within the Church. In fact, the prophecy was directed to *all* the remnants of Israel, not just one. Furthermore, the censuring is to be among "all the nations of the Gentiles" (3 Nephi 20:20) not just those in the New World. This is not a matter of someone posing as one mighty and strong coming forward to purge the Church.

This warning, as it is given in 3 Nephi 16, may be directed at the United States and those who were members of the Church but have drifted from it. It invites the Gentiles to "turn" to the Lord and speaks of those who fail to do so as "salt that hath lost its savor" (3 Nephi 16:15), thus intimating that a covenant had once been made. The twentieth chapter speaks in the broader context of all the house of Israel and all the nations of the earth. It then speaks of the New Jerusalem that is to be built in the Americas. It intimates that all the land will be a New Zion or New Jerusalem (see 3 Nephi 20:22).[11] In this chapter, the Savior reminds the Nephites that they are the children of the prophets, that they are of Israel and are rightful heirs of the covenant. He further notes that in and through them all the families of the earth are to receive the blessings of the gospel (see 3 Nephi 20:27).

In 3 Nephi 21 the Lord promises a sign whereby the things He has promised might be confirmed. The sign is the establishment of a free people in the United States of America, the Restoration of the gospel, the coming forth of the Book of Mormon, the martyrdom of the Prophet Joseph Smith, and His own eternal triumph. The Lord declares that those who reject the testimony of the Book of Mormon will, as Moses promised, "be cut off" from the Lord's people, meaning they will be left without root or branch in the eternities to come (see 3 Nephi 11:1–26).

Again the passages from Micah are quoted, and this time the announcement is made that those who repent will be members of Christ's Church and numbered among those of the covenant. These, the Lord said, will be called on to assist the remnant of Jacob in building the New Jerusalem (see 3 Nephi 21:12–24). Then, in what is clearly a millennial context, the announcement is made that the work of the Father in gathering Israel will commence. Four times the word *commence* is used relative to the gathering of Israel in the context of the Millennium (see 3 Nephi 21:26–28).

SEEING THE SALVATION OF OUR GOD

Third Nephi could be seen as a type for the Second Coming of Christ: it establishes the pattern. First will come the destruction of the wicked, those who have rejected the prophets and who have the blood of the Saints on their hands. Then, the Savior will come suddenly, as Malachi prophesied, to His temple, where He will greet His covenant people. Here the assurance will again be given that the promises made to the fathers will all be fulfilled and the ancient covenant renewed. At this time, all Gentile governments will end and the day of the Israelites will begin. In the Millennium, the gathering of Israel will begin in earnest as the lost tribes are gathered into the fold, and those waiting to join the Church will far outnumber those who have already embraced the covenant of salvation. Thus, it will be necessary to enlarge the place of Israel's tent, to lengthen the cords and strengthen the stakes (see 3 Nephi 21:23–29; 22).

GUIDELINES FOR UNDERSTANDING THE PROMISES TO THE COVENANT PEOPLE IN 3 NEPHI

Third Nephi contains some key passages relative to the promises of the Lord to the house of Israel. I have particular reference to chapters 16, 20, and 21. These passages have been misunderstood and misused. Often this happens innocently, sometimes not. Unstable views frequently strain the meaning of these texts to justify speculative or personally aggrandizing views. To that end, perhaps these observations ought to be made:

1. The Book of Mormon came forth to gather Israel—all Israel, not a particular or exclusive part of Israel. On the title page Moroni states that the purpose of the book is "to show unto the remnant of the House of Israel what great things the Lord hath done for their fathers;

and that they may know the covenants of the Lord, that they are not cast off forever." Note that the emphasis is on *the* remnant of Israel, not *a* remnant. Long before Christ visited the Nephites, Israel had been scattered throughout the earth (see 1 Nephi 22:4), thus Christ's announcement to the Nephites that there were still others whom He had been commanded of the Father to visit. All these scattered remnants of Jacob have claim on the promises made to their fathers. Each is "a remnant of Jacob," and collectively they are "the remnant." We can be confident that the same promises given to the remnant of Jacob in the Americas were also given to the rest of Jacob's children, wherever they may have been when the resurrected Christ visited them.

2. These chapters cannot be properly understood in isolation from the rest of the covenant sermon. They assume an understanding of the call and ordination of the Twelve (see 3 Nephi 18:36; Moroni 2:2). The whole idea of there being "twelve" instead of some other number is their symbolic representation of the twelve tribes of Israel. The unity with which they stand at the head of the Church was and is to be a constant reminder of the Lord's promise to unite all of Israel in His millennial kingdom. The gathering of Israel and building of Zion must take place under their direction. Any doctrine that holds that some remnant of Israel can do some portion of the gathering or the building of Zion independent of the direction of the Twelve, or likewise any leader who comes on the scene to do some marvelous thing independent of their direction, is out of harmony with the covenant of baptism and the covenant to sustain the Twelve, with which the Savior began His instruction to the Nephites (see 3 Nephi 12:1).

It ought also to be observed that the same pattern and principle exists in our dispensation. The keys of the gathering of Israel and the building of Zion rest with the First Presidency and the Twelve but no others. The Church is governed by modern revelation, not the writings of ancient prophets. Isaiah may have stood at the head of the Church in his day but he does not stand at the head of the Church in our day. The Book of Mormon unlocks the book of Isaiah, not the other way around.

3. Spiritual stability and sound understanding are not found in strained phrases. We ought to be inherently suspicious of interpretations

that aggrandize a particular group or some marvelous or mighty leader who is going to come onto the scene to straighten out the Church. The Twelve are in place. I have read the agreement that the phrase "the arm of the Lord" was reference to a special servant of the Lord who is to come on the scene and save the day when present leaders fall short of their calling. It rather strains the idea of "the arm of the Lord" to suppose that it no longer needs to be attached to the body. In the realm of my experience, arms are always an appendage to a body and do not operate without it. Nor is it reasonable to suppose that the keys given the Twelve will be taken from them or surrendered by them to some individual who supposes himself to be the one mighty and strong called to set the Church in order.

4. Wisdom suggests moderation and caution in scriptural interpretation. In discussing chapters 16, 20, and 21, Elder McConkie suggested that there were things contained therein that the Lord had not chosen to make plain at the present time. It would be unwise for us to attempt to clarify what the Lord or His covenant spokesmen have not. In writing on these chapters Elder McConkie observed: "It is not always possible for us in our present state of spiritual enlightenment to put every event into an exact category or time frame." He also noted that some of these texts "apply to both pre- and post-millennial events; some have an initial and partial fulfillment in our day and shall have a second and grander completion in the days ahead."[12]

5. In a past general conference we were warned about false views relative to the gathering. The warning was specifically against "cults" and "colonies."[13] The caution was to beware of those who think themselves a part of some inner circle, who think their understanding is ahead of those called to hold the keys of the gathering of Israel and thus think they are to preside over all that takes place relative to it.

CONCLUSION

Moroni told Joseph Smith that the "fulness of the everlasting Gospel" was to be found in the instruction given by the Savior to the Nephites (see JS–H 1:34). The message of Christ recorded there centers on the blessings and obligations of a covenant people. "Ye are the children of the prophets," Christ told them, "and ye are of the house of Israel; and ye are of the covenant which the Father made with your fathers, saying unto Abraham: And in thy seed shall all the kindreds of the earth be blessed" (3 Nephi 20:25).

The chosen seed of Abraham have the promise that they will be endowed with the fulness of all gospel blessings. Such is their right by birth. It is the obligation of those so endowed to carry those same blessings of salvation to all others that all the kindreds of the earth might be blessed. According to the Abrahamic covenant, Christ endowed the Nephites with the fulness of His gospel and the promise that in and through them all nations of the earth would be blessed. This becomes literally so as their testament, or record of Christ, in the form of the Book of Mormon, goes forth in these the last days to gather the honest in heart out of all nations. That gathering, as the Book of Mormon attests, will be to the covenants of salvation which bring with them the fulness of all gospel blessings.

We too are the seed of Abraham and as such are heirs of the same promises and thus recipients of the same obligations as have been the faithful Saints in all ages. Like our ancient counterparts we have been blessed with the fulness of the gospel and the obligation to declare it among all nations and peoples. As ours is the God of our fathers, so ours is the gospel of our fathers. Their hearts were turned to us, and ours turn to them. Their covenant is our covenant, and their testimony becomes our testimony as we boldly declare the message of the Book of Mormon to all the nations of the earth.

NOTES

1. Bruce R. McConkie, *The Mortal Messiah* (Salt Lake City: Deseret Book, 1980), 2:102.

2. I was interested to find the following by A. B. Bruce: "The number twelve was recommended by obvious symbolic reasons. It happily expressed in figures what Jesus claimed to be, and what He had come to do, and thus furnished a support to the faith and a stimulus to the devotion of His followers. It significantly hinted that Jesus was the divine Messianic King of Israel, come to set up

the kingdom whose advent was foretold by prophets in glowing language, suggested by the balmy days of Israel's history, when the theocratic community existed in its integrity, and all the tribes of the chosen nation were united under the royal house of David" (*The Training of the Twelve* [Grand Rapids: Krogel, 1971], 32).

3. *A Dictionary of Christ and the Gospels* (New York: Charles Scribner's Sons, 1908), 1:105.

4. See Joseph Smith, *History of the Church of Jesus Christ of Latter-day Saints,* ed. B. H. Roberts, 2d ed., rev. (Salt Lake City: Deseret Book, 1980), 4:538.

5. See McConkie, *Mortal Messiah,* 3:218–19.

6. E. W. Nicholson, "The Interpretation of Exodus XXIV 9–11," *Vesta Testamentum,* January 1974, 84.

7. Dianne Bergant and Robert J. Karris, eds., *The Collegeville Bible Commentary* (Collegeville, Minn.: Liturgical Press, 1989), 104.

8. See John F. Walvoord and Roy B. Zuck, eds., *The Bible Knowledge Commentary: Old Testament* (Wheaton, Ill.: Victor, 1985), 2:146. Examples would include the covenant made between Isaac and Abimelech (see Genesis 26:26–31); the statement in Genesis 31:54, which reads, "Then Jacob offered sacrifice upon the mount, and called his brethren to eat bread: and they did eat bread, and tarried all night in the mount"; and the meeting in the king's dale between Melchizedek and Abraham (see Genesis 14:17–20). The Joseph Smith Translation of this last example reads, "and he *break bread and blest it; and he blest the wine,* he being the priest of the most high God (Joseph Smith Translation, Genesis 14:17; emphasis added).

9. See Paul J. Achtemeier, ed., *Harper's Bible Dictionary* (San Francisco: Harper & Row, 1985), 616.

10. Dennis J. McCarthy, *Treaty and Covenant* (Rome: Biblical Institute Press, 1978), 254.

11. See Bruce R. McConkie, *The Millennial Messiah* (Salt Lake City: Deseret Book, 1982), 301.

12. McConkie, *The Millennial Messiah,* 251.

13. Boyd K. Packer, "'To Be Learned Is Good If . . .'" *Ensign,* November 1992, 71.

22

One by One: The Fifth Gospel's Model of Service

Richard Neitzel Holzapfel

The New Testament portrays Jesus Christ's mortal work as a mission not only to large groups but also to individuals. The Gospel narratives indicate that in many cases there was direct physical contact between Jesus and individuals as He ministered among the people. For example, when He healed Peter's mother-in-law of a fever, Jesus "*touched* her hand" (Matthew 8:14–15; emphasis added; see also Mark 1:30–31; Luke 4:38–39). Jesus again "put forth his hand, and *touched*" a man with leprosy to make him whole (Matthew 8:1–3; emphasis added). He touched the eyes of two blind men as He healed them (see Matthew 9:27–31). He healed deafness and a speech impediment when He put His fingers "into" a man's ears (Mark 7:32–37). He "put his hands upon" a blind man (Mark 8:22–26). He healed a demoniac child when He "took him by the hand and lifted him up" (Mark 9:14–29; see also Matthew 17:14–21; Luke 9:37–43). The Savior healed Jarius' daughter when He "took her by the hand" and raised her from the dead (Matthew 9:23–26; see also Mark 5:35–42; Luke 8:49–55). The New Testament Gospels record many more miracles in which direct physical contact may have been possible.[1]

Richard Neitzel Holzapfel is an associate professor of Church history and doctrine at Brigham Young University.

Occasionally, individuals reached out to touch the Savior, as was the case when the woman with an issue of blood "*touched* the border of his garment" (see Luke 8:43–46; emphasis added). In some instances, however, there was more involved than the simple act of touching. In the case of the woman just cited, Jesus said He knew "that virtue is gone out of me" (Luke 8:46). Joseph Smith explained that "the virtue here referred to is the spirit of life" and that we sometimes become weakened when giving blessings.[2] These remarks by Jesus and Joseph Smith imply a transfer of power in such ministrations.

According to Mark and Luke, Jesus often healed not merely by touching the individual but through a more formal laying on of hands (see Mark 5:23; 6:5; 7:32; 8:22–25; Luke 4:40; 13:13), and He enjoined the disciples to do the same (see Mark 16:18). Healing was also often conveyed through this laying on of hands in the post-Resurrection Church (see Acts 9:12, 17; 28:8). Jesus also blessed children by laying hands on them (see Mark 10:13–16). *Laying on of hands* has a distinct meaning and purpose in the Bible. Authority or power was not passed literally through the arms and hands to the individual, but laying on of hands was a symbolic representation of who or what was the focus of the ritual action. The Old Testament usage of laying on of hands related to sacrifice and succession in office. In the New Testament, it was associated with healing, with baptism with the Holy Spirit, and with assignment to specific administrative tasks in the Church. All the examples mentioned in the New Testament of the laying on of hands have the following underlying unifying characteristics: the context is always sacred, as frequent mention of prayer shows, and in each instance something is achieved through the practice, even though the laying on of hands is a symbolic action.

3 NEPHI—THE FIFTH GOSPEL

Third Nephi, sometimes referred to as the fifth Gospel in Latter-day Saint circles, describes Christ's post-Resurrection ministry to the Nephites in terms similar to those used in the four New Testament Gospels. It emphasizes the individual experiences of the Nephite people with the resurrected Messiah, noting their direct physical contact with

Him as well as His laying on of hands as the symbolic act of transmitting authority and power. In addition, various forms of the word *minister* are used in connection with these experiences. In his introduction to the appearance narrative, Mormon states, "Behold, I will show unto you that the people . . . did have great favors shown unto them, and great blessings poured out upon their heads, insomuch that soon after the ascension of Christ into heaven he did truly manifest himself unto them—showing his body unto them, and *ministering* unto them; and an account of his *ministry* shall be given hereafter" (3 Nephi 10:18–19; emphasis added).

The Book of Mormon account of Jesus' ministry among the Nephites sharpens our understanding of the principle of service by showing how true disciples should minister to others. That account is clearer and more precise than the New Testament account on many points relating to the Gospel. It focuses not only on the words of Jesus (doctrine) but also on His actions (application of the doctrines). By the power of Christ, Mormon saw into the future—our day (see Mormon 3:16–22). It therefore seems fair to assume that He carefully selected material to provide lessons rooted in our own situation. After Jesus revealed Himself to the Nephites, He taught by word and example the correlation among individual experience, touching (laying on of hands in many cases), and ministry. The Book of Mormon uses the term *minister* and its variants to mean both giving individual attention and symbolically transferring power through touching or the laying on of hands.

When Christ appeared to the ancient inhabitants of America, He invited them to "thrust your hands into my side, and also that ye may feel the prints of the nails in my hands and in my feet, that ye may know that I am the God of Israel, and the God of the whole earth, and have been slain for the sins of the world" (3 Nephi 11:14). All the people gathered at the temple in Bountiful "went forth, and thrust their hands into his side, and did feel the prints of the nails in his hands and in his feet" (3 Nephi 11:15), and when they had brought their sick and afflicted and their children, there were as many as 2,500 people (see 3 Nephi 17:25). To emphasize the experience, Mormon states, "And this they did do, going forth *one by one* until they had all gone forth [until they all saw] with their eyes and did feel with their hands" (3 Nephi 11:15; emphasis added). The cumulative effect of the personal experience left them all worshiping Jesus and crying, "Hosanna! Blessed be the name of the Most High God!" (3 Nephi 11:17).

ORDINANCES ONE BY ONE

The resurrected Savior then taught that holy ordinances were to be performed individually. He detailed the procedure for performing the ordinance of baptism:

"Verily I say unto you that whoso repenteth of his sins through your words, and desireth to be baptized in my name, on this wise shall ye baptize them—Behold, ye shall go down and stand in the water, and in my name shall ye baptize them.

"And now behold, these are the words which ye shall say, calling them by name, saying:

"Having authority given me of Jesus Christ, I baptize you in the name of the Father, and of the Son, and of the Holy Ghost. Amen.

"And then shall ye immerse them in the water, and come forth again out of the water" (3 Nephi 11:23–26).

It is significant that each person was to be specifically called by name and then immersed individually in the water by the one performing the ordinance.

Nephi baptized the disciples in the manner prescribed—one by one. The record states,

"And it came to pass that Nephi went down into the water and was baptized. And he came up out of the water and began to baptize. And he baptized all those whom Jesus had chosen" (3 Nephi 19:11–12). The Book of Mormon confirms that those baptized were ministered to further: "And it came to pass when they were all baptized and had come up out of the water, the Holy Ghost did fall upon them, and they were filled with the Holy Ghost and with fire. And behold, they were encircled about as if it were by fire; and it came down from heaven, and the multitude did witness it, and did bear record; and angels did come down out of heaven and did *minister* unto them. And it came to pass that while the angels were *ministering* unto the disciples, behold, Jesus came and stood in the midst and *ministered* unto them" (3 Nephi 19:13–15; emphasis added).

Like the New Testament paradigm (see Mark 1:31; 15:41; Luke 8:3), ministry in the Book of Mormon appears to be something spontaneous. As the disciples baptized others, each believer received the gift of the Holy Spirit and was further ministered unto.

Christ also blessed the sick among the Nephites as He had done during His mortal ministry in the Holy Land: "For I perceive that ye desire that I should show unto you what I have done unto your brethren at Jerusalem, for I see that your faith is sufficient that I should heal you" (3 Nephi 17:8). The sacred record continues, "And it came to pass that when he had thus spoken, all the multitude, with one accord, did go forth with their sick and their afflicted, and their lame, and with their blind, and with their dumb, and with all them that were afflicted in any manner; and he did heal them every one as they were brought forth unto him" (3 Nephi 17:9). It seems reasonable to assume that the Savior had power to heal all present among the Nephites without their being brought forth to Him. Even before His resurrection, the Savior healed people in groups without touching them and was able to heal those not within a specific proximity to Himself (see Mark 7:24–30; Luke 7:1–9). The Lord chose among the Nephites, however, to have the sick brought close to Him, and as the record implies, He touched each one personally.

Following this great healing occasion, Jesus commanded the people to bring "their little children and set them down upon the ground round about him." Then "he took their little children, *one by one,* and blessed them, and prayed unto the Father for them.

"And when he had done this he wept again;

"And he spake unto the multitude, and said unto them: Behold your little ones.

"And as they looked to behold they cast their eyes towards heaven, and they saw the heavens open, and they saw angels descending out of heaven as it were in the midst of fire; and they came down and encircled those little ones about, and they were encircled about with fire; and the angels did *minister* unto them" (3 Nephi 17:12, 21–24; emphasis added).

The book of 3 Nephi continues to record the words and deeds of Christ as He instructed the disciples regarding the sacrament. "And this shall ye do . . . , which I have shown unto you. And it shall be a testimony unto the Father that ye do always remember me. And if ye do always remember me ye shall have my Spirit to be with you" (3 Nephi 18:7). He gave similar instructions regarding the cup of wine (see 3 Nephi 18:11). A day later, Jesus provided bread and wine miraculously and again administered the sacrament unto the people (see 3 Nephi 20:1–9). Both sacramental experiences included the giving of bread and wine to each individual.

After Jesus instituted the sacrament among the Nephites, He gave the disciples power to confer the Holy Ghost: "And it came to pass that when Jesus had made an end of these sayings, he *touched* with his hand the disciples whom he had chosen, *one by one,* even until he had *touched* them all, and spake unto them as *he touched* them" (3 Nephi 18:36; emphasis added). Although the multitude did not hear what Jesus said, the disciples "bare record that he gave them power to give the Holy Ghost" (3 Nephi 18:37).

Though it is probable that Jesus ordained the New Testament apostles through the laying on of hands, the present New Testament text does not allude to that event, nor is there evidence that Matthias was assigned Judas' place among the Twelve through the laying on of hands. Here again, the fifth Gospel highlights Jesus' actions and clarifies the New Testament procedure of calling and ordaining the Twelve to minister. Moroni adds to our understanding of their calling:

"The words of Christ, which he spake unto his disciples, the twelve whom he had chosen, as he laid his hands upon them—

"And he called them by name, saying: Ye shall call on the Father in my name, in mighty prayer; and after ye have done this ye shall have power that to him upon whom ye shall lay your hands, ye shall give the Holy Ghost; and in my name shall ye give it, for thus do mine apostles. Now Christ spake these words unto them at the time of his first appearing; and the multitude heard it not, but the disciples heard it; and on as many as they laid their hands, fell the Holy Ghost" (Moroni 2:1–3).

THE NEPHITE DISCIPLES' MINISTRY

In the New Testament period, Jesus chose His own disciples (see John 6:70; 15:16, 19). Likewise, in the Book of Mormon account, it is Christ who initiated the call to ministry (see 3 Nephi 11:18–22; 12:1; 18:36). This point was emphasized when Jesus said, while looking on the newly called twelve, "For behold, ye are they whom I have chosen to *minister* unto these people" (3 Nephi 13:25; emphasis added). Once called, the Lord touched the disciples individually as they began a ministry similar to what Jesus had already done among them:

"And it came to pass that when Jesus had made an end of these sayings, *he touched* with his hand the disciples whom he had chosen, one by one, even until he had *touched* them all, and spake unto them as *he touched* them. . . .

"And it came to pass that when Jesus had touched them all, there came a cloud and overshadowed the multitude" (3 Nephi 18:36, 38; emphasis added).

Thus, a conceptual thread weaves together the themes of calling, touching, and laying on of hands (see 3 Nephi 17:24; 19:14).

The disciples' ministry was not limited to the righteous; but a ministry to the "unworthy" was also enjoined by the Savior. Although strict commandments were given to those administering the holy ordinances regarding the need for holiness in receiving such blessings, the Lord stated concerning the unworthy, "Ye shall not cast him out from among you, but ye shall *minister* unto him and shall pray for him unto the Father, in my name." When the individual came forward with a broken heart and contrite spirit, then the true disciple was to "*minister* unto him of my flesh and blood" (3 Nephi 18:30; emphasis added). Even if a person continued in an unrepentant state, Christ commanded that "ye shall not cast him out of your synagogues, or your places of worship, for unto such shall ye continue to *minister;* for ye know not but what they will return and repent, and come unto me with full purpose of heart" (3 Nephi 18:32; emphasis added). Taking the model of ministering to the physically infirm, the Lord applied the same principle to the spiritually infirm; the disciples should bring them to Jesus, who promised, "I shall heal them" (3 Nephi 18:32).

Almost immediately thereafter, Jesus "departed from them, and ascended into heaven" (3 Nephi 18:39). When the people left for their homes, "it was noised abroad among the people immediately, before it was yet dark, that the multitude had seen Jesus, and that he had *ministered* unto them, and that he would also show himself on the morrow unto the multitude" (3 Nephi 19:2; emphasis added). On the following day, the numbers grew "so great that [the disciples] did cause that they should be separated into twelve bodies" (3 Nephi 19:5). Mormon summarizes the experience:

"Therefore, I would that ye should behold that the Lord truly did teach the people, for the space of three days; and after that he did show himself unto them oft, and did break bread oft, and bless it, and give it unto them.

"And it came to pass that he did teach and *minister* unto the children of the multitude of whom hath been spoken. . . .

"And it came to pass that after he had ascended into heaven—the second time that he showed himself unto them . . . after having healed all their sick, and their lame, and opened the eyes of their blind and unstopped the ears of the deaf, and even had done all manner of cures among them, and raised a man from the dead, and had shown forth his power unto them. . . .

"Behold, it came to pass on the morrow that the multitude gathered themselves together. . . .

"And it came to pass that the disciples whom Jesus had chosen began from that time forth to baptize and to teach as many as did come unto them; and as many as were baptized in the name of Jesus were filled with the Holy Ghost. . . .

"And they taught, and did *minister* one to another; and they had all things common among them, every man dealing justly, one with another.

"And it came to pass that they did do all things even as Jesus had commanded them.

"And they who were baptized in the name of Jesus were called the church of Christ" (3 Nephi 26:13–17, 19–21; emphasis added).

On a later visit with the Nephite disciples, the Savior spake unto them *"one by one"* and asked each one, "What is it that ye desire of me, after that I am gone to the Father?" (3 Nephi 28:1; emphasis added). Nine of them responded, "We desire that after we have lived unto the age of man, that our *ministry,* wherein thou hast called us, may have an end, that we may speedily come unto thee in thy kingdom" (3 Nephi 28:2; emphasis added). The remaining three desired to stay on the earth and continue their labors until Jesus would come again. Then He "*touched* every one of them with his finger save it were the three who were to tarry, and then he departed" (3 Nephi 28:12; emphasis added). These three were then miraculously "caught up into heaven," but when they returned to earth they "did again *minister* upon the face of the earth" (3 Nephi 28:13, 16; emphasis added).

These special disciples, Mormon indicates, "did go forth upon the face of the land, and did *minister* unto all the people" (3 Nephi 28:18; emphasis added). Nearly four hundred years later, Mormon testified that He knew they were still on earth: "I have seen them, and they have *ministered* unto me" (3 Nephi 28:26; emphasis added). He notes that their mission would be among Jews and Gentiles, where "they shall *minister* unto all the scattered tribes of Israel, and unto all nations, kindreds, tongues and people" (3 Nephi 28:29; emphasis added).

The disciples of Jesus were to duplicate the experiences they had shared with Christ: "Verily, verily, I say unto you, this is my gospel; and ye know the thing that ye must do in my church; for the works which ye have seen me do that shall ye also do; for that which ye have seen me do even that shall ye do" (3 Nephi 27:21).

Mormon introduces the entire appearance narrative (see the note before 3 Nephi 11) with these words, "Jesus Christ did show himself unto the people of Nephi, as the multitude were gathered together in the land Bountiful, and did *minister* unto them" (emphasis added). According to Mormon's introduction, Jesus did two things: first, He showed Himself to the people, and second, He ministered unto them.

Ministering was obviously an essential element of the visit of Christ among the Nephites.

CONCLUSION

During His New Testament labors, Jesus often addressed multitudes and performed miracles among them. On many occasions He spoke directly to individuals, and in several cases He touched them and healed them. But in several instances, He laid His hands on people, symbolizing the action taken to the individual. The 3 Nephi record replicates and emphasizes Christ's New Testament model of ministry by words and deeds.

According to the Book of Mormon model, ministering often occurs "one by one" as disciples come in contact with the Savior and with one another. In many cases a personal "touch" is a symbolic means of transmitting God's love and power to an individual. In several instances, however, the touch is another way of expressing that hands were laid upon an individual. The context of these several examples among the Nephites seems to indicate that an ordinance is being performed by the *laying on of hands* (see 3 Nephi 18:36). Being chosen to minister is also a call to serve innocent and pure children and the faithful Saints, just as Jesus and the angels did during His appearance among the Nephites.

As disciples of Jesus Christ, we should recognize that Jesus swept away the legalistic regulations of the Mosaic code and touched those who had been considered "untouchable" under the law (see 3 Nephi 17:7, see also Leviticus 13; 3 Nephi 15:2–9). He commanded the Nephite disciples to do the same and encouraged them to invite everyone to join with them in worship as they ministered to one another. Likewise, for the modern believer, a call to discipleship is more than just joining a study class. It is a call to perform the work of the Lord and His angels spontaneously, to minister as a servant among mortals. In particular, it is a call to serve the physically, mentally, emotionally, economically, and spiritually infirm, modern society's "untouchables." These individuals should not be "cast out from among" us but should be ministered to and touched by true disciples, as Jesus demonstrated.

Through the ordinances of the gospel performed individually, and as prescribed by the resurrected Savior by His chosen disciples, "the power of godliness is manifest" (D&C 84:20).

NOTES

1. See Matthew 8:28–32; 9:2–8; 20:30–34; Mark 1:21–28; 5:1–20; 10:46–52; Luke 4:31–37; 6:6–11; 7:11–17; 8:26–36; 11:14; 13:11–13; 14:1–4; 18:35–43; 22:50–51; John 5:1–9; and 9:1–17.

2. Joseph Smith, *Teachings of the Prophet Joseph Smith,* comp. Joseph Fielding Smith (Salt Lake City: Deseret Book, 1976), 281.

23

"This Is My Gospel"

Robert L. Millet

After at least two days of instruction, worship, and intense spiritual experience, the risen Lord appeared once again to His American Hebrews. The twelve disciples of the Nephites "were gathered together and were united in mighty prayer and fasting." When Jesus appeared, He inquired as to their desires. "Lord," they answered, "we will that thou wouldst tell us the name whereby we shall call this church; for there are disputations among the people concerning this matter" (3 Nephi 27:1–3). In this context the living Christ sets forth some of the most straightforward yet profound doctrine to be found in the entire Book of Mormon concerning the name and mission of His Church.

HIS NAME AND HIS CHURCH

It is not clear why disputations arose among the Nephites concerning the name of the Church. Since the days of Alma, in which a formal church structure and organization had been established, it appears that the Saints had been called the members of the "church of Christ" or the "church of God" (see Mosiah 18:17; 25:18, 23; Alma

---

Robert L. Millet is the Richard L. Evans Professor of Religious Understanding and former dean of Religious Education at Brigham Young University.

4:5; 3 Nephi 26:21). With the end of the Mosaic dispensation and the initiation of the Messianic, a new day had dawned; it was the meridian or focal point of salvation history, the age in which the Lord Omnipotent, the long-awaited promised Messiah, would "come down from heaven among the children of men, and . . . dwell in a tabernacle of clay" (Mosiah 3:5). We recall that Jesus had earlier given the priesthood authority to baptize to Nephi and the twelve disciples (see 3 Nephi 11:22) when in fact they already held authority from God to perform the saving ordinances. Likewise, Jesus baptized those who had previously been baptized (see 3 Nephi 19:10–12). But it was a new day, a new light, and a new revelation.[1]

Even though the Nephites had held the fulness of the priesthood and had enjoyed the blessings of the everlasting gospel from the days of Lehi and Nephi, they continued to observe the law of Moses. That is, they offered sacrifice just as Adam had done two and a half millennia before, and they conformed to the law's "myriad moral principles and its endless ethical restrictions. . . . There is . . . no intimation in the Book of Mormon that the Nephites offered the daily sacrifices required by the law or that they held the various feasts that were part of the religious life of their Old World kinsmen."[2] Because the faithful among the Nephites accepted and treasured the blessings of the gospel, because they looked forward with an eye of faith to the coming of the Holy One, because they knew full well the central message of the law and thus comprehended with certainty the law as a means to Him who was and is the great End, the law of Moses had become dead unto them. They were "alive in Christ because of [their] faith" in Him (2 Nephi 25:25) and because they had learned to distinguish tokens from covenants and ritual from religion. It was a new era—the beginning of the Dispensation of the Meridian of Time—and they had only recently been initiated anew into the covenants and ordinances (see 3 Nephi 11:22). Perhaps for these reasons the people had begun to wonder if there was a new or different name by which the congregation of Christians in this new dispensation was to be called and known.

The Master's words to His chosen twelve suggest that there may have been some among the Nephites who proposed to name the church something other than the Church of Jesus Christ:

"Verily, verily, I say unto you, why is it that the people should murmur and dispute because of this thing?

"Have they not read the scriptures, which say ye must take upon you the name of Christ, which is my name? For by this name shall ye be called at the last day;

"And whoso taketh upon him my name, and endureth to the end, the same shall be saved at the last day" (3 Nephi 27:4–6).

Our Lord's words are most instructive. The Church or body of Christ is a true and living thing only to the degree that it is imbued and animated by Christ. Like an individual, the Church must take upon it the name of Christ—His divine influence, attributes, and nature—in order to enjoy His transforming powers. Those who are noble in character, kindly in deed and manner, considerate and compassionate—what the bulk of the Western world would call "Christian" in nature—but who refuse to take upon themselves the name of Christ (and all that such a commitment entails), are not fully Christ's, nor are they Christians in the total and complete sense. They remain in a lost and fallen state, yielding to the enticings of the spirit of the evil one and to the nature of things in a fallen world. They are without God in the world (see Alma 41:11) and, as such, are without tie to the family of God. They are spiritual orphans, nameless and family-less, in a lone and dreary world. And what of the Church? It is made up of people, and to the degree that those congregants are as yet unredeemed and unregenerated, the Church cannot be the light that is so desperately needed in a darkened world, cannot make available that life and that energy that flow from its great Head.

From the days of Adam, the divine decree has gone forth: "Thou shalt do all that thou doest in the name of the Son, and thou shalt repent and call upon God in the name of the Son forevermore" (Moses 5:8). *All* things are to be done in His holy name—*all* things. We are to speak, act, preach, and prophesy in the name of the Son. We are to heal the sick and raise the dead in the name of the Son. We are to conduct the business of the Church and perform the ordinances of salvation in the name of the Son. We are to do what we do in the name of Jesus Christ and speak and act the way our blessed Master would under similar circumstances. The holy scriptures—as vital an instrument as they are in pointing us to the words and works of the Perfect One—do not provide us with the only pattern by which we gauge our actions and direct our labors. The people of God seek to be led by the power of the Holy Ghost, the oldest and most enduring "book" of living scripture, that sure and certain guide that shows and tells all things that need to be done (see 2 Nephi 32:3, 5).

Through baptism and rebirth we signify, according to Elder Dallin H. Oaks, "our commitment to do all that we can to achieve eternal life in the kingdom of our Father. We are expressing our candidacy—our determination to strive for—exaltation in the celestial kingdom." Further, we "take upon us [Christ's] name as we publicly profess our belief in him, as we fulfill our obligations as members of his Church, and as we do the work of his kingdom. But there is something beyond these familiar meanings, because what we witness [in the sacrament prayers] is not that we *take* upon us his name but that we are *willing* to do so. In this sense, our witness relates to some future event or status whose attainment is not self-assumed, but depends on the authority or initiative of the Savior himself."[3] That is, we have presently announced our righteous desires, and have entered into a covenant with God. We have announced our candidacy for exaltation, but have not yet received it. When the time comes that we have received the fulness of the Father, and have qualified for the highest of eternal rewards, we shall have the name of Christ sealed upon us forever. King Benjamin thus pleaded with his people: "I would that ye should be steadfast and immovable, always abounding in good works, that Christ, the Lord God Omnipotent, may seal you his, *that you may be brought to heaven, that ye may have everlasting salvation and eternal life*" (Mosiah 5:15; emphasis added).

Only the children of Christ will be called by the name of Christ. Only those who have by covenant adoption taken upon them the holy name shall receive the rewards of holiness. Alma declared, "Behold, I say unto you, that the good shepherd doth call you; yea, and in his own name he doth call you, which is the name of Christ; and if ye will not hearken unto the voice of the good shepherd, to the name by which ye are called, behold, ye are not the sheep of the good shepherd.

"And now if ye are not the sheep of the good shepherd, of what fold are ye? Behold, I say unto you, that the devil is your shepherd, and ye are of his fold" (Alma 5:38–39).

In the same way, the Redeemer taught in a modern revelation:

"Behold, Jesus Christ is the name which is given of the Father, and there is none other name given whereby man can be saved;

"Wherefore, all men must take upon them the name which is given of the Father, for in that name shall they be called at the last day;

"Wherefore, if they know not the name by which they are called, they cannot have place in the kingdom of my Father" (D&C 18:23–25).

The Lord's Church, with His name upon it, administers His gospel. It teaches His doctrine and makes available His ordinances. The Church of Jesus Christ is a service agency, an auxiliary if you will, established for the blessing and edification of individuals and families. Elder Russell M. Nelson observed: "The Church is the way by which the Master accomplishes His work and bestows His glory. Its ordinances and related covenants are the crowning rewards of our membership. While many organizations can offer fellowship and fine instruction, only His church can provide baptism, confirmation, ordination, the sacrament, patriarchal blessings, and the ordinances of the temple—all bestowed by authorized priesthood power. That power is destined to bless *all* children of our Heavenly Father."[4]

In summary, then, the Savior directed: "Therefore, whatsoever ye shall do, ye shall do it in my name; therefore ye shall call the church in my name; and ye shall call upon the Father in my name that he will bless the church for my sake" (3 Nephi 27:7). We ever pray for the growth and proliferation of the Church of Jesus Christ, which is the kingdom of God on earth. We plead mightily for the expansion of the work of the Lord in all nations, and among all kindreds, tongues, and people. We petition the Father in the name of the Son, and when our prayers meet the divine standard they are offered under the direction of the Holy Ghost. We pray for the Church that bears the name of the Son, and we pray for special outpourings of light and power. More particularly, we pray for those who constitute the sheep of His fold. We ask sincerely that the judgments of God may be turned away and the mercies of heaven extended, all through the mediation and intercession of the Holy One of Israel (see Alma 33:11, 16).

BUILT UPON HIS GOSPEL

We learn, however, that although being called after Christ's name is a necessary condition for it to be His church, such is not sufficient. The resurrected Lord stated that *"if it be called in my name then it is my church, if it so be that they are built upon my gospel"* (3 Nephi 27:8; emphasis added). Anyone can organize a church. Anyone can name that church the Church of Jesus Christ. And yet, as the Master affirms, it will not be His church unless it is built upon His gospel. I will note in this brief section when a church is *not* built upon His gospel, and then discuss the principles of Christ's gospel in the next.

We cannot really be built upon Christ's gospel if we do not believe in the divinity of Jesus Christ. Those who labor tirelessly to lighten burdens or alleviate human suffering but at the same time deny that Jesus Christ is God cannot have the lasting impact on society that they could have through drawing upon those spiritual forces that center in the Lord Omnipotent. Those in our day who focus endlessly on the moral teachings of Jesus but downplay His divine sonship miss the mark dramatically. C. S. Lewis warned us about saying that Jesus was nothing more than a moral teacher:

"'I'm ready to accept Jesus as a great moral teacher, but I don't accept His claim to be God.' That is the one thing we must not say. A man who was merely a man and said the sort of things Jesus said would not be a great moral teacher. He would either be a lunatic—on a level with the man who says he is a poached egg—or else he would be the Devil of Hell. You must make your choice. Either this man was, and is, the Son of God: or else a madman or something worse. You can shut Him up for a fool, you can spit at Him and kill Him as a demon; or you can fall at His feet and call Him Lord and God. But let us not come with any patronising nonsense about His being a great human teacher. He has not left that open to us. He did not intend to."[5]

In the absence of the real thing—the fulness of the gospel—many ideas and movements seek to occupy center stage. Among the more popular in today's world is a focus upon Jesus as a loving teacher, guide, and moral leader. For some persons, Jesus stands as the preeminent example of kindness, the ultimate illustration of social and interpersonal graciousness and morality. A favorite text for this group is the Sermon on the Mount, and their highest aspiration is to live the Golden Rule. A Roman Catholic philosopher has observed: "According to the theological liberal, [the Sermon on the Mount] is the essence of Christianity, and Christ is the best of human teachers and examples. . . . Christianity is essentially ethics. What's missing here? Simply, the essence of Christianity, which is *not* the Sermon on the Mount. When Christianity was proclaimed throughout the world, the proclamation (*kerygma*) was not 'Love your enemies!' but 'Christ is risen!' This was not a new *ideal* but a new *event,* that God became man, died, and rose for our salvation. Christianity is first of all not ideal but real, an event, news, the gospel, the 'good news.' The essence of Christianity is not Christianity; the essence of Christianity is Christ."[6]

For many, the doctrine of Christ has been replaced by the ethics of Jesus. Those who insist that ethics must be discussed or taught or enforced point toward the declining moral standards of our day, the increase of drug abuse or teenage pregnancy, the prevalence of our inhumanity to each other. They contend that if Christianity is to make a difference in the world, we must find ways to transform ethereal theology into religious practice in a decaying society. They thus promote a social gospel—a relevant religion. The problem with a social gospel is that it is inherently and forevermore deficient as far as solving the real problems of human beings. It almost always focuses on symptoms rather than causes. Ethics is not the essence of the gospel, nor is it necessarily righteousness. The very word *ethics* has come to connote socially acceptable standards based on current consensus, as opposed to absolute truths based on divinely established parameters. Ethics is too often to virtue and righteousness what theology is to religion—a pale and wimpy substitute. Indeed, ethics without the virtue that comes through the cleansing powers of the Redeemer is like religion without God, at least the true and living God.

Elder Bruce R. McConkie has written, "It is one thing to teach ethical principles, quite another to proclaim the great doctrinal verities, which are the foundation of true Christianity and out of which eternal salvation comes. True it is that salvation is limited to those in whose souls the ethical principles abound, but true it is also that Christian ethics, in the full and saving sense, automatically become a part of the lives of those who first believe Christian doctrines." In summary, "It is only when gospel ethics are tied to gospel doctrines that they rest on a sure and enduring foundation and gain full operation in the lives of the saints."[7]

Latter-day Saints are often criticized for expending so much of the Church's resources on missionary work or the construction of temples, indicating that the institutional Church should be more involved in leading or officially supporting a crusade or social cause. Where is your charity? they ask. Of what avail are your noble theological principles? they inquire. I agree with Elder Bruce C. Hafen of the Seventy, who pointed out that "the ultimate purpose of the gospel of Jesus Christ is to cause the sons and daughters of God to become as Christ is. Those who see religious purpose only in terms of ethical service in the relationship between man and fellowmen may miss that divinely ordained possibility. It is quite possible to render charitable—even 'Christian'—service without developing deeply ingrained and permanent Christlike character. Paul understood this when he warned against giving all one's goods to feed the poor without true charity. . . . *While religious philosophies whose highest aim is social relevance may do much good, they will not ultimately lead people to achieve the highest religious purpose, which is to become as God and Christ are.*"[8]

The Savior declared to His Nephite followers that "if it so be that the church is built upon my gospel then will the Father show forth his own works in it" (3 Nephi 27:10). When the Saints of God have been true to their trusts and live worthy of the gifts and influence of the Holy Ghost, then the works of the Father—the works of righteousness, including deeds of Christian service, manifested in the actions and behavior of the faithful—flow forth from regenerate hearts. Those works are not the works of mortals alone but rather the doings of persons who have become new creatures in Christ. Their works are therefore the works of the Lord, for they have been motivated by the power of the Spirit. "I am crucified with Christ," the Apostle Paul wrote: "nevertheless I live; yet not I, but Christ liveth in me" (Galatians 2:20). To the Philippian Saints he likewise beckoned: "Work out your own salvation with fear and trembling. For *it is God which worketh in you* both to will and to do of his good pleasure" (Philippians 2:12–13; emphasis added).

It is true that much of the time we do the works of righteousness simply out of a sense of duty and not always as a result of some overwhelming spiritual motivation within us. Such efforts attest to our willingness to be obedient, but along the way we must strive in prayer for a change of heart, for the Lord to prompt and direct our labors through His Spirit. Otherwise we spend our days operating merely in terms of expectation and requirement when we could be operating in terms of pure love and enjoyment. Without the Spirit and power of God providing impetus, meaning, purpose, and staying power for our poor efforts, we eventually experience a type of spiritual burnout; we continue to work to exhaustion, but our hearts are not in it. Though for a season we may serve because of good companionship, out of fear of punishment, because of duty or loyalty, and even as a part of a hope for an eternal reward, "if our service is to be most efficacious, it must be accomplished for the love of God and the love of his children. . . . [Laboring] with all of our heart and mind is a high challenge for all of us. Such service must be free of selfish ambition. It must be motivated only by the pure love of Christ."[9]

The Master warned what will happen if we seek to be His but are not built upon His gospel. If our effort "be not built upon my gospel," He said, "and is built upon the works of men, or upon the works of the devil, verily I say unto you they have joy in their works for a season, and by and by the end cometh, and they are hewn down and cast into the fire, from whence there is no return" (3 Nephi 27:11). God's work and glory is "to bring to pass the immortality and eternal life of man" (Moses 1:39). Our most noble work will be accomplished and our greatest glory will come to the degree that we are similarly occupied with this overarching objective. The works of the devil obviously pertain to carnality and devilishness, what Paul called "the works of the flesh"—such sins as adultery, fornication, idolatry, witchcraft, hatred, strife, and heresy (see Galatians 5:19–21). They bring pleasure and telestial titillation for a season, but they result inevitably in shrinkage of the soul, followed in time by bitter loneliness and that awful alienation from things of lasting worth. Indeed, "their works do follow them, for it is because of their works that they are hewn down" (3 Nephi 27:12).

The works of humankind may refer to what we know as honorable endeavors, worthwhile efforts to improve humanity and society, but labors whose focus is not truly on the Lord or His work and glory. So often the works of humankind bring glory to humankind. More often than not, the works of humankind hack away at the leaves of the inconsequential while ignoring the spiritual roots of attitudes and behavior. The poignant message of the Savior is that happiness, meaning lasting joy, comes only to those who are built upon His gospel and whose works are really the Lord's works. So many people, as C. S. Lewis observed, "seek to invent some sort of happiness for themselves without God. And out of that hopeless attempt has come nearly all that we call human history—money, poverty, ambition, war, prostitution, classes, slavery—the long terrible story of people trying to find something other than God which will make them happy. The reason why it can never succeed is this. God made us: invented us as a man invents an engine. A car is made to run on gasoline, and it would not run properly on anything else. *Now God designed the human machine to run on Himself. He Himself is the fuel our spirits were designed to burn, or the food our spirits were designed to feed on. There is no other. That is why it is just no good asking God to make us happy in our own way without bothering about religion. God cannot give us a happiness and peace apart from Himself,* because it is not there. There is no such thing."[10]

Because we are so very limited in our vision, we are tempted to envy the financial success of those who spurn the laws and commandments of God. "They look happy and free," Elder Glenn L. Pace remarked, "but don't mistake telestial pleasure for celestial happiness and joy. Don't mistake lack of self-control for freedom. Complete freedom without appropriate restraint makes us slaves to our appetites. Don't envy a lesser and lower life."[11]

"THIS IS MY GOSPEL"

Some things simply matter more than others. Some topics of discussion, even intellectually stimulating ones, must take a back seat to more fundamental verities. It is just so in regard to what the scriptures call the gospel or the doctrine of Christ, those foundational truths associated with the person and powers of Jesus the Messiah. Who He is and what He has done are paramount and central issues; all else, however supplementary, is secondary. The Prophet Joseph Smith was once asked about the basic tenets of Mormonism. "The fundamental principles of our religion," he answered, "are the testimony of the Apostles and Prophets, concerning Jesus Christ, that He died, was buried, and rose again the third day, and ascended into heaven; and all other things which pertain to our religion are only appendages to it."[12]

This statement by the Prophet highlights our duty as to what we ought to teach and what ought to receive the greatest stress in the Church. It suggests that occasionally it may be helpful, relative to our Church involvement, to ask the question, why are we doing what we are doing? If in fact our efforts do not (directly, or at least indirectly) assist the Saints in their quest to come unto Christ, then perhaps the particular program or activity has no place in the Church.

The Church of Jesus Christ of Latter-day Saints is, in the language of revelation, "the only true and living church upon the face of the whole earth" (D&C 1:30). The true Church administers the gospel; salvation in this day and age will come through the covenants and ordinances administered and made available by the Church or it will not come at all. To speak of coming unto Christ independent of Christ's Church or in defiance of His anointed servants is foolishness. It is, however, the gospel of Jesus Christ that saves (see Romans 1:16) and not the Church per se. Auxiliaries and programs and policies and procedures—though inspired from heaven and essential for the everyday operation and continuing expansion of the Lord's kingdom—are of efficacy, virtue, and force only to the degree that they encourage and motivate the Saints to trust in and serve the Lord and thus receive His matchless mercy and grace.

The word *gospel* means, literally, God-news or good news. The gospel is the good news that Christ came, that He lived and died, and that He rose again to immortal glory. The gospel is the good news that through Christ we may be cleansed and renewed, transformed into new creatures. The gospel is the good news that through our Savior and Redeemer we can be delivered from death and sin to the abundant life. In short, the gospel is the "glad tidings . . .

"That he came into the world, even Jesus, to be crucified for the world, and to bear the sins of the world, and to sanctify the world, and to cleanse it from all unrighteousness;

"That through him all might be saved whom the Father had put into his power and made by him" (D&C 76:40–42).

To the Nephites, the risen Lord declared: "Behold I have given unto you my gospel, and this is the gospel which I have given unto you—that I came into the world to do the will of my Father, because my Father sent me" (3 Nephi 27:13).

The gospel is a sacred covenant, a two-way promise between God and humankind. Christ does for us what we could never do for ourselves. He offers Himself as a ransom for sin; He descends below all things that He and we might have the privilege of ascending to celestial heights; and He dies and rises from the tomb that we—in a way that is completely incomprehensible to the finite mind—might likewise come forth from death into resurrected, immortal glory. On our part, we agree to do those things that we can do for ourselves: we make a solemn promise to accept and receive Him as our Lord and Savior; to believe on His name and rely wholly upon His merits, mercy, and grace; to accept and receive the principles and ordinances of His gospel; and to strive all the days of our lives to endure faithfully to the end, meaning keep our covenants and walk in paths of truth and righteousness.

"Viewed from our mortal position," Elder Bruce R. McConkie wrote, "the gospel is all that is required to take us back to the Eternal Presence, there to be crowned with glory and honor, immortality and eternal life." He continued: "To gain these greatest of all rewards, two things are required. The first is the atonement by which all men are raised in immortality, with those who believe and obey ascending also unto eternal life. This atoning sacrifice was the work of our Blessed Lord, and he has done his work. The second requisite is obedience on our part to the laws and ordinances of the gospel. Thus *the gospel is, in effect, the atonement. But the gospel is also all of the laws, principles, doctrines, rites, ordinances, acts, powers, authorities, and keys needed to save and exalt fallen man in the highest heaven hereafter.*"[13]

It is probably the case that if one hundred Protestants were asked *where* the Atonement of Christ took place, those one hundred persons would answer: At Golgotha, on the cross. It is also no doubt true that if one hundred Latter-day Saints were asked the same question, a large percentage would respond: In Gethsemane, in the garden. In fact, the sufferings of Jesus Christ that began in the Garden of Gethsemane were consummated on the cross. Between noon and 3:00 P.M. on that fateful Friday, all of the agonies of Gethsemane returned, as the Spirit of our Heavenly Father was once again withdrawn from the Suffering Servant (see Matthew 27:46).[14] Truly, the lowly Nazarene has trodden the winepress, meaning Gethsemane or the garden of the oilpress, alone (see D&C 76:107; 88:106; 133:50; Isaiah 63:3). In His own words, that awful agony in the Garden "caused myself, even God, the greatest of all, to tremble because of pain, and to bleed at every pore, and to suffer both body and spirit—and would that I might not drink the bitter cup, and shrink—

"Nevertheless, glory be to the Father, and I partook and finished my preparations unto the children of men" (D&C 19:18–19).

And as to the final phase of His redemptive labor, His foreordained place on the cross, He explained to the Nephites: "My Father sent me that I might be lifted up upon the cross; and after that I had been lifted up upon the cross, that I might draw all men unto me" (3 Nephi 27:14).

The scriptures—especially 3 Nephi 27—clearly and consistently teach that the principles of the gospel are as follows:

1. *Faith in the Lord Jesus Christ.* Those who seek to enjoy the benefits of the Atonement of Christ must first learn to exercise faith in Christ. They must believe in Him, believe that He is, "that he created all things, both in heaven and in earth; believe that He has all wisdom, and all power, both in heaven and in earth; believe that man doth not comprehend all the things which the Lord can comprehend" (Mosiah 4:9). In the *Lectures on Faith,* Joseph Smith taught that three things are necessary in order for rational and intelligent beings to exercise saving faith in God or Christ. First, they must accept the idea that God actually exists; they must plant the seed of the word of God in their hearts and experiment upon (pray over and labor with) the fact that there actually is a Savior (see Alma 32–33). Second, they must have a correct idea of God's character, attributes, and perfections; they must, from serious study and personal revelation, seek to understand what God is like. Third, they must gain an actual knowledge that the course of life they are pursuing accords with the will of God; they must know that their lives are worthy of divine approbation and thus of the blessings of heaven. The Prophet explained that the third requisite for faith—the peaceful assurance that we have pleased God—comes only through our willingness to sacrifice all things for the kingdom's sake.[15] Faith in Jesus Christ, the first principle of the gospel, is thus based on evidence. And the more evidence we amass—external and internal—the greater our faith. We may, like the Zoramites, begin with the simple hope that there is a Christ and that salvation is available (see Alma 32:27), but in time that hope can, by the power of the Holy Ghost, ripen into the knowledge that one day we will not only be *with* Christ but *like* Him (see Moroni 7:41, 48; 1 John 3:2). The Savior teaches plainly that no person enters into His rest save their garments are washed in His blood, which cleansing comes by faith and repentance (see 3 Nephi 27:19).

2. *Repentance.* Once we come to know the Lord—of His power and greatness and perfections—we automatically sense our own inadequacies. We feel to shrink before the Lord Omnipotent; we cry out for mercy and pardon from the Holy One of Israel. And thus it is that

repentance follows on the heels of faith; as we encounter the Master, we begin to discern the vast chasm between the divine realm and our own unholy state. Repentance is literally an "afterthought," "a change of mind," a change in perspective and lifestyle. Repentance is the process by which we discard the rags of uncleanness and through Christ begin to adorn ourselves in the robes of righteousness. It is the means by which we incorporate into our lives a power beyond our own, an infinite power that transforms us into new creatures, new creatures in Christ. It is only through "the repentance of all their sins" (3 Nephi 27:19) that the followers of Christ are enabled to go where God and Christ are.

3. *Baptism by water and by fire.* Jesus and His prophets have declared in unmistakable terms that salvation comes only to those who have been born again (see John 3:1–5; Mosiah 27:24–26; Alma 7:14). People must be born again or born from above in order to see and enter the kingdom of God. When the Spirit of the Lord brings about a change of heart and takes the veil of darkness and unbelief from our eyes, we are born again to see and are thereby enabled to recognize and acknowledge the Lord's Church and His servants. We are born again to enter the kingdom only as we subscribe to the "articles of adoption," meaning the first principles and ordinances of the gospel, the legal requirements for entrance into Christ's family kingdom.[16] Joseph Smith taught, "Baptism is a sign to God, to angels, and to heaven that we do the will of God, and there is no other way beneath the heavens whereby God hath ordained for man to come to Him to be saved, and enter into the Kingdom of God, except faith in Jesus Christ, repentance, and baptism for the remission of sins, and any other course is in vain; then you have the promise of the gift of the Holy Ghost."[17]

Baptism becomes the physical token of our acceptance of the atoning graces of our Lord. We go down into the "watery grave" and come forth as initiates, new citizens of the kingdom, as a sign of our ready acceptance of the Lord's burial in the tomb and His subsequent rise to newness of life in the Resurrection (see Romans 6:3–5). The baptism of fire takes place as the Holy Ghost, who is a sanctifier, takes from our souls the filth and dross of worldliness. The Prophet explained that "you might as well baptize a bag of sand as a man, if not done in view of the remission of sins and getting of the Holy Ghost. Baptism by water is but half a baptism, and is good for nothing without the other half—that is, the baptism of the Holy Ghost."[18] That is to say, "Sins are remitted not in the waters of baptism, as we say in speaking figuratively, but when we receive the Holy Ghost. It is the Holy Spirit of God that erases carnality and brings us into a state of righteousness."[19] Men and women who come unto Christ through the appropriate ordinances are in time "sanctified by the reception of the Holy Ghost" (3 Nephi 27:20), meaning they are made pure and holy. Filth and dross—the elements of the natural world—are burned out of their souls as though by fire, thus giving rise to the expression "the baptism of fire." The Holy Ghost, that *revelator* who is the means by which we come to know the truth, is also a *sanctifier* and thus the means whereby we become people who are true. In time, through being sanctified, members of the Church come to abhor sin and cleave unto righteousness (see Alma 13:12).

4. *Enduring to the end.* Disciples of Christ in all ages are instructed to be baptized of water and of fire and to labor to maintain their worthy standing before God. The scriptures teach that to the degree the Saints of the Most High trust in the will and purposes of God and lean upon His mighty arm, as well as extend themselves in Christian service to the needy, they are able to *retain* that remission of sins from day to day (see Mosiah 4:11–12, 26; Alma 4:13). To endure to the end is to remain true to our covenants after baptism and live the life of Saints to the best of our ability, throughout the remainder of our lives. The commission is for members of the household of faith "to stand as witnesses of God at all times and in all things, and in all places that ye may be in, even until death, that ye may be redeemed of God, and be numbered with those of the first resurrection, that ye may have eternal life" (Mosiah 18:9). To endure to the end is to be "steadfast and immovable"—the scriptural phrase for spiritual maturity—and to press toward the high prize of eternal life (see Mosiah 5:15; 2 Nephi 31:16, 20; 33:4; D&C 6:13; 14:7). The scriptures plainly affirm that "whoso repenteth and is baptized in [Christ's] name shall be filled; and if he endureth to the end, behold, him will [the Lord] hold guiltless before

[the] Father at that day when [Christ] shall stand to judge the world" (3 Nephi 27:16).

People of the covenant are able to endure to the end, not just through personal grit and will power, not just by holding white-knuckled to the iron rod, but by cultivating the gift of the Holy Ghost. It is the Spirit that provides direction while we are encircled by the mists of darkness. It is the Spirit that provides moral courage to proceed along the gospel path while the tauntings and temptations emanating from the great and spacious building ring out loud and clear. And it is the Spirit that brings peace to the weary, hope to the faithful, and the promise of eternal life to those who continue to hunger and thirst after righteousness and are willing to serve God at all hazards.[20]

5. *Resurrection and eternal judgment.* In 1839 Joseph Smith observed that "the Doctrines of the Resurrection of the Dead and the Eternal Judgment are necessary to preach among the first principles of the Gospel of Jesus Christ."[21] Through the Atonement of Jesus Christ, as an unconditional benefit, all men and women will, in a limited sense, be redeemed from spiritual death. They will be raised from the grave and thereafter be brought to stand in the presence of the Almighty to be judged according to the deeds done in mortality. This principle of the gospel illustrates both the mercy and justice of God. Samuel the Lamanite testified that Christ "surely must die that salvation may come; yea, it behooveth him and becometh expedient that he dieth, to bring to pass the resurrection of the dead, that thereby men may be brought into the presence of the Lord" (Helaman 14:15; see also 2 Nephi 9:15, 21–22; Mormon 9:13). Christ reinforced this doctrinal teaching to His Nephite disciples:

"And my Father sent me that I might be lifted up upon the cross; and after that I had been lifted up upon the cross, that I might draw all men unto me, that as I have been lifted up by men even so should men be lifted up [that is, raised from the dead] by the Father, to stand before me, to be judged of their works, whether they be good or whether they be evil—

"And for this cause have I been lifted up; therefore, according to the power of the Father I will draw all men unto me, that they may be judged according to their works" (3 Nephi 27:14–15).

WHAT GOSPEL SHALL WE TEACH?

The Book of Mormon is said to contain the fulness of the gospel (see D&C 20:9; 27:5; 35:12, 17; 42:12). Some have wondered how the Lord and His prophets could state this, when in fact the Book of Mormon contains no specific reference to such matters as eternal marriage, degrees of glory in the Resurrection, vicarious work for the dead, and so forth. Again, let us focus on what the gospel is. The Book of Mormon contains the fulness of the gospel in the sense that it teaches the doctrine of redemption—that salvation is in Christ and in Him alone—and the principles of the gospel (faith, repentance, rebirth, enduring, resurrection, and judgment) more plainly and persuasively than any other book of scripture. The Book of Mormon does not necessarily contain the fulness of gospel doctrine. Rather, it is a sacred repository of eternal truth relative to the most fundamental and far-reaching doctrine of all—the doctrine of Christ.[22]

We have received a divine commission from our Lord to teach one another the doctrine of the kingdom (see D&C 88:77). What is it that we should teach? Above and beyond all that might be said in sermons and lessons and seminars and discussions, what should be the walk and talk of the Latter-day Saints? Simply stated, we are to teach the gospel. Our primary message, like Paul's, must be "Jesus Christ, and him crucified" (1 Corinthians 2:2). If we have any hope of preserving the faith of our fathers among our people, of building firmly on the rock of revelation and the doctrines Joseph Smith taught, then we must ground and settle ourselves in Jesus Christ and His atoning sacrifice. We must, of course, teach all the doctrines of the gospel when it is appropriate to do so. But above all, we must see to it that "we talk of Christ, we rejoice in Christ, we preach of Christ, we prophesy of Christ, . . . that our children may know to what source they may look for a remission of their sins" (2 Nephi 25:26). President Boyd K. Packer testified: "Truth, glorious truth, proclaims there is . . . a Mediator. . . . Through Him mercy can be fully extended to each of us without offending the eternal law of justice. *This truth is the very root of Christian doctrine. You may know much about the gospel as it branches out from there, but if you only know the branches and those branches do not touch that root, if they have been cut free from that truth, there will be no life nor substance nor redemption in them.*"[23]

We frequently hear that the gospel is universal, that Mormonism welcomes and embodies all that is true and good and ennobling. From this perspective, then, the gospel embraces the truths of the sciences, the arts, and great literature. Would it not follow, then, that whatever we taught in the meetings of the Church, so long as it were true, would be the gospel? If a man should address the congregation in sacrament meeting and speak for twenty minutes on the laws of motion or the process of photosynthesis, would he then be preaching the gospel? If a woman should decide to speak at length to her Spiritual Living class on the laws of genetics or the manner in which sentences may be properly diagrammed, would she then be bearing witness of the gospel? Certainly not. For although in a rather vague sense the gospel may be said to contain all truth, it should be clear to most discerning minds that the constant and consistent witness of the scripture is that only those truths tied to the doctrine of Christ have power to touch and lift and transform human souls. These are those of which the Holy Ghost will bear testimony, those which, when preached by that Spirit, result in mutual edification of both speaker and listener.

In 1984 Commissioner Henry B. Eyring delivered an address to teachers in the Church Educational System. He spoke soberly of the "sea of filth" which today's youth encounter and of the absolute necessity for solid and sound gospel instruction in the effort to immunize the youth against the waywardness of the world:

"Now I would like to say this: There are two views of the gospel—both true. They make a terrific difference in the power of your teaching.

"One view is that the gospel is all truth. It is. The gospel is truth. With that view I could teach pretty well anything true in a classroom, and I would be teaching the gospel. The other view is that the gospel is the principles, commandments, and ordinances which, if kept, conformed with, and accepted, will lead to eternal life. That is also true.

"When I choose which of these views I will let dominate my teaching, I take a great step. If I take the view that the gospel is all truth, rather than that it is the ordinances and principles and commandments which, if kept, conformed with, and accepted, lead to eternal life, I have already nearly taken myself out of the contest to help a student withstand the sea of filth. Why? Because he needs to have his eyes focused on light, and that means not truth in some abstract sense but the joy of keeping the commandments and conforming with the principles and accepting the ordinances of the gospel of Jesus Christ. If I decide I will not make that my primary vision of the gospel, I am already out of the contest to help my student with his capacity to see good and to want and desire it in the midst of filth."[24]

CONCLUSION

The Master summarized the gospel or doctrine of Christ for us and beautifully elucidated each of the principles of that gospel:

"And no unclean thing can enter into his kingdom; therefore nothing entereth into his rest save it be those who have washed their garments in my blood, because of their faith, and the repentance of all their sins, and their faithfulness unto the end.

"Now this is the commandment: Repent, all ye ends of the earth, and come unto me and be baptized in my name, that ye may be sanctified by the reception of the Holy Ghost, that ye may stand spotless before me at the last day.

"Verily, verily, I say unto you, this is my gospel; and ye know the things that ye must do in my church; for the works which ye have seen me do that shall ye also do; for that which ye have seen me do even that shall ye do;

"Therefore, if ye do these things blessed are ye, for ye shall be lifted up at the last day" (3 Nephi 27:19–22).

These matters are sacred. They are among the mysteries of the kingdom, meaning they are to be known and understood only by revelation from God.[25] I add a personal witness to the effect that other great and marvelous things, further mysteries, are made known unto us, not as we wade in the morass of the unknown or the esoteric, but rather as we ponder upon, teach from, and focus on those plain and precious truths we know as the principles of the gospel. Profundity thus grows naturally out of simplicity.

Just thirteen days before his death, Elder McConkie affirmed the vital importance of teaching the doctrine of atonement. He stated: "Now, the atonement of Christ is the most basic and fundamental doctrine of the gospel, and it is the least understood of all our revealed truths. Many of us have a superficial knowledge and rely upon the Lord and his goodness to see us through the trials and perils of life. But if we are to have faith like Enoch and Elijah we must believe what they believed, know what they knew, and live as they lived. May I invite you to join with me in gaining a sound and sure knowledge of the Atonement. We must cast aside the philosophies of men and the wisdom of the wise and hearken to that Spirit which is given to us to guide us into all truth. We must search the scriptures, accepting them as the mind and will and voice of the Lord and the very power of God unto salvation."[26]

The gospel is the glad tidings concerning the infinite and eternal atoning sacrifice of the Lord Jesus Christ. The Atonement is central. It is the hub of the wheel; all other matters are spokes at best. The good news is that we can be changed, be converted, become different people in and through Christ. The good news is that we can come to perceive an entirely new realm of reality, a realm unknown to the world at large. It is a new life, a new life in Christ. In a time of stress and great uncertainty, thanks be to God for the peace and joy of the Spirit that can come to us through Christ and His gospel. In a day when we encounter somber and soul-stirring headlines on almost every page of the newspaper, God be praised that the good news of the gospel has been restored in our day through modern witnesses of Christ. "In the world ye shall have tribulation," the Master acknowledged, and then He added, "but be of good cheer; I have overcome the world" (John 16:33). Christ our Lord has overcome the world, and He has opened the door and made available to us the power to do the same. And surely there could be no better news, no more joyful tidings, than that.

NOTES

1. Joseph Fielding Smith, *Doctrines of Salvation,* comp. Bruce R. McConkie (Salt Lake City: Bookcraft, 1954–56), 2:336.

2. Bruce R. McConkie, *The Promised Messiah* (Salt Lake City: Deseret Book, 1978), 427.

3. Dallin H. Oaks, "Taking upon Us the Name of Jesus Christ," *Ensign,* May 1985, 82–83.

4. Russell M. Nelson, "'Thus Shall My Church Be Called,'" *Ensign,* May 1990, 18.

5. C. S. Lewis, *Mere Christianity* (New York: Macmillan, 1952), 55–56.

6. Peter Kreeft, *Back to Virtue* (San Francisco: Ignatius, 1992), 83; emphasis in the original.

7. Bruce R. McConkie, *A New Witness for the Articles of Faith* (Salt Lake City: Deseret Book, 1985), 699–700.

8. Bruce C. Hafen, *The Broken Heart* (Salt Lake City: Deseret Book, 1989), 196–97; emphasis added.

9. Dallin H. Oaks, "Why Do We Serve?" *Ensign,* November 1984, 14–15.

10. Lewis, *Mere Christianity,* 53–54; emphasis added.

11. Glenn L. Pace, "They're Not Really Happy," *Ensign,* November 1987, 40.

12. Joseph Smith, *Teachings of the Prophet Joseph Smith,* comp. Joseph Fielding Smith (Salt Lake City: Deseret Book, 1976), 121.

13. McConkie, *A New Witness for the Articles of Faith,* 34; emphasis added.

14. See James E. Talmage, *Jesus the Christ* (Salt Lake City: Deseret News Press, 1963), 661; see also Bruce R. McConkie, *The Mortal Messiah* (Salt Lake City: Deseret Book, 1979–81), 4:224, 226; Bruce R. McConkie, "The Purifying Power of Gethsemane," *Ensign,* May 1985, 9–10; Brigham Young, in *Journal of Discourses* (London: Latter-day Saints' Book Depot, 1854–86), 3:205–6.

15. See Joseph Smith, *Lectures on Faith* (Salt Lake City: Deseret Book, 1985), 38 (3:2–5).

16. See Smith, *Teachings,* 328; see also Orson Pratt, *Orson Pratt's Works* (Salt Lake City: Deseret News Press, 1965), 48.

17. Smith, *Teachings,* 198.

18. Smith, *Teachings,* 314.

19. McConkie, *A New Witness for the Articles of Faith,* 290; see also 239; see also 2 Nephi 31:17; Moroni 6:4.

20. See Smith, *Teachings,* 150.

21. Smith, *Teachings,* 149; see also 365.

22. See Ezra Taft Benson, *A Witness and a Warning* (Salt Lake City: Deseret Book, 1988), 18–19.

23. Boyd K. Packer, "The Mediator," *Ensign,* May 1977, 56; emphasis added.

24. Henry B. Eyring, "Eyes to See, Ears to Hear," in *Supplement: Eighth Annual Church Educator's Symposium: A Symposium on the New Testament* (Salt Lake City: The Church of Jesus Christ of Latter-day Saints, 1984), 11.

25. See Harold B. Lee, *Ye Are the Light of the World* (Salt Lake City: Deseret Book, 1974), 211.

26. McConkie, "The Purifying Power of Gethsemane," 10.

24

The Doctrine of God the Father in the Book of Mormon

Andrew C. Skinner

No other ancient record does what the Book of Mormon does. When it comes to testifying of Jesus as Messiah, the Book of Mormon is unparalleled. It boldly proclaims to a modern world that Jesus was the Great Jehovah before He came to earth (see 3 Nephi 15:5); that as the Messiah He was born into mortality a real flesh-and-blood being (see Mosiah 3:5–7); that He was literally the Son of God and the son of a mortal woman named Mary (see Mosiah 3:8; Alma 7:9–10); and that through His suffering and sacrifice an infinite and eternal atonement was made for all humankind (see Alma 34:8–15; 3 Nephi 11:10–15). While secular scholarship ofttimes tries to allegorize or explain away these truths, the Book of Mormon restores to both Jew and Gentile descriptions of the Atonement that were lost for centuries. And it places the Atonement at the very center of our understanding of God's plan *and* our religion. But the Book of Mormon also does something else in a profound and unrelenting way—it stands as a pivotal witness of God the Eternal Father.

A Witness of God the Father

Perhaps we do not reflect a great deal on the notion that the Book of Mormon stands as a premier witness of God the Father. This may

---

Andrew C. Skinner is dean of Religious Education at Brigham Young University.

be so because we spend so much time emphasizing the Book of Mormon as a witness of Christ (and rightly so). But if we are not vigilant, we may miss the significance of the foundational corollary doctrine restored by the ancient record—the Messiah literally had a divine Father and the prophets of the Book of Mormon knew it! No matter how carefully, how often, or how long one studies the Book of Mormon, its message is constantly hammered home: Jesus the Messiah is the literal Son of God the Father, who also figures prominently in its pages. We cannot ignore this, wish it away, or twist it into something that does not square with the Prophet Joseph Smith's First Vision.

Joseph Smith translated and pondered the doctrines of the Book of Mormon through the lenses of his experience in the Sacred Grove. He said he saw and interacted with two personages, whose brightness and glory defied all description. Everything in the Book of Mormon fits perfectly with, and ultimately supports, the Prophet's experience and understanding. There is no confusion over this or shred of evidence to the contrary in the Book of Mormon. In fact, there is evidence to indicate that the Prophet Joseph Smith carefully reviewed the text of the Book of Mormon with the doctrine of the fatherhood of God specifically in mind. For example, the first edition (1830) of 1 Nephi 11:21 contained the words, "Behold the Lamb of God, yea, even the Eternal Father!" By the time of the 1837 edition, Joseph Smith had inserted a clarifying phrase so that the verse then read, "Behold the Lamb of God, yea, even *the Son of* the Eternal Father!" The Prophet also inserted this same clarifying phrase in verse 32 of chapter 11 so that the 1837 edition read, "And I looked and beheld the Lamb of God, that he was taken by the people; yea, *the Son of* the everlasting God was judged of the world."

Without question, these two verses were doctrinally correct as they stood in the original 1830 edition of the Book of Mormon. Jesus Christ is indeed the Eternal Father and the everlasting God, as is explained by the prophet Abinadi in Mosiah 15. But Joseph Smith, prophet, seer, and revelator of the Lord in this modern (and last) dispensation, also knew the doctrine of the Godhead (from firsthand experience, we might add), and also knew that the Book of Mormon was to stand as a sure and clear witness of that doctrine *in* the latter days and *among* the Latter-day Saints. The changes he made to the texts of 1 Nephi 11:21 and 11:32 are appropriate, appreciated, and much needed in our day to clear up misunderstandings. The fundamental truth that there exists a divine Father, separate from other beings, is taught no less powerfully in the Book of Mormon than the doctrine that there exists a divine Son whom we worship as our Messiah and Savior. Therefore, let us explore two of the seminal ways in which the reality of God the Father is taught in the Book of Mormon.

NUMEROUS EXPLICIT VERSES

First of all, the doctrine of God the Father is taught in the Book of Mormon through explicit references to Jesus Christ as the Son of an Eternal Father. The language used to teach the divine sonship of Jesus is plentiful and varied, as well as obvious and subtle. He is called the Son (see 2 Nephi 31:18), the Beloved Son (see 2 Nephi 31:11), the Son of God (see 1 Nephi 10:17), the Holy Child (see Moroni 8:3), the Son of the most high God (see 1 Nephi 11:6), the Son of the living God (see Mormon 5:14), Son of our great God (see Alma 24:13), Son of the everlasting God (see 1 Nephi 11:32), Son of the Eternal Father (see 1 Nephi 11:21; 13:40), the Only Begotten of the Father (see Alma 5:48), the Only Begotten Son (see Jacob 4:5, 11; Alma 12:33), Christ the Son (see Alma 11:44), and the Son of Righteousness (see 3 Nephi 25:2). One would be hard pressed to find a more explicit and consistent list of titles that testifies of the obvious—Jesus is regarded as the Son of a divine Father.

The phrase "Son of God" alone is used fifty-one times throughout the Book of Mormon text, with variations of this phrase occurring several more times. The phrase "Only Begotten Son" is used five times, "Only Begotten of the Father" four times, and "Son of the living God" four times. The prophets Mormon and Moroni use this very powerful and expressive phrase (i.e., "Son of the living God") always in tandem with the specific mention of the name of Jesus (see 3 Nephi 30:1; Mormon 5:14; 9:29). And Nephi uses it when discussing the baptism of Christ (see 2 Nephi 31:16).

Here are Mormon's words in describing the purpose of the doctrines and teachings of the Book of Mormon: "And behold, they shall go unto the unbelieving of the Jews; and for this intent shall they go—that they may be persuaded that Jesus is the Christ, the Son of the living God; that the Father may bring about, through his most Beloved, his great and eternal purpose, in restoring the Jews, or all the house of Israel, to the land of their inheritance, which the Lord their God hath given them, unto the fulfilling of his covenant" (Mormon 5:14).

As implied in this verse, Jesus, the earthly Messiah or Anointed One, who was the Firstborn of all of our Heavenly Father's spirit sons and daughters (see D&C 93:21), and who became the literal Son of that same divine Father, was also the designated agent of His Father's plan—the One chosen to carry out and put into effect His Father's will—all of His Father's aims and desires for this earth and the people who live upon it. This even included the Father's desire that the family known as Israel be established in lands appointed for their habitation and use while living on this earth. Thus, Abinadi could teach that the will of the Son was "swallowed up" in the will of the Father (Mosiah 15:7).

It is instructive to note that occurrences of the phrase "Son of God" often appear grouped together in certain specific chapters of the Book of Mormon which specifically focus on aspects of the Atonement. The Book of Mormon prophets understood well that the Atonement, brought about by the matchless sacrifice of God's earthly Son, was the central feature of the Father's plan for His children from the beginning. As Alma testifies, "God did call on men, in the name of his Son, (this being the plan of redemption which was laid) saying: If ye will repent, and harden not your hearts, then will I have mercy upon you, through mine Only Begotten Son" (Alma 12:33).

Those chapters where mention of the "Son of God" figures prominently include 1 Nephi 11, Alma 11, Alma 33, Alma 34, Helaman 8, and Helaman 14. In 1 Nephi 11 Nephi describes his vision of the birth and ministry of the Son of God, who was Himself God before He came to earth as a mortal being. In Alma 11 Amulek teaches that a universal resurrection comes through the Son of God. In Alma 33 Zenos and

Zenock teach that mercy is bestowed because of the Son of God. In Alma 34 Amulek teaches that the Son of God would become the great and last sacrifice, and would provide an infinite and eternal atonement for all. In Helaman 8, Nephi teaches that Abraham, Moses, Zenos, Zenock, Ezias, Isaiah, Jeremiah, Lehi, and Nephi all testified that the Son of God would come to earth as the Messiah and bring salvation. And in Helaman 14 Samuel the Lamanite testifies of the mortal birth of the Son of God, who would redeem human beings from temporal and spiritual death.

Even after only a cursory reading of the Book of Mormon it becomes apparent that the most consistent and persistent teaching by Book of Mormon prophets about the Savior-Messiah is that He is the Son of God. What Amulek said specifically to one of his audiences could well be said to every soul after they have read the Book of Mormon: "My brethren, I think that it is impossible that ye should be ignorant of the things which have been spoken concerning the coming of Christ, who is taught by us to be the Son of God" (Alma 34:2).

EPISODES DESCRIBING THE FATHER AS DISTINCT FROM THE SON

The doctrine of God the Father is taught in specific, unique episodes of the Book of Mormon where the Father and the Son are described as separate divine personages. One of the most powerful and impressive of these is found in Nephi's prophetic discourse regarding the baptism of Christ in 2 Nephi 31. Nephi was shown in vision both the ministry of John the Baptist, "that prophet . . . that should baptize the Lamb of God" (2 Nephi 31:4), as well as the actual baptismal scene of the Messiah (see 2 Nephi 31:17). The text makes clear that Nephi was also given an explicit and detailed understanding of the doctrinal basis of the ordinance of baptism and the reason for Christ's baptism (see 2 Nephi 31:5–10). But what also comes out of a careful reading of 2 Nephi 31 is the unmistakable conclusion that Nephi had a profound understanding of, and encounter with, the Godhead. In stunning detail Nephi tells his readers that he was privileged to hear the voices of both the Father and the Son.

As a way of introducing His Son, God the Father commanded Nephi to repent "and be baptized in the name of my Beloved Son" (2 Nephi 31:11). The Son, our Savior, then told Nephi that those who would follow the Father's command would be given the Holy Ghost, just as the Father had given the Holy Ghost to the Son (see 2 Nephi 31:12). After he presents some of his own words of exhortation, Nephi then relates how he heard the voice of the Savior a second time: "But, behold, my beloved brethren, thus came the voice of the Son unto me, saying: After ye have repented of your sins, and witnessed unto the Father that ye are willing to keep my commandments, by the baptism of water, and have received the baptism of water, and have received the baptism of fire and of the Holy Ghost, and can speak with a new tongue, yea, even with the tongue of angels, and after this should deny me, it would have been better for you that ye had not known me" (2 Nephi 31:14).

Immediately after this instruction from the premortal Savior, Nephi again heard the voice of God the Father bearing record of His Son, in a manner that fits the pattern established and repeated in the rest of the standard works. "And I heard a voice from the Father, saying: Yea, the words of my Beloved are true and faithful. He that endureth to the end, the same shall be saved" (2 Nephi 31:15). Only on certain special occasions have certain select humans on this earth had the privilege of hearing the voice of God the Father, and then it has been to hear Him introduce and bear record of His Son, who is His executor and the creator of those worlds He calls His own (see Joseph Smith Translation, John 1:19; Moses 1:31–33).[1] These special occasions include, interestingly, the actual baptism of Christ (see Matthew 3:17); the episode on the Mount of Transfiguration (see Matthew 17:5); the Savior's appearance at the temple after His triumphal entry (see John 12:28); the Savior's appearance in the New World after His Resurrection (see 3 Nephi 11:7); and the First Vision (see JS–H 1:17).

In each of these instances, the sentiments expressed by God the Father are so similar to one another as to be considered virtually identical: "This is my Beloved Son, in whom I am well pleased; listen to him." While it is possible that Nephi's encounter with the Father is an example of the premortal Savior (Jehovah) speaking as though He were God the Father, a more compelling case is made for this being the actual voice of God the Father. It fits the pattern of the Father bearing witness of the Son as seen elsewhere. It uses almost the same language, certainly the same sentiment, of the other examples. And it concerns the baptism of the Son, which we know evoked the Father's voice when the Savior experienced the ordinance in the flesh.

If 2 Nephi recounts the actual utterance of God the Father, then it is unique in our scriptural library for it is our only record of the Father's actual voice being heard by a mortal being *before* His Son, our Redeemer, was born into mortality. In other words, 2 Nephi 31 is the only recorded instance in scripture of the Father bearing testimony of the premortal Savior. Were we to judge the value of the Book of Mormon based on this episode alone, we would be compelled to label the sacred text not only unique but truly invaluable.

Another invaluable contribution to our understanding of the doctrine of the fatherhood of God is made by Alma in his discourse to the people of Gideon. He describes the context or background of Christ's birth into mortality in these words: "And behold, he shall be born of Mary, at Jerusalem which is the land of our forefathers, she being a virgin, a precious and chosen vessel, who shall be overshadowed and conceive by the power of the Holy Ghost, and bring forth a son, yea, even the Son of God" (Alma 7:10).

Here we learn not only that the earthly name of the Savior's mortal mother was foreknown by prophets long before the actual events occurred, but also that Mary herself was specially chosen during her sojourn in our premortal state to perform her special role of motherhood. (It will be remembered that the Prophet Joseph Smith taught that every man, and by implication every woman, who has a calling to minister to the inhabitants of this world was foreordained to that calling in the Grand Council before the world was created.[2] What greater calling could any individual have than to be the mother of the literal Son of God in mortality?) In addition, we understand from Alma's comment that the third member of the Godhead had a role in the mortal birth of the Son of God. On this point, Elder Melvin J. Ballard has offered the following commentary:

"Joseph Smith made it perfectly clear that Jesus Christ told the absolute truth, as did those who testify concerning him, the Apostles of the Lord Jesus Christ, wherein he is declared to be the very Son of God. And if God the Eternal Father is not the real Father of Jesus Christ, then we are in confusion; then he is not in reality the Son of God. But we declare that he *is* the Only Begotten of the Father in the flesh. Mary told the story most beautifully when she said that an angel of the Lord came to her and told her that she had found favor in the sight of God and had come to be worthy of the fulfillment of the promises heretofore made, to become the virgin mother of the Redeemer of the world. She afterwards, referring to the event, said: 'God hath done wonderful things unto me.' 'And the Holy Ghost came upon her,' in the story, 'and she came into the presence of the highest.' No man or woman can live in mortality and survive the presence of the Highest except by the sustaining power of the Holy Ghost. So it came upon her to prepare her for admittance into the divine presence, and the power of the Highest, who is the Father, was present, and overshadowed her, and the holy Child that was born of her was called the Son of God."[3]

Perhaps the most compelling text in the Book of Mormon that discusses God the Father is found in the section that details the post-Resurrection appearance of the Savior in the New World, namely 3 Nephi 11:3–28:15. These chapters contain the Savior's personal teachings and testimony given to His American Israelites and give to us in modern times important insights regarding His relationship with His divine Father as well as the Father's will concerning us. Of the eighteen chapters comprising this section, only two do not mention the Father: 3 Nephi 22 (which is the Savior's recitation of Isaiah 54) and 3 Nephi 25 (wherein the Savior quotes Malachi 4). A list of a few of the references to the Father in each of the other sixteen chapters may be profitable.

3 Nephi 11. The voice of the Father introduces and bears witness of the Savior (see 3 Nephi 11:7).

The Savior tells His disciples that He and the Father are one (see 3 Nephi 11:27).

The Savior testifies that His doctrine was given to Him by the Father; He also bears record of the Father, and the Father and the Holy Ghost, in turn, bear witness of Him (see 3 Nephi 11:31–32, 35–36).

3 Nephi 12. The Savior exhorts all to let their light shine and, thus, glorify their Father in Heaven (see 3 Nephi 12:16).

The Savior exhorts all disciples to be perfect just as He or their Father in Heaven is perfect (see 3 Nephi 12:48).

3 Nephi 13. The Savior teaches the order of prayer—instructing His disciples to address their Father who already knows all things they need before they ask (see 3 Nephi 13:8–9).

3 Nephi 14. The Savior describes the Father's concern for His children as being much greater than mortal parents' concern for their children; the Father will give good things to those who ask (see 3 Nephi 14:11).

The Savior declares that only those who actually do the will of their Father in Heaven will be able to enter the kingdom of heaven (see 3 Nephi 14:21).

3 Nephi 15. The Savior testifies that it is the Father who has given the house of Joseph its land of inheritance (see 3 Nephi 15:12–13).

The Savior explains that at no time did the Father give Him a commandment to teach the Jerusalem disciples about the other tribes of the house of Israel, whom the Father led away out of their lands (see 3 Nephi 15:15).

The Savior declares that He received commandments of the Father to teach some things and not others because of the unbelief manifested by the Israelites in the Old World (see 3 Nephi 15:15–18).

The Savior tells His disciples in the New World that they, as well as other tribes, were separated from the Old World Israelites by the Father (see 3 Nephi 15:19–20).

3 Nephi 16. The Savior reiterates that He was commanded by the Father to give the American Israelites the land on which they were residing as their land of inheritance (see 3 Nephi 16:16).

3 Nephi 17. The Savior commands the people to go to their homes and ask the Father in His (Jesus') name for understanding concerning the teachings that the Father commanded the Savior to give to them (see 3 Nephi 17:3).

The Savior tells the multitude that He is going to the Father and then to the lost tribes of Israel (see 3 Nephi 17:4).

The Savior speaks directly to the Father, calling Him "Father" (see 3 Nephi 17:14).

After calling out to the Father, the Savior then kneels and prays to the Father, speaking words so great and marvelous they cannot be repeated (see 3 Nephi 17:15–18).

The Savior prays to the Father on behalf of the little children (see 3 Nephi 17:21).

3 Nephi 18. The Savior teaches His disciples to partake of the sacrament as a testimony to the Father that they do always remember the Savior and His sacrifice, and as a witness to the Father that they are willing to do the things the Savior has commanded (see 3 Nephi 18:1–11).

The Savior tells the Nephites that He must go unto His Father to fulfill other commandments that the Father has given Him (see 3 Nephi 18:27).

3 Nephi 19. The twelve special disciples divide the multitude into twelve groups and teach them to pray unto the Father in the name of Jesus (see 3 Nephi 19:5–9).

The Savior prays to the Father in a manner that resembles the great High Priestly prayer He offered in Jerusalem (see 3 Nephi 19:20–23, 27–29; compare John 17).

The Savior again prays to the Father in words that cannot be recorded (see 3 Nephi 19:31–32).

3 Nephi 20. The Savior speaks of the covenant which He says the Father made with the house of Israel through Abraham and the patriarchs (see 3 Nephi 20:12–13, 25). That He is speaking of Himself acting in the role of the Father seems unlikely when one considers the subsequent verse where He also declares that the Father raised Him up and sent Him to the Nephites to bless them because they are the children of the covenant (see 3 Nephi 20:26).

The Savior teaches the people that the Father is behind the gathering of Israel and will fulfill the covenant which He made with Abraham (see 3 Nephi 20:27–34).

The Savior declares that with the fulfillment of the covenant, all the ends of the earth shall see the salvation of the Father. He also reiterates that He and the Father are one (see 3 Nephi 20:35).

3 Nephi 21. The Savior teaches the Nephites that the Gentiles will be established in their land and be set up as a free people by the power of the Father. Furthermore, the Gentiles will be instrumental in fulfilling the covenant of the Father with a remnant of the Nephite and Lamanite peoples (see 3 Nephi 21:2–5).

The Savior speaks of the work of the Father (see 3 Nephi 21:26).

3 Nephi 23. The Savior commands that certain things be added to the Nephites' records, which will go forth to the Gentiles according to the time and will of the Father (see 3 Nephi 23:4).

3 Nephi 24. The Savior commands the disciples to write down the words which the Father had given to Malachi (see 3 Nephi 24:1).

3 Nephi 26. The Savior tells the multitude that the Father commanded Him to restore to them those scriptures which they did not have in their possession because the Father wants the scriptures to go forth to future generations (see 3 Nephi 26:2).

The narrative explains that the Savior did go back to the Father after the end of the second day that He was with the people (see 3 Nephi 26:15).

3 Nephi 27. The Savior shows Himself to the disciples as they are praying unto the Father in His (Jesus') name (see 3 Nephi 27:2).

The Savior defines the gospel in its simplest form as His act of doing the will of the Father. He says His Father sent Him into the world to be lifted up on the cross. And just as men would lift Him up, so would men be lifted up by the Father because of the Son's atoning act (see 3 Nephi 27:13–14).

The Savior declares that He will act as a mediator, holding men guiltless before His Father if they will endure in righteousness. He was given this power as mediator by His Father (see 3 Nephi 27:15–16).

3 Nephi 28. The Savior tells the Three Nephites that because of their selfless request to tarry on the earth and not taste death, just as the Apostle John had requested, they shall have a fulness of joy, sit down in the kingdom of His Father, and be even as He is, that is, like the Father. "I am even as the Father; and the Father and I are one" (3 Nephi 28:10).

CLARIFYING SOME POSSIBLE CONFUSION

Reflection on the Savior's references to the Father in 3 Nephi raises an interesting issue. From the Savior's statements it would seem that the Father is much more involved than we may have previously thought in matters of salvation history that are usually ascribed to Jehovah. For example, the Savior said it was the Father who made the covenant with the house of Israel through Abraham (see 3 Nephi 20:12–13, 25).

It is the Father who is intimately involved in the scattering and gathering of the house of Israel. And it was the Father who gave the prophet Malachi the words recorded in Malachi 3:1. Yet we know that the scriptures teach that it was Jehovah who covenanted with Abraham (see Abraham 1:16; 2:6–8), that it was Jehovah who inspired the prophets of old like Malachi, and that only on rare occasions has God the Father been directly involved with mortals on this earth. Given those truths, it might almost sound like the Father being spoken of by the Savior in 3 Nephi is Jehovah, and that Jehovah is a being separate from Jesus Christ, or on the other hand if Jehovah and Jesus are one and the same, that Christ in 3 Nephi is speaking to or about Himself and praying to Himself as Jehovah, that He suffered His own will on the cross, and that it was He who caused Himself to be raised from the dead.

Resolution of the seeming confusion may be found by integrating the Savior's statements in 3 Nephi with other revelations of the Restoration. Through the Prophet Joseph Smith we know that the Father, Son, and Holy Ghost are separate and distinct personages (see D&C 130:22; JS–H 1:17). From the Book of Mormon itself we know that Jesus Christ was the premortal Jehovah come to earth as the long-awaited Messiah (see 3 Nephi 15:5). We also know that the plan of salvation was Heavenly Father's plan and that Jesus Christ put into effect or executed all the terms and conditions of His Father's plan (see Moses 4:1–4), whether acting in premortality as Jehovah or acting in mortality as Christ. We further know from the Savior's emphasis of the point He makes in 3 Nephi, as well as from modern revelation, that even though the Godhead is composed of individual beings, their unity in perfection is far more intertwined and intense than we mortals might comprehend.

The Savior Himself told the Nephites several times that He and the Father are one—not in personage or physical form, but in purpose. But even more than that, says the Savior, "I am *in* the Father, and the Father *in* me, and the Father and I are one" (3 Nephi 11:27; emphasis added; see also 3 Nephi 9:15; 19:23; and 28:10). In other words, the Father and the Son, whether the Son is acting as Jehovah or Christ, are so unified in mind and will that what one thinks, says, and does, the other one thinks, says, and does exactly.

This concept has been described in part by modern prophets as the principle of divine investiture of authority. President Joseph Fielding Smith taught:

"Christ is also our Father because his Father has given him of his fulness; that is, he has received a fulness of the glory of the Father. This is taught in Doctrine and Covenants 93:1–5, 16–17, and also by Abinadi in the 15th chapter of Mosiah. Abinadi's statement that he is 'the Father, because he was conceived by the power of God,' harmonizes with the Lord's own words in section 93 that he is the Father because he has received of the fulness of the Father. Christ says he is the Son because, 'I was in the world and made flesh my tabernacle, and dwelt among the sons of men.' Abinadi expresses this truth by saying he is 'the Son because of the flesh.'

"The Father has honored Christ by placing his name upon him, so that he can minister in and through that name as though he were the Father; and thus, so far as power and authority are concerned, his words and acts become and are those of the Father."[4]

Thus, when the Savior visited His American Israelites He testified with perfect propriety of His Father's intimate involvement in those matters of salvation history (covenanting with Abraham, speaking through Old Testament and Book of Mormon prophets, and establishing laws and commandments on the earth) with which Jehovah was also intimately involved. And yet there are also some actions and sayings attributed to the Father in the text of 3 Nephi that are uniquely God the Father's. When His voice bears witness of His Beloved Son, in whom He is "well pleased," it is the Father's voice and no other (3 Nephi 11:7). When the Savior testifies that it was by the power of the Father that He was raised up, it is the power of God the Father and no other (see 3 Nephi 27:14–15). When the Savior declares that He will hold the righteous guiltless before the Father (acting as a mediator representing us to the Father), it is the Father before whom the Savior will stand and no other (see 3 Nephi 27:16; see also D&C 45:3–5). And when the Savior declares that He received the doctrine that He teaches from the Father, it is ultimately God the Father from whom all doctrine originates, for it was originally the Father's plan by which we live (see 3 Nephi 11:31–32; Moses 4:1–4).

CONCLUSION

The words of the Book of Mormon and modern prophets describe a doctrine of the Godhead and a doctrine of God the Eternal Father that is so much more profound, and at the same time so much simpler, than Trinitarian formulations. Joseph Smith said that he had "*always* declared God to be a distinct personage, Jesus Christ a separate and distinct personage from God the Father, and that the Holy Ghost was a distinct personage and a Spirit: and these three constitute three distinct personages and three Gods."[5] Both the Book of Mormon and Joseph Smith's personal experience and teaching are monumental witnesses of God the Father.

The Book of Mormon is not an elementary treatise on, nor does it contain a confused notion of, the doctrine of the Godhead. It does not display an evolving concept of the Godhead, where only later Book of Mormon prophets knew of three separate Deities. Nor does it support the idea of a prophet-translator who only later in his ministry came to understand a clear picture of three distinct personages. From its beginning, the Book of Mormon teaches what Joseph Smith knew from the beginning. God the Father, God the Son, and God the Holy Ghost are separate and distinct personages, though they think, speak, and act as one God. And they testify of each other, as the Book of Mormon so powerfully demonstrates. "And in the mouth of three witnesses shall these things be established; and the testimony of three, and this work, in the which shall be shown forth the power of God and also his word, of which the Father, and the Son, and the Holy Ghost bear record—and all this shall stand as a testimony against the world at the last day" (Ether 5:4).

NOTES

1. President Joseph Fielding Smith taught: "All revelation since the fall has come through Jesus Christ, who is the Jehovah of the Old Testament. In all of the scriptures, where God is mentioned and where he has appeared, it was Jehovah who talked with Abraham, with Noah, Enoch, Moses and all the prophets. . . . The Father has never dealt with man directly and personally since the fall, and he has never appeared except to introduce and bear record of the Son. Thus the *Inspired Version* records that 'no man hath seen God at any time, except he hath borne record of the Son'" (Joseph Fielding Smith, *Doctrines of Salvation,* comp. Bruce R. McConkie [Salt Lake City: Bookcraft, 1970], 1:27).

2. See Joseph Smith, *Teachings of the Prophet Joseph Smith,* comp. Joseph Fielding Smith (Salt Lake City: Deseret Book, 1972), 365.

3. Bryant S. Hinckley, ed., *Sermons and Missionary Services of Melvin Joseph Ballard* (Salt Lake City: Deseret Book, 1949), 166–67.

4. Joseph Fielding Smith, *Doctrines of Salvation,* 1:29–30.

5. Smith, *Teachings,* 370; emphasis added.

25

The Jaredites: A Case Study in Following the Brethren

Douglas E. Brinley

A distinguishing feature of The Church of Jesus Christ of Latter-day Saints is the principle of continuous revelation: God speaks to His children through prophet-servants today as well as in former times (see Amos 3:7). The principle of revelation separates Latter-day Saints from all other religions, for our claim of administering the true gospel is based on this premise: In 1820 God called a young man to the prophetic office and subsequently sent eight angels to restore the gospel and priesthood keys that enable men and women to qualify for exaltation. Moroni restored the gospel in the form of a set of plates that contain the everlasting gospel. John the Baptist; Peter, James, and John; Moses, Elias, and Elijah restored priesthood keys for the salvation and exaltation of God's children. President John Taylor explained that true religion has a heavenly connection:

"A good many people, and those professing Christians, will sneer at the idea of present revelation. Whoever heard of true religion without communication with God? To me the thing is the most absurd thing that the human mind could conceive of. I do not wonder, when the people generally reject the principle of present revelation, that

---

Douglas E. Brinley is a professor of Church history and doctrine at Brigham Young University.

skepticism and infidelity prevail to such an alarming extent. I do not wonder that so many men treat religion with contempt, and regard it as something not worth the attention of intelligent beings, *for without revelation religion is a mockery and a farce.* If I can not have a religion that will lead me to God, and place me *en rapport* with him, and unfold to my mind the principles of immortality and eternal life, I want nothing to do with it."[1]

A BOOK OF MORMON MESSAGE

A prominent theme of the Book of Mormon is, however, that people seldom follow the Lord's servants when they are sent, especially when living conditions are soft, comfortable, and easy and prosperity abounds. During these periods people ignore God, reject His prophets, and become distracted from their goal to obtain "immortality and eternal life" (Moses 1:39).

From the rebellion of Laman and Lemuel against Lehi and against Nephi to the fall of Moroni's people, the Book of Mormon is replete with examples of people who ignored the counsel of their living prophets. The result was a "ripening in iniquity" until the inhabitants were destroyed by civil war or natural disasters (see 2 Nephi 28:16; Alma 10:19; Helaman 5:2; 6:40; 8:26; 11:37; 13:14; 3 Nephi 8; Ether 2:9; 9:20).

THE PEOPLE OF JARED

One of the most poignant examples of the destruction of an entire civilization who failed to follow their prophets is found in the book of Ether. The fall of the people of Jared was especially tragic in light of the numerous times God sent prophets to warn them that they were bringing a curse upon the land that would end in their "utter destruction" if the people did not repent. Eventually the entire nation was engulfed in a civil war that brought about their extinction as a people, leaving only Coriantumr and the prophet-recorder Ether as lone survivors. Moroni warned the latter-day inhabitants of the land to avoid the pattern that destroyed the former occupants of the land: "And this cometh unto you, O ye Gentiles, that ye may know the decrees of God—that ye may repent, and not continue in your iniquities until the fulness come, that ye may not bring down the fulness of the wrath of God upon you as the inhabitants of the land have hitherto done" (Ether 2:11).

THE PATTERN OF DESTRUCTION

One way to view the fall of the Jaredites is to observe the four points of sequence that led to their downfall:

1. God sent prophets to call the people to repentance.
2. They warned the people of destruction if they did not repent.
3. The people chose either to repent or reject the prophetic message.
4. They received the consequences of their decision.

This pattern was repeated at least six times in the Jaredite record until the people were destroyed under the reign of Coriantumr, who ignored the counsel of Ether until repentance was no longer possible (see Ether 15:1–2). Moroni explained that it was the Lord who brought about the destruction of this people: "And now," wrote the abridger, "I . . . proceed to give an account of those ancient inhabitants who were destroyed *by the hand of the Lord* upon the face of this north country" (Ether 1:1; emphasis added). Let us now examine these six episodes that ended in the destruction of an entire nation.

JAREDITES IN THE LAND

The Jaredites were led to the land of promise by the Lord at the time of the "great tower" and the confusion of tongues (see Genesis 11; Ether 1:33).[2] As they multiplied and spread throughout the land, they became a large and prosperous people. They began as a righteous colony, having been "taught to walk humbly before the Lord; and they were also taught from on high" (Ether 6:17).

As they grew in number, the people desired a king over the objections of the brother of Jared, who cautioned them that having a king would be unwise in the long run (see Ether 6:22–23; 7:5). At a much later date, Mosiah, the Nephite seer who first translated the record of this fallen people from twenty-four gold plates, also warned the Nephites of the dangers of a kingship. His counsel came from the antics of king Noah, son of Zeniff, and also from translating the record of the people of Jared. He observed:

"How much iniquity doth one wicked king cause to be committed, yea, and what great destruction! . . .

"Now I say unto you, ye cannot dethrone an iniquitous king save it be through much contention, and the shedding of much blood.

"For behold, he has his friends in iniquity, and he keepeth his guards about him; and he teareth up the laws of those who have reigned in righteousness before him; and he trampleth under his feet the commandments of God;

"And he enacteth laws, and sendeth them forth among his people, yea, laws after the manner of his own wickedness; and whosoever doth not obey his laws he causeth to be destroyed; and whosoever doth rebel against him he will send his armies against them to war, and if he can he will destroy them; and thus an unrighteous king doth pervert the ways of all righteousness.

"And now behold I say unto you, it is not expedient that such abominations should come upon you" (Mosiah 29:17, 21–24).

EPISODE 1: THE REIGN OF KINGS

Like their later Israelite counterparts, the people of Jared wanted a king. After the brother of Jared warned against this form of government, he relented but no one wanted the office until finally one of the sons of Jared, Orihah, consented and was anointed ruler (see Ether 6:22–27). Orihah and his successor-son, Kib, were righteous kings, but Kib's son, Corihor, rebelled against his father, overthrowing him and taking him captive. While in prison—more likely a house arrest—Kib fathered a son, Shule, who "became mighty as to the strength of a man" (Ether 7:8). This son was sympathetic to his father and succeeded in repelling Corihor and restoring Kib to his throne. Kib passed his office on to Shule. However, one of Corihor's sons, Noah, in attempting to overthrow Shule, took him captive and would have executed him except the sons of Shule "crept into the house of Noah by night and slew him, and broke down the door of the prison and brought out their father, and placed him upon his throne in his own kingdom" (Ether

7:18). Thus men began to covet the throne, and rebellion and mischief among the people continued. The son of Noah, Cohor, succeeded in dividing the people into two groups: "And there were two kingdoms, the kingdom of Shule, and the kingdom of Cohor" (Ether 7:20). In a subsequent battle, Shule killed Cohor and united the kingdom.

It was in this setting that prophets came forth to warn the people that their wickedness violated their covenant on the land with God and that judgments were imminent unless swift repentance followed. This was the first of six episodes where prophets were sent to warn the Jaredites that their wickedness was offensive to the Lord (see Ether 2:7–12). This first episode follows four steps in the sequence to destruction: (1) prophets are sent, (2) a message of warning is given, (3) the people respond, and on this occasion (4) the outcome is favorable.

Sequence to Destruction

1. *Prophet(s):* Unnamed, but "sent from the Lord" (Ether 7:23).
2. *Message:* "The wickedness and idolatry of the people was bringing a curse upon the land, and they should be destroyed if they did not repent" (Ether 7:23).
3. *Response of the People:* "The people did revile against the prophets, and did mock them" (Ether 7:24).
4. *Outcome:* Before judgments began, King Shule "did execute a law throughout all the land, which gave power unto the prophets" to "go whithersoever they would; and by this cause the people were brought unto repentance" (Ether 7:25), and "there were no more wars in the days of Shule" (Ether 7:27). In this case, the government supported freedom of religion. Unfortunately, this principle, protected by kingly edict under Shule, was withdrawn by later rulers.

EPISODE 2: THE DAYS OF JARED

Two men, Jared, the son of Omer, and Akish, conspired to the throne and organized a secret combination to kill Omer. But the Lord warned Omer "in a dream that he should depart out of the land," leaving the throne to Jared (Ether 9:3). Having tasted power, however, Akish decided to kill Jared so that he himself could become king.

Internal dissent among his sons led to Akish's death, restoring Omer to the kingship. His son, Emer, followed him as ruler, and governed in peace for the next sixty-two years. The people multiplied and prospered, insomuch that the Lord "began again to take the curse from off the land" (Ether 9:16). Emer's sons, Coriantum and Com, also became kings and ruled in righteousness and the people were blessed.

However, after several generations of peace, wickedness returned. "The people had spread again over all the face of the land, and there began again to be an exceedingly great wickedness upon the face of the land, and Heth began to embrace the secret plans again of old, to destroy his father" (Ether 9:26). Heth became king by murdering his father, Com, and prophets were sent forth to warn the people of impending judgments.

Sequence to Destruction

1. *Prophets:* Unnamed, but from the Lord (Ether 9:28).

2. *Message:* "That [the people] must prepare the way of the Lord or there should come a curse upon the face of the land; yea, even there should be a great famine, in which they should be destroyed if they did not repent" (Ether 9:28).

3. *Response of the People:* "But the people believed not the words of the prophets, but they cast them out; and some of them they cast into pits and left them to perish" (Ether 9:29).

4. *Outcome:* This time the government did not protect the prophets to teach repentance freely in the land, but instead threatened the lives of the prophets. "And it came to pass that they did all these things according to the commandment of the king, Heth" (Ether 9:29). Consequently, judgments ensued: "And it came to pass that there began to be a great dearth upon the land, and the inhabitants began to be destroyed exceedingly fast" (Ether 9:30). Upon threat of destruction by poisonous serpents and drought, the people "began to repent of their iniquities and cry unto the Lord. And it came to pass that when they had humbled themselves sufficiently before the Lord he did send rain upon the face of the earth; and the people began to revive again" (Ether 9:34–35).

EPISODE 3: THE DAYS OF COM

Peace and prosperity reigned in the land for another generation before Heth's grandson Riplakish came to power. Unfortunately, he introduced polygamy, whoredoms, and high taxes and built prisons to house those who would not pay taxes, putting to death those who would not labor. The people rebelled against his policies and killed him. His son Morianton restored a measure of peace again among the people for several generations until the reign of Com.

Sequence to Destruction

1. *Prophets:* "Many prophets" (Ether 11:1).

2. *Message:* "The destruction of that great people except they should repent, and turn unto the Lord, and forsake their murders and wickedness" (Ether 11:1).

3. *Response of the People:* "The prophets were rejected by the people, and they fled unto [Com] for protection, for the people sought to destroy them" (Ether 11:2).

4. *Outcome:* Com protected the prophets, and there was a delay in the judgments of the Lord. Com was "blessed in all the remainder of his days" (Ether 11:3).

Com was a righteous ruler as was his son Shiblom. One of Shiblom's brothers, however, rebelled against Shiblom and caused that "all the prophets who prophesied of the destruction of the people should be put to death" (Ether 11:5). Thus, "there began to be an exceedingly great war in all the land" (Ether 11:4). Moroni describes the situation:

"There was great calamity in all the land, for [these prophets] had testified that a great curse should come upon the land, and also upon the people, and that there should be a great destruction among them, such an one as never had been upon the face of the earth, and their bones should become as heaps of earth upon the face of the land except they should repent of their wickedness.

"And they hearkened not unto the voice of the Lord, because of their wicked combinations; wherefore, there began to be wars and contentions in all the land, and also many famines and pestilences, insomuch that there was a great destruction, *such an one as never had been known upon the face of the earth;* and all this came to pass in the days of Shiblom" (Ether 11:6–7; emphasis added).

This great destruction resulted in "heaps" of bodies upon the earth which eventually caused the people to repent, and "inasmuch as they did [repent] the Lord did have mercy on them" (Ether 11:8).

EPISODE 4: THE DAYS OF ETHEM

Three generations later, Ethem ascended to the throne and did "execute judgment in wickedness all his days" (Ether 11:14). Prophets renewed their cry for repentance.

Sequence to Destruction

1. *Prophets:* "In the days of Ethem there came many prophets, and prophesied again unto the people" (Ether 11:12).

2. *Message:* "They did prophesy that the Lord would utterly destroy them from off the face of the earth except they repented of their iniquities" (Ether 11:12).

3. *Response of the People:* "The people hardened their hearts, and would not hearken unto their words; and the prophets mourned and withdrew from among the people" (Ether 11:13).

4. *Outcome:* The prophets were silenced and the Lord withdrew His spirit from the people. A series of wars began to decimate the people. The Lord provided numerous opportunities for the people to repent and change their ways, but they would not.

EPISODE 5: THE DAYS OF CORIANTOR

A series of political power struggles resulted in further war, and the Lord sent prophets to warn the people to repent (see Ether 11:20). Moron was taken captive and fathered a son named Coriantor who spent his days in captivity also. Coriantor was the father of the prophet Ether (see Ether 11:23).

Sequence to Destruction

1. *Prophets:* "In the days of Coriantor there also came many prophets" (Ether 11:20).

2. *Message:* "[These prophets] prophesied of great and marvelous things, and cried repentance unto the people, and [said that] except they should repent the Lord God would execute judgment against them *to their utter destruction;* and that the Lord God would send or bring forth another people to possess the land, by his power, after the manner by which he brought their fathers" (Ether 11:20–21; emphasis added).

3. *Response of the People:* "And they did reject all the words of the prophets, because of their secret society and wicked abominations" (Ether 11:22).

4. *Outcome:* Civil war began to destroy the inhabitants of the land.

Though Coriantor fathered Ether in captivity, it appears that the prophet-writer of the Jaredite record should rightfully have been the king. But his grandfather, Moron, had been deposed by an unnamed "descendant of the brother of Jared" (Ether 11:17–18). We do not know who this man was. The record is not clear if this person is Coriantumr's father or even his grandfather. If it was, it makes the relationship between Ether and Coriantumr more delicate and may account for Coriantumr's rejection of Ether's message to him. He may have seen Ether as trying to bring his kingdom down so that he could assume the mantle of leadership.

Ether cried "from the morning, even until the going down of the sun, exhorting the people to believe in God unto repentance lest they should be destroyed" (Ether 12:3).

"He truly told them of all things, from the beginning of man; and that after the waters [of the flood] had receded from off the face of this land it became a choice land above all other lands, a chosen land of the Lord; wherefore the Lord would have that all men should serve him who dwell upon the face thereof;

"And that it was the place of the New Jerusalem, which should come down out of heaven, and the holy sanctuary of the Lord.

"Behold, Ether saw the days of Christ, and he spake concerning a New Jerusalem upon this land" (Ether 13:2–4).

But the people rejected Ether's message and "esteemed him as naught, and cast him out; and he hid himself in the cavity of a rock by day, and by night he went forth viewing the things which should come upon the people" (Ether 13:13).

EPISODE 6: THE REIGN OF CORIANTUMR

Many sought to wrest the kingdom from Coriantumr. Although there was constant warfare, the people refused to humble themselves, even when Ether explained to Coriantumr how he could save his life and the lives of his family and subjects as well.

Sequence to Destruction

1. *Prophet:* Ether, son of Coriantor.

2. *Message:* "Prophesy unto Coriantumr that, if he would repent, and all his household, the Lord would give unto him his kingdom and spare the people—otherwise they should be destroyed, and all his household save it were himself. And he should only live to see the fulfilling of the prophecies which had been spoken concerning another people receiving the land for their inheritance; and Coriantumr should receive a burial by them; and every soul should be destroyed save it were Coriantumr" (Ether 13:20–21).

3. *Response of Coriantumr:* "Coriantumr repented not, neither his household, neither the people; and the wars ceased not; and they sought to kill Ether, but he fled from before them and hid again in the cavity of the rock" (Ether 13:22).

4. *Outcome:* The destruction of the Jaredite civilization—Coriantumr and Ether were the only survivors.

ETHER'S PROPHECY

Ether's prophecy becomes a remarkable example of how prophets are able to see the end from the beginning and give inspired and detailed utterances long before such particulars could be known rationally. The extent of this prophecy by Ether becomes evident as we follow Coriantumr to the end of his reign and view how improbable Ether's prediction was at the time he first confronted the king.

To illustrate how implausible Ether's prophecy must have seemed to Coriantumr, the record shows that numerous times the king should have died from wounds and loss of blood, if not infection. But Ether had told him that he alone of all of his subjects would survive and be buried by another people who would inhabit the land (see Ether 13:20–21; Omni 1:14–22).

The magnitude of Ether's prediction deepened as Coriantumr confronted his antagonist, Shiz. After an especially fierce battle, Moroni wrote:

"When Coriantumr had recovered of his wounds, he began to remember the words which Ether had spoken unto him.

"He saw that there had been slain by the sword already nearly two millions of his people, and he began to sorrow in his heart; yea, there had been slain two millions of mighty men, and also their wives and their children.

"He began to repent of the evil which he had done; he began to remember the words which had been spoken by the mouth of all the prophets, and he saw them that they were fulfilled thus far, every whit; and his soul mourned and refused to be comforted" (Ether 15:1–3).

BATTLE CASUALTIES

Millions of people died before Coriantumr admitted that Ether had spoken the truth to him, but by then it was too late. To provide some perspective of the magnitude of the slaughter among Coriantumr's people, we note that at the time Ether approached him with a solution to save people, Coriantumr presided over a kingdom numbering millions of inhabitants. The record says that "there had been slain two millions of mighty men, and also their wives and their children" (Ether 15:2). If even half of these men were married and the average family size included a wife and only two to three children, there would have been six to eight million people in his kingdom. From the American Revolutionary War through the Vietnam conflict (including the Civil War)—wars that introduced weapons of mass destruction—"only" 652,769 Americans died on the battlefield[3] compared to the millions killed in these final Jaredite struggles where the people died in hand-to-hand combat.

THE FULFILLMENT OF ETHER'S PROPHECY

The magnitude of Ether's prophecy deepens. At the time he approached Coriantumr and delivered his inspired ultimatum, Coriantumr could have reasonably scoffed at Ether's prediction because of the vast numbers of inhabitants comprising his kingdom. To believe that all of his subjects could be killed before he was—given the fact that he apparently *led* his troops into battle and would be one of the first to engage the enemy—would no doubt seem preposterous. Surely Ether's prophecy could not be fulfilled. For example, the record states: "Shared . . . also gave battle unto Coriantumr; and he did . . . bring him into captivity" (Ether 13:23); yet Coriantumr was not killed. Coriantumr's sons retook the kingdom by beating Shared and restoring the kingdom to their father. He and Shared later fought again, and before Coriantumr finally killed Shared, "Shared wounded Coriantumr in his thigh, that he did not go to battle again for the space of two years" (Ether 13:31).

On another occasion Coriantumr fought against Lib, who wounded him. When he recovered from that wound, he killed Lib. However, Lib's brother Shiz swore that he would avenge his brother's blood, and "pursued after Coriantumr, and he did overthrow many cities, and he did slay both women and children, and he did burn the cities. And there went a fear of Shiz throughout all the land" (Ether 14:12, 17–18). He was so barbaric that many people fled to his camp, thinking that he surely would conquer Coriantumr—for Shiz had "sworn to avenge himself upon Coriantumr of the blood of [Lib]" (Ether 14:24), determined that Ether's prophecy that Coriantumr would not fall by the sword would never be fulfilled. "Shiz smote upon Coriantumr that he gave him many deep wounds; and Coriantumr, having lost his blood, fainted, and was carried away [by his people] as though he were dead" (Ether 14:30). Shiz must have thought he had killed Coriantumr at that time, but Coriantumr recovered to fight another day.

The ensuing battles became so fierce that Coriantumr offered to give up the kingdom if they would only spare his people (Ether 15:4–5). But Shiz's condition that Coriantumr "give himself up, that [Shiz] might slay him with his own sword," was not acceptable, and more battles ensued (Ether 15:5, 7).

THE FINAL BATTLE

As Coriantumr saw his people being decimated, he again offered Shiz the kingdom if he would simply cease fighting, but Shiz would not relent. They fought again "and when the night came they had all fallen by the sword save it were fifty and two of the people of Coriantumr, and sixty and nine of the people of Shiz" (Ether 15:23). The next day's battle reduced those numbers to twenty-seven and thirty-two (see Ether 15:25), and the last battle left only Shiz and Coriantumr facing each other.

"When they had all fallen by the sword, save it were Coriantumr and Shiz, behold Shiz had fainted with the loss of blood.

"And it came to pass that when Coriantumr had leaned upon his sword, that he rested a little, he smote off the head of Shiz.

"And it came to pass that after he had smitten off the head of Shiz, that Shiz raised up on his hands and fell; and after that he had struggled for breath, he died.

"And it came to pass that Coriantumr fell to the earth, and became as if he had no life" (Ether 15:29–33).

Ether "went forth, and beheld that the words of the Lord had all been fulfilled" (Ether 15:33). Now his remarkable prophecy, uttered in detail many years earlier, was almost complete. "Coriantumr was discovered by the people of Zarahemla; and he dwelt with them for the space of nine moons" before he died (Omni 1:21).

The Jaredites had had many opportunities to turn their civilization around and avoid the judgments that eventually destroyed them. From the beginning they had been warned that "this is a land which is choice above all other lands; wherefore he that doth possess it shall serve God or shall be swept off; for it is the everlasting decree of God. And it is not until the fulness of iniquity among the children of the land, that they are swept off" (Ether 2:10). Many prophets had warned that their doom would come when they refused to repent and "serve the God of the land, who is Jesus Christ" (Ether 2:12). Thus a great people destroyed themselves because they refused to follow the counsel of the Lord's prophets.

A MESSAGE FOR OUR DAY

Moroni saw our day in vision when his people, much like Ether's, were gone (see Mormon 8:34–35). He felt impressed to point out parallels between his own people, the Jaredites, and us as latter-day inhabitants of the promised land. He pleaded for us to "repent, and not continue in [our] iniquities until the fulness come, that [we] may not bring down the fulness of the wrath of God upon [us] as the *inhabitants of the land have hitherto done*" (Ether 2:11; emphasis added). Will we follow the counsel of God's prophets any better than the former inhabitants did? If we are not wiser than they were, we will suffer their same fate.

We must heed the prophets of our day. The Lord has organized His Church and kingdom on the earth with a First Presidency and a Quorum of Twelve Apostles, each member sustained as a prophet, seer, and revelator. Every six months we have the opportunity to listen to their counsel and warnings on how we should improve our lives so we can avoid the tragedies that destroyed this land's former inhabitants.

CONCLUSION

The principle of following God's prophets has always been a test for the children of God. It continues to be the principle that will determine whether or not Zion will be established on the earth in the latter days. Zion can be built up only as individuals who are pure in heart accept counsel and direction from living prophets. In a day of relative ease and prosperity, that is not an easy task. The Prophet Joseph Smith acknowledged that even the Saints wrestle with this principle: "There are those who profess to be Saints who are too apt to murmur and find fault, when any advice is given, which comes in opposition to their feelings, even when they, themselves, ask for counsel; much more so when counsel is given unasked for, which does not agree with their notion of things; but brethren, we hope for better things from the most of you; we trust that you desire counsel, from time to time, and that you will cheerfully conform to it, whenever you receive it from a proper source."[4]

Our destiny in this dispensation, as it was for the Nephites and Jaredites, will be determined by our willingness to heed the counsel of the living prophets. President Wilford Woodruff warned the Latter-day Saints of going against prophetic counsel: "We, as a people, should not treat lightly this counsel, for I will tell you in the name of the Lord—and I have watched it from the time I became a member of this Church—there is no man who undertakes to run counter to the counsel of the legally authorized leader of this people that ever prospers, and no such man ever will prosper. . . . You will find that all persons who take a stand against this counsel will never prosper. . . . When counsel comes we should not treat it lightly, no matter to what subject it pertains, for if we do it will work evil unto us."[5]

Only when people are willing to follow God's prophets can Zion be established. They must be pure in heart, willing, and anxious to receive and implement inspired counsel, and thereby carry out the will of God, or they must face the judgments of the Almighty.

NOTES

1. John Taylor, in *Journal of Discourses* (London: Latter-day Saints' Book Depot, 1854–86), 6:371; emphasis added.

2. The tower of Babel incident is thought to have occurred in approximately 2200 B.C. (see Bible Dictionary, "Chronology," 635). Later editions of the dictionary delete the years of specific events from Adam to King Saul. Also, the term "tower of Babel" is not used in the Book of Mormon record.

3. When other war-related deaths are included—sickness and infections from wounds—a total of 1,178,066 deaths are attributable to all wars that the United States has fought as a nation (see Mark S. Hoffman, ed., *The World Almanac and Book of Facts* [New York: Pharos Books, 1993], 698).

4. Joseph Smith, *History of the Church of Jesus Christ of Latter-day Saints,* ed. B. H. Roberts (Salt Lake City: Deseret Book, 1962), 4:45.

5. Wilford Woodruff, in *Journal of Discourses,* 14:33.

26

The Spirit of Christ: A Light amidst the Darkness

Daniel K Judd

Those prophets who wrote, compiled, and abridged the Book of Mormon did so with the inhabitants of our day in mind. President Ezra Taft Benson stated: "We must make the Book of Mormon a center focus of study because it was written for our day. The Nephites never had the book, neither did the Lamanites of ancient times. It was meant for us. Mormon wrote near the end of the Nephite civilization. Under the inspiration of God, who sees all things from the beginning, he abridged centuries of records, choosing the stories, speeches, and events that would be most helpful to us."[1]

Moroni, the last of the Book of Mormon prophets, saw our day:

"The Lord hath shown unto me great and marvelous things concerning that which must shortly come, at that day when these things shall come forth among you.

"Behold, I speak unto you as if ye were present, and yet ye are not. But behold, Jesus Christ hath shown you unto me, and I know your doing,

" . . . the pride of your hearts . . . envying, and strifes, and malice, and persecutions, and all manner of iniquities" (Mormon 8:34–36).

Daniel K Judd is chair of the Department of Ancient Scripture at Brigham Young University.

In the *Wall Street Journal,* we read a sobering description of the problems in today's society that is consistent with Moroni's vision: "Since 1960 . . . there has been a 560% increase in violent crime; a 419% increase in illegitimate births; a quadrupling in divorce rates; a tripling of the percentage of children living in single-parent homes; more than a 200% increase in the teenage suicide rate."[2]

We live in difficult times, and my heart goes out to all those whose lives embody these statistics in any way. While some of the problems of our day do not involve questions of morality, most do. We have all been influenced in some way by the moral decay of our culture. Many things which were once considered evil are now celebrated as "good," and numerous things which were once reverenced as good are now called inappropriate or evil. Isaiah has written, "Wo unto them that call evil good, and good evil; that put darkness for light, and light for darkness; that put bitter for sweet, and sweet for bitter!" (Isaiah 5:20; see also 2 Nephi 15:20).

A LIGHT IN THE DARKNESS

Not only have prophets provided descriptions of the problems of our day, but they have also given counsel as to how to address them. As part of his record, the prophet Moroni included his father's teaching on the most fundamental means by which God sustains man: the Spirit of Christ: "For behold, the *Spirit of Christ* is given to every man, that he may know good from evil; wherefore, I show unto you the way to judge; for every thing which inviteth to do good, and to persuade to believe in Christ, is sent forth by the power and gift of Christ; wherefore ye may know with a perfect knowledge it is of God" (Moroni 7:16; emphasis added). The Spirit of Christ is not merely a source of truth; it is an integral part of what we are as human beings (see John 14:6, 20; D&C 93:29).

While the Book of Mormon does not provide detailed information concerning the Spirit of Christ, it does describe its purposes and its influence upon the lives of people. From modern scriptures, we learn that the Spirit of Christ is the *power* that "proceedeth forth from the presence of God to fill the immensity of space" (D&C 88:12; see also

2 Nephi 16:3). It is the *light* of the sun, the moon, and the stars, and the *power* by which all things were made (see D&C 88:7–10). It is a *spirit* that "giveth life to all things" and the "*law* by which all things are governed" (D&C 88:13; emphasis added). Also, this spirit is the power which enables God to comprehend all things (see D&C 88:41). The Spirit of Christ is also that which "giveth light to every man that cometh into the world" (D&C 84:46) and is given to everyone that they "may know good from evil" (Moroni 7:15).

THE SPIRIT OF CHRIST AND THE HOLY GHOST

The Spirit of Christ is often confused with the Holy Ghost, the gift of the Holy Ghost, and the spirit personage of Jesus Christ. Some of the confusion obviously comes because terms such as "Spirit of the Lord," "Spirit of God," and "Spirit of Christ" are often used interchangeably in both scripture and conversation, and it is often difficult to determine to which personage or gift the passage refers. The term "Spirit of Christ" is used only twice in the Book of Mormon (see Moroni 7:16 and 10:17) while the term "Holy Ghost" is used ninety-five times. The term "Spirit of the Lord" is used forty times, "Spirit of God" twenty times, and "power of God" fifty-four times. An analysis of the use of these terms reveals that only in a few instances is the differentiation of these terms made clear.

It is from the prophets of this dispensation that we learn that the Spirit of Christ is neither the Holy Ghost, the gift of the Holy Ghost, nor the spirit personage of Jesus Christ, but it is the primary means by which each of these entities operate. President Joseph F. Smith taught: "The question is often asked, Is there any difference between the Spirit of the Lord and the Holy Ghost? The terms are frequently used synonymously. We often say the Spirit of God when we mean the Holy Ghost; we likewise say the Holy Ghost when we mean the Spirit of God. The Holy Ghost is a personage in the Godhead, and is not that which lighteth every man that cometh into the world. It is the Spirit of God which proceeds through Christ to the world, that enlightens every man that comes into the world, and that strives with the children of men, and will continue to strive with them, until it brings them to a knowledge of the truth and the possession of the greater light and testimony of the Holy Ghost."[3]

Elder James E. Talmage taught that the Spirit of Christ is the "divine essence" by means of which the Godhead operates upon man and in nature."[4] Elder Bruce R. McConkie added, "Before and after baptism, all men are endowed to one degree or another with that Spirit which is the light of Christ." He said that a "testimony before baptism, speaking by way of analogy, comes as a flash of lightning blazing forth in a dark and stormy night . . . to light the path." Then he compared the gift of the Holy Ghost to the "continuing blaze of the sun at noonday, shedding its rays on the path of life and on all that surrounds it."[5] Perhaps it would be appropriate to liken the Spirit of Christ to the faint and yet fixed light of the moon and stars that precedes the brighter light of dawn.

Prophets, both ancient and modern, have taught that the Spirit of Christ is *preparatory* in purpose. It prepares God's children to receive the temporary witness of the Holy Ghost, followed by the more constant gift of the Holy Ghost, which is bestowed upon those who are baptized (see D&C 130:23). An example of this progression can be identified in the Book of Mormon account of the conversion of King Lamoni. Even though Lamoni had the autocratic authority of a king and had been taught that "whatsoever [he] did was right," the text suggests that he still knew it was wrong to slay those servants he judged had not served him well: "Notwithstanding [King Lamoni and his father] believed in a Great Spirit, they supposed that whatsoever they did was right; nevertheless, Lamoni began to fear exceedingly, with fear lest he had done wrong in slaying his servants" (Alma 18:5).

We may conclude from this verse that the Spirit of the Lord is *not* simply the internalization of the expectations of the culture in which one lives (see Joseph Smith Translation, John 7:24), but it is a part of what we are as human beings (see Romans 2:14). Though the truth was eclipsed by tradition and sin, a spirit was working upon King Lamoni that revived his sense of right and wrong.

King Lamoni's experience continued and intensified as he "fell unto the earth, as if he were dead" (Alma 18:42). Note the description of

Lamoni's experience during the time he was overcome: "Ammon . . . knew that king Lamoni was under the power of God; he knew that the dark veil of unbelief was being cast away from his mind, and the *light* which did *light* up his mind, which was the *light* of the glory of God, which was a marvelous *light* of his goodness—yea, this *light* had infused such joy into his soul, the cloud of darkness having been dispelled, and that the *light* of everlasting life was lit up in his soul, yea, he knew that this had overcome his natural frame, and he was carried away in God" (Alma 19:6; emphasis added).

Ammon seems to be describing the Light of Christ that was working on the king, preparing him to receive the constant companionship of the Holy Ghost. King Lamoni and all of his servants were then baptized, and even though it is not detailed in this scriptural account we can be confident that precedent was followed and, after being baptized, they were given the gift of the Holy Ghost (see 2 Nephi 31:14).

The additional light that comes with the reception of the gift of the Holy Ghost is demonstrated by Ammon's experiences as he worked with King Lamoni. In addition to the great physical power demonstrated by Ammon, he was also "filled with the *Spirit of God,* therefore he *perceived the thoughts of the king*" (Alma 18:16; emphasis added). Ammon also described additional blessings in the following:

"I am called by his *Holy Spirit* to teach these things unto this people, that they may be brought to a knowledge of that which is just and true;

"And a portion of that *Spirit* dwelleth in me, which giveth me knowledge, and also power according to my faith and desires which are in God" (Alma 18:34–35; emphasis added).

THE LIGHT OF CREATION

The scriptures also teach us that one of the fundamental functions of the Spirit of Christ was in the creation of the earth (see D&C 88:10). This strongly suggests that the Spirit of God that "moved upon the face of the water" mentioned by Moses in the various Creation accounts was the Spirit of Christ (see Moses 2:2–5; Genesis 1:2–5). Elder Parley P. Pratt wrote that it is the "true light," or the Spirit of

Christ, that permeates all nature and provides the life-sustaining instincts found in both men and animals.[6] As stated earlier, the Spirit of Christ is not always something that is external to us; it is also a part of what we are as living creatures. The scriptures imply that without the Spirit of Christ, which gives us life "from one moment to another," life would cease to exist (see Mosiah 2:21; D&C 88:50).

THE LIGHT OF DISCOVERY AND INTELLECT

The Spirit of Christ is also the power that enlightens our intellects as we seek to discover the mysteries of heaven and earth (see D&C 88:11). Nephi tells us that "the *Spirit of God* . . . wrought upon the man" Columbus in his discovery of the New World and that "the *Spirit of God* . . . wrought upon other Gentiles [i.e., Pilgrims]; and they went forth out of captivity, upon the many waters" (1 Nephi 13:12–13; emphasis added). We also read of the Lord's promise to Nephi to be his "*light* in the wilderness" as he sought to find the promised land (1 Nephi 17:13; emphasis added).

Alma wrote of hearts being changed and souls being "illuminated by the *light* of the everlasting word" (Alma 5:7; emphasis added). He also described the "discernible" nature of light in the following passage: "O then, is not this real? I say unto you, Yea, because it is *light;* and whatsoever is *light,* is good, because it is discernible, therefore ye must know that it is good" (Alma 32:35; emphasis added).

Many of the world's great leaders, scientists, artists, and philosophers have also been influenced by "a portion of God's light." In 1978 the First Presidency stated: "The great religious leaders of the world such as Mohammed, Confucius, and the Reformers, as well as philosophers including Socrates, Plato, and others, received a portion of God's light. Moral truths were given to them by God to enlighten whole nations and to bring a higher level of understanding to individuals."[7]

It was also the Spirit of Christ that led to the scientific discoveries of Gutenberg, Edison, and Bell, and others. President Joseph Fielding Smith wrote: "Those who make these discoveries are inspired of God or they would never make them. The Lord gave inspiration to Edison, to Franklin, to Morse, to Whitney and to all of the inventors and discoverers, and through their inspiration they obtained the necessary knowledge and were able to manufacture and invent as they have done for the benefit of the world. Without the help of the Lord they would have been just as helpless as the people were in other ages."[8]

THE LIGHT OF CONSCIENCE

Though the Spirit of Christ is manifest in a multitude of ways, the remainder of this chapter will be dedicated to the dimension of the Spirit of Christ that deals with conscience, the knowing of "good from evil." In addition to what was stated earlier concerning "every thing which inviteth to do good" being "sent forth by the power and gift of Christ" (Moroni 7:16), Mormon also teaches us about discerning that which is evil: "But whatsoever thing persuadeth men to do evil, and believe not in Christ, and deny him, and serve not God, then ye may know with a perfect knowledge it is of the devil; for after this manner doth the devil work, for he persuadeth no man to do good, no, not one; neither do his angels; neither do they who subject themselves unto him" (Moroni 7:17).

Though we live in marvelous times when the gospel of Christ has been restored to the earth in its fulness, many have come to a distorted view of good and evil for they "denieth the *power* of God" because of the "precepts of men" (2 Nephi 28:26; emphasis added). The good and evil spoken of in scripture has been replaced by the dogmatism of some and the relativism of others. The Book of Mormon anti-Christ Korihor taught that "every man prospered according to his genius" and justified his own evil deeds and those of others by teaching that "whatsoever a man did was no crime" (Alma 30:17). The Apostle Paul warned of those who would come to associate righteousness with prosperity and competence (see 1 Timothy 6:5). All of these false philosophies lead to serious distortions of conscience.

The Lord has warned us that the day would come when men would "perceive not the light" (D&C 45:29) and reject the fulness of the gospel because they would come to believe in false philosophies. President Joseph Fielding Smith warned of relying solely on the power of intellect: "*The worship of reason, of false philosophy,* is greater now than it was [in the days of the Son of God]. Men are depending upon their own research to find out God, and that which they cannot discover and which they cannot demonstrate to their satisfaction through their own research and their *natural senses,* they reject. They are not seeking for the Spirit of the Lord; they are not striving to know God in the manner in which he has marked out by which he may be known; but they are walking in their own way, believing in their own man-made philosophies, teaching the doctrines of devils and not the doctrines of the Son of God."[9]

We ought not interpret this to say that reason and intellect should be rejected but rather that reason should not be exercised without regard to the morality of which it is inextricably a part. Nephi taught that we should not "hearken unto the precepts of men, *save their precepts shall be given by the power of the Holy Ghost*" (2 Nephi 28:31; emphasis added). His brother Jacob taught that "to be learned is good if [the learned] hearken unto the counsels of God" (2 Nephi 9:29). Note the following counsel from Elder Hugh B. Brown: "The Church of Jesus Christ of Latter-day Saints accepts newly revealed truth, whether it comes through direct revelation or from study and research. We deny the common conception of reality that distinguishes radically between the natural and the supernatural, between the temporal and the eternal, between the sacred and the secular. For us, there is no order of reality that is utterly different in character from the world of which we are a part, that is separated from us by an impassable gulf. We do not separate our daily mundane tasks and interests from the meaning and substance of religion. We recognize the spiritual in all phases and aspects of living and realize that this life is an important part of eternal life."[10]

We need to make "righteous judgment[s]" (Joseph Smith Translation, Matthew 7:2) concerning the knowledge we obtain, whether it comes from secular or sacred sources. Mormon teaches us that the way to make these judgments is as plain as day and night: "For every thing which inviteth to do good, and to persuade to believe in Christ, is sent forth by the power and gift of Christ; wherefore ye may know with a perfect knowledge it is of God" (Moroni 7:16). However, this does not say that we will always be able to discern right from wrong in the present moment. From the Doctrine and Covenants we read: "But as you cannot always judge the righteous, or as you cannot always tell the wicked from the righteous, therefore I say unto you, hold your peace until I shall see fit to make all things known unto the world concerning the matter" (D&C 10:37). There will be times when we must exercise patience and faith as we "wait upon the Lord" for the understanding that is sought (2 Nephi 18:17).

MORAL AGENCY

We live in a day when many are claiming that all truth is relative and that there are no absolutes. Moral agency, which invites the choice between right and wrong, has been replaced by a distorted notion of agency—the choice between alternatives. President Boyd K. Packer clarifies this point of doctrine in his discussion of the "pro-choice" philosophy in his conference talk entitled "Our Moral Environment": "Regardless of how lofty and moral the 'pro-choice' argument sounds, it is badly flawed. With that same logic one could argue that all traffic signs and barriers which keep the careless from danger should be pulled down on the theory that each individual must be free to choose how close to the edge he will go. . . . The phrase '*free* agency' does not appear in scripture. The only agency spoken of there is *moral agency,* 'which,' the Lord said, 'I have given unto him, that every man may be *accountable* for his own sins in the day of judgment' (D&C 101:78; italics added)."[11]

Just as the scriptures contain accounts of lives being changed for the better in days of old, lives continue to be changed in the present as we come to understand and exercise the moral agency we have been given. Elder Spencer J. Condie has shared the following story of a man whose life was changed as he was true to the light within:

"I know [a] good man who was reared in a family without the blessings of the gospel. Through a series of unfortunate events in his early youth, he was introduced to homosexuality, and gradually he became a prisoner of this addictive behavior.

"One day two young missionaries knocked on his door and asked if he would be interested in learning of the restored gospel of Jesus Christ.

In his heart of hearts he wanted to be freed from his prison of uncleanness, but feeling unable to change the direction his life had taken, he terminated the missionary discussions. Before leaving his apartment, the two elders left a copy of the Book of Mormon with him, and testified of its truthfulness.

"My friend placed the book on his bookshelf and forgot about it for several years. He continued acting out his homosexual tendencies, assuming that such relationships would bring him happiness. But alas, with each passing year, his misery increased.

"One day in the depths of despair, he scanned his bookshelf for something to read which might edify and uplift him and restore his self-worth. His eye caught hold of the book with a dark-blue cover, which the missionaries had given him several years before. He began to read. On the second page of this book, he read of Father Lehi's vision in which he was given a book to read, and 'as he read, he was filled with the Spirit of the Lord' (1 Nephi 1:12). And as my good friend continued reading, he too was filled with the Spirit of the Lord.

"He read King Benjamin's benedictory challenge to undergo a mighty change of heart—not a little change, but a mighty change. He was given hope by the comforting conversion stories of Enos, Alma, Ammon, and Aaron. He was also inspired by the account of the Savior's visit to the ancient Nephites. By the time he reached the final page of the Book of Mormon, he was prepared to accept Moroni's loving invitation to 'come unto Christ, and be perfected in him, and deny yourselves of all ungodliness' (Moroni 10:32).

"My friend contacted the Church and was taught the gospel and was baptized. Within a relatively short time, he married a lovely young woman, and they are the parents of several beautiful children. He and his wife are very dynamic and committed servants of the Lord, influencing many others for good."[12]

In the following passage, the prophet Mormon summarizes for us the great sorrow of those who reject the light of Christ, and the great rejoicing experienced by all who follow him: "And thus we see the great reason of sorrow, and also of rejoicing—sorrow because of death and destruction among men, and joy because of the *light of Christ* unto life" (Alma 28:14; emphasis added).

PROMPTINGS OF CONSCIENCE

It is through our conscience we first come to perceive the love of a Father in Heaven who does "all things for the welfare and happiness of his people" (Helaman 12:2). The word "conscience" literally means to know within oneself. President Packer has written about the word *conscience:*

"It is made up of the prefix *con,* meaning 'with,' and the word *science,* meaning 'to know.' The *Oxford English Dictionary* says it comes from the Latin *conscientia,* meaning 'knowledge [knowing] within oneself.' The first definition listed there is 'inward knowledge, consciousness, inmost thought, mind.' The second one is 'consciousness of right and wrong,' or in just two words, 'moral sense.'

"Our conscience might be described as a memory, a residual awareness of who we really are, of our true identity. *It is perhaps the best example of the fact that we can become aware of truths because we feel them rather than by knowing them because we perceive them through the physical senses.*"[13]

We can experience our conscience *or* "light of Christ" or "Spirit of Christ"—in different ways. If we are living *truth-full-y* (consistent with light and truth), we will experience our conscience as a gentle invitation persuading us to follow its prompting to do good. We may have even reached a point of *self-less-ness,* where we aren't even cognizant that we are being prompted or acting upon the prompting. When this is the case, we will live spontaneously, without self-regard (see 3 Nephi 9:20). When we are not living truthfully, we will experience our conscience as a demanding and irritating mandate.

Following our conscience leads us to peace and greater understanding, while acting against what we know to be right leads to distress and confusion and is often the beginning of greater problems. Large, ominous problems typically begin as small, simple ones. While the problems most of us face are neither as dramatic as Lamoni's nor as complicated as the individual's described by Elder Condie, we still confront them on a daily basis. A friend told me the following example of a prompting of conscience with which most of us can identify:

"My wife had asked if I would rock the baby to sleep. I knew I should, but I really wanted to watch the football game. I quickly settled on a compromise, I could take the baby into my room, watch the football game on the portable television and rock her to sleep at the same time. A real 'win/win' situation! I would miss the color screen, but what a small price to pay for being a good Dad.

"The problem came after about two minutes of watching the game. My daughter began to fuss. The thought came in my mind that if I turned the television off, walked with her and sang to her, she might be soothed. I knew it was the right thing to do, but did I do it? No, I spent the next thirty minutes struggling to watch the game and rock my child, all the while resenting the fact that I couldn't do what I wanted to!"

One of the characteristics of persons who go against their conscience is that they have to justify their actions. These justifications come in the forms of rationalizations, thoughts, blaming emotions, and in some cases, physiological responses. In Proverbs we read, "The way of a fool is right in his own eyes" (Proverbs 12:15). Having discussed this story with the individual who lived it, I can detail for you what his self-justifications were: (1) "I've been working with difficult situations all day, I need some time to myself"; (2) "My wife is much better suited to deal with children than I am, she should be doing this"; (3) "My wife doesn't appreciate all that I do; it's really unfair she would have me do this"; (4) "I'm so tired, I need to lie down"; and finally, (5) "Why did we have all these kids anyway?"

We often think of "sin" as being something grievous like murder, adultery, or some other form of gross immorality, and while they are among the most serious of sins, the scriptures teach that anytime we "knoweth to do good, and doeth it not, . . . it is sin" (James 4:17). When my friend did not arise and walk with his child, he went against that which he knew was right (conscience), and that in a word is sin.

I know from personal, professional, and ecclesiastical experience that most of the problems we face in life begin when we deny the promptings of conscience we experience daily. President Spencer W. Kimball made this same observation in the following:

"There are many causes for human suffering—including war, disease, and poverty—and the suffering that proceeds from each of these is very real, but I would not be true to my trust if I did not say that *the most persistent cause of human suffering, that suffering which causes the deepest pain, is sin*—the violation of the commandments given to us by God. . . . If any of us wish to have more precise prescriptions for ourselves in terms of what we can do to have more abundant lives, all we usually need to do is to consult our conscience."[14]

While many of us go against our conscience by not doing those things we know are right, others of us confuse conscience with societal expectations and get lost in the artificial light of perfectionism. Consider the following story of Esther, published in the Sunday School manual *Teach Them Correct Principles:*

"Esther was trying to be the perfect wife and mother. Every morning she woke up announcing to herself: 'This is the day I will be perfect. The house will be organized, I will not yell at my children, and I will finish everything important I have planned.' Every night she went to bed discouraged, because she had failed to accomplish her goal. She became irritable with everyone, including herself, and she began to wonder what she was doing wrong.

"One night Esther knelt in prayer and asked for guidance. Afterward, while lying awake, a startling thought came to her. She realized that in focusing on her own perfection she was focusing on herself and failing to love others, particularly her husband and children. She was being not loving, therefore not Christlike, but essentially selfish. She was trying to be sweet to her children, but not freely, out of love for them, but because she saw it as a necessary part of *her* perfection. Furthermore, she was trying to get a feeling of righteousness by forcing her husband and children to meet her ideal of perfection. When her children got in the way of her 'perfect' routine, she blamed them for making her feel 'imperfect,' and she became irritated with them and treated them in a most unloving way. Likewise, if her husband did not meet her idea of perfection when he came home from work, she judged him as failing and was critical of him as a way of reinforcing her sense of her own righteousness.

"Esther remembered the Savior's commandment to be perfect *as he is perfect* (see 3 Nephi 12:48). She realized that this perfection includes loving as he loved (see John 13:34), and realized she had been pursuing the wrong goal."[15]

As with Esther, most of us who have challenges with perfectionism are not committed to selflessly serving others, but in serving ourselves by showing the world how competent we are. We are constantly on the run, doing a lot of things for a lot of people and sometimes becoming physically ill in the process. Like Martha of New Testament times, those who struggle with perfectionism are "careful and troubled about many things" (Luke 10:41). A perfectionist's flurry of activity is often a type of "virtuous" excuse for not being true to simple promptings of conscience.

It is through these simple promptings of conscience that the Lord continually attempts to get us to be one with Him. He will never invite us to fall short or go "beyond the mark" (see Jacob 4:14). He promises us that if we are true to the light given us, He will give us greater light: "That which is of God is light; and he that receiveth light, and continueth in God, receiveth more light; and that light groweth brighter and brighter until the perfect day" (D&C 50:24).

CONCLUSION

In conclusion, I give you my own witness that I have felt the love and direction of Father in Heaven through both the Spirit of Christ and the Holy Ghost. I have also been privileged to work with many people who have experienced a "mighty change" (Mosiah 5:2) by first coming to recognize and then by being true to the Spirit of Christ within them. I know that if we are true to the portion of the light given us, we will receive more. "Wherefore, I beseech you, brethren [and sisters], that ye should search diligently in the light of Christ that ye may know good from evil; and if ye will lay hold upon every good thing, and condemn it not, ye certainly will be a child of Christ" (Moroni 7:19).

NOTES

1. Ezra Taft Benson, *The Teachings of Ezra Taft Benson* (Salt Lake City: Bookcraft, 1988), 58.

2. William J. Bennett, "Quantifying America's Decline," *Wall Street Journal,* 15 March 1993.

3. Joseph F. Smith, *Gospel Doctrine,* 5th ed. (Salt Lake City, Utah: Deseret Book, 1939), 67–68.

4. James E. Talmage, *Articles of Faith* (Salt Lake City: The Church of Jesus Christ of Latter-day Saints, 1949), 488.

5. Bruce R. McConkie, *A New Witness for the Articles of Faith* (Salt Lake City: Deseret Book, 1984), 262.

6. Parley P. Pratt, *Key to the Science of Theology* (Salt Lake City: George Q. Cannon and Sons, 1891), 41.

7. Statement of the First Presidency, 15 February 1978.

8. Joseph Fielding Smith, *Doctrines of Salvation* (Salt Lake City: Bookcraft, 1954), 1:147.

9. Smith, *Doctrines of Salvation,* 3:275.

10. Hugh B. Brown, in Conference Report, April 1964, 81–82.

11. Boyd K. Packer, "Our Moral Environment," *Ensign,* May 1992, 66–68.

12. Spencer J. Condie, "A Mighty Change of Heart," *Ensign,* November 1993, 15–17.

13. Boyd K. Packer, "The Law and the Light," in *The Book of Mormon: Jacob through Words of Mormon, To Learn with Joy,* ed. Monte S. Nyman and Charles D. Tate Jr. (Provo, Utah: Religious Studies Center, Brigham Young University, 1990), 3–4.

14. Spencer W. Kimball, *The Teachings of Spencer W. Kimball,* ed. Edward L. Kimball (Salt Lake City: Bookcraft, 1982), 155.

15. *Teach Them Correct Principles: A Study in Family Relations* (Salt Lake City: The Church of Jesus Christ of Latter-day Saints, 1987), 7.

27
Faith, Hope, and Charity

Larry E. Dahl

As part of his final appeal to his future readers to come unto Christ and be perfected in Him, Moroni testified: "Wherefore, there must be faith; and if there must be faith there must also be hope; and if there must be hope there must also be charity. And except ye have charity ye can in nowise be saved in the kingdom of God; neither can ye be saved in the kingdom of God if ye have not faith; neither can ye if ye have no hope" (Moroni 10:20–21).

Faith, hope, and charity are familiar terms often spoken of together, and nearly always in the same order. Paul indicates that the order has significance, charity being the last and also the greatest of the three (see 1 Corinthians 13:13). A perusal of Church manuals and magazines shows that faith is discussed the most, charity next, and hope the least. In fact, it has been my experience that hope, which is as necessary to our salvation as faith or charity, is rarely discussed as a gospel principle. Furthermore, treatment of faith and charity is often limited to simply reading the words of Paul or Alma or Moroni without a careful analysis of what these apostles and prophets said or what their intended meaning was. To add to our understanding, we will

---

Larry E. Dahl is an emeritus professor of Church history and doctrine at Brigham Young University.

explore some of the teachings of the Book of Mormon concerning faith, hope, and charity—their meanings, their relationships to each other, how they are acquired, and what their fruits are.

FAITH

The word *faith* appears some 260 times in the Book of Mormon. Except for perhaps a half dozen instances—such as Alma 32; 48:15–16; 57:26–27 and Ether 12:6—the writers use the word without defining or describing it, apparently assuming that the reader understands its meaning.

The word *faith* is used in several contexts. At least sixteen times it refers to one's system of belief, the Church, or the gospel, as in "He had hope to shake me from the faith" (Jacob 7:5); "This judge was after the order and faith of Nehor" (Alma 14:16); and "A few of the Lamanites who were converted unto the true faith" (3 Nephi 6:14). At least six references deal with one's having strong faith. For example, Ammon rejoiced over the Lamanite queen, saying, "Blessed art thou because of thy exceeding faith; I say unto thee, woman, there has not been such great faith among all the people of the Nephites" (Alma 19:10). And concerning the Nephite multitude to whom the Savior appeared after His Resurrection, He told His disciples, "So great faith have I never seen among all the Jews" (3 Nephi 19:35). In at least nineteen instances, the Book of Mormon peoples and the reader are encouraged or charged to acquire or exercise faith. At least twenty-seven times, the word refers to someone's spiritual status. For instance, the Lamanite converts known as the people of Ammon are described as being "firm in the faith of Christ" (Alma 27:27), and Jarom records, "Our kings and our leaders were mighty men in the faith of the Lord" (Jarom 1:7). These are a few of the contexts in which the word *faith* appears in the Book of Mormon.

The rest of the 260 references to faith testify to the fruits of faith, the great blessings that flow from acquiring, retaining, and exercising it. Faith brings the power of the Holy Ghost to reveal truths, change hearts, remit sins, and sanctify (see Jarom 1:4; Mosiah 4:3; 5:4–7; Alma 9:20; 3 Nephi 27:19). Only through faith can miracles take place (see Ether 12:16, 18). Through faith confining cords are broken (see 1 Nephi 7:11–12; Alma 14:26–28), prison walls tumble (see Ether 12:13), military victories are won (see Alma 57:21–22), mountains move (see Jacob 4:6; Mormon 8:24; Ether 12:30), ancient records come forth (see 2 Nephi 3:19–21; Ether 12:22), and angels manifest themselves (see Moroni 7:30). Exceeding faith allows some to see Christ and have all things revealed to them (see Ether 3:9; 4:7; 12:8, 19–20, 31). Ultimately, the Savior "claimeth all those who have faith in him; and they who have faith in him will cleave unto every good thing" (Moroni 7:28), and He grants them eternal life (see Helaman 8:15). The list goes on and on. We are reminded several times that "the Lord is able to do all things according to his will, for the children of men, if it so be that they exercise faith in him" (1 Nephi 7:12; see also 2 Nephi 1:10; Moroni 10:23). It seems that the inspired writers of the Book of Mormon longed for later readers to understand clearly that the fruits of faith are both precious and possible.

How to Acquire Faith

The Book of Mormon also contains several passages about how one acquires faith. Consider the following in the order they appear.

Alma recorded that the keeping of the law of Moses by certain converted Lamanites served to "strengthen their faith in Christ" (Alma 25:16). He also taught a group of Zoramites that faith comes and is increased by experimenting with the word of God, by planting the word in one's heart, then by nourishing it with diligence and patience (see Alma 32–33). When his listeners asked how to do that, Alma admonished them to search the scriptures and cry unto the Lord through prayer, to soften their hearts and to "begin to believe in the Son of God" (Alma 33:22).

Amulek added his plea to those same Zoramites "that ye may begin to exercise your faith unto repentance, that ye begin to call upon his holy name" (Alma 34:17). He also reminded them that such prayer is vain unless it is accompanied by active concern for others (see Alma 34:28–29).

Growing in faith is tied to fasting and praying "oft" (Helaman 3:35). "You must repent, and cry unto the voice, even until ye shall have faith in Christ" (Helaman 5:41). Nephi, the son of Helaman, was similarly told that he would be made mighty in faith because of his unwearyingness in declaring the gospel, in seeking the Lord's will instead of his own, and in keeping the commandments (see Helaman 10:4–5).

The Lamanite prophet Samuel reminded the Nephites that coming to a knowledge of the truth and to a belief in the holy scriptures leads to faith (see Helaman 15:7).

Mormon testified that "the Lord God prepareth the way that the residue of men may have faith in Christ" by sending angels to minister unto the children of men, by declaring by His own mouth to prophets that Christ should come, by manifesting things in diverse ways unto the children of men, and by sending angels to declare "the word of Christ unto the chosen vessels of the Lord, that they may bear testimony of him" (Moroni 7:21–25, 28–32).

It seems clear from these verses that faith is a gift bestowed by God, and that a person can, and indeed must, qualify himself or herself to receive that gift by learning of Christ through studying the scriptures and listening to the prophets; by offering honest, humble, and persistent prayers; by patiently obeying the commandments he or she has been given; and by fasting. Gaining faith is assured with such an approach.

Defining Faith

Undoubtedly it is much more important to know how to acquire faith and experience its fruits than to be able to give a technical definition of it. However, many minds ache to understand clearly and to be able to explain principles precisely. What help, then, does the Book of Mormon give us in defining faith?

Alma 32 contains pertinent information. Three times Alma tells us what faith is not. He says, "Faith is not to have a perfect knowledge," for "if a man knoweth a thing he hath no cause to believe, for he knoweth it" (Alma 32:21, 18; see also 32:17, 26). As both evidence and explanation of this notion, Alma gives the example of planting a seed and observing it sprout. When a person has actually experienced the sprouting, Alma says his knowledge is perfect and his faith is dormant in that thing (see Alma 32:34). The phrase "in that thing" is an important key, for Alma is quick to remind us that our knowledge is not perfect in *all* things, but only in *that thing,* that is, that the seed is good. He adds, "Neither must ye lay aside your faith, for ye have only exercised your faith to plant the seed that ye might try the experiment to know if the seed was good" (Alma 32:36).

This explanation helps us better understand Ether 3:19, which says that after the brother of Jared saw the finger of the Lord, "he had faith no longer, for he knew, nothing doubting." This does not mean that he no longer had need for faith and that he knew all things, but he did know specifically that Christ lived and had a spirit body. "In that thing" his knowledge was perfect and his faith dormant. However, he still needed to have faith concerning a myriad of other things he had not yet seen or experienced. Hence, whatever else it is, faith includes an element of anticipation of unseen reality. It is oriented toward the future.

What other elements does faith possess besides anticipation? The following three passages about the two thousand stripling warriors are illuminating. First, after explaining that the Nephites were taught to defend themselves but never to be aggressors, the record states:

"And this was their faith, that by so doing God would prosper them in the land, or in other words, if they were faithful in keeping the commandments of God that he would prosper them in the land; yea, warn them to flee, or to prepare for war, according to their danger;

"And also, that God would make it known unto them whither they should go to defend themselves against their enemies, and by so doing, the Lord would deliver them; and this was the faith of Moroni" (Alma 48:15–16).

Then, concerning the fact that all survived a vicious battle, Helaman explains:

"And now, their preservation was astonishing to our whole army, yea, that they should be spared while there was a thousand of our brethren who were slain. And we do justly ascribe it to the miraculous power of God, because of their exceeding faith in that which they had been taught to believe—that there was a just God, and whosoever did not doubt, that they should be preserved by his marvelous power.

"Now this was the faith of these of whom I have spoken; they are young, and their minds are firm, and they do put their trust in God continually" (Alma 57:26–27).

Finally, in response to fervent prayers for strength against their enemies, the righteous Nephites received this welcome answer:

"Yea, it came to pass that the Lord our God did visit us with assurances that he would deliver us; yea, insomuch that he did speak peace to our souls, and did grant unto us great faith, and did cause us that we should hope for our deliverance in him" (Alma 58:11).

The sense of the word *faith* in these instances is that of assurance, trust, lack of doubt, and confidence. Also, in every instance, doing or a sense of obeying is present. "And thus they went forth" (Alma 48:20); "and they did obey and observe to perform every word of command with exactness" (Alma 57:21); "and we did take courage . . . and were fixed with a determination. . . . And thus we did go forth with all our might" (Alma 58:12–13). Thus the Book of Mormon teaches that faith is an assurance, confidence, and trust in unseen reality that impels one to act.

What of Alma 32:21, which says, "If ye have faith ye hope for things which are not seen, which are true"? Is this not a definition of faith? I suggest that it is more a statement of what follows faith than it is a definition of faith. If we define *faith* solely with the word *hope,* then they are the same. But it is clear from many other passages in the Book of Mormon that hope is something different from, even beyond, faith. If one views Alma 32:21 as a statement that hope follows faith, then that view is consistent with other passages that treat hope as distinct from faith.

HOPE

The word *hope* is used fifty times in the Book of Mormon. It is used in two senses: (1) a general one, consistent with common usage and meaning a "desire accompanied by expectation of fulfillment," or wanting or longing for something that may be a possibility, or a kind of wishing and wondering; and (2) a specific, theological sense, meaning a state of mind, heart, and spirit necessary for salvation, a gift of God given through the Holy Ghost.

Some examples of the general use of the word *hope* are found in Jacob and 3 Nephi. Jacob said that Sherem "had hope to shake me from the faith" (Jacob 7:5), and Giddianhi wrote to Lachoneus, "I hope that ye will deliver up your lands and your possessions, without the shedding of blood" (3 Nephi 3:10). Likewise, by gathering into one body and having provisions for seven years, the Nephites "did hope to destroy the robbers from off the face of the land" (3 Nephi 4:4).

These examples speak of a different hope from the second type: that which one must have in order to be saved (see Moroni 10:21), the hope that "cometh of faith, [and] maketh an anchor to the souls of men," making them "sure and steadfast, always abounding in good works" (Ether 12:4).

What does the Book of Mormon say about this saving hope? Saving hope follows, comes from, and grows out of faith, as Moroni states:

"Whoso believeth in God might with surety hope for a better world, yea, even a place at the right hand of God, which hope *cometh of faith*" (Ether 12:4; emphasis added).

"Wherefore, ye may also have hope, and be partakers of the gift, if ye will but have faith" (Ether 12:9).

"And again, my beloved brethren, I would speak unto you concerning hope. How is it that ye can attain unto faith, save ye shall have hope?

"And what is it that ye shall hope for? Behold I say unto you that ye shall have hope through the atonement of Christ and the power of his resurrection, to be raised unto life eternal, and this because of your faith in him according to the promise.

"Wherefore, if a man have faith he must needs have hope; for without faith there cannot be any hope" (Moroni 7:40–42).

A casual reading of these verses can lead to some confusion, however. Does Moroni 7:40 say that one must have hope before faith? What, then, does verse 42 mean, which states that without faith there cannot be any hope? The intended meaning, I submit, is that if one exercises faith, hope must follow, which hope is the sure and natural consequence of faith. The sense of verse 40 would then be, "How is it that ye can attain unto faith, save ye shall *then* [naturally, automatically, as an outgrowth and reward of your faith] have hope?" If one takes such a view, Moroni 7:40–42 is consistent internally and also with other Book of Mormon passages that speak of the sequential relationship of faith and hope.

Others have taken a somewhat different view. They speak of faith and hope as having reciprocal relationships at various levels. Applying such an understanding to Moroni 7:40–42 would suggest that verse 40 refers to one level of hope, which leads to faith, which in turn leads to a second level of hope noted in verses 41 and 42. This pattern then repeats itself in an upward cycle. A careful examination of the scriptural record, however, shows reasons in favor of the idea that saving hope is a result, not an initial cause, of faith.

Taking the sequential view that faith precedes hope does not deny that something must precede faith. If it is not hope, what is it? Alma called it a "desire to believe" (Alma 32:27). Perhaps this could be thought of as a type of hope, relating to a general "wishing and wondering." But it is not the saving hope that I believe Mormon and Moroni refer to in Moroni 7:40–42. Saving hope *follows* faith.

In addition to teaching that saving hope comes as a result of faith, the Book of Mormon supports the idea that saving hope is a desire, a longing, a hungering and thirsting after righteousness with a full expectation of eventual fulfillment. Consider the following. The prophet Ether explained that hope "maketh an anchor to the souls of men, which would make them sure and steadfast, always abounding in good works, being led to glorify god" (Ether 12:4), and the Lamanite prophet Samuel taught that those who experience a change of heart "are firm and steadfast in the faith" (Helaman 15:7–8).

If hope makes men steadfast, and those who have experienced a change of heart are steadfast, can we not then link hope with a change of heart? It is interesting to examine the Book of Mormon references to a convert's change of heart in relation to the idea that hope consists of a desire for righteousness. After hearing King Benjamin's great address, his people testified, "We believe all the words which thou hast spoken unto us; and also, we know of their surety and truth, because of the Spirit of the Lord Omnipotent, which has wrought a mighty change in us, or in our hearts, that we have no more disposition to do evil, but to do good continually" (Mosiah 5:2). We learn from Mosiah 4:3 and 5:7 that this change of heart came as a result of their being "spiritually begotten," including having their sins remitted, which brought them peace of conscience and great joy. The same testimony comes from King Lamoni and his people at their conversion: "And they did all declare unto the people the selfsame thing—that their hearts had been changed; that they had no more desire to do evil" (Alma 19:33).

It is clear that such a change is required of all who are to inherit the kingdom of God, for the voice of the Lord said to Alma at the time of his spiritual awakening: "Marvel not that all mankind, yea, men and women, all nations, kindreds, tongues and people, must be born again; yea, born of God, changed from their carnal and fallen state, to a state of righteousness, being redeemed of God, becoming his sons and daughters" (Mosiah 27:25). Before his conversion Alma desired to destroy the church of God (see Alma 36:6); after his conversion he longed to build His church and to be with God and angels (see Alma 36:22, 24).

It all seems to fit. Faith (including prayer, repentance, and obedience) prepares a person to receive a spiritual rebirth, which brings a remission of sins and changes the heart so that it desires righteousness. This desire for righteousness is a primary ingredient of hope.

But there is more to hope than longing for righteousness. The Holy Ghost, who plays a major role in bringing about that desire, remains to fill the converted soul with staying power, a spiritual confidence, an assurance that his longings will be realized. Such confidence was reflected in King Benjamin's people when they said, "We . . . have great views of that which is to come; and were it expedient, we could prophesy of all things" (Mosiah 5:3). Similarly, Alma testified, "I know that he will raise me up at the last day, to dwell with him in glory; yea, and I will praise him forever" (Alma 36:28).

Heaven would not be heaven if we did not want to be there—if our hearts and our very natures were not in complete harmony with the righteousness that is there. Imagine the incongruity of someone struggling white-knuckle-like to keep what he regards as burdensome commandments in order to be saved in the kingdom of God, and once there to feel similarly burdened by the necessity of living those same principles eternally. Indeed, "ye can in nowise be saved in the kingdom of God . . . if ye have no hope" (Moroni 10:21).

CHARITY

Though spoken of explicitly the fewest number of times (twenty-seven), *charity* is defined and explained in the Book of Mormon more directly and clearly than either faith or hope. Nephi said simply, "Charity is love" (2 Nephi 26:30). Mormon, as quoted by Moroni, expanded this definition to "Charity is the pure love of Christ" (Moroni 7:47). The verses that speak of charity indicate that if we are to be saved in the kingdom of God, we must experience charity in two dimensions, which I will call vertical and horizontal.

Vertical charity refers to the love of Christ has for us, which love motivated the Atonement. Moroni explained:

"And again, I remember that thou hast said that thou hast loved the world, even unto the laying down of thy life for the world, that thou mightest take it again to prepare a place for the children of men.

"And now I know that this love which thou hast had for the children of men is charity; wherefore, except men shall have charity they cannot inherit that place which thou hast prepared in the mansions of thy Father" (Ether 12:33–34).

Horizontal charity refers to that love we must feel and extend to others of mankind. Nephi spoke of this dimension when he said:

"I have charity for my people. . . .

"I have charity for the Jew. . . .

"I also have charity for the Gentiles" (2 Nephi 33:7–9).

Mormon explained both dimensions of charity in these words:

"Charity suffereth long, and is kind, and envieth not, and is not puffed up, seeketh not her own, is not easily provoked, thinketh no evil, and rejoiceth not in iniquity but rejoiceth in the truth, beareth all things, believeth all things, hopeth all things, endureth all things. . . . Charity never faileth" (Moroni 7:45–46).

When our hearts are filled with charity, we love as Christ loved, His goals become our goals, His work becomes our work, and ultimately His glory becomes our glory, for we will become "joint-heirs with Christ" (Romans 8:17) of "all that [the] Father hath" (D&C 84:38).

With this thought in mind, and thinking of charity in relation to hope, it might be said that hope is a hungering and thirsting after righteousness for oneself, and charity is essentially a hungering and thirsting after righteousness for others. Not surprisingly, therefore, we find that Lehi, after tasting the fruit of the tree of life, "began to be desirous that [his] family should partake of it also" (1 Nephi 8:12) and that Nephi wrote, "I pray continually for [my people] by day, and mine eyes water my pillow by night, because of them" (2 Nephi 33:3).

Enos, after experiencing the joy of hearing his own sins were remitted, "pour[ed] out [his] whole soul unto God" for "the welfare of [his friends], the Nephites." And when he had obtained a promise of blessings for them, he then "prayed . . . with many long strugglings for [his enemies], the Lamanites" (Enos 1:9, 11). Following their conversion, Alma and the sons of Mosiah "were desirous that salvation should be declared to every creature, for they could not bear that any human soul should perish; yea, even the very thoughts that any soul should endure endless torment did cause them to quake and tremble" (Mosiah 28:3). This same commitment to serving to bless others is shown by all the prophet-leaders of the Book of Mormon.

Charity, like faith and hope before it, is bestowed by God upon those who prepare themselves to receive it. Mormon instructed members of the Church in his day, whom he described as "the peaceable followers of Christ, . . . that have obtained a sufficient hope by which ye can enter into the rest of the Lord" (Moroni 7:3), to "pray unto the Father with all the energy of heart, that ye may be filled with this love, which he hath bestowed upon all who are true followers of his Son, Jesus Christ" (Moroni 7:48). Mormon's plea and his earlier explanation of the characteristics of charity (see Moroni 7:45) show that charity is an outgrowth of faith and hope and encompasses them both. How appropriate it is, then, to speak of these three principles in the order given—faith leads to hope, and then the two develop into charity—charity being the "greatest" (1 Corinthians 13:13).

LINE UPON LINE

It is worthwhile to ponder and discuss the gradually unfolding nature of faith, hope, and charity. Alma instructed Zeezrom that men are given a "lesser" or "greater" portion of the "word," and they enlarge or diminish that portion "according to the heed and diligence which they give unto" it. Those who obey will receive more and more until they know the mysteries of God "in full"; those who harden their hearts receive less and less "until they know nothing concerning his mysteries" (Alma 12:9–11). In this light, Book of Mormon phrases such as "a particle of faith" (Alma 32:27), "much faith" (Mosiah 27:14), "strong" faith (Alma 7:17), "exceeding faith" (Mosiah 4:3), and even "exceedingly great faith" (Moroni 10:11) are clearer and more meaningful.

Similarly, when we receive the baptism of fire that remits sin and brings hope, we do not suddenly vault into full spiritual maturity. In Peter's words, we are "newborn babes" in need of milk that we "may grow thereby" (1 Peter 2:2). In this connection, it is intriguing to consider the implications of the Savior's statement that certain Lamanites, "because of their faith in me at the time of their conversion, were baptized with fire and with the Holy Ghost, and they knew it not" (3 Nephi 9:20). Undoubtedly, they knew something had happened, for "they were encircled about, yea every soul, by a pillar of fire," and "they could speak forth marvelous words" (Helaman 5:43, 45), but their understanding of what they were experiencing may have come later.

There is no guarantee that the change of heart involved here will remain forever. Alma asks, "And now behold, I say unto you, my brethren, if ye have experienced a change of heart, and if ye have felt to sing the song of redeeming love, I would ask, can ye feel so now?" (Alma 5:26). We can lose the desire for righteousness. That desire comes from the companionship of the Holy Ghost, and when we become disobedient, or even casual about the gospel, we feel less and less of His power. On the other hand, awareness and obedience bring to us more and more of the power of the Spirit, intensifying our desire for righteousness. Hence, we read of "sufficient hope" (Moroni 7:3), "firm hope" (Alma 34:41), "a more excellent hope" (Ether 12:32), and "a perfect brightness of hope" (2 Nephi 31:20).

I have not found specific evidence in the Book of Mormon that there are portions of charity. Obviously, vertical charity, Christ's love for us, is pure, full, perfect, consistent. However, I suspect that horizontal charity, our love for each other, functions on a continuum as do faith and hope.

FAITH, HOPE, AND CHARITY CENTERED IN CHRIST

The Savior said, "I will show unto them that faith, hope and charity bringeth unto me—the fountain of all righteousness" (Ether 12:28). The first principle of the gospel is not just "faith," but "faith in the Lord Jesus Christ" (Articles of Faith 1:4). Similarly, we must obtain not just hope, but a "hope in Christ" (Jacob 2:19), a "hope of his glory" (Jacob 4:4), and "hope for our deliverance in him" (Alma 58:11). Likewise, by simple definition, charity is not just "love," but "the pure love of Christ" (Moroni 7:47).

To say that true faith, hope, and charity must be centered in Christ may seem to be an unnecessary statement of the obvious. However, as with all other gospel principles, faith, hope and charity have their counterfeits. President Spencer W. Kimball has said, "Whatever thing a man sets his heart and his trust in most is his god; and if his god doesn't also happen to be the true and living God of Israel, that man is laboring in idolatry."[1] There are many causes in the world to which men give their allegiance. They trust (have faith) in their chosen cause; they long for (hope for) the purposes of that cause to be fulfilled, and eagerly desire that others share their commitment and rewards (charity). Many of these causes are commendable, but all are ultimately inadequate to provide permanent solutions to the problems in this world and salvation in the world to come. As the angel instructed King Benjamin, "There shall be no other name given nor any other way nor means whereby salvation can come unto the children of men, only in and through the name of Christ, the Lord Omnipotent" (Mosiah 3:17).

CONCLUSION

We began with Moroni's testimony that faith, hope, and charity are necessary for salvation. We close with Moroni's testimony that these gifts will always be available to those who believe: "And I would exhort you, my beloved brethren, that ye remember that he is the same yesterday, today, and forever, and that all these gifts of which I have spoken, which are spiritual, never will be done away, even as long as the world shall stand, only according to the unbelief of the children of men" (Moroni 10:19). May we have the good sense to believe and realize these marvelous gifts in our lives.

NOTE

1. Spencer W. Kimball, "The False Gods We Worship," *Ensign,* June 1976, 4.

INDEX